DEADLY INJUSTICE

Deadly Injustice

Trayvon Martin, Race, and the
Criminal Justice System

Edited by
Devon Johnson, Patricia Y. Warren,
and Amy Farrell

With a Foreword by Lawrence D. Bobo

NEW YORK UNIVERSITY PRESS
New York and London

NEW YORK UNIVERSITY PRESS
New York and London
www.nyupress.org

References to Internet websites (URLs) were accurate at the time of writing.
Neither the author nor New York University Press is responsible for URLs
that may have expired or changed since the manuscript was prepared.

ISBN: 978-1-4798-7345-6 (hardback)
ISBN: 978-1-4798-9429-1 (paperback)

For Library of Congress Cataloging-in-Publication data, please contact the
Library of Congress.

New York University Press books are printed on acid-free paper,
and their binding materials are chosen for strength and durability.
We strive to use environmentally responsible suppliers and materials
to the greatest extent possible in publishing our books.

Manufactured in the United States of America

10 9 8 7 6 5 4 3 2 1

Also available as an ebook

This book is dedicated to the Racial Democracy, Crime and Justice Network, and to all the scholars, activists, teachers, writers, and organizations that work to both understand and speak out against injustice.

CONTENTS

Acknowledgments ix

Foreword: The Racial Double Homicide of Trayvon Martin xi
  Lawrence D. Bobo

Introduction: Race, Criminal Justice, and the Death of
Trayvon Martin 1
  Devon Johnson, Patricia Y. Warren, and Amy Farrell

PART I. WHO IS IN DANGER?

1. Profiling Trayvon: Young Black Males, Suspicion,
   and Surveillance 7
   Jacinta M. Gau and Kareem L. Jordan

2. Presumed Danger: Race, Bias, Stigma, and Perceptions of
   Crime and Criminals 23
   Kevin M. Drakulich and Laura Siller

3. Policed, Punished, Dehumanized: The Reality for
   Young Men of Color Living in America 59
   Victor M. Rios

4. Threat, Danger, and Vulnerability: Trayvon Martin and
   Gwen Araujo 81
   Toya Like, Lori Sexton, and Savannah Porter

PART II. WHERE DO YOU STAND?

5. Go Ahead and Shoot—The Law Might Have Your Back:
   History, Race, Implicit Bias, and Justice in Florida's
   Stand Your Ground Law 115
   Katheryn Russell-Brown

6. The Dangers of Racialized Perceptions and Thinking
   by Law Enforcement 146
   David A. Harris

7. The Acquittal of George Zimmerman: Race and Judges'
   Perceptions about the Accuracy of Not Guilty Verdicts   165
   Amy Farrell, Patricia Y. Warren, Devon Johnson,
   Jordyn L. Rosario, and Daniel Givelber

8. Up to No Good: The Context of Adolescent Discrimination
   in Neighborhoods   185
   Bryan L. Sykes, Alex R. Piquero, Jason Gioviano, and
   Nicolas Pittman

PART III. WHICH VOICES COUNT?

9. From *Simpson* to *Zimmerman*: Examining the Effects of
   Race, Class, and Gender in the Failed Prosecution of
   Two Highly Publicized, Racially Divisive Cases   215
   Delores Jones-Brown and Henry F. Fradella

10. Divided by Race: Differences in the Perception of Injustice   245
    Isaac Unah and Valerie Wright

11. The Zimmerman Verdict: Media, Political Reaction, and
    Public Response in the Age of Social Networking   275
    Chenelle A. Jones and Mia Ortiz

12. Read between the Lines: What Determines Media Coverage
    of Youth Homicide?   298
    Heather M. Washington and Valerie Wright

    Afterword: Reducing Racialized Violence and
    Deracializing Justice   323
    Doris Marie Provine and Ruth D. Peterson

    About the Contributors   335

    Index   343

ACKNOWLEDGMENTS

The idea for this book developed from discussions at the Racial Democracy, Crime and Justice Network (RDCJN) workshop in July 2013, just after the verdict in the George Zimmerman case. We thank the RDCJN members who contributed to the brainstorming discussions, and are indebted to those who volunteered to write the chapters that appear in the volume. These scholars worked extremely hard under short deadlines, and we are grateful to have their work and their ideas included here. We also thank the members of the RDCJN Steering Committee for their unwavering support of us and for their belief in the importance of this volume. We extend a special acknowledgment to Ruth Peterson and Marie Provine for their advice throughout the process, and for writing the afterword to the volume. Larry Bobo also deserves a significant note of thanks for contributing the foreword. Finally, we owe a special thank you to John Hagan for supporting the volume and including it in his New York University Press series: New Perspectives in Crime, Deviance, and Law.

Our job was made much easier by the excellent contributions of the members of our editorial advisory board, each of whom reviewed one or more chapters for this volume. We thank Elsa Chen, Shaun Gabbidon, Charis Kubrin, Jody Miller, Ruth Peterson, Marie Provine, Eric Stewart, and Maria Velez for their thoughtful comments, for sticking to our tight time frame, and for their support of this project.

We feel very fortunate to be members of the RDCJN and to be linked to colleagues across the country who focus scholarly attention on critical issues of race/ethnicity, crime, and justice in their research and teaching. This collection is one of many important attempts to create space for informed discussion about race and justice in America.

Devon Johnson
Patricia Y. Warren
Amy Farrell

FOREWORD: THE RACIAL DOUBLE HOMICIDE
OF TRAYVON MARTIN

LAWRENCE D. BOBO

The murder of Trayvon Martin was a tragedy. The acquittal of George Zimmerman on murder charges was an unspeakable national shame and travesty. I referred to it at the time as the second murder of Trayvon Martin. Yet, to mention these events does as much to stir controversy and dissension as it does to generate a shared sense of community and moral outrage. It is hard now even to fashion a language and terminology that is not immediately read as signaling what "side" one is on in the matter; the places where race, crime, and policing meet are simply that acutely and instantly polarizing. And make no mistake, I have chosen language that makes clear where I stand.

Both murders of Trayvon Martin are of a piece with deep problems of discrimination, racism, and class bias woven into the fabric of our criminal justice system and of the American social order writ large. Indeed, perhaps the situation's most numbing aspect is not the loss of a young man's life and the subsequent failure of police, prosecutors, juries, and the courts, but rather the disturbing continuity of these events with so many others like it that both preceded and will surely follow them. One need only list the names of the unjustly dead to capture the long and national scope of this problem, such as Jimmie Lee Jackson, Eleanor Bumpurs, Tyisha Miller, Rodney King, Amadou Diallo, Michael Brown, Eric Garner, Tamir Rice, and more.

What is the fundamental nature of that problem? The simple polarizing answers are easy enough to invoke. We hear "racist cops" from one side. From the other side we hear of a very real problem of "black criminality." The core of the problem, to my mind, is the wedding of socioeconomic, legal-political, and cultural racism. To say this, however, is to immediately point to complex historical conditions and social process that require very careful analysis and dissection if we are to truly understand the challenges before us. Finding vocabularies that allow effective communication is no easy task, especially regarding matters of crime and policing, where the views of black Americans and those of their fellow white Americans are often far, far apart.[1]

For the moment I want to continue with the framing of the issue as one of a racial double homicide. The first homicide involved the shooting of Trayvon Martin by George Zimmerman. The second homicide involved a series of escalating failures of the legal system and process that resulted in the acquittal of Zimmerman: the slowness of police to arrest and prosecutors to bring charges against Zimmerman; the impaneling of a jury containing no African Americans; the vicious distortion of reality embedded in the assertion that Trayvon Martin used "the sidewalk as a weapon"; and the ultimate failure to convict Zimmerman under Florida's dubious Stand Your Ground law.

We have now seen this pattern of "double homicides" play out again and again since the Zimmerman verdict. Nowhere was this dynamic more evidently in play than in the case of Michael Brown in Ferguson, Missouri. As distinguished historian and African Americanist scholar Robin D. G. Kelley put it, "For a grand jury to find no probable cause even on the lesser charge of involuntary manslaughter is a stunning achievement in a police shooting of an unarmed teenager with his hands raised, several yards away."[2] The equally stunning failure to bring charges against the officers involved in the death of Eric Garner in New York only adds to the acute sense that a situation demanding urgent invention looms before us.

The work of social change and of social justice takes place at many levels and over long stretches of time. One important step in that process is the production of knowledge, indeed ways of seeing and understanding, that clarify the nature of the problem. It is precisely in this way that social scientists have a special obligation to illuminate, in as systematic, conceptually clear, and methodologically rigorous a fashion as possible, significant social problems. Devon Johnson, Patricia Y. Warren, and Amy Farrell have assembled an impressive array of scholars to focus on the set of thorny issues for our criminal justice system and for the vitality of American democracy raised by events like both murders of Trayvon Martin. This volume, bringing together new research and fresh analyses from sociologists, criminologists, legal scholars, and political scientists, takes huge steps toward the all-important new knowledge base and reframing of issues that needs to happen if we are to prevent the next set of "double homicides."

Reading these chapters brings home two critical observations for me. First and foremost, Devon Johnson and her collaborators hone to fine precision the idea that in America we remain immersed in a culture of contempt, derision, and, at bottom, profound dehumanization of African Americans, men and women, but especially of young black males. We know from major social surveys that negative stereotypes of African Americans remain commonplace, particularly views of blacks as less capable, less hardworking, and more inclined to crime and violence than whites. A variety of experimental studies reveal a potentially deep basis to these stereotypes in widely shared psychological associations between blackness and primitive animals like apes, as well as with guns and violence.

Second, the work in this volume clarifies how this "cultural racism" gets normalized and becomes a source of routinely mobilized bias in the functioning of the criminal justice system; how from my point of view it results in the first of the racial double homicides noted above. It affects the quality of interaction between police and members of the black community. It does so in ways that can result in much greater readiness and, in fact, much higher actual recourse to the use of deadly force in dealings with African Americans on the part of police. Thus, a recent report by ProPublica shows a shocking twenty-one times greater risk of being killed by police for African Americans than for their white counterparts. As the researchers explained, "The 1,217 deadly police shootings from 2010 to 2012 captured in the federal data show that blacks, age 15 to 19, were killed at a rate of 31.17 per million, while just 1.47 per million white males in that age range died at the hands of police."[3]

But as we know, the problem neither really begins nor stops with this "first homicide." The second homicide then involves a series of scenes where the culture of racism permeates decision making, as we saw in the Trayvon Martin murders. Should the officer (individual) involved in killing a civilian be arrested? Should the officer (individual) face criminal charges? If ever an indictment is handed down, what is the right charge, who will serve on a jury, and where will the trial take place?

How will the terms of the relevant law be explained to a jury, and what standard of legal culpability should they apply? The "second homicide" then involves the repeated failure of the criminal justice system to treat the lives of African Americans, particularly poor African American males, in the same way it would middle-class white Americans. These repeated failures receive various justifications, some more obvious and potentially defensible than others.

Law and the criminal justice system in the United States have long operated in ways that could be characterized not merely as racially biased, but as explicitly racially oppressive.[4] In the post–civil rights era, particularly in the age of Obama and under the nation's first African American attorney general in Eric Holder, many had hoped we would decisively turn back the problem of race bias in matters of law, policing, and criminal justice. Yet, we know from careful sociological analyses,[5] legal-political assessments,[6] and recent public opinion research as well,[7] that the racialized character of law enforcement in the United States remains a deeply etched feature of the criminal justice system. It could hardly be otherwise in a society and economy once based on slavery and still exhibiting high levels of racial residential segregation and concomitant patterns of racialized poverty and unemployment.

Getting beyond the current state of polarization and discontent requires building the evidentiary base and analytical perspectives necessary to end this pattern of double homicide. Devon Johnson and her colleagues have assembled an impressive and important set of new thinking and research that constitutes a strong social scientific input to righting the wrongs of racial double homicide; to putting the needless death of Trayvon Martin and many, many like him into a meaningful framework and arming us with a potential resource for action. It is time now for the rest of us to put this rich material and valuable information to good and impactful use.

NOTES
1. Thompson and Bobo 2011.
2. Kelley 2014.
3. Gabrielson, Jones, and Sagara 2014.
4. Kennedy 1997.
5. Western 2006.

6. Alexander 2010.
7. Bobo and Thompson 2010.

REFERENCES

Alexander, Michelle. 2010. *The New Jim Crow: Mass Incarceration in the Age of Color-blindness*. New York: New Press.

Bobo, Lawrence D., and Victor Thompson. 2010. "Racialized Mass Incarceration: Poverty, Prejudice, and Punishment." In *Doing Race: 21 Essays for the 21st Century*, edited by Hazel R. Markus and Paula M. Moya, 322–55. New York: Norton.

Gabrielson, Ryan, Ryann Grochowski Jones, and Eric Sagara. 2014. "Deadly Force, in Black and White: A ProPublica Analysis of Killings by Police Shows Outsize Risk for Young Black Males." http://www.propublica.org/article/deadly-force-in-black-and-white?utm_source=et&utm_medium=email&utm_campaign=dailynewsletter#. Accessed February 10, 2015.

Kelley, Robin D. G. 2014. "Why We Won't Wait: Resisting the War Against the Black and Brown Underclass." *Counterpunch*. http://www.counterpunch.org/2014/11/25/75039/print. Accessed February 10, 2015.

Kennedy, Randall. 1997. *Race, Crime and the Law*. New York: Vintage.

Thompson, Victor R., and Lawrence D. Bobo. 2011. "Thinking about Crime: Race and Lay Accounts of Lawbreaking Behavior." *Annals of the American Academy of Political and Social Science* 634:16–38.

Western, Bruce. 2006. *Punishment and Inequality in America*. New York: Russell Sage Foundation.

Introduction

Race, Criminal Justice, and the Death of Trayvon Martin

DEVON JOHNSON, PATRICIA Y. WARREN, AND AMY FARRELL

On Sunday, February 26, 2012, George Zimmerman, a neighborhood watch volunteer in a gated Sanford, Florida, community, called the police to report a suspicious person walking in his neighborhood. Mr. Zimmerman, a twenty-eight-year-old man of mixed Hispanic ethnicity, was instructed by the dispatcher not to approach the person in question. Mr. Zimmerman disregarded those instructions, engaged in an altercation with the individual, and then fatally shot and killed Trayvon Martin, a seventeen-year-old unarmed African American teenager. Martin had been walking back to his father's house after buying snacks at a local convenience store.

Zimmerman told the Sanford police that he killed Martin in self-defense. He was taken into custody but was soon released, and no charges were immediately filed. In an effort to spur an investigation and arrest, Martin's parents launched an online petition that eventually garnered over two million signatures. Stories about Martin's death soon appeared on national and social media and prompted demonstrations and rallies across the country. Participants wearing hoodies (as Martin was the night he died) and carrying placards with the phrase "I am Trayvon Martin" called for Zimmerman's arrest. Attention to the case was so prominent that even President Barack Obama commented, telling reporters, "If I had a son, he'd look like Trayvon." Within several days, the U.S. Department of Justice and the Federal Bureau of Investigation (FBI) announced investigations into the shooting, the Sanford police chief stepped down amid controversy over the department's handling of the shooting, and a special prosecutor was appointed. On April 11, 2012, forty-three days after Trayvon Martin was killed, Zimmerman was arrested and charged with second-degree murder. His trial began on June 10, 2013, and on July 13, 2013, George Zimmerman was acquitted of all charges by a Florida jury of six women. Weeks of public outcry and protests followed the announcement of the verdict.

The killing of Trayvon Martin and the subsequent trial of George Zimmerman for his murder sparked an intense national debate about race and criminal justice in America. High-profile criminal cases such as the murder of Trayvon Martin both shape and reflect the public's views about offenders, the criminal process, and justice more generally. These cases also provide a window into how our criminal justice system operates, and raise important questions about whether justice is administered fairly and effectively. This particular case raised issues at the intersection of race, ethnicity, crime, and justice that have a long history in our country, and which remain salient today.

This volume is composed of twelve chapters that use the Martin/ Zimmerman case as a foundation to examine the racialization of justice in contemporary society. Authors were asked to address the causes and consequences of Martin's death and Zimmerman's acquittal in order to highlight the larger social, political, and legal processes that influence both the administration of justice and perceptions of its legitimacy in the United States. Reflecting upon this high-profile case, the authors in this volume explore the broader issues associated with race, ethnicity, crime, and justice that are at the heart of the American justice system.

The book is divided into three topical areas. Chapters in the first section ("Who Is in Danger?") focus on the role of race, ethnicity, and gender in shaping perceptions of criminality and the views of participants in the criminal process. Jacinta Gau and Kareem Jordan argue that George Zimmerman's targeting of Trayvon Martin reflects pervasive stereotypes about blacks' criminality and discuss how his actions are "legitimized" by police activity that promotes the extra scrutiny of African Americans. Kevin Drakulich and Laura Siller examine how race directly and indirectly shapes public perceptions of crime and criminals, with an emphasis on implicit racial bias. In an adaptation from his book *Punished: Policing the Lives of Black and Latino Boys*, Victor Rios provides insight into the multiple ways that surveillance of and assumptions about the dangerousness of young men of color decrease community security and create social distance between police and minority communities. Moreover, he argues, the symbols of crime and dangerousness that are often attributed to young men of color foster fear, which may give rise to situations such as Zimmerman's deadly pursuit of Trayvon Martin. In the final chapter in this section, Toya Like, Lori Sexton, and Savannah Porter compare the Trayvon Martin case to the murder of Gwen Araujo, a transgendered teenager who was killed in Newark, California, in 2002. They highlight how the intersections of race, ethnicity, class, and gender influence perceptions of others as threatening or dangerous.

The second section of the volume ("Where Do You Stand?") examines the role of race in the development of Stand Your Ground laws, in criminal investigations, and in court processes. Katheryn Russell-Brown explores the evolution of Stand Your Ground laws in Florida and how such laws place perceived threats of harm above human life. David Harris examines how the racialization of policing and employment of Stand Your Ground defenses negatively affect criminal investigations by leading officers to focus on the wrong people and thereby misallocate police resources. In light of arguments that race played a role in the Zimmerman verdict, Amy Farrell, Patricia Y. Warren, Devon Johnson, Jordyn Rosario, and Daniel Givelber explore how the racial and ethnic backgrounds of defendants and jurors influence judges' perceptions about the accuracy of acquittals in routine criminal trials. The final chapter in this section, written by Bryan Sykes, Alex Piquero, Jason Gioviano, and Nicolas Pittman, examines how perceptions of neighborhood safety are related to experiences of discrimination, which might provide a contextual frame for the encounter between Zimmerman and Martin.

In the third section of the book ("Which Voices Count?"), authors address public opinion, political responses, and media accounts of the Martin/Zimmerman case. Delores Jones-Brown and Henry Fradella argue that the combined influences of race, class, and gender influence the sociolegal environment in which Trayvon Martin died and George Zimmerman was tried and acquitted. The authors further analyze the divergent social views around the justifiability of Trayvon Martin's death, and the legal validity of Zimmerman's prosecution. For Isaac Unah and Valerie Wright, responses to the Zimmerman trial symbolize long-standing differences among whites, blacks, and Hispanics in their attitudes toward the criminal justice system and perceptions of its legitimacy. Chenelle Jones and Mia Ortiz explore public reactions to the Zimmerman verdict, with a particular emphasis on the role of social media and social protests in organizing calls for federal involvement in the case. This section closes with a chapter by Heather Washington and Valerie Wright where they examine media accounts of young homicide victims. The authors find significant race and gender differences in how these victims are characterized and in the amount of media coverage they receive.

Ultimately, the chapters in this volume provide a scholarly exploration of race, ethnicity, crime, and justice. This approach complements and adds evidence to the discussions about race and justice that occur on news broadcasts, across social media, and in everyday life. To be sure, the debates about the role of race in the administration of justice that emerged in the wake of Trayvon Martin's death and George Zimmerman's acquittal have a long history in this country. And, unfortunately, they likely have a long future. As we compile this edited collection three years after Trayvon Martin's death, high-profile incidents in places like Ferguson, Missouri, Staten Island, New York, and Baltimore, Maryland, have prompted groups across the United States to hold near-daily protests expressing concern that our society does not value black lives, and that justice is too often elusive for people of color. The chapters in this volume provide context for understanding the social, political, and legal processes that contribute to these views, and help explain why so many in our society question the legitimacy of our system of justice. By carefully examining and presenting the social scientific evidence, the scholars in this volume provide a critical perspective at an important historical moment.

PART I

Who Is in Danger?

1

Profiling Trayvon

Young Black Males, Suspicion, and Surveillance

JACINTA M. GAU AND KAREEM L. JORDAN

On February 26, 2012, the police dispatch center in Sanford, Florida, received a call. The caller, George Zimmerman, block watch coordinator for his gated community, told the dispatcher that there was a suspicious person walking through the neighborhood. The purported suspect was a young black male sporting a hooded sweatshirt who appeared, to Zimmerman, to be ambling aimlessly down the sidewalk. In fact, the individual was seventeen-year-old Trayvon Martin and he was visiting his father, who resided in the neighborhood. Martin was returning to his father's home after completing a snack run to a local convenience store. He was chatting on his cell phone with a friend. He was unarmed. Zimmerman, apparently convinced that the teenager was an imminent threat to neighborhood security, concealed his handgun on his person, entered his car, and, ignoring the dispatcher's admonitions that his actions were unnecessary, began following Martin. At this point in the story, the details get murky. There were no direct witnesses, so the narrative had to be cobbled together with bits and pieces of accounts from a variety of sources. The only clear fact is that the two ended up embroiled in a physical struggle and that Trayvon Martin died when George Zimmerman, fearing he was losing the fight, shot Martin in the abdomen. Several months later, Zimmerman was tried for second-degree murder; the six-person jury acquitted him. They were unconvinced that Zimmerman's actions amounted to anything more than a tragic but understandable mistake, or that Martin did not somehow bring his demise upon himself.

The Martin-Zimmerman case raises a multitude of thorny issues about race, Florida's broad self-defense statutes, and the role of the media and advocacy groups in the delivery of justice. The present chapter analyzes the actions of Zimmerman and jury as being situated within a larger culture of suspicion aimed at young black males. Zimmerman's actions against Martin—and the jury's subsequent leniency toward Zimmerman—can be viewed as microcosms of the prevalent assumption nationwide that black males are inherently unpredictable and dangerous. This assumption is the foundation for police policies that encourage—whether explicitly or as a (predictable) side effect—enhanced police scrutiny of members of this group, and is also evident in the tendency for juries to treat black defendants with particular severity. Public opinion studies have revealed widespread bias—be it overt or latent—against young black males. This bias, endemic to (white) society, perpetuates racialized justice system activities, and these activities, in turn, feed public opinion by making these biases seem factual and justified. Viewed through the lens of a racially stratified society, Zimmerman's actions and those of the jury seem unremarkable, perhaps even inevitable.

The Subtext of Racial Profiling: Symbolic Assailants and the Accoutrements of the Criminal

A pioneering study of police officers' habits, preferences, and styles in performing their jobs introduced the notion of the symbolic assailant:[1] "Police officers, because their work requires them to be occupied continually with potential violence, develop a perceptual shorthand to identify certain kinds of people as symbolic assailants, that is, as persons who use gestures, language, and attire that the police have come to recognize as a prelude to violence. This does not mean that violence by a symbolic assailant is necessarily predictable. On the contrary, the police officer responds to the vague indication of danger suggested by appearance." This "perceptual shorthand" allows experienced police officers to quickly organize large quantities of incoming information, much of it ambiguous, into predefined categories of "threatening" and "nonthreatening." When a potential suspect's behavioral cues do not allow officers to determine immediately that the person is a threat, proxy indicators (e.g., race, sex, age, clothing style) are substituted for more direct measures of character and intent. Police then infer dangerousness on the basis of outward symbols that they have come to equate with unpredictability and violence.

While there is nothing inherently insidious about perceptual shorthand (what social psychologists would call heuristic devices, experience-based learning that permits new information to be organized efficiently), trouble arises on the basis of the historically tumultuous relationship between police and black Americans. After the Civil War, police forces were explicitly deployed to prevent blacks from entering whites' claimed territories and institutions. Police often turned a blind eye toward—or even actively participated in—mob violence aimed at instilling terror and submission in the black community. As time wore on, the severity and obviousness of the oppression lessened, but the racial angle did not disappear. It merely changed form.

The unique tensions between police and black Americans sit amid a context of implicit bias wherein blacks and crime have become heavily intertwined in public imagery and dialogue.[2] Black males, especially, are at the center of discussions about crime and violence. News media feed the public a steady diet of crime stories that disproportionately feature black offenders, and hopeful politicians gunning for office exploit campaign rhetoric with more or less obvious racial overtures as a means of exciting their electorates.[3] The stereotype of black males as the poster children for violence in America lingers tenaciously because it seems correct based on crime statistics. As with most stereotypes, a distortion of facts, combined with a few examples of carefully selected confirmatory cases, can make the stereotype appear less like a bias and more like a data-derived, evidence-based conclusion. The black crime stereotype is pernicious precisely because the facts are so easy to manipulate.

At an ecological level, violent crime rates and black populations overlap spatially. Most black Americans reside in metropolitan areas, and many cities' residential patterns remain racially segregated (sometimes dramatically so). Social and economic isolation—fueled by past and present racial discrimination as well as by employment discrimination and unequal access to educational institutions—has created pockets of impoverished blacks nationwide, particularly in urban areas.[4] Crime, especially violent crime, flourishes in these islands of poverty and economic stagnation.[5] Disillusionment with society's primary institutions (e.g., education, job markets) has spurred the rise of an oppositional culture that leads poor black youths growing up in these isolated areas of concentrated disadvantage to reject the values espoused by these institutions and to develop their own codes, norms, and value systems.[6] Conflict and violence are forms of currency in this underground economy that prizes self-help and rewards strategic acts of aggression.

Not everyone in these majority-black, impoverished areas commits violence or endorses aggression as an acceptable means of conflict resolution, of course—the majority do not. Those who do not, however, nonetheless bear equal stigma as those who do. The assumption that an individual person's character or behavior can be predicted on the basis of information about the group to which he or she belongs is an example of a type of faulty logic called the ecological fallacy. The ecological fallacy occurs when a certain statistic that captures a general trend at the group level is (erroneously) used to infer something about an individual member of that group. Claims that high rates of crime commission among black males justify increased suspicion of them as a group are logically flawed. It is true that black males, especially those in their youth and young adult years, have a higher rate of violent crime commission than any other demographic group; however, most black males do not commit acts of aggression. As with any other demographic group, some young black males engage in crime and violence, but most do not.

Police profiling of young black males occurs when officers assume that the high rates of criminal justice involvement among this group mean that each of them, individually, is potentially dangerous. Research reveals that officers working high-crime beats do not adequately distinguish between those who are involved in crime and those who are not.[7] In the context of relations between police officers and young black males, perceptual shorthand is created on the basis of characteristics that officers come to associate with violence, and the "symbolic assailant" is the young black male who does stereotypical things like dressing in baggy clothes and hanging out on street corners.[8] Under this heuristic device, a young black male need not do anything overtly suspicious to be considered suspect; instead, his clothing, hairstyle, and mannerisms—mimicking the accoutrements of gang members and drug dealers—are considered sufficient proof of his potential dangerousness. Furthermore, because the danger is always potential rather than certain, the stereotype can never be refuted or falsified. An officer need not revisit his underlying prejudice about black males' criminal proclivities when he encounters a member of this group who does not assault him and or give him legal grounds for arrest; rather, the officer can rationalize this event in any number of ways (e.g., he handled the situation well and prevented violence, or the suspect is truly guilty but there is not sufficient evidence to prove it). Because the stereotype is fluid, and because dangerousness is framed as potential rather than certain, police officers can maintain their stereotypes even after encountering numerous young black males who are innocent of wrongdoing.

Due to their elevated rates of offending and officers' failure to adequately distinguish the guilty from the innocent, young minority males are the demographic group most likely to be singled out for stops and frisks. A stop is a brief detention wherein an officer, her suspicions having been aroused by a person's seemingly aberrant behavior, questions the suspect about who he is, what he is doing, where he is going, and other details designed to obtain information that would either confirm or dispel the officer's suspicion that the individual is up to mischief. Frisks sometimes, but not always, accompany stops. A frisk is a pat down of the outer layer of a suspect's clothing; the purpose of the search is to detect contraband such as guns or drugs. These intrusions upon liberty and privacy are minor compared to those entailed in full-blown arrests and searches, but they are significant and emotionally meaningful violations of one's dignity. They can be seen as demeaning and as a sign of disrespect. Minorities, especially males, are stopped and frisked more often than whites are,[9] and often on shakier evidentiary grounds.[10] Disproportionate exposure to this negative encounter type contributes to young minority males' hostility toward police. This pattern of racially lopsided policing continues, however, because it is backed up by public opinion and stereotypes about black criminality.

Public Opinion: Cause and Consequence of Racialization in the Justice System

Racialized policing could not exist without a broad base of public support both for the police and for race-based practices. Attitudes about the police are divided, sometimes sharply, along racial lines. Whites

TABLE 1.1. General Social Survey Results: White Respondents' Attitudes toward Whites and Blacks

Survey item	"How well does this describe . . ."	
	Whites	Blacks
"Rich . . . poor"[a]	3.65	4.77
"Hardworking . . . lazy"[a]	3.52	4.26
"Self-supporting . . . live off welfare"[b]	2.71	4.79
"Intelligent . . . unintelligent"[a]	3.42	3.79
"Not violent . . . violence prone"[c]	3.86	4.50

[a] 2012 GSS; [b] 1990 GSS; [c] 2000 GSS

consistently report more favorable attitudes toward police than do blacks. Blacks are more likely to believe that the police sometimes act unfairly, are rude, or provide lower-quality services to racial minorities.[11] Whites are more likely to view police as operating in a race-neutral fashion.[12] In one survey, 70 percent of black respondents reported feeling that police treat blacks less fairly than they do whites; just 37 percent of white respondents echoed this sentiment.[13]

Paralleling their support for police is whites' lingering tendency to view blacks disparagingly. Overt racial bias is no longer politically correct in most circles, but implicit bias—assumptions and stereotypes that people hold even when they might not be aware that they harbor these prejudices—remains prevalent.[14] A recent national poll revealed persistent overt and implicit bias.[15] Further evidence of lingering negative stereotypes about blacks can be found in the General Social Survey, which is administered to a randomly selected, nationally representative sample every two years by the National Opinion Research Center. Table 1.1 shows results from survey questions tapping into respondents' attitudes toward whites versus toward blacks. These survey items asked respondents to rate, on a scale of 1 to 7, how they would describe whites and blacks on these social measures. The table presents the results for white respondents' answers to each question. The numbers reflect the mean on each scale, with higher values indicative of more negative attitudes.

This table shows that whites, as a group, consistently rated blacks more negatively than they did other whites. The differences, moreover, were not limited to stereotypes about violent propensities; to the contrary, they spanned a spectrum of unseemly characteristics and social behaviors. Whites rated blacks higher on measures of poverty, laziness, welfare dependency, and unintelligence. Of course, this does not mean that every white person in this sample viewed blacks unfavorably; as a group, however, white respondents displayed clear signs of implicit bias. Implicit bias can be as threatening to the public welfare as explicit bias is, as those who hold implicit negative stereotypes are often not aware of their prejudices and can rationalize their beliefs as being based on fact rather than on racism or stereotypes.

Whites' faith in the police, coupled with their predominantly unfavorable views about blacks, provides the groundwork for racialized policing. To the extent that whites do believe that police engage in racial profiling, they tend to approve of this practice on the argument that blacks are heavily involved in crime and prone to violence.[16] There is a certain amount of hypocrisy surrounding racial profiling, even within the law enforcement community. On the one hand, police and their vocal advocates stolidly reject the term "racial profiling" and maintain the position that profiling on the basis of race is always and absolutely wrong. On the other hand, however, there is a prevalent belief that minorities are more likely to commit crime and that someone's race is a reliable indicator of his or her criminal potential. This hypocrisy is often enshrouded in a sense of gloomy resignation: minority status is an unfortunate predictor of criminal propensity, but a predictor nonetheless. White Americans, then, appear willing to tolerate police surveillance of black Americans because this accords with their beliefs about black criminality. Profiling might not get ringing endorsement, but the fundamental acceptance of it as "what needs to be done" allows the practice to continue.

Young Black Males' Experiences with Surveillance

Enhanced police surveillance takes a toll on the already tense, volatile relationship between police and young black males and, indeed, between whites and blacks in society at large. Turmoil is perpetuated when policing strategies and officer actions revolve around assumptions about these youths' and young adults' character, integrity, and human worth. To be sure, the animosity is reciprocated; young black males often treat officers rudely or with defiance, which can inflame officers' tempers and serve as confirmation of the apparent validity of officers' assumption that they are all miscreant. On the other hand, police officers are one of the most visible symbols of mainstream society. Society codifies its morals and values into law and then charges police officers with upholding not only those laws but also the cultural values they embody. As such, officers are not merely enforcers of the law—they are representatives of mainstream society. Their symbolic importance has implications for their interactions with members of the public. As police officers are official representatives of society, their actions toward the individuals with whom they come into contact convey suggestions about those individuals' worth and value to society.[17] When a police officer degrades a person, that person does not only feel poorly toward that officer—he can feel that society itself has rejected him.

Substantial research has documented the profound and lasting impact that repeated degradation and abuse by police officers has on young black males. Members of this group are particularly vulnerable to the psychological effects of police mistreatment because they experience high rates of alienation from other mainstream institutions such as schools and the labor market.[18] Many already feel devalued by society, and many internalize these feelings in a manner that leads them to devalue themselves and others in their group.[19] Police scrutiny, rudeness, and abuse can add to existing feelings of isolation, rejection, and frustration.

Young black males living in urban areas consistently report feeling monitored, harassed, and mistreated by police. Many have personally experienced police maltreatment and have also witnessed or heard about others' unpleasant encounters. These additive effects accumulate over time; repeated exposure to personal and vicarious victimization instills a sense of mistrust in, and hostility toward, police.[20] Black communities nationwide experience the ramifications each time one of their own is mistreated by police.

Racialized policing also continues to be a wedge issue separating whites from communities of color. Whites' stereotypes and fears about black criminality allow them to feel that police surveillance of minorities (particularly young males) is rational and necessary as a means of keeping this "dangerous" group in check. Individuals and communities of color, by contrast, experience feelings of frustration, anger, and alienation at the indignities visited upon them by police in the name of public safety. This problem is a direct result of the wide social gap between whites and minorities, and it also perpetuates the problem by keeping the two sides at constant odds with each other.

Taking It to Court: Biases against Black Defendants and Victims

On April 11, 2012, George Zimmerman was indicted on second-degree murder charges for the death of Trayvon Martin. On June 25, 2012, the trial began. Nobody disputed that Zimmerman had killed Martin, so the case turned on whether the jury believed that Zimmerman had reasonably thought, in the heat of the physical altercation, that he was in imminent danger of being seriously injured. The question for the jury to decide was whether they found Zimmerman's claim of self-defense credible and sufficiently compelling to justify acquitting him of murder. As such, Martin was on trial as much as Zimmerman was, arguably even more so. Zimmerman's defense team introduced evidence intended to impeach Martin's character and to paint him as a violent delinquent who might have hurt or killed Zimmerman had Zimmerman not acted first. The six jurors impaneled on the case were thus placed in a position not merely of having to consider whether a white/Hispanic man had reasonably acted in self-defense—they also had to decide whether (black) Trayvon Martin was dangerous.

Race has been found to influence the decision making of prosecutors, judges, and juries. Prosecutors, for instance, are more likely to pursue the death penalty against black defendants, particularly those accused of killing white victims.[21] The focal concerns perspective offers a theoretical understanding of how race and ethnicity affect judicial decision making.[22] This perspective contends that when making decisions, judges consider three factors: blameworthiness, dangerousness to the community, and practical constraints and concerns. Blameworthiness is assessed through such legal variables as offense severity and prior record. Variables such as type of offense, employment status, and use of a weapon signify a defendant's level of dangerousness to the community. Practical constraints and concerns include both organizational and individual considerations. Organizational factors include such things as adequate correctional space and court case flow. Individual determinants include factors that affect judges' determination of a defendant's ability to serve time in jail or prison (e.g., family and community responsibilities).

Because judges must often make decisions with limited time and incomplete information, they develop a perceptual shorthand not unlike that developed by police officers, as described earlier. This shorthand is based on stereotypes evoked by extralegal factors such as race, ethnicity, gender, and age. Defendants who meet the stereotypical image of a dangerous offender tend to be sentenced more harshly.[23] This particularly disadvantages males, blacks, Hispanics, and younger offenders, as they are more often associated with supposedly crime-prone groups.[24] In fact, research has demonstrated that young black males are among the most harshly treated demographic groups in the criminal justice system.[25]

Experimental studies using mock juries have uncovered evidence that defendants' race is salient to jurors and can affect their decision making. A meta-analysis of research examining the influence of race in jury decision making in simulated trials indicated that race was a factor in the decision to convict a defendant.[26] Another study found that mock jurors were more likely to impose death sentences on black defendants than on white ones; this effect was even more pronounced when the black defendants' victims were white. Jurors offered the greatest leniency in scenarios where white defendants were accused of murdering black victims.[27] Similarly, another team of researchers discovered that mock jurors were more lenient on white defendants than on black ones, particularly when a white defendant's victim was black.[28] These findings tap into an underlying dynamic in the Zimmerman-Martin trial: even though, technically, a white man was on trial for murdering a black man, the logic was reversed such that the jury was attempting to discern whether the white man had actually been the victim of an attack by the black man. Based on the research suggesting that jurors are more punitive toward blacks (as both defendants and as victims) and more sympathetic toward whites (as both defendants and victims), the racial dyad between Zimmerman and Martin was problematic from the outset of the trial. The selection of a majority-white jury virtually guaranteed that the defense would have an easy time vilifying Martin and making Zimmerman appear to be the true victim.

Compounding this problem was the fact that, during the trial, the prosecution was limited to discussing certain character evidence about Trayvon Martin. The jurors, lacking full and thorough knowledge of Martin's actions during the event, had to look beyond the facts of the case to make a decision about his culpability and potential dangerousness. As such, the Zimmerman trial may have been an instance of the liberation hypothesis in action. The liberation hypothesis predicts that jurors are most likely to take extralegal factors (e.g., defendant race or gender) into account when the facts of the case are ambiguous.[29] According to this line of logic, when the evidence is strong and unequivocal, jurors will render a verdict based solely upon that evidence; however, when the evidence is not clearly in favor of either guilt or innocence, and when jurors are hunting for additional information to help them make a decision, defendant and victim characteristics can enter the equation. It was discussed earlier that whites attribute negative behaviors and characteristics to blacks; this tendency bleeds over to jurors because jurors are a sample drawn from society's general population. In the Zimmerman trial, where Martin's actions received more attention than did Zimmerman's, the absence of a full understanding and knowledge of Martin created an opportunity for stereotypes, prejudices, and biases to influence courtroom decision making. The role of race in jury decision making may be due to not only biases against the victim, but also the jury's way of identifying with the defendant. Jurors typically relate to defendants on two levels. First, jurors generally are more empathetic toward defendants with whom they can personally identify on the basis of shared characteristics, including race.[30] This is typically referred to as in-group favoritism.[31] Second, jurors possess empathy on a more cognitive level.[32] If jurors are able to vicariously experience the feelings of the defendant (e.g., circumstances that lead to a killing), they are more likely to be empathetic. Neither of these levels is favorable when there is a nonblack jury and a black victim. There is a lower likelihood of jurors feeling empathy toward a black victim, because they may have difficulty identifying with that person. This, too, may have materially impacted the verdict in the Zimmerman trial, as five of the jurors were white and one was Hispanic. The jury may therefore have identified with Zimmerman more than with Martin on the basis of group similarity.

Where Do We Go from Here? Changing the Landscape of Racism in a "Postracial" Era

In recent years, particularly with the election (and reelection) of the nation's first black president, it has become common to hear claims that racism is a vestige of the past. Those who propose that the country has entered a "postracial" era argue that race is no longer a predictor of a person's experiences or opportunities in life. They contend that everyone sinks or swims on the basis of personal merit, not the lottery of genetic determinants of skin color. These claims represent willful ignorance of certain clear facts: Black and Latino Americans continue to bear the burdens of broken school systems and employment discrimination, race-based residential segregation persists throughout urban and rural areas, and there is a yawning chasm between the wealth and assets enjoyed by the average white family and those possessed by the average black family. To be sure, white hoods and burning crosses are no longer acceptable—yet Confederate flags still fly and middle-class blacks still get stopped by police while walking in their neighborhoods of residence. There is an urgent need for a national discussion of race and its material impacts on the lives of all Americans, not just persons of color. In particular, the conversation should involve an open dialog about race and the justice system.

It might seem counterintuitive to propose reducing racial disparities in the justice system—and in public opinion—by making race *more* prominent, but doing so could help unbury implicit biases and bring them into the light so that their influence can be admitted, examined, and, ultimately, dispelled. Modern notions of political correctness (usually) prevent people from expressing openly racist opinions, but this does not mean that these feelings have vanished. They linger, yet they are not talked about, and as such they are free to infect various aspects of social thought, so long as they are cloaked in seemingly race-neutral language. Deliberate blindness to race also ensures the continuation of a social wedge between whites and people of color. White Americans' insistence that race is immaterial conflicts sharply with minorities' lived experiences.

The solution is a candid dialogue about race and its impact. Distrust and distance between the groups will linger until there is widespread admission that people's skin color does impact their lives in significant ways. Implicit biases can be addressed in steps, the first one being to admit that they exist. Greater understanding of how implicit bias operates—and how people can harbor these beliefs without even being aware of it—can help people reexamine their own beliefs and consider how racial prejudice might be affecting their thinking, even if on a subconscious level. As one set of authors put it, "The aversive nature of modern racism suggests that Whites are motivated to appear non-prejudiced when racial issues are salient."[33] That is, while implicit bias can lead whites to act in a prejudiced manner toward blacks, whites who are sensitized to the racial dynamics of a particular situation become more self aware and tend to monitor their attitudes and behaviors more closely. Indeed, it has been found that white mock jurors' negative attitudes toward black defendants are significantly reduced when race was made salient.[34] When race is out in the open, people's implicit biases have nowhere to hide.

Conclusion

This chapter reviewed the evidence demonstrating that race-based treatment is endemic to the criminal justice system. Public opinion continues to reflect clear divides between whites and minorities— particularly between whites and blacks—on attitudes toward the justice system and its agents; moreover, despite overt racism being a relic of the past, implicit biases maintain a strong grasp on the public conscience. Large portions of whites continue to view blacks in a negative light and, especially, to believe that they are prone to crime and violence. Racialized policing whereby officers closely scrutinize blacks' movement and behavior—even that which appears innocuous—is supported by public sentiment and, likewise, has the effect of making public hostility toward and suspicion of black males appear rational. In the courtroom, black defendants and victims frequently receive short shrift. This is due in part to (white) jurors' stereotypes about blacks' criminal tendencies, and in part to the fact that nonblack jurors have trouble identifying and empathizing with black victims. Viewed against the backdrop of society-wide implicit biases and ingrained suspicion of young black males, Zimmerman's actions against Martin are far from surprising; they seem, rather, to be a logical outgrowth of existing widespread prejudice and large-scale acceptance of racial profiling. The first step in solving this dilemma is to admit the existence of these deeply engrained biases—continuing to deny them serves only to perpetuate racially disparate treatment and ensure the endurance of a social wedge between white and black Americans. As is frequently the case, the first step to fixing something that is broken is to admit that the problem exists.

NOTES

1. Skolnick 2011, 42.
2. Olusanya and Gau 2012.
3. Gest 2001.
4. Massey and Denton 1993; Wilson 1987.
5. Massey 1995.
6. Anderson 1999.
7. Ibid.
8. Skolnick 2011, 42.
9. Fagan and Davies 2000.
10. Harris 1994.
11. Tyler 2005.
12. Patten 2013.
13. Pew Research Center 2013.
14. Olusanya and Gau 2012.
15. Associated Press 2012.
16. Weitzer 2000.
17. Tyler 1997.
18. Anderson 1999.
19. Butler 1995.
20. Brunson 2007.
21. Sorensen and Wallace 1999.
22. Steffensmeier 1980; Steffensmeier, Ulmer, and Kramer 1998.
23. Eberhardt et al. 2006.
24. Kennedy 1997; Steffensmeier, Ulmer, and Kramer 1998.
25. Steffensmeier, Ulmer, and Kramer 1998.
26. Mitchell et al. 2005.
27. Lynch and Haney 2009.

28. ForsterLee et al. 2006.
29. Kalven and Zeisel 1966.
30. Brewer 2004; Olsen-Fulero and Fulero 1997.
31. Hewstone, Rubin, and Willis 2002.
32. Olsen-Fulero and Fulero 1997; Brewer 2004.
33. Sommers and Ellsworth 2000, 1367.
34. Ibid.

REFERENCES

Anderson, E. 1999. *Code of the Streets: Decency, Violence, and the Moral Life of the Inner City.* New York: Norton.

Associated Press. 2012. "Racial Attitudes Survey." http://surveys.ap.org/data%5CGfK%5CAP_Racial_Attitudes_Topline_09182012.pdf.

Brewer, T. W. 2004. "Race and Jurors' Receptivity to Mitigation in Capital Cases: The Effect of Jurors, Defendants', and Victims' Race in Combination." *Law and Human Behavior* 28 (5): 529–45.

Brunson, R. K. 2007. " 'Police Don't Like Black People': African-American Young Men's Accumulated Police Experiences." *Criminology & Public Policy* 6 (1): 71–102.

Butler, P. 1995. "Racially Based Jury Nullification: Black Power in the Criminal Justice System." *Yale Law Journal* 105 (3): 677–725.

Eberhardt, J. L., P. G. Davies, V. J. Purdie-Vaughns, and S. L. Johnson. 2006. "Looking Deathworthy: Perceived Stereotypicality of Black Defendants Predicts Capital-Sentencing Outcomes." *Psychological Science* 17 (5): 383–86.

Fagan, J. T., and G. Davies. 2000. "Street Stops and Broken Windows: Terry, Race, and Disorder in New York City." *Fordham Urban Law Journal* 28 (2): 457–504.

ForsterLee, R., L. ForsterLee, I. A. Horowitz, and E. King. 2006. "The Effects of Defendant Race, Victim Race, and Juror Gender on Evidence Processing in a Murder Trial." *Behavioral Sciences and the Law* 24:179–98.

Gest, T. 2001. *Crime & Politics: Big Government's Erratic Campaign for Law and Order.* Oxford: Oxford University Press.

Harris, D. A. 1994. "Factors for Reasonable Suspicion: When Black and Poor Means Stopped and Frisked." *Indiana Law Journal* 69:659–87.

Hewstone, M., M. Rubin, and H. Willis. 2002. "Intergroup Bias." *Annual Review of Psychology* 53:575–604.

Kalven, H., and H. Zeisel. 1966. *The American Jury.* Boston: Little, Brown.

Kennedy, R. 1997. *Race, Crime and the Law.* New York: Vintage.

Lynch, M., and C. Haney. 2009. "Capital Jury Deliberation: Effects on Death Sentencing, Comprehension, and Discrimination." *Law & Human Behavior* 33:481–96.

Massey, D. S. 1995. "Getting Away with Murder: Segregation and Violent Crime in Urban America." *University of Pennsylvania Law Review* 143 (5): 1203–32.

Massey, D. S., and N. A. Denton. 1993. *American Apartheid: Segregation and the Making of the Underclass.* Cambridge, MA: Harvard University Press.

Mitchell, T. L., R. M. Haw, J. E. Pfeifer, and C. A. Meissner. 2005. "Racial Bias in Mock Juror Decision-Making: A Meta-Analytic Review of Defendant Treatment." *Law and Human Behavior* 29 (6): 621–37.

Olsen-Fulero, L., and S. M. Fulero. 1997. "Commonsense Rape Judgments: An Empathy Complexity Theory of Rape Juror Story Making." *Psychology, Public Policy and Law* 3:402–20.

Olusanya, O., and J. M. Gau. 2012. "Race, Neighborhood Context, and Risk Prediction." *Criminal Justice Studies* 25 (2): 159–75.

Patten, E. 2013. "The Black-White and Urban-Rural Divides in Perceptions of Racial Fairness." Washington, DC: Pew Research Center.

Pew Research Center. 2013. "King's Dream Remains an Elusive Goal: Many Americans See Racial Disparities." Washington, DC: Pew Research Center.

Skolnick, J. H. 2011. *Justice Without Trial: Law Enforcement in Democratic Society.* 4th ed. New York: John Wiley.

Sommers, S. R., and P. C. Ellsworth. 2000. "Race in the Courtroom: Perceptions of Guilt and Dispositional Attributions." *Personality and Social Psychology Bulletin* 26 (11): 1367–79.

Sorensen, J., and D. H. Wallace. 1999. "Prosecutorial Discretion in Seeking Death: An Analysis of Racial Disparity in the Pretrial Stages of Case Processing in a Midwestern County." *Justice Quarterly* 16 (3): 559–78.

Steffensmeier, D. 1980. "Assessing the Impact of the Women's Movement on Sex-Based Differences in the Handling of Adult Criminal Defendants." *Crime & Delinquency* 26 (3): 344–58.

Steffensmeier, D., J. Ulmer, and J. Kramer. 1998. "The Interaction of Race, Gender, and Age in Criminal Sentencing: The Punishment Cost of Being Young, Black, and Male." *Criminology* 36 (4): 763–97.

Tyler, T. R. 1997. "The Psychology of Legitimacy: A Relational Perspective on Voluntary Deference to Authorities." *Personality and Social Psychology Review* 1 (4): 323–45.

Tyler, T. R. 2005. "Policing in Black and White: Ethnic Group Differences in Trust and Confidence in the Police." *Police Quarterly* 8 (3): 322–42.

Weitzer, R. 2000. "Racialized Policing: Residents' Perceptions in Three Neighborhoods." *Law and Society Review* 34 (1): 129–55.

Wilson, W. J. 1987. *The Truly Disadvantaged: The Inner City, the Underclass, and Public Policy.* Chicago: University of Chicago Press.

2

Presumed Danger

Race, Bias, Stigma, and Perceptions of Crime and Criminals

KEVIN M. DRAKULICH AND LAURA SILLER

The shooting of Trayvon Martin and the subsequent trial of George Zimmerman prompted heated national conversations and garnered massive media coverage. As Martin was unarmed, a core question that emerged in its coverage was the role race played in Zimmerman's evaluation of the dangerousness of the situation.[1]

The incredible volume of media coverage appeared disproportionate to its specific consequences. Trayvon Martin's death was tragic to those who cared for him, but, in a larger tragedy, shooting deaths of young African American men are not uncommon in this country, and few of them rise to this level of media attention. Research on moral panics suggests that when media attention to an incident seems disproportionate to its direct consequences, it is likely that the public interest is motivated by a concern about what the case symbolizes—what it tells us about ourselves as a society.[2] Thus, the real interest was not just in the role race played in Zimmerman's evaluation of danger, but whether race continues to play a sizeable role in general in how we evaluate the criminal dangerousness of people or places, as well as what this role means.[3]

Our goal is to pose a broader explanation for this question of how race colors perceptions of crime and communities. We do not have any special insight into the mind of George Zimmerman. What we can speak to is how people *in general* evaluate criminal danger and the ways that race may influence these judgments. This discussion is particularly complicated in the modern era—characterized by persistent racial inequalities but also by historically low levels of overtly racist attitudes.[4] To explain this seeming paradox, a variety of scholars have suggested some form of "modern" racism in which overt animus or bias is eschewed while subtler views couched in nonracial ideological language persist.[5] Thus, as Elijah Anderson has argued, the Trayvon Martin case may reflect a different kind of prejudice within a different environment of racial attitudes and race relations than that involved in the 1955 death of Emmett Till, another case that sparked a national conversation about race.[6] In this modern era of racial attitudes, a simple story about overt racial crime stereotypes may not be sufficient.

In this chapter we extend prior work to propose a two-part explanation for how race influences perceptions of criminal danger in this modern era. First, race may matter in more *indirect* ways than simple racial crime stereotypes. For example, we know that perceptions of minor disorder play an important role in people's perceptions of more serious criminal danger, but we also know that perceptions of disorder are strongly influenced by the neighborhood racial composition.[7]

Second, the direct role of racial bias may simply be *hidden* from view. While explicit admissions of racial bias have indeed declined, new work has revealed that many people hold racial biases but do not report them in surveys, either because of concerns about social desirability or because they are not consciously aware of their biases. Thus, those who hold such biases may be more likely to perceive crime as increasing, but this effect may not be captured in traditional surveys.

The question of how race influences our perceptions of criminal danger is both interesting and complicated because it exists at the intersection of several different fields of study. First, it involves questions about social context: how we perceive and react to the social and physical environments of the communities in which we live. Second, it involves cognitive processes: the ways we evaluate risk and judge threats. Finally, of course, it also invokes the complicated history of race relations in this country.

In this chapter we shed light on some of the indirect and hidden ways race influences perceptions of criminal danger. We begin with a review of relevant work from each of the fields of study outlined above. The first section provides an overview of research on the role of race in perceptions of crime and communities, focusing in particular on unresolved questions. The second draws on social-psychological research to help us understand more generally how we evaluate risk and perceive danger and what role race may play in this process. The third provides a brief overview of *why* race might matter at all for these perceptions, outlining two "ideal type" explanations.

Following this, we draw on data from two separate sources to investigate our two-part explanation for the role of race in perceptions of crime and communities. First, we use a single-city neighborhood survey to investigate one of the indirect ways race may matter to perceptions of local criminal danger: by influencing perceptions of minor disorder. Second, we employ a measure of *implicit* racial bias included in a national survey to explore a potential hidden role of race on perceptions of local criminal danger.

Perceptions of Neighborhoods

People perceive more risk of victimization and express more fear of crime in neighborhoods with larger numbers of African Americans. Studies have reported an effect of the perceived or actual racial composition—the percentage of residents of the local area belonging to different racial groups—on assessments of criminal danger,[8] even after accounting for differences in the actual threat posed by crime.[9]

While this research convincingly suggests that the racial composition matters to people's perceptions of crime, it leaves largely unanswered the question of *why* this is the case. Perhaps the simplest and most straightforward explanation involves *racial crime stereotypes*: people believe that racial and ethnic minorities are more involved in crime and thus perceive neighborhoods with more racial and ethnic minorities to be more dangerous. Prior research has shown evidence of a relationship between perceptions of criminal danger and general measures of racial prejudice,[10] as well as stereotypes specifically about crime.[11] However, this work is largely not able to investigate whether racial crime stereotypes or other negative racial attitudes *explain* why people perceive more crime in neighborhoods with larger numbers of racial/ethnic minorities. In other words, we know that some people have racial stereotypes and that these people tend to report perceiving more crime, but we do not know whether the inverse is true: do all of those people who overestimate crime in neighborhoods with more African Americans do so because they have stereotypes of African Americans as criminals?

Two recent studies have sought to investigate whether racial crime stereotypes explain (or "mediate") the relationship between the racial composition and some measure of the perceived risk of criminal danger. Neither found evidence that stereotypes do much to explain why people overestimate crime in neighborhoods with larger numbers of African Americans.[12] In short, then, the simplest and most direct explanation for why people perceive more crime in neighborhoods with more racial minorities—that they hold crime stereotypes about racial minorities—does not seem to be supported in existing data.

So what does explain the relationship between the racial composition and perceptions of crime? This chapter suggests two different—though not necessarily competing—explanations.

The first is that race may act in a less direct fashion. For instance, a large variety of prior work has suggested that perceptions of minor disorder play a major role in perceptions of crime. The idea is that while people will rarely see visible evidence of serious crimes, they will be much more likely to be able to assess the presence or absence of minor kinds of disorder, from trash and graffiti to unruly teenagers and loud neighbors. It may be, then, that people use these minor signs of disorder as a proxy: a way to estimate the likelihood of more serious crimes they may have less direct information about. This is, in fact, a relatively old idea in criminology and is part of the premise behind "broken windows theory."[13] A variety of research provides evidence of a link between perceptions of minor disorder and more serious crime.[14]

Of course, perceptions of disorder, superficially, should not carry information about race and thus should not be a good candidate for explaining the relationship between the racial composition and perceptions of crime. However, recent work has suggested that perceptions of disorder may not always be based on the actual presence of disorder, and instead may be influenced by other social cues, such as the race or class of the neighborhood.[15] In this case, perceptions of disorder—along with other purportedly nonracial pieces of information—may in fact be influenced by the racial composition of the neighborhood in ways that help explain the connection between race and perceptions of crime within communities.[16]

There is also another possibility. It may be that surveys that directly ask respondents about their racial stereotypes or other racial feelings or attitudes are failing to truly capture these feelings and attitudes and the way they influence people's perceptions. Some people may be concerned that prejudicial or stereotypical views are not socially desirable, and thus may hide the truth when taking a survey. It is also possible that people are influenced by racial affect or bias without being consciously aware of its influence. As described in the following section, social psychologists have discovered that our perceptions are influenced by a variety of factors, not all of which operate on a conscious level. Thus, in addition to race influencing perceptions of crime and criminals in an indirect fashion, it may also influence such perceptions in a more direct but harder to detect manner.

Evaluations of Criminal Danger: Cognitive Processes

As we go about our daily lives, we frequently, though not always consciously or purposefully, assess the potential for danger posed by people and places. Presumably, George Zimmerman perceived danger in the situation he found himself in with Trayvon Martin, but it is not just members of neighborhood watches who are on the lookout for potential threats. Evaluations of danger may occur within the context of decisions about walking through a park at night, crossing to a sidewalk on the other side of a street, letting one's children play outside, and moving into or out of neighborhoods.

Assessing the danger of a place or situation is a difficult task. We rarely if ever have all the information necessary: few of us are aware of the exact frequency of crimes that have occurred in an area in the past, let alone have a sense of the likelihood of them happening again in the near future. Cognitive psychologists have long been interested in how we make judgments in the face of uncertain information,[17] and some of their findings may be helpful in sorting out how people assess the danger posed by people or places.

When trying to estimate the likelihood of something like criminal danger in the face of incomplete information, individuals will frequently employ a particular cognitive shortcut. *Availability* describes the ease with which previous instances of or occurrences can be brought to mind: those who have frequently or recently witnessed or heard stories about crimes in the neighborhood will have an easy time accessing these memories and may thus be more likely to rate the neighborhood as a dangerous place.[18] For the many who have not frequently or recently witnessed or heard about a serious crime occurring in the neighborhood, this question—"how dangerous is my neighborhood?"—may be more difficult. When faced with a difficult question, we often *substitute* in an easier question.[19] So in trying to answer a question about the likelihood of a serious (but generally infrequent) crime occurring in the local area, we might instead try to answer what we see as a related question: how many instances we can recall of less serious but more frequent and visible crimes or even informal rule infractions.

A second important tool we employ is *representativeness*: the degree to which we believe something fits or belongs in a particular group or class. This is related to the cognitive process of stereotyping, a tool that aids information processing by organizing people into categories and associating categories with universal traits. When we encounter someone who appears to fit within a category, we use the trait information to develop expectations.[20] Thus, when we encounter people on the street, we might take note of their skin color or the way they are dressed and use that information to fit them into categories like "black" or "poor." If we associate those categories with traits like "criminal" or "dangerous," we are likely to proceed with caution. In this same way we may also try to fit places into categories like "run-down," which we may associate with traits like "dangerous."

Another relevant development is the discovery that many of our evaluations, judgments, and even actions are governed by processes that are far less deliberate or conscious than was suggested by early work on risk evaluation and decision making.[21] This newer work suggests we often make evaluations or decisions based on subtle cues in an automatic fashion without conscious awareness that this has happened.[22] One major dimension of this is the idea of a priming effect, that we are influenced by words or images that set us up to respond in particular ways to subsequent situations, even when we are not consciously aware that the priming has occurred.

We can be primed by subtle cues and by our environmental context. For example, people exposed to images of lockers or classrooms were more likely to vote to increase school funding, as were those assigned to voting locations inside school buildings.[23] One important component of this is *affect*: the degree to which we let our likes and dislikes influence our perceptions, including our evaluations of risk, even when we do not know what inspired the affect in the first place.[24]

Building on this premise, a wide variety of recent work has sought to identify the kinds of biases we hold *implicitly*: those feelings or stereotypes that affect our judgments without our conscious awareness.[25] Though these biases are often related to explicitly expressed biases or attitudes, they are also distinct from them, in some cases even conflicting with them.[26] These implicit biases influence actions; for instance, implicit measures more strongly predict discriminatory behavior than explicit measures.[27] Recent work has begun detailing the various ways these implicit biases may influence our criminal justice system through the actions of the courts as well as law enforcement officers.[28]

Each of these ideas from cognitive psychology helps shed light on the process by which we judge the danger posed by people or places. These tools are useful: many are related to basic fight-or-flight response systems developed to protect us in early human history.[29] However, most are also imperfect and will lead us to incorrect judgments about safety in systematic ways.[30] These biases may help us understand why people perceive more criminal danger in neighborhoods with more African Americans, even after actual differences in crime are accounted for.[31] Stereotypes, for instance, are useful tools for processing the large amount of information we must often take in and evaluate quickly—we must often judge the danger posed by a stranger we encounter in public without the benefit of getting to know the individual's personal history. But stereotypes will often be based on inaccurate information, for instance the overrepresentation of black faces on TV crime reports.[32] Even when stereotypes are based on relatively accurate estimates of average behavior by a group, they may still cause problems. Statistical discrimination exists when people, due to a lack of other relevant information, make judgments based on average group characteristics. This may be completely rational in the aggregate but will frequently be incorrect in individual cases.[33]

Similarly, the substitution of an easier question for a more difficult one—answering "have I seen visible instances of minor crimes?" rather than "what is the likelihood of a serious crime happening?"—is useful only to the degree that the answer to the easier question serves as an accurate proxy for the harder one. It also depends on the answer to the easier question being correct. If the answer is based not on careful calculation or assessment but instead on subtle primes that set us up to feel more negatively or positively or which trigger some automatic association, then even the answer to this easier question may be biased. As Kahneman suggests, "we can be blind to the obvious, and we are also blind to our blindness."[34]

This section, then, outlines basic cognitive tools—and accompanying cognitive errors—that may help us understand some of the findings from research on perceptions of criminal danger discussed in the previous section. When trying to evaluate the criminal danger posed by a person or place, we may draw on stereotypes and ask ourselves whether the person or place can be matched to a category associated with criminal danger. We may try to recall whether serious crimes happen frequently in this area, and if we struggle to find an answer for this we may instead ask ourselves an easier question about whether we have seen evidence of less serious but more visible disorder in the local area. In each case these judgments will be informed not only, or even necessarily primarily, by conscious and rational calculations but also by implicit and automatically activated associations and biases.

A Role for Race: Historical Stigma and Intergroup Conflict

At the heart of the Zimmerman case are latent concerns about race relations in this country. Much of the media coverage of the case focused on the question of whether George Zimmerman was racist or whether his actions reflected racism or racial bias.[35] Zimmerman's attorney, alternatively, implied the real issue was Martin's racism toward Zimmerman and whites.[36] This case highlights the complicated role of race and racism in the modern era, where racial inequalities persist despite sharp declines in overtly racist attitudes.

If race did play a role in Zimmerman's evaluation of the situation, does this mean he was racist? If race plays a significant role more generally in our perceptions of neighborhoods as criminally dangerous, does that imply a role for racism? To some degree the answers to these questions are semantic—it matters exactly how we define racism. However they also contain potentially important substantive distinctions.

In this section we review literature on race, race relations, and racism to develop two distinct "ideal type" explanations for why race might matter to people's perceptions of crime. We have intentionally simplified these perspectives to highlight places where they may be contrasted. In the real world, as we discuss in the conclusion, both explanations may operate in concert. The first explanation draws on the idea of a racial stigma rooted in the historical association between race and class. The second draws on the notion of prejudice as a by-product of intergroup conflict.

Social scientists have long been interested in the idea of stigma—an attribute or identity labeled as discrediting or otherwise disapproved of by the greater society. In the seminal work on the subject, Goffman develops an understanding of the role of stigma in social identity by drawing on the social-psychological conception of categorizing persons and assigning group-wide attributes.[37] In addition to stigmas associated with physical or personal divergences from norms, Goffman also identifies a "tribal" stigma associated with group membership or identity—including both race and class.

When groups are residentially segregated and geographically concentrated on the basis of race or class, and this spatial distribution remains stable over time, stigma may be seen as applying not just to people but also to places themselves,[38] something potentially implicated in racial residential preferences and segregation.[39] Anderson suggests this stigma of place—what he terms the "iconic ghetto"—is carried by African Americans outside of these most disadvantaged neighborhoods, even among some of those who have cultural distance from such places.[40] If black people's "place" is in the ghetto, then they may cause concern when they are outside of this realm, something Anderson has suggested may have been at work in the case of Trayvon Martin and George Zimmerman.[41]

Sampson argues that such stigma does not necessarily suggest prejudice or group hostility.[42] Instead, historical processes like racial residential segregation and the concentration of African Americans in industrial jobs at the advent of deindustrialization have produced stable communities characterized by extreme disadvantage, crime, and other social problems.[43] This visible and durable link between race, place, and crime has reinforced the connection among these factors in the public mind. As Sampson notes by drawing on work on implicit bias, it may even be that such stigma is possessed without conscious recognition by some who would personally reject prejudice toward blacks.[44] This echoes Goffman's suggestion that stigma is driven more by ignorance than by intentions of harm.[45] Finding that the racial composition of a neighborhood affects whites' and blacks' perceptions of disorder equally, Sampson concludes that the racial stigma of disorder, at least, appears more the product of statistical discrimination than racial prejudice or hostility.[46]

It may be worthwhile, however, to consider this other possibility as either a complementary or an alternative explanation: that racial stigma *is* rooted in prejudice or active group hostility. This explanation is rooted in Blumer's conception of prejudice as a sense of group position.[47] In this view, members of dominant groups will be concerned by members of subordinate groups when such groups are perceived to be interested in a greater share of privileges and resources. This concern will be manifest in stereotypical views of subordinate group members as intrinsically different and inferior. Given the racial hierarchy in the United States,[48] this suggests non-Hispanic whites will be especially likely to hold such views of African Americans.

In the time since Blumer's classic work,[49] overt expressions of racial prejudice have declined substantially.[50] This may mean, however, that the group processes described by Blumer have merely been moved out of public view. Jackman and Muha, for instance, suggest that open prejudice and discrimination are appropriate only in social situations in which relative intergroup inequalities are accepted, or at least not openly challenged.[51] Once such challenges occur, the dominant group will develop a new ideology that continues to serve their interests by deemphasizing group distinctions in favor of individualism, while discounting the role of historical inequalities that have ensured that members of the different groups will not have the same opportunities. This has resulted in a phenomenon that has been variously described as "symbolic," "laissez-faire," or "color-blind" racism.[52] Extending the logic of these perspectives to perceptions of crime and communities, it may be that views of blacks and black communities as criminal serve to preserve intergroup relative positions even in an era when those holding such views may deny possessing motivations rooted in intergroup hostilities. The consequences of stigma are consistent with this: stigma appears to reinforce and extend existing inequalities.[53]

Thus, while both perspectives—racial stigma as prejudice versus a version of statistical discrimination—suggest that race will color perceptions of crime and communities, they can be distinguished along at least two dimensions. The first distinction involves intergroup hierarchy and power. Blumer's suggestion is that dominant groups will possess prejudice toward subordinate groups growing out of concerns about changes in the relative positions of the two groups.[54] This suggests disproportionality in intergroup views based on their relative position and power. Bobo argues for the continuing relevance of these concerns about relative intergroup positions even as possessors of such laissez-faire racist attitudes might explicitly deny any racist motivations.[55] Similarly, Link and Phelan remind us that it takes power to stigmatize.[56] As such, the first distinction is that the intergroup conflict perspective expects differences in the attitudes groups hold about the subordinate group—specifically that the dominant group will be disproportionately likely to hold negative views of this group. In contrast, if a general stigma exists about the subordinate group, then all groups may hold equally negative views of this group.

The second distinction involves negative affect. Prejudice is, as Allport suggests, "antipathy based on a faulty or inflexible generalization . . . [which] may be felt or expressed . . . [and] directed toward a group as a whole, or toward an individual because he is a member of that group."[57] Thus, while the idea of a stigma rooted in historical associations between race and class does not suggest active hostility, prejudice born of intergroup conflict does directly implicate negative affect. As noted above, our descriptions of these two perspectives are intentionally simplified, but they do point toward potential distinctions that may help sort out the *meaning* of the role of race in perceptions of criminal danger.

The Present Study: Investigating Indirect and Hidden Roles for Race in Perceptions of Crime and Communities

Our goal is to pose a broader explanation for the way race colors perceptions of crime and communities. Toward this end, we present evidence in two stages from two different sources that address the two different dimensions to our explanation. First, using a neighborhood-level study of a single city, we contrast two potential sources of perceptions of crime: racial crime stereotypes and perceptions of disorder. In both cases we examine whether they help explain the effect of the racial composition—in particular the proportion of local residents who are African American—on perceptions of criminal danger. Second, we use a nationally representative survey to explore a potential hidden role for race, drawing on an implicit measure of relative racial affect.

Direct and Indirect Roles for Race: Stereotypes and Disorder

Data to examine a potential indirect role for race come from the Seattle Neighborhoods and Crime Survey (SNCS), a survey of roughly six thousand residents of Seattle conducted in 2002 and 2003.[58] This survey is combined with contextual information on the race and class composition and the prevalence of crime from the U.S. Census Bureau and the Seattle Police Department. The main outcome of interest is individual assessments of the danger posed by crime within people's neighborhood, specifically how unsafe they feel their neighborhood is from crime and criminals. The survey also includes a measure of racial crime stereotypes, contrasting stereotypes of blacks relative to whites to capture perceptions of how much more blacks tend to be involved in drugs and gangs relative to whites.[59] Finally, the survey also includes a measure of perceptions of physical and social disorder.[60]

Our first question concerns the influences on people's perceptions of the criminal danger of their neighborhoods. Figure 2.1 presents selected standardized coefficients and confidence intervals from a model predicting perceptions of the local danger posed by crime among non-Hispanic whites with a variety of both individual- and neighborhood-level factors.[61] The vertical line running through the middle of figure 2.1 represents zero. For each row in the figure, the distance between this zero line and the dot represents the strength of the relationship; dots to the left of the line represent a negative relationship, while dots to the right represent a positive relationship. Within each row the horizontal line represents the confidence interval; crossing the zero line indicates that the relationship is not significantly different from zero.[62] For example, the results suggest that people who have been

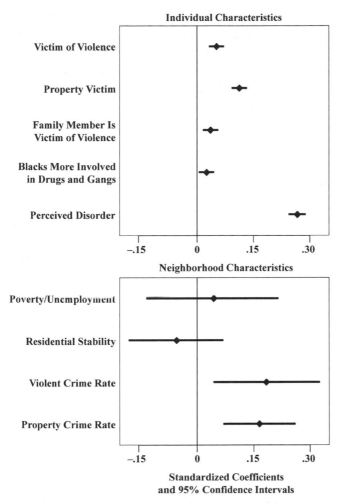

Figure 2.1. Selected standardized coefficients and confidence intervals from multilevel model predicting perceptions of local criminal danger. Data from the Seattle Neighborhoods and Crime Survey.

the victim of violent or property crimes are more likely to perceive their neighborhood as criminally dangerous, as are those who live in neighborhoods with higher violent and property crime rates.

After accounting for all of these factors, those residents who more strongly believe that blacks are more involved in drugs and gangs than whites—those who possess *crime stereotypes* about blacks—perceive more criminal danger in their communities. As figure 2.1 reveals, this effect is significantly different from zero, but it is also relatively modest: smaller than the effects of any of the victimization experiences. Perceptions of disorder are also significantly and positively related to perceptions of criminal danger, but this effect is substantially stronger than the effect of stereotypes or victimization experiences.

Our second question involves the degree to which these factors help explain the role of the racial composition in perceptions of criminal danger. To explore this question, figure 2.2 presents standardized coefficients and confidence intervals for the effect of the proportion African American on perceptions of criminal danger from three separate models. The first line (labeled "Basic Controls") presents the standardized coefficient and confidence interval from a model including all of the individual and neighborhood covariates from the model presented in figure 2.1 with the exception of stereotypes and perceptions of disorder. This line shows a significant and positive role for the proportion African American in people's perceptions of the neighborhood as criminally dangerous. The second line shows the same effect from a model that also includes a control for racial crime stereotypes about blacks

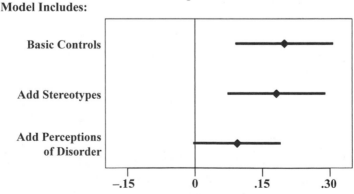

Figure 2.2. Coefficients for the effect of the proportion African American on perceptions of criminal danger from models with different controls. Data from the Seattle Neighborhoods and Crime Survey.

relative to whites. This line is essentially unchanged from the first, revealing that stereotypes do little to explain why people perceive more crime in neighborhoods with more African Americans. The final line shows the same effect but from a model which also includes perceptions of disorder. The results reveal a smaller effect which is not significantly different from zero. In other words, while racial crime stereotypes do little to explain why the racial composition of a neighborhood matters to perceptions of criminal danger, people's perceptions of disorder do appear to explain much of this relationship.

A final question is whether these processes differ for black versus white respondents. To test this we explored interactions between black and white respondents in these models. The results suggest the black and white respondents perceive similar levels of criminal danger when they possess stereotypes of blacks as more criminal than whites, when they perceive high levels of disorder in their neighborhoods, and when they live in neighborhoods with a higher proportion African American.[63] However, while white and black respondents who held stereotypes were similarly affected by them, they did differ in their overall likelihood of possessing such stereotypes. Figure 2.3 compares the means (represented as dots) and confidence intervals (represented by vertical lines) for these two groups. The results suggest that both groups were more likely to believe that blacks are involved in drugs and gangs than are whites. However, the difference is significantly larger for white respondents than it is for African American respondents.[64]

Thus, the data from Seattle suggest that the influence of living in a neighborhood with more African Americans on perceptions of criminal danger may be less direct (through racial crime stereotypes) and more indirect (through perceptions of minor disorder). The results also suggest that these processes do not differ for black and white residents, although white residents overall were more likely to believe that blacks are more involved in drugs and gangs than are whites.

A Hidden Role for Racial Affect

Data to examine a potential hidden role for race come from the 2008–9 American National Election Studies (ANES) Panel Study, a representative sample of the American electorate.[65] The survey includes a question

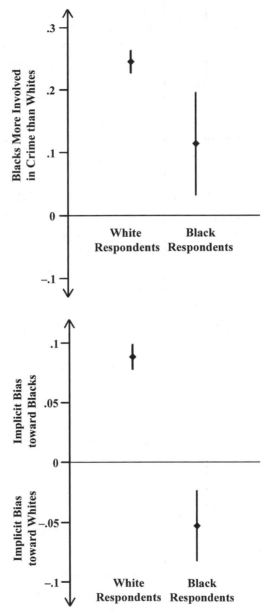

Figure 2.3. Means and 95 percent confidence intervals for white and black respondents for the question of how much more involved in drugs and gangs are blacks versus whites. Data from the Seattle Neighborhoods and Crime Survey.

about local crime, asking respondents whether crime rates in their city or town are increasing. The survey also includes a measure of racial crime stereotypes (the difference between perceptions of blacks versus whites as violent) and two measures of relative racial affect. The first is captured in an overt and explicit fashion: respondents were asked how warm or cold they felt toward both whites and blacks as a group, and the resulting measure captures how much colder the respondents felt toward blacks relative to whites.[66]

The second measure of relative racial affect is captured implicitly via the Affect Misattribution Procedure (AMP). This procedure, administered on a computer, works by exposing the respondent to a suboptimal prime—an image shown so briefly the respondent is unlikely to register it consciously—which may produce an affective response (in this case an image of either a black or a white face). The respondent is then shown a second neutral image (in this case a Chinese ideogram) and asked to rate it as more or less pleasant than average. The idea is that the respondent is *primed* with a more positive or negative feeling based on the image of the black or white face and then he or she *projects* this feeling onto the second picture, not unlike the projection that occurs in Rorschach inkblot tests.[67] This test is repeated forty-eight times with different pairings of black and white faces with Chinese ideograms. The resulting measure captures the average affective response to neutral images primed with black versus white faces. Unlike the explicit measure, the AMP has the potential to capture two additional kinds of relative racial affect: that of which the respondent is not aware and that of which the respondent is aware but chooses to not admit.

Our first question is whether racial crime stereotypes and racial biases are associated with perceived increases in local crime. Figure 2.4 presents selected standardized coefficients and confidence intervals from a model predicting perceptions that crime in one's city or town is increasing.[68] The first two lines suggest that the belief that blacks are more violent than whites is not associated with perceptions of local crime increasing, nor is explicit bias against blacks relative to whites: the degree to which the respondent admitted he or she felt colder toward blacks relative to whites. The final line, however, reveals that the implicit measure of bias—the degree to which the respondent rated black-face-primed images more unfavorably than white-face-primed images—is

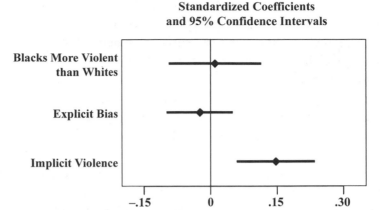

Figure 2.4. Selected standardized coefficients and confidence intervals from model predicting perceived increase in city violent crime. Data from the American National Election Studies.

significantly and positively related to perceptions that the local crime rate is increasing.

The second question is whether these effects differ for black versus white respondents. Interactions with the respondent's race revealed that stereotypes and explicit bias do not appear to matter for blacks or for whites. There is, however, a marginally significant interaction between implicit bias and race that suggests that implicit bias against blacks has a more strongly positive effect on perceptions of the local crime rate increasing for whites than for blacks.[69] There are also significant differences in the prevalence of implicit bias toward African Americans. Figure 2.5 presents means and confidence intervals for black versus white respondents. The results suggest that white respondents were more likely to rate images primed by black faces as unpleasant while black respondents were more likely to rate images primed by white faces as more unpleasant.[70] In other words, both groups revealed an in-group preference.

Thus, the data from this national survey suggest that there may also be a more direct role of racial affect or bias, but that it may be partially hidden. Specifically, while explicit measures of racial stereotypes and racial bias are not strongly related to perceptions of local crime, an implicit measure of racial bias—capturing disproportionate negative affect toward blacks relative to whites—is positively related to such perceptions. The results also suggest that implicit bias may play a marginally stronger positive role in perceptions of crime among whites, and that biases specifically against blacks are more common among white respondents.

Discussion and Conclusion

We will never know with any confidence exactly what George Zimmerman was thinking on the night he fatally shot Trayvon Martin or the role that race may have played in how he viewed the situation. The resulting surge of media coverage—much of it focused on this question—seemed to tap into latent concerns about race relations generally, and specifically

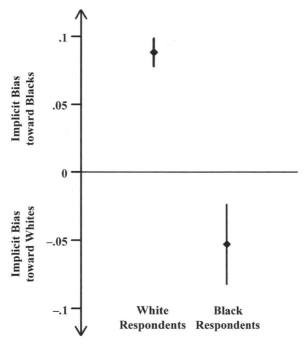

Figure 2.5. Means and 95 percent confidence intervals for white and black respondents for the question of how much more violent are blacks versus whites, and explicit and implicit bias against blacks versus whites. Data from the American National Election Studies.

the degree to which the public associates race and criminal danger. As discussed in this chapter, criminological work has also struggled with this question. Research has frequently suggested that race matters for perceptions of crime and communities, but it has been unclear exactly *how* race matters. This chapter has suggested some preliminary answers.

The broad answer is that while conscious racial crime stereotypes and explicit and overt racial biases play at best a minimal role, perceptions of disorder and implicit biases appear to play more major roles. Below we explore the meanings and consequences of each of these two findings as well as of the role of race more broadly.

The Indirect Influence of Race

So why is it that people perceive more criminal danger in neighborhoods with greater numbers of African Americans? It does not appear that people make an explicit and rational calculation in which they compare their evaluation of how frequently African Americans are involved in crime with the presence of African Americans in the community. Or, at minimum, it does not appear that this is a particularly important component of the broader explanation. Instead, one of the ways that race seems to influence perceptions of criminal danger is more indirect: through race-influenced perceptions of minor signs of disorder and deviations from social norms.

This is consistent with what we know about people's evaluations of risk from a cognitive perspective, which often turn out to be governed not by conscious rational calculations, but by automatic reactions to subtle cues that occur without conscious intervention. Several of these cognitive processes may be at work here. First, it may be that in trying to answer the difficult question of how dangerous a neighborhood is in terms of serious crime, people may instead be substituting an easier question about whether they've seen more visible signs of minor disorder; indeed a wide variety of work has suggested the two may be associated in people's minds. Second, given prior work suggesting that the presence of African Americans plays a more important role in perceptions of disorder than does the actual presence of disorder,[71] it may also be that people's perceptions of this minor disorder are biased in systematic ways. In this sense, it is possible that the racial composition of a neighborhood acts as a prime, setting people up to be hyperaware of minor infractions of social norms or other disorder. In fact, experiments have shown evidence consistent with this: people tend to have an easier time recognizing degraded images of crime-relevant objects like guns when they are primed with images of a black face.[72]

The Hidden Influence of Race

The second part of the answer also draws on this more nuanced understanding of how we evaluate risk and make judgments about the presence of criminal danger. Specifically, explicit measures of racial bias and overt and self-reported racial crime stereotypes did not seem to be related to people's estimates of whether crime was going up or down in their city or town. However, an implicit measure of racial bias—capturing disproportionate negative affect toward blacks relative to whites—is strongly and positively related to perceptions of crime increasing. These models account for the direct role of explicit bias and stereotypes, suggesting that this captures some people who explicitly deny holding stereotypes of or bias against African Americans. This is consistent with work that suggests that implicit biases may reflect something distinct from explicitly stated biases and preferences.[73]

During coverage of the Trayvon Martin case, a frequent question was whether there was proof that George Zimmerman acted in a racially biased way. Stories reported that Zimmerman was cleared of racial bias by FBI investigators.[74] Even Bill Cosby weighed in to suggest that since it was not possible to prove that Zimmerman had acted in a biased way, we should focus on other aspects of the case like the presence of a gun.[75] These stories, however, focus on explicit racial bias or overt discriminatory behavior. The role for implicit bias shown here suggests that bias *does* still play a role in general in our perceptions of crime, even if it is a role that is more difficult to see.

These results suggest one or both of two possible stories. On the one hand, some of those who explicitly deny any bias against blacks but show implicit evidence of such a bias may be unaware they hold such biases; this would be consistent with the suggestion that we are frequently unaware of the kinds of information or associations we draw upon when evaluating people or places.[76] Alternatively, some people may be aware that they hold such biases but choose not to admit to them due to concerns about social desirability. If the goal is to reduce the role race plays in shaping perceptions of crime and communities, it may be important to distinguish between the two. Exposing people to counterstereotypical information, for instance, may be a more promising strategy among the first group than among the second.

The Meaning of the Role of Race

The reasons *why* race matters are also consequential. If these biases in perceptions are the simple product of statistical discrimination rooted in the historical association between race, structure, and crime, then the solution may be a simple matter of helping people overcome or gain awareness of such biases. There is promising work in this vein suggesting that even when automatic responses to stimuli cannot be overcome, people can consciously intervene and prevent themselves from acting on those responses if they are aware they exist,[77] and that exposure to counterstereotypes can reduce biases, at least in the short term.[78] If these biases are the product of concerns about group positions, on the other hand, the solution may not be so simple. As Jackman and Muha suggest, the dominant group may simply construct new ideologies that conform to current norms while continuing to justify and perpetuate intergroup inequalities.[79]

Earlier in the chapter we developed two simplified "ideal type" explanations for the role of race in perceptions of crime. One was based on a general stigma rooted in historical inequalities and akin to statistical discrimination. Under this explanation, the relationship between race and perceptions of criminal danger is not rooted in intergroup antipathy and should affect all people relatively equally. The second explanation was rooted in the idea of prejudice as a function of concern about relative group positions. Under this explanation, the relationship between race and perceptions of criminal danger *is* rooted in intergroup antipathy and perceptions of criminal danger should disproportionately be directed at members of subordinate groups by members of dominant groups.

While the overall findings about *how* race matters—through indirect and hidden paths—is clear, the story about the *meaning* of the role of race is less clear. On the one hand, consistent with a general stigma, both white and black respondents tended to report more crime in neighborhoods with larger numbers of African Americans. In addition, white and black respondents tended to be equally affected by perceptions of disorder and racial crime stereotypes. On the other hand, white respondents were more likely to report stereotypes of blacks as criminals, and were substantially more likely to possess implicit biases against blacks. This is especially important given that the measures of bias is a measure of affect—specifically relative differences in the negative affect engendered by being primed with black faces versus white faces. This implicit bias, in turn, played at least a marginally larger role in increasing perceptions of local crime among whites than it did among African Americans.

The role of negative intergroup affect and the differences between white and black respondents in their stereotypes of and bias toward blacks seem to suggest that group processes are relevant. However, the facts that white and black respondents judged African American neighborhoods to be similarly dangerous—and that they seemed equally affected by perceptions of disorder and the possession of stereotypes about blacks as criminal—are at least consistent with the idea of stigma.

Further complicating the story is the idea that while negative affect toward African Americans may play a role in perceptions of criminal danger, not everyone will be aware of this affect and some will explicitly denounce it. This raises difficult but important questions about intent. Both dimensions of Allport's definition of prejudice seem to be at work here: antipathy—or at minimum some form of negative intergroup affect—and faulty or inflexible generalizations about a group.[80] But what does it mean that some people may not be aware they possess negative affect toward African Americans? It is clear these findings suggest something distinct from the virulent and overt prejudice of the Jim Crow era but also distinct from the suggestion of a postracial society where group processes are no longer relevant.

Racial feelings and attitudes, we know, are complicated and heterogeneous. It is likely that the implicit measure captures both some unconscious biases but also some purposefully concealed biases. It is likely that both some kind of statistical discrimination and some kind of intergroup conflict are at play—and that some of the dynamics of the concerns over group positions will play out in more overt ways and some will be more subtle and hidden. An important step for future work will be to disentangle how this heterogeneity is distributed: where and among whom each of the different processes seems more important.

Conclusion: Similar Views of Communities, Differing Views of Racial Bias

More than fifty years after the civil rights movement and the death of Emmett Till, the shooting death of Trayvon Martin sparked a national debate about the state of race relations and the role of racial bias in contemporary American life. This chapter sheds light on the indirect and hidden roles race plays in perceptions of criminal danger. It also suggests both some similarities and differences in this role among whites and African Americans.

Among the notable similarities is the finding that both whites and blacks perceived more crime in neighborhoods with larger numbers of African Americans. This is consistent with the previous finding that both whites and blacks perceived more *disorder* in neighborhoods with larger numbers of African Americans.[81] The similar size of the effect, however, does not necessarily imply that it *means* the same thing for members of the different groups. Specific differences in the average perspectives of African Americans and whites may tell us something about the different meanings the connection between race, disorder, and crime may hold.

Speaking about the Trayvon Martin case, President Obama said, "I think it's important to recognize that the African American community is looking at this through a set of experiences, a history, that doesn't go away . . . those sets of experiences inform how the African American community interprets what happened one night in Florida."[82] Social science research confirms this: African Americans tend to see the role of a history of slavery and discrimination as more relevant to present-day inequalities than do whites.[83] African Americans are also more likely to view the criminal justice system as biased against them.[84] As W.E.B. Du Bois suggested, African Americans are also aware of how they are viewed by the larger society and must reconcile this with their understanding of themselves. African Americans thus view themselves, the crime within their community, and racially charged incidents like the Trayvon Martin case through this unique lens.[85]

Whites, on the other hand, tend to minimize the role of historical factors like slavery or Jim Crow laws, as well as contemporary discrimination or prejudice, in the relative inequalities between blacks and whites.[86] In fact, while both blacks and whites believe that discrimination against blacks has declined since the civil rights era, whites on average believe this drop has been both incredibly steep and accompanied by a corresponding increase in discrimination against whites.[87] Thus, while African Americans tend to see social problems through a lens that highlights both historical and contemporary mistreatments and injustices, whites tend to view the same issues through a lens that minimizes this context.

These very different perspectives are helpful in understanding the differences in how whites and blacks view the criminal danger posed by black neighborhoods. They may also be useful in understanding the very different meanings the Trayvon Martin case holds for these two groups. On average, African Americans followed the case more closely and were substantially more likely than whites to believe that the shooting was racially biased, that Zimmerman had committed a crime, and that the police acted in a racially biased manner by not immediately arresting him.[88] Even though the case lacked strong evidence of *overt* racial bias, the African American community's history of exposure to racism remains a salient part of the everyday lives of African Americans and, in turn, informs public perceptions of the role of race and racial bias in contemporary American life. In this sense, many African Americans may have reached the same conclusion as this chapter: that race continues to influence perceptions of communities, crime, and criminals in profound ways, but that the influence it exerts is less overt and visible than it was in the past, and is instead more indirect and hidden.

NOTES

1. Lee 2012; Alvarez 2013; Fox 2013; Meade 2014. A similar question has been at the heart of other recent high-profile shooting deaths of unarmed African American men including Oscar Grant, Jordan Davis, and Michael Brown. Perceptions of dangerousness are at the heart of legal concepts like self-defense and Stand Your Ground.

2. Goode and Ben-Yehuda 2010.

3. Although George Zimmerman's mother was born in Peru and although he has an Afro-Peruvian great-grandfather, much of the media story tended to treat the shooting as a white versus black racial issue. Reflecting this and with the goal of presenting a simple and concise story, we also restrict ourselves in this chapter to a comparison of non-Hispanic blacks and whites (a note on language: we use "whites" as shorthand for non-Hispanic whites and use "blacks" and "African Americans" interchangeably to refer to non-Hispanic blacks). Nonetheless, this *is* a simplification, and it deserves to be complicated by fitting it within a larger racial hierarchy in the United States—something we explicitly encourage future work to do.

4. E.g., Schuman et al. 1997; Bobo and Charles 2009; Krysan 2011.

5. Kinder and Sears 1981; Jackman and Muha 1984; Kinder 1986; Sears 1988; Bobo, Kluegel, and Smith 1997; Bonilla-Silva 2010.

6. Anderson 2013. Emmett Till broke an "unspoken rule" of the segregated South during the Jim Crow era: whistling at a white woman. Three days after the incident, Till's badly beaten body was pulled from the Tallahatchie River, identified only by a ring on his hand (Anderson 2008).

7. Sampson and Raudenbush 2004; Drakulich 2013.

8. Lizotte and Bordua 1980; Stinchcombe et al. 1980; Moeller 1989; Covington and Taylor 1991; Chiricos, Hogan, and Gertz 1997; Chiricos, McEntire, and Gertz 2001.

9. Quillian and Pager 2001; 2010; Drakulich 2012. Related to this, people also appear more afraid of encountering strangers in public settings when those strangers are black rather than white (St. John and Heald-Moore 1995; 1996).

10. Stinchcombe et al. 1980; Skogan 1995; St. John and Heald-Moore 1996—though see Mears and Stewart 2010.

11. Merry 1981; St. John and Heald-Moore 1996; Lee and Ulmer 2000.

12. Pickett et al. 2012 use perceptions of the racial composition. Drakulich 2012 uses the actual racial composition and controls for a variety of measures of the incidence of crime.

13. Hunter 1978; Garofalo and Laub 1979; Lewis and Maxfield 1980; Lewis and Salem 1986. Broken windows theory suggests that when minor forms of disorder are left unattended (e.g., not fixing a broken window, not removing graffiti), the neighborhood will look unregulated, which in turn can lead to serious crime and ultimately to the decline of the neighborhood (Wilson and Kelling 1982; Skogan 1990). While researchers have frequently challenged the notion that disorder is causally linked to more serious crime (Sampson and Raudenbush 2004; Harcourt 2001), research has consistently noted a strong association between *perceptions* of disorder and *perceptions* of crime.

14. Greenberg 1986; Taylor and Hale 1986; Covington and Taylor 1991; Lagrange, Ferraro, and Supancic 1992; Taylor and Covington 1993; Brunton-Smith and Sturgis 2011—though see Skogan 1990; Wilcox, Quisenberry, and Jones 2003.

15. Piquero 1999; Sampson and Raudenbush 2004; Sampson 2009; Drakulich 2013.

16. Drakulich 2013.

17. E.g., Tversky and Kahneman 1974.

18. E.g., ibid.
19. Kahneman and Frederick 2002; 2004.
20. E.g., Hilton and von Hippel 1996; Macrae and Bodenhausen 2000.
21. E.g., Kahneman 2011.
22. E.g., Greenwald and Banaji 1995.
23. Berger, Meredith, and Wheeler 2008.
24. E.g., Slovic 2006.
25. E.g., Greenwald, McGhee, and Schwartz 1998; Payne et al. 2005.
26. E.g., Greenwald and Banaji 1995.
27. Greenwald et al. 2009.
28. See review in Staats 2013.
29. E.g., Cannon 1932; Kahneman 2011.
30. Tversky and Kahneman 1974.
31. Quillian and Pager 2001; Drakulich 2012.
32. Gilliam, Valentino, and Beckmann 2002.
33. Phelps 1972; Quillian and Pager 2010.
34. Kahneman 2011, 23.
35. E.g., Jonsson 2012.
36. E.g., Benn and Burch 2013; Alcindor 2013.
37. Goffman 1963.
38. E.g., Sampson 2009; Peterson and Krivo 2010.
39. Charles 2000; 2003.
40. Anderson 2012.
41. Anderson 2013.
42. Sampson 2009.
43. E.g., Wilson 1987; Massey and Denton 1993; Peterson and Krivo 2010.
44. Sampson 2009.
45. Goffman 1963, 116.
46. Sampson 2009.
47. Blumer 1958.
48. E.g., Peterson and Krivo 2010.
49. Blumer 1958.
50. E.g., Schuman et al. 1997; Krysan 2011.
51. Jackman and Muha 1984.
52. Bobo, Kluegel, and Smith 1997; Bonilla-Silva 2010; Kinder and Sears 1981; Kinder 1986; Sears 1988.
53. Link and Phelan 2001; Sampson 2009.
54. Blumer 1958.
55. Bobo 1983; 1999; Bobo, Kluegel, and Smith 1997.
56. Link and Phelan 2001.
57. Allport 1954, 9.
58. A more detailed description of the data and of Seattle itself can be found in Matsueda 2010; Drakulich 2012; 2013.

59. More information on this measure can be found in Drakulich 2012.

60. This is a simple index based on items indicating how big of a problem the respondent sees five different examples of disorder as being within their neighborhood. More information on these individual items can be found in Drakulich 2013.

61. Respondents' perceptions of their neighborhood are not independent—they are clustered in neighborhoods and react to the same contextual conditions and crime rates. For these reasons we use a simple random-intercept multilevel model to model the variability among individuals within neighborhoods as a product of individual characteristics and the variability between neighborhoods as a product of neighborhood characteristics. The outcome is captured on an ordinal scale, but with the goal of simplifying interpretation we chose to present results from a linear multilevel model after finding that the results from an ordered logit multilevel model were substantively identical. In addition to the measures depicted in Figure 2.1, the full model also includes individual-level controls for gender, age, marital and child status, years of education, income, home ownership, length of residence, and race and ethnicity, as well as neighborhood-level controls for the proportions Asian, African American, and Latino. The model includes information for 3,828 individuals and 123 census tracts. An intraclass correlation indicates that about 16 percent of the variation in perceptions of criminal danger occurs between rather than within neighborhoods. As a whole, this model explains 20 percent of the variation among individuals and nearly all (91 percent) of the variation between neighborhoods.

62. There are a smaller number of neighborhoods than individuals, so the confidence intervals for the neighborhood-level factors are longer than those for the individual factors, reflecting more uncertainty.

63. As the interactions were not significant, we do not show them here. Caution is recommended in interpreting differences in the effect of the racial composition given that black respondents tended to be from a more narrow range of neighborhoods in this regard than did white respondents.

64. The difference in means is significant at $p < .01$. The larger confidence interval for black respondents is a function of the smaller number of black respondents: 228 versus 3,830 white respondents.

65. More information about this study can be found in DeBell, Krosnick, and Lupia 2010 and Drakulich 2015.

66. Sample weights are employed in all reported results to adjust for factors affecting the probability of selection into the sample and to make the sample more representative of the population in the United States who was eligible to vote in the November 2008 election. As the interest of this chapter is a comparison of non-Hispanic whites and blacks, the analyses restrict the sample to these groups. The outcome was measured in wave 17. The measure of implicit bias comes from waves 9 and 10. The measure of stereotypes is from wave 20—several months after the outcome—and thus should be interpreted with caution. The control variables are largely captured from the base survey.

67. Payne et al. 2005.

68. This model differs in several important ways from that presented for the neighborhood-level survey, including the reference scale for perceived crime (the respondent's city or town versus neighborhood), the question asked by the outcome (perceptions of crime increasing rather than overall criminal danger), and the ability to examine the local crime and racial context. However, given the lack of measures of implicit racial affect in communities and crime surveys, we believe the current results represent an important exploratory step despite these limitations, and we strongly recommend future work that explores the potential interaction between implicit affect and the race and crime context. The model does control for a standard set of demographic factors, including gender, age, marital status, education, income, employment status, and race. The outcome is captured on an ordinal scale, but with the goal of simplifying interpretation we chose to present results from a linear model after finding that the results from an ordered logit model were substantively identical.

69. Given the marginal significance ($p < .05$, one-tailed) and the inability to account for potentially different crime contexts for white and black respondents, we recommend caution interpreting this interaction without further replication.

70. The difference in means is significant at $p < .001$. The comparison includes 2,067 non-Hispanic whites and 207 non-Hispanic blacks. Although stereotypes and explicit racial bias were not associated with perceptions of local crime, there were significant differences in the means of both of these items as well, revealing that white relative to black respondents were more likely to report that blacks are violent and to express explicit bias toward blacks.

71. Sampson and Raudenbush 2004; Sampson 2009; Drakulich 2013.

72. Eberhardt et al. 2004.

73. E.g., Greenwald and Banaji 1995.

74. E.g., Jonsson 2012.

75. Wilstein 2013.

76. E.g., Kahneman 2011.

77. Fazio and Towles-Schwen 1999; Blair 2002; Towles-Schwen and Fazio 2003; Olson and Fazio 2004; Ito et al. 2006; Kawakami et al. 2007.

78. Dasgupta and Greenwald 2001; Olson and Fazio 2004; also see Lane, Kang, and Banaji 2007.

79. Jackman and Muha 1984.

80. Allport 1954.

81. Sampson 2009.

82. Obama 2013.

83. E.g., Bonilla-Silva 2010.

84. E.g., Hagan and Albonetti 1982; Matsueda and Drakulich 2009; Peffley and Hurwitz 2010.

85. Du Bois 1903.

86. E.g., Bonilla-Silva 2010.

87. Norton and Sommers 2011.

88. Newport 2012; Gabbidon and Jordan 2013.

REFERENCES

Alcindor, Yamiche. 2013. "Trayvon Martin's Friend: Encounter Was Racially Charged." *USA Today*, June 27. http://www.usatoday.com/story/news/nation/2013/06/27/trayvon-martin-sanford-zimmerman-florida-race/2462403/. Accessed March 11, 2014.

Allport, Gordon W. 1954. *The Nature of Prejudice*. New York: Doubleday Books.

Alvarez, Lizette. 2013. "Zimmerman Acquitted in Trayvon Martin Killing." *New York Times*, June 14. http://www.nytimes.com/2013/07/14/us/george-zimmerman-verdict-trayvon-martin.html?pagewanted=all&_r=0. Accessed February 22, 2014.

Anderson, Devery S. 2008. "A Wallet, a White Woman, and a Whistle: Fact and Fiction in Emmett Till's Encounter in Money, Mississippi." *Southern Quarterly* 45 (4): 10–21.

Anderson, Elijah. 2012. "The Iconic Ghetto." *Annals of the American Academy of Political and Social Science* 42:8–24.

———. 2013. "Emmett and Trayvon: How Racial Prejudice in America Has Changed in the Last Sixty Years." *Washington Monthly*, January/February. http://www.washingtonmonthly.com/magazine/january_february_2013/features/emmett_and_trayvon042036.php?page=all. Accessed March 5, 2014.

Benn, Evan S., and Audra D. S. Burch. 2013. "Trayvon Martin's Childhood Friend Back on the Witness Stand in Zimmerman Trail." *Miami Heard*, June 26. http://www.miamiherald.com/2013/06/26/3471243/alternate-juror-dismissed-in-trayvon.html. Accessed February 22, 2014.

Berger, Jonah, Marc Meredith, and S. Christian Wheeler. 2008. "Contextual Priming: Where People Vote Affects How They Vote." *Proceedings for the National Academy of Sciences of the United States of America* 105 (26): 8846–49.

Blair, Irene V. 2002. "The Malleability of Automatic Stereotypes and Prejudice." *Personality and Social Psychology Review* 6:242–61.

Blumer, Herbert. 1958. "Race Prejudice as a Sense of Group Position." *Pacific Sociological Review* 1:3–7.

Bobo, Lawrence. 1983. "Whites' Opposition to Busing: Symbolic Racism or Realistic Group Conflict?" *Journal of Personality and Social Psychology* 45:1196–10.

———. 1999. "Prejudice as Group Position: Microfoundations of a Sociology Approach to Racism and Race Relations." *Journal of Social Issues* 55 (3): 445–72.

Bobo, Lawrence, and Camille Z. Charles. 2009. "Race in the American Mind: From the Moynihan Report to the Obama Candidacy." *Annals of the American Academy of Political and Social Sciences* 621:243–59.

Bobo, Lawrence, James R. Kluegel, and Ryan A. Smith. 1997. "Laissez-Faire Racism: The Crystallization of a Kinder, Gentler, Antiblack Ideology." In *Racial Attitudes in the 1990s: Continuity and Change*, edited by S. A. Tuch and J. K. Martin, 15–41. Westport, CT: Praeger.

Bonilla-Silva, Eduardo. 2010. *Racism without Racists: Color-Blind Racism and the Persistence of Racial Inequality in the United States*. 3rd ed. New York: Rowman & Littlefield.

Brunton-Smith, Ian, and Patrick Sturgis. 2011. "Do Neighborhoods Generate Fear of Crime? An Empirical Test Using the British Crime Survey." *Criminology* 49: 331–69.

Cannon, Walter. 1932. *The Wisdom of the Body*. New York: Norton.

Charles, Camille Z. 2000. "Neighborhood Racial-Composition Preferences: Evidence from a Multiethnic Metropolis." *Social Problems* 47 (3): 379–407.

———. 2003. "The Dynamics of Racial Residential Segregation." *Annual Review of Sociology* 29:167–207.

Chiricos, Ted, Michael Hogan, and Marc Gertz. 1997. "Racial Composition of Neighborhood and Fear of Crime." *Criminology* 35:107–32.

Chiricos, Ted, Ranee McEntire, and Marc Gertz. 2001. "Perceived Racial and Ethnic Composition of Neighborhood and Perceived Risk of Crime." *Social Problems* 48:322–40.

Covington, Jeanette, and Ralph B. Taylor. 1991. "Fear of Crime in Urban Residential Neighborhoods: Implications of Between- and Within-Neighborhood Sources for Current Models." *Sociological Quarterly* 32:231–49.

Dasgupta, Nilanjana, and Anthony G. Greenwald. 2001. "On the Malleability of Automatic Attitudes: Combating Automatic Prejudice with Images of Admired and Disliked Individuals." *Journal of Personality and Social Psychology* 81:800–814.

DeBell, Matthew, Jon A. Krosnick, and Arthur Lupia. 2010. *Methodology Report and User's Guide for the 2008–2009 ANES Panel Study*. Palo Alto, CA and Ann Arbor: Stanford University and the University of Michigan.

Drakulich, Kevin M. 2012. "Strangers, Neighbors, and Race: A Contact Model of Stereotypes and Racial Anxieties about Crime." *Race and Justice* 2:322–55.

———. 2013. "Perceptions of the Local Danger Posed by Crime: Race, Disorder, Informal Control, and the Police." *Social Science Research* 42:611–32.

———. 2015. "Explicit and Hidden Racial Bias in the Framing of Social Problems." *Social Problems* 62 (1). doi:http://dx.doi.org/10.1093/socpro/spu003.

Du Bois, W.E.B. 1903. *The Souls of Black Folk: Essays and Sketches*. Chicago: Maestro.

Eberhardt, Jennifer L., Phillip Atiba Goff, Valerie J. Purdie, and Paul G. Davies. 2004. "Seeing Black: Race, Crime, and Visual Processing." *Journal of Personality and Social Psychology* 87:876–93.

Fazio, Russell H., and Tamara Towles-Schwen. 1999. "The MODE Model of Attitude-Behavior Processes." In *Dual-Process Theories in Social Psychology*, edited by S. Chaiken and Y. Trope, 97–116. New York: Guilford.

Fox, Lauren. 2013. "Racial Profiling Bill Gets Another Chance because of Trayvon Martin." *U.S. News & World Report*, July 30. http://www.usnews.com/news/articles/2013/07/30/racial-profiling-bill-gets-another-chance-because-of-trayvon-martin. Retrieved February 22, 2014.

Gabbidon, Shaun L., and Kareem L. Jordan. 2013. "Public Opinion on the Trayvon Martin Killing: A Test of the Racial Gradient Thesis." *Journal of Crime & Justice* 36:283–98.

Garofalo, James, and John Laub. 1979. "The Fear of Crime: Broadening Our Perspective." *Victimology* 3:242–53.

Gilliam, Franklin D., Nicholas A. Valentino, and Matthew N. Beckmann. 2002. "Where You Live and What You Watch: The Impact of Racial Proximity and Local Television News on Attitudes about Race and Crime." *Political Research Quarterly* 55:755–80.

Goffman, Erving. 1963. *Stigma: Notes on the Management of Spoiled Identity*. Englewood Cliffs, NJ: Prentice Hall.

Goode, Erich, and Nachman Ben-Yehuda. 2010 *Moral Panics: The Social Construction of Deviance*. Cambridge, MA: Blackwell.

Greenberg, Stephanie W. 1986. "Fear and Its Relationship to Crime, Neighborhood Deterioration, and Informal Social Control." In *The Social Ecology of Crime*, edited by J. M. Byrne and R. J. Sampson, 97–116. New York: Springer-Verlag.

Greenwald, Anthony G., and Mahzarin R. Banaji. 1995. "Implicit Social Cognition: Attitudes, Self-Esteem, and Stereotypes." *Psychological Review* 102:4–27.

Greenwald, Anthony G., Debbie E. McGhee, and Jordan L. K. Schwartz. 1998. "Measuring Individual Differences in Implicit Cognition: The Implicit Association Task." *Journal of Personality and Social Psychology* 74:1464–80.

Greenwald, Anthony G., T. Andrew Poehlman, Eric L. Uhlmann, and Mahzarin R. Banaji. 2009. "Understanding and Using the Implicit Association Test: III. Meta-analysis of Predictive Validity." *Journal of Personality and Social Psychology* 97 (1): 17–41.

Hagan, John, and Celesta Albonetti. 1982. "Race, Class, and the Perception of Criminal Injustice in America." *American Journal of Sociology* 88:329–55.

Hagan, John, Carla Shedd, and Monique R. Payne. 2005. "Race, Ethnicity, and Youth Perceptions of Criminal Injustice." *American Sociological Review* 70:381–407.

Harcourt, Bernard. 2001. *Illusions of Order: The False Promise of Broken Windows Policing*. Cambridge, MA: Harvard University Press.

Hilton, James L., and William von Hippel. 1996. "Stereotypes." *Annual Review of Psychology* 47:237–71.

Hunter, Albert J. 1978. "Symbols of Incivility: Social Disorder and Fear of Crime in Urban Neighborhoods." Washington, DC: U.S. Department of Justice.

Ito, Tiffany A., Krystal W. Chiao, Patricia G. Devine, Tyler S. Loring, and John T. Cacioppo. 2006. "The Influence of Facial Feedback on Race Bias." *Psychological Science* 17:256–61.

Jackman, Mary R., and Michael J. Muha. 1984. "Education and Intergroup Attitudes: Moral Enlightenment, Superficial Democratic Commitment, or Ideological Refinement?" *American Sociological Review* 49:751–69.

Jonsson, Patrick. 2012. "FBI Report: No Evidence George Zimmerman Is Racist." *Chris-*

tian Science Monitor, July 12. http://www.csmonitor.com/USA/Justice/2012/0712/ FBI-report-No-evidence-George-Zimmerman-is-racist. Accessed March 4, 2014.

Kahneman, Daniel. 2011. *Thinking, Fast and Slow*. New York: Farrar, Straus and Giroux.

Kahneman, Daniel, and Shane Frederick. 2002. "Representativeness Revisited: Attribute Substitution in Intuitive Judgment." In *Heuristics and Biases: The Psychology of Intuitive Judgment*, edited by T. Gilovich, D. Griffin, and D. Kahneman, 49–81. New York: Cambridge University Press

———. 2004. "Attribute Substitution in Intuitive Judgment." In *Models of Man: Essays in Memory of Herbert Simon*, edited by Mie Augier and James G. March, 411–32. Cambridge, MA: MIT Press.

Kawakami, Kerry, Curtis E. Phills, Jennifer R. Steele, and John F. Dovidio. 2007. "(Close) Distance Makes the Heart Grow Fonder: Improving Implicit Attitudes and Interracial Interactions through Approach Behaviors." *Journal of Personality and Social Psychology* 92 (6): 957–71.

Kinder, Donald R. 1986. "The Continuing American Dilemma: White Resistance to Racial Change 40 Years after Myrdal." *Journal of Social Issues* 42:151–71.

Kinder, Donald R., and David O. Sears. 1981. "Prejudice and Politics: Symbolic Racism versus Racial Threats to the Good Life." *Journal of Personality and Social Psychology* 40:414–31.

Krysan, Maria. 2011. "Race and Residence from the Telescope to the Microscope." *Contexts* 10:38–42.

LaGrange, Randy L., Ken Ferraro, and M. Supancic. 1992. "Perceived Risk and Fear of Crime—Role of Social and Physical Incivilities." *Journal of Research in Crime and Delinquency* 29:311–34.

Lane, Kristin A., Jerry Kang, and Mahzarin R. Banaji. 2007. "Implicit Social Cognition and Law." *Annual Review of Law and Social Science* 3:427–51.

Lee, Min Sik, and Jeffrey T. Ulmer. 2000. "Fear of Crime among Korean Americans in Chicago Communities." *Criminology* 38:1173–1206.

Lee, Trymaine. 2012. "George Zimmerman Case's Newly Released Evidence Suggests No Racial Bias." *Huffington Post*, July 12. http://www.huffingtonpost.com/2012/07/12/george-zimmerman-case_n_1669153.html. Accessed February 19, 2014.

Lewis, Dan A., and Michael G. Maxfield. 1980. "Fear in the Neighborhoods: An Investigation of the Impact of Crime." *Journal of Research in Crime and Delinquency* 17:160–89.

Lewis, Dan A., and Greta Salem. 1986. *Fear of Crime: Incivilities and the Production of a Social Problem*. Oxford: Transaction Books.

Link, Bruce G., and Jo C. Phelan. 2001. "Conceptualizing Stigma." *Annual Review of Sociology* 27:363–85.

Lizotte, Alan J., and David J. Bordua. 1980. "Firearms Ownership for Sport and Protection: Two Divergent Models." *American Sociological Review* 45:229–44.

Macrae, C. Neil, and Galen V. Bodenhausen. 2000. "Social Cognition: Thinking Categorically about Others." *Annual Review of Psychology* 51:93–120.

Massey, Douglas S., and Nancy A. Denton. 1993. *American Apartheid: Segregation and the Making of the Underclass.* Cambridge, MA: Harvard University Press.

Matsueda, Ross L. 2010. "Seattle Neighborhoods and Crime Survey, 2003–2003" (ICPSR28701-v1). Ann Arbor, MI: Inter-University Consortium for Political and Social Research [distributor].

Matsueda, Ross L., and Kevin M. Drakulich. 2009. "Perceptions of Criminal Injustice, Symbolic Racism, and Racial Politics." *Annals of the American Academy of Political and Social Science* 623:163–78.

Meade, Desmond. 2014. "Trayvon Martin, Jordan Davis, Who's Next? It's Time for Us to Heal the Wound of Racism." *Huffington Post*, February 18. http://www.huffingtonpost.com/desmond-meade/trayvon-martin-jordan-davis_b_4810080.html. Accessed February 22, 2014.

Mears, Daniel P., and Eric A. Stewart. 2010. "Interracial Contact and Fear of Crime." *Journal of Criminal Justice* 38:34–41.

Merry, Sally Engle. 1981. *Urban Danger: Life in a Neighborhood of Strangers.* Philadelphia: Temple University Press.

Moeller, Gertrude L. 1989. "Fear of Criminal Victimization: The Effect of Neighborhood Racial Composition." *Sociological Inquiry* 59:208–21.

Newport, Frank. 2012. "Blacks, Nonblacks Hold Sharply Different Views of Martin Case." *Gallup Politics*, April 5. http://www.gallup.com/poll/153776/blacks-nonblacks-hold-sharply-different-views-martin-case.aspx. Accessed March 4, 2014.

Norton, Michael I., and Samuel R. Sommers. 2011. "Whites See Racism as a Zero-Sum Game That They Are Now Losing." *Perspectives on Psychological Science* 6:215–18.

Obama, Barak. 2013. "President Obama Speaks on Trayvon Martin." http://www.whitehouse.gov/photos-and-video/video/2013/07/19/president-obama-speaks-trayvon-martin. Accessed February 22, 2014.

Olson, Michael A., and Russell H. Fazio. 2004. "Trait Inferences as a Function of Automatically Activated Racial Attitudes and Motivation to Control Prejudiced Reactions." *Basic and Applied Social Psychology* 26:1–11.

Payne, B. Keith, Clara M. Cheng, Oleysa Govorun, and Brandon D. Stewart. 2005. "An Inkblot for Attitudes: Affect Misattribution as Implicit Measurement." *Journal of Personality and Social Psychology* 89:277–93.

Peffley, Mark A., and Jon Hurwitz. 2010. *Justice in America: The Separate Realities of Blacks and Whites.* New York: Cambridge University Press.

Peterson, Ruth D., and Lauren J. Krivo. 2010. *Divergent Social Worlds: Neighborhood Crime and the Racial-Spatial Divide.* New York: Russell Sage Foundation.

Phelps, Edmund S. 1972. "The Statistical Theory of Racism and Sexism." *American Economic Review* 62:659–61.

Pickett, Justin T., Ted Chiricos, Kristin M. Golden, and Marc Gertz. 2012. "Reconsidering the Relationship between Perceived Neighborhood Racial Composition and Whites' Perceptions of Victimization Risk: Do Racial Stereotypes Matter?" *Criminology* 50:145–86.

Piquero, Alex. 1999. "The Validity of Incivility Measures in Public Housing." *Justice Quarterly* 16:793–18.

Quillian, Lincoln, and Devah Pager. 2001. "Black Neighbors, Higher Crime? The Role of Racial Stereotypes in Evaluations of Neighborhood Crime." *American Journal of Sociology* 107:717–67.

———. 2010. "Estimating Risk: Stereotype Amplification and the Perceived Risk of Criminal Victimization." *Social Psychology Quarterly* 73:79–104.

Sampson, Robert J. 2009. "Disparity and Diversity in the Contemporary City: Social (Dis)order Revisited." *British Journal of Sociology* 60:1–31.

Sampson, Robert J., and Stephen W. Raudenbush. 2004. "Seeing Disorder: Neighborhood Stigma and the Social Construction of 'Broken Windows.'" *Social Psychology Quarterly* 67:319–42.

Schuman, Howard, Charlotte Steeh, Lawrence Bobo, and Maria Krysan. 1997. *Racial Attitudes in America: Trends and Interpretations.* Rev. ed. Cambridge, MA: Harvard University Press.

Sears, David O. 1988. "Symbolic Racism." In *Eliminating Racism: Profiles in Controversy*, edited by P. Katz and D. Taylor, 53–84. New York: Plenum.

Skogan, Wesley G. 1990. *Disorder and Decline: Crime and the Spiral of Decay in American Communities.* Berkeley: University of California Press.

———. 1995. "Crime and the Racial Fears of White Americans." *Annals of the American Academy of Political and Social Science* 539:59–71.

Slovic, Paul. 2006. "Perceived Risk, Trust, and Democracy." *Risk Analysis an International Journal* 13 (6): 675–82.

Staats, Cheryl. 2013. "State of the Science: Implicit Bias Review 2013." Columbus: Ohio State University, Kirwan Institute for the Study of Race and Ethnicity. http://kirwan institute.osu.edu/docs/SOTS-Implicit_Bias.pdf. Accessed February 22, 2014.

Stinchcombe, Arthur L., Rebecca Adams, Carol A. Heimer, Kim Lane Scheppele, Tom W. Smith, and D. Garth Taylor. 1980. *Crime and Punishment: Changing Attitudes in America.* San Francisco: Jossey-Bass.

St. John, Craig, and Tamara Heald-Moore. 1995. "Fear of Black Strangers." *Social Science Research* 24:262–80.

———. 1996. "Racial Prejudice and Fear of Criminal Victimization by Strangers in Public Settings." *Sociological Inquiry* 66:267–84.

Taylor, Ralph B., and Jeanette Covington. 1993. "Community Structural Change and Fear of Crime." *Social Problems* 40:374–97.

Taylor, Ralph B., and Margaret Hale. 1986. "Testing Alternative Models of Fear of Crime." *Journal of Criminal Law and Criminology* 77:151–89.

Towles-Schwen, Tamara, and Russell H. Fazio. 2003. "Choosing Social Situations: The Relation between Automatically Activated Racial Attitudes and Anticipated Comfort Interacting with African Americans." *Personality and Social Psychology Bulletin* 29:170–82.

Tversky, Amos, and Daniel Kahneman. 1974. "Judgment under Uncertainty: Heuristics and Biases." *Science* 185 (4157): 1124–31.

Wilcox, Pamela, Neil Quisenberry, and Shayne Jones. 2003. "The Built Environment and Community Crime Risk Interpretation." *Journal of Research in Crime and Delinquency* 40:322–45.

Wilson, James Q., and George L. Kelling. 1982. "Broken Windows: The Police and Neighborhood Safety." *Atlantic Monthly,* March, 29–38.

Wilson, William Julius. 1987. *The Truly Disadvantaged: The Inner City, the Underclass, and Public Policy.* Chicago: University of Chicago Press.

Wilstein, Matt. 2013. "Bill Cosby: 'You Can't Prove' That George Zimmerman Is 'Racist.'" *Mediaite,* July 19. http://www.mediaite.com/online/bill-cosby-you-cant-prove -that-george-zimmerman-is-racist/. Accessed March 5, 2014.

3

Policed, Punished, Dehumanized

The Reality for Young Men of Color Living in America

VICTOR M. RIOS

In attempting to maintain the existing order, the powerful commit crimes of control. . . . At the same time, oppressed people engage in . . . crimes of resistance.
—Meda Chesney-Lind and Randall G. Shelden,
Girls, Delinquency, and Juvenile Justice

Growing up, I experienced constant police harassment and brutality, making me normalize police violence in my community. I personally had my face stomped to the cement by police at age fifteen. My younger brother had been dragged out of a car through the window and beaten at age fourteen by a gang of notorious police officers who called themselves "the Riders." When we filed complaints with the Oakland Police Department or talked to lawyers for help we were ignored. It seemed then that there was nothing we could do about unsanctioned police violence, that no one else cared, and that there were no avenues for getting the word out; until now. The difference between 1997 and today is that a critical mass of young black and Latino men being killed by police and vigilantes has come to the national spotlight through social and mainstream media. This provides a new opportunity to expose the problem of state-sanctioned violence on marginalized populations and on cultivating a social movement that turns against the brutal punitive state.

The state-sanctioned police and vigilante violence on men of color like Oscar Grant (California), Trayvon Martin (Florida), Eric Garner (New York), Andy Lopez (California), and Michael Brown (Missouri)—to name a few high-profile cases—stems from an unchecked system of punitive social control that criminalizes young people of color from early ages. While some marginalized men of color are murdered by police and vigilantes, many more, a large number who live in poverty throughout the United States, experience a kind of social death or social incapacitation in which they are rendered as criminal suspects not just by police but by schools, community centers, social workers, merchants, community members, and even family members. By the time that these young men become young adults, their lives have been policed, punished, and dehumanized by various institutions. This hypercriminalization empowers and emboldens the criminal justice system, law enforcement, and vigilantes to harass, arrest, and shoot these young men at will. This youth control complex—the coalescing of various social institutions to punish, stigmatize, and dehumanize marginalized young people—provides the justification for law enforcement to render young black and Latino bodies as disposable. Society criminalizes marginalized young people so much that by the time a police officer or vigilante shoots them, they have already been rendered as deserving of draconian punishments, even death.

In the midst of this brutal treatment that marginalized young people experience in many communities throughout the United States, there is hope. In my twelve years of collecting data on young people who have been entangled in the criminal justice system, I have found that this very system of punitive social control that has socially incapacitated so many young people and killed many others has, paradoxically, become the most viable impetus for the marginalized masses to generate a viable social movement, one that dismantles the punitive state, in the twenty-first century. When calls are made to resist against police brutality, these very same individuals who have been rendered as apolitical and criminal by their communities become engaged and politicized. The marginalized masses will continue to resist, on their own terms, until a more just and dignifying system is created: "The paradox of punitive social control is that it socially incapacitates too many marginalized populations; at the same time, this system of repression may just be the catalyst for the next wave of massive social movements from below."[1]

In this chapter I discuss how the inner-city men I have followed over the years engage in both acts of survival and crimes of resistance.[2] Sociologist Howard Becker finds that labeled youths resist by internalizing their label and committing more crime.[3] My study finds a missing link in this analysis: the internalization of criminality is only one outcome in the labeling process; another outcome that young people who are labeled partake in is resistance—they internalize criminalization, flip it on its head, and generate action that seeks to change the very system that oppresses them. This is apparent in day-to-day contestations to hyperpolicing but also in recent mass protests around the country in the wake of multiple police killings of young black and Latino men.

Punitive Social Control and Social Incapacitation

A black man is killed by police or vigilantes at least every twenty-eight hours in the United States.[4] Many of these killings are dismissed by the legal system as legitimate. Even the U.S. Supreme Court has been involved in sanctioning police brutality. In a recent decision it ruled that even egregious police misconduct is not a violation of individual constitutional rights.[5] This rampant state-sanctioned deadly force is only the tip of a larger iceberg: punitive social control. Young African American and Latino males suffer a plethora of police and vigilante harassment and brutality on the streets throughout the United States. Many scholars and activists have argued that to date little has been done by police departments, politicians, or the community to halt the everyday use of excessive force and racial profiling by police departments and private security on African American and Latino youths.

Vigilantes, those "everyday citizen" wannabe cops and security guards who are involved in criminalizing and punishing young males of color, have learned that the law places little value on the lives of the black population. This has emboldened individuals to take the law into their own hands. The punitive state is so powerful that it has now been embodied by those "everyday citizens" who seek to punish those considered criminal suspects. The killing of young men of color like Trayvon Martin is a consequence of an extremely punitive criminal justice system and negative public sentiment about inner-city minority boys. To prevent another brutal killing of yet another innocent minority teenager, the public and policy makers must urge police departments to change their differential treatment practices: to eliminate profiling, excessive force, and the vigilante mentality that many officers display.

Many of the young people I have followed, some for over a decade, have not been shot and killed by police but instead have experienced a slow but devastating process of social death, the systematic process by which individuals are denied their humanity.[6] While individuals remain alive, they are socially isolated, violated, and prevented from engaging in social relations that affirm their humanity. Ethnic studies scholar Dylan Rodriguez argues that incarceration is a form of social death, which is "the political and organizational logic of the prison."[7] But beyond finding that incarceration produces a certain kind of social death, criminalization begins at a young age and injects young black and Latino boys with microdoses of social death. I refer to this "microaggression" form of social death as "social incapacitation." Social incapacitation is the process of dehumanization by which punitive social control becomes an instrument that prevents marginalized populations from becoming "productive" citizens who can feel dignity and affirmation from institutions of socialization. Culture scholar George Lipsitz reminds us of Malcolm X's brilliant analysis of racism: "Racism is like a Cadillac, they bring out a new model every year."[8] Malcolm X might agree that if race and class stratification form the highway by which marginalized populations are excluded from important material and symbolic resources in American society, then punitive social control is the Cadillac that cruises them deeper into social exclusion, marginalization, and ultimately social or justified physical death.

As many young working-class black and Latino boys come of age, they realize that they are being systematically punished for being poor, young, black or Latino, and male. In the era of mass incarceration, when punitive social control has become a dominant form of governance, some young people are systematically targeted as criminal risks. "Under this insufferable climate of increased repression and unabated exploitation," Henry Giroux argues, "young people and communities of color become the new casualties in an ongoing war against justice, freedom, social citizenship, and democracy. Given the switch in public policy from social investment to containment, it is clear that young people for whom race and class loom large have become disposable."[9] This process has created a generation of marginalized young people, who are prevented from engaging in a full affirmation of their humanity, let alone from gaining entry into roles that might give them social mobility. The logic and practice of punitive social control has prevented many marginalized young people from gaining acceptance in school, landing a job, or catching a break for minor transgressions from police and probation officers.

Criminalization does not only occur in the law; it crosses boundaries and follows the young people in this study across an array of institutions, including school, the neighborhood, the community center, and the family. In other words, the young men I have studied often found themselves in situations in which their deviant and nondeviant behaviors were constantly treated as threats, risks, and crimes by the various dominant institutions they attempted to navigate. I define this ubiquitous criminalization as the *youth control complex*, a system in which schools, police, probation officers, families, community centers, businesses, and other institutions collaborate to treat young people's everyday behaviors as criminal activity. Young people, who become pinballs within this youth control complex, experience what I refer to as *hypercriminalization*, the process by which an individual's nondeviant behavior and everyday interactions become treated as risk, threat, or crime and, in turn, have an impact on his or her perceptions, worldview, and life outcomes. The youth control complex creates an overarching system regulating the lives of young people, what I refer to as *punitive social control*. Criminalization results in punishment. Punishment, in this study, is understood as any outcome resulting from criminalization that makes young people feel stigmatized, outcast, shamed, defeated, or hopeless.

The youth control complex is not a new phenomenon. Poor and racialized populations have been criminalized in the United States since its inception. The black body has been one of the objects on which criminalization, punishment, social incapacitation, and social death have been executed and perfected. The transatlantic slave trade, savage whippings by slave owners, lynching, and police brutality have been a few of the many historical forms, often state-sanctioned if not state-imposed, of violent punishments executed on the black body. The state-sanctioned brutal police and vigilante murders of unarmed men of color in the twenty-first century can be understood as modern-day lynching by bullet. These killings serve the expressive function of sending a message to other men of color that they are to obey de facto and de jure rules of racial, gendered, and economic exclusion and subjugation.

Punishment of the brown body has been executed through the genocide of indigenous populations; appropriation of Mexican territory by the United States; and vigilante and police brutality against "bandidos," "immigrants," zoot-suiters, and gang youths.[10] In an era of mass incarceration, developed over the past thirty years, punitive social control has fed an out-of-control minotaur, allowing it to expand its labyrinth by embedding itself into traditionally nurturing institutions, punishing young people at younger ages, and marking many for life. Criminalization is well disguised as a protective mechanism: zero-tolerance policies at schools are declared to provide the students who want to learn protection from bullies and disruptions; increased punitive policing is sold as protecting good citizens from violent gang members; longer incarceration sentences and adult sentencing appear to keep the bad guys from victimizing others and send a clear message to potential criminals; and so on.

Labor historian Robin Kelley argues that marginalized young people become involved in "play"—the seeking of personal enjoyment despite their detrimental circumstances. Social scientists, according to Kelley, have confused this "play" for a form of social disorder: "The growing numbers of young brown bodies engaged in 'play' rather than work (from street-corner bantering, to 'malling' [hanging out at shopping malls], to basketball) have contributed to popular constructions of the 'underclass' as a threat and shaped urban police practices. The invention of terms such as *wilding*, as Houston Baker points out, reveal a discourse of black male youth out of control, rampaging teenagers free of the disciplinary structures of school, work, and prison."[11] In 2010, groups of black youth in Philadelphia were placed in the national media spotlight when the city called in the FBI, made student transportation passes invalid after four o'clock in the afternoon, and implemented a policy to cite parents when their children broke curfew laws. This crackdown occurred in response to "flash mobs," large numbers of people who gather after being organized through text messaging. Although the majority of these gatherings did not involve delinquency, a few events, where violence and vandalism took place, led to the criminalization of young black people gathering in groups in downtown Philadelphia. These flash mobs can be analyzed as creative responses to social isolation and a lack of recreation spaces. According to Kelley, and consistent with my findings, marginalized young people's "play" has become criminalized. Sometimes young people of color are killed because their play is confused as threatening behavior, as was the case when thirteen-year-old Andy Lopez was shot seven times by police while he played with a toy gun and when twelve-year-old Tamir Rice was shot and killed by police for the same reason.

The young men in this study compare encounters with police, probation officers, and prosecutors with interactions they have with school administrators and teachers who place them in detention rooms; community centers that attempt to exorcise their criminality; and even parents, who feel ashamed or dishonored and relinquish their relationship with their own children altogether. It seems, in the accounts of the boys, that various institutions collaborate to form a system that degrades and dishonors them on an everyday basis. As such, these young men's understanding of their environment as a punitive one, where they are not given a second chance, leads them to believe that they have no choice but to resist. These institutions, though independently operated with their own practices, policies, and logics, intersect with one another to provide a consistent flow of criminalization. The consequences of this formation are often brutal. Young Ronny, from Oakland, explains: "We are not trusted. Even if we try to change, it's us against the world. It's almost like they don't want us to change. Why they gotta send us to the ghetto alternative high school? We don't deserve to go to the same school down the street? When we try to apply for a job, we just get looked at like we crazy. If we do get an interview, the first question is, 'Have you been arrested before?' . . . We got little choice." Ronny understands his actions as responses to this system of punishment, which restricts his ability to survive, work, play, and learn. As such, he develops coping skills that are often seen as deviant and criminal by the system. Sociologist Elijah Anderson reminds us that young men in these kinds of situations react by demonstrating mistrust of the system: "Highly alienated and embittered, they exude generalized contempt for the wider scheme of things, and for a system they are sure has nothing but contempt for them."[12]

This web of punishment, the youth control complex, adds to young people's blocked opportunities but also generates creative responses, which allow the boys to feel dignified. Sometimes these responses even lead to informal and formal political resistance. However, some responses jeopardize the boys' ability to remain free and negatively impact their social relations with others.

Resistance

A paradox exists among the youths in my studies: criminalization becomes a vehicle by which they develop a political consciousness and resistant identities. Unjust interactions with the youth control complex create blocked opportunities, but they also ignite the boys' social consciousness and help them develop worldviews and identities diametrically opposed to the youth control complex, punitive social control, and the punitive state. Some boys develop a more formal political identity that calls for a change to the system that so oppresses them. Ronny's story, as explained below, exemplifies the process by which marginalized young people develop resistance against punitive social control.

Criminologist Yasser Payne argues that some marginalized black youth who have been excluded from mainstream institutions find affirmation, fulfillment, and resilience in practices associated with street life. These practices, according to Payne, provide young men with "sites of resilience," spaces where they feel empowered and affirmed.[13] Some boys in my studies wholeheartedly believed that they were making a formidable attempt to tap into mainstream institutions, using every possible resource to do so, but, in return, they often received negative responses. They used the resilience skills they had learned on the streets in spaces that could not value the respectability and morals that they brought to the table. These morals and values were often rendered deviant, and the boys were excluded or criminalized. One of their responses was to manifest a resistance to this perceived exclusion and criminalization, a stance that could place value on their self-developed survival skills. This resistance developed in the form of deviance, "irrational behavior," breaking rules, or committing crime. The resistance became more methodical for some of the boys, as they turned to more formal ways of organizing and resisting punitive social control.

Resistance Identities

Resistance identities, according to sociologist Manuel Castells, are those identities created by subordinated populations in response to oppression. These identities operate by "excluding the excluder."[14] In feeling excluded from a network of positive credentials, education, and employment opportunities, young people develop creative responses that provide them with the necessary tools to survive in an environment where they have been left behind and where they are consistently criminalized. They develop practices that seem to embrace criminality as a means of contesting a system that sees them as criminals. Sociologist Richard Quinney argues that poor people engage in crimes such as stealing, robbing, and pirating as "acts of survival," in an economic system where they have been left behind and where their well-being is not fulfilled by other collective means. He further argues that some poor and working-class people engage in "crimes of resistance," such as sabotaging workplace equipment and destroying public property, as a form of protest against their economic conditions.[15] Sociologist John Hagedorn argues that one promising avenue for transforming the lives of marginalized young people is to embrace their resistance, "Encouraging cultural 'resistance identities' and linking them to social movements, like those in the United States opposing gentrification, police brutality, or deportations, may present the best opportunity to reach out to our alienated youth."[16] Sociologist Felix Padilla finds that gang-involved youths hold a "conscious understanding of the workings of social institutions."[17] Padilla quotes education scholar Henry Giroux to frame his analysis of the critical consciousness developed by marginalized young people: "In some cases . . . youngsters may not be fully aware of the political grounds of the position toward the conventional society, except for a general awareness of its dominating nature and the need to somehow escape from it without relegating themselves to a future they do not want. Even this vague understanding and its attendant behavior portend a politically progressive logic."[18]

I build on this work by demonstrating how the young men in my studies engage in both acts of survival and crimes of resistance. Furthermore, I argue that some of their nonserious offenses were committed as acts of resistance to being criminalized. The boys in this study were clearly aware of, recognized, and had an analysis of the system that criminalized them. Consequently, youth labeled as deviants participated in everyday practices of resistance. Sociologist Howard Becker finds that labeled youths resist by internalizing their label and committing more crime.[19]

The young men in my studies constantly participated in everyday acts of resistance that did not make sense to the adults in their community. Teachers, police officers, and community center workers were often baffled by the deviant acts committed by the boys. From the perspective of adults, these transgressions and small crimes were ridiculous and irrational because the risk of being caught was high and the benefit derived from committing the deviant act was minuscule. This frustration led adults to abandon empathy for the boys and to apply the toughest sanctions on them. "If they're going to act like idiots, I am going to have to give them the axe," explained one gang task force officer in Oakland.

Many of the adults I interviewed believed that the boys' defiance was, as some called it, "stupid." Sarcastic remarks such as "that was smart" often followed when a youth purposely broke a simple rule, leading him to be ostracized, kicked out of class, or even arrested. Why would the boys break the simplest of rules knowing that there would be grave consequences? From their perspective, the boys were breaking the rules in order to resist a system that seemed stacked against them. In many ways, breaking the rules was one of the few resources that the boys could use in response to criminalization.

Why would these boys steal a twenty-five-cent bag of chips when they had money in their pocket? Curse out a police officer who was trying to befriend them? Act indifferent to a potential employer? Or purposely not answer their probation officer's call during curfew time, even though they were sitting next to the phone? These seemingly irrational transgressions often created meaning that gave these youngsters dignity in an environment that already saw them as criminal prior to their committing the act. But working for dignity does not necessarily translate to working for freedom. In other words, when the boys sought out dignity, they were often at risk of losing their freedom; when they worked for freedom, they were making an attempt to stay out of jail or prison but often felt that they had lost their dignity in the process.

Patterns of behavior that are often misrecognized as ignorant, stupid, and self-defeating by authority figures, policy makers, and scholars are often young people's attempt to use the resources provided by their environment to transform their social conditions. Sociologist Anne Swidler's concept of "culture as repertoire" contends that individuals deploy different, often contradicting actions in the social world based on the needs demanded by specific social situations.[20] For Swidler, culture influences action by providing a tool kit of actions to choose from. This notion of culture is important in the study of working-class populations because it provides a space for scholars to "study culture and poverty without blaming the victim."

The boys used the resources around them to develop a response to what they perceived as punitive treatment. Their responses where often misinterpreted by authority figures. Ronny, for example, responded to his potential employer's cold gestures by using the tools he had learned from others in the community: to avoid being perceived as aggressive toward white women. Whereas the protocols of mainstream culture would have provided him with the understanding that he should shake a potential employer's hand, his racialization had conditioned him to remain passive and avoid physical contact of any kind, even a seemingly innocuous handshake. The youths in this study demonstrated a yearning for being accepted by mainstream society and used the resources available to them in an attempt to do so. However, their actions were misinterpreted as acts of deviance. This in turn led the system to further criminalize them.

The Stolen Bag of Chips

One fall afternoon, I met with fifteen-year-old Flaco, a Latino gang-associated young man from east Oakland. We joined three of his friends as they walked to their usual after-school hangout, Walnut Park. They decided to make a stop at Sam's Liquor Store. I walked in with them, noticing a sign on the outside that read, "Only two kids allowed in store at one time." I realized that they were breaking the store rule by entering in a group of four. I pretended to walk in separately from the group to see how the store clerk would respond to their transgression. I stood in the back of the store next to the soft drink and beer refrigerators. Flaco walked up to the candy bar aisle—keeping a good distance between himself and the Snickers, Twix, and Skittles, to show the clerk, who was already staring him down, that he was not attempting to steal. He grabbed a candy bar, held it far away from his body, walked a few steps, and placed it on the counter. Many of the boys in this study often maintained their distance in the candy or soda aisles at stores. This may have been a way for them to show the store that they were not attempting to steal. Store clerks in the neighborhoods I studied were always apprehensive of customers. They watched people from the moment they walked in and had surveillance cameras set up, and some had personal pictures of AK-47 rifles taped on their counters to indicate to customers that they were prepared. This particular clerk may have been concerned that too many kids in his store meant that he could not keep an eye on all of them at the same time.

The store clerk, a balding, middle-aged, Asian American male, pointed to the door and yelled, "Only two kids allowed in the store at a time!" The three youths who were in line to pay for their items looked at the store clerk and at each other. I could see in their faces the look of despair as their most pleasurable moment of the day, to bite into a delicious candy bar, fell apart. Mike, who stood closest to the entrance of the door, responded, "We ain't doing shit." The store clerk looked at him and replied, "I am going to call the police!" Mike grabbed a twenty-five-cent bag of Fritos Flamin' Hot chips, lifted it up in front of the clerk's face, and said, "You see this? I was gonna pay for it, but now I ain't paying for shit, stupid mothafucka." He rushed out of the store with the bag of chips. The clerk picked up the phone and called the police. The rest of the youngsters dropped the snacks they were in line to purchase and ran out of the store. I walked up to the store clerk and gave him a quarter for Mike, who had stolen the chips. With an infuriated look, the clerk responded, "It's too late. The police are on their way to get the robbers."

When I walked out of the store, the boys had all disappeared. I was not able to track them down until a few days later. When I ran into Flaco, he informed me that the police had arrested Mike that day for stealing the twenty-five-cent bag of chips. After interviewing the boys and observing the store clerk's interactions with them soon after this event, I found that Mike's "irrational" behavior had changed the way the store clerk interacted with the boys. The boys believed that the store clerk had begun to treat them with more respect. The store clerk avoided provoking negative interactions with the boys, even if it meant allowing a few more boys into the store than his store policy demanded. While even Mike's peers believed that his actions were "crazy," they also acknowledged that something significant had changed in their inter-actions with the store clerk. For example, Flaco thought that Mike had overreacted, but he also rationalized Mike's actions. Because of Mike, Flaco felt respected by the store clerk the next time he went in the store: "Mike fucked up. He was acting hyphee [crazy] that day. He should have paid the guy. . . . But because of what he did, me and my dogs go into the sto', and the guy don't say shit. We all go in like five deep— like 'what?'—and dude [the store clerk] don't say shit no more." When I asked Mike why he had stolen the bag of chips, he responded, "That fool was trippin'. He should've come correct. I was gonna pay him. You saw, I had the money in my hand. . . . That fool knows not to fuck with us anymore. . . . I did get taken in for that, but it don't matter. They gave me probation and shit. I'll just keep it cool now since that fool will keep it cool now too." In Mike's worldview, his strategy of fighting for dignity at the cost of giving up his freedom had paid off. Mike's actions resulted in his commitment to the criminal justice system. According to him, he was very aware of this risk when he stole the bag of chips. He had grown frustrated at the treatment he had received at school and by police, which culminated at the store. This frustration, and a deep desire to feel respected, led Mike to willfully expose himself to incarceration. In the end, Mike lost his freedom, becoming supervised by the criminal justice system. Nonetheless, he gained a sense of dignity for himself and his peers, which made it worth exchanging his freedom. This scenario is representative of many of the crimes that the other boys committed. Demanding dignity from the system generated a paradox for the boys: they all indicated wanting to be free of incarceration, policing, and sur-veillance, while, at the same time, punitive surveillance, policing, and discipline led many of them to consciously act in a way that pipelined them into the criminal justice system.

The boys took control of their criminalization by using the few resources they had at hand. In this example, Mike and his friends changed the interactional dynamic between themselves and the store clerk. The store clerk would no longer yell or enforce the two-boys-max rule, which the youths perceived as ridiculous. Instead, he adjusted his practices by allowing the boys into the store, as long as they did not steal. However, the price that Mike paid was steep. This arrest later led him deeper into the criminal justice system.

I asked Mike, "Why didn't you steal something more expensive?" He told me that he thought about it, but, in the moment, he didn't care what he took. He wanted to prove a point to the clerk: "not to fuck with me." For Mike, stealing the bag of chips wasn't about saving the quarter he had to pay for the chips; it wasn't about accumulating the most valuable commodity he could get his hands on; it wasn't about stealing because he was poor and wanted to eat a bag of chips. Although he may have had a desire for all of the above, the purpose of stealing the bag of chips was to redeem himself for being shamed and feeling disrespected. In the end, despite facing further punishment, Mike and his friends felt that their actions were not in vain; they had won a small battle in a war they were so tired of losing. While authority figures expected the boys to desist and follow the rules, and while the boys expressed a deep desire "to be left alone" and remain free, one of the only resources they had to feel respected within the system was to actively engage in behaviors that defied the rules of the game. This in turn led to further criminalization.

Crimes of Resistance

Much of the deviance and crime committed by the boys could be understood as a form of resistance, which, despite its negative repercussions, brought about self-empowerment for the boys. Many of the young men self-consciously "acted stupid" in order to diminish the significance of a system that had excluded and punished them. These deviant politics garnered attention from the youth control complex, frustrating its agents: the police, school personnel, and others. This frustration led to more punishment, which in turn led to a deeper crisis of control in the community. In the end, it was this crisis of control, when institutions were not able to provide a sufficient amount of social order, which the young men consciously perceived to be a successful result of their defiance. As Flaco put it, "They trying to regulate me, right? So if they can't regulate me, then that means they not doing their job. So my job is to not—what's that word?—confirm [conform]."

Youth Mobilization against Punitive Social Control

As the youths in this study experienced firsthand the punitive grip of the state, they fought back in whatever way they could. Instead of remaining passive and allowing the system to shame, criminalize, and exclude them, the boys continued to produce scattered acts of resistance. From stealing at the store to cursing out police officers who had once brutalized them, the boys engaged themselves in deviant politics.

We should not romanticize the petty crimes or rebellious acts committed by the boys in this study. Boys who resisted often suffered real and drastic consequences. Sometimes they did not even realize that they were resisting. Often they were simply, as they called it, "getting stupid," meaning that they acted "bad" for the sake of being "bad." Moreover, deviant politics were often messy—one example is the perpetuation of misogyny discussed in the following chapter. These kinds of practices had no long-term positive outcomes for any of the boys in the study. However, these deviant politics may have been a means to an end, the development of oppositional consciousness and political activism, which, in turn, empowered some boys to become agents who fought to dismantle punitive social control and transform other forms of oppression. This is what happened to nine of the boys in this study, who became involved in an organization that protested police brutality and what they called, using feminist scholar Angela Davis's term, "the prison industrial complex," a system of private and government agencies that economically benefit from the incarceration of marginalized populations. These boys had joined grassroots organizations in Oakland after meeting community organizers who had recruited them because of their status as what the community organizers called "survivors of the juvenile justice system." The boys related to and recognized this analysis of the system, which compelled them to join the community organizers in meetings and marches that protested police brutality and the building of incarceration facilities.

During a revisit to Oakland in 2009 soon after the police killing of Oscar Grant, I found that all nine of these young men, four black and five Latino, continued to participate in formal dissent. They took part in marches, vigils, and meetings that demanded justice for the killing of Oscar Grant by a police officer. Grant was unarmed and handcuffed when the officer shot him in the back. The incident was caught on video and became national headline news. Although none of the boys knew Oscar Grant, all nine boys described Oscar Grant as "one of us." Kobe described a rally that he attended after the killing: "The march for *my boy* Oscar Grant, man, was downtown on Wednesday, that Wednesday when we was riding it [marching] or whatever, and we gave up. We was in, like, a little part of, like, an alley street, so the crew I was with, we gave in. We was gonna lay down, and they [police] came up to us and was hitting us in the head with the guns and pinned their knees to our backs and twisted my arm. I thought he was gonna break it." The fact that Kobe continued to be brutalized by police, now as a protestor, bolstered his worldview that all police are part of a system of criminalization and brutality. Prior to Grant's killing, many of these boys had been brutalized or had witnessed friends or family brutalized or killed by police. Eleven of the boys claimed to know a friend or family member who had been severely injured or killed by police. Smoky Man reflected on why he became politically active: "I fight 'cause all the stuff they been doing. They [the police] took [killed] two of my cousins in 2004, for no reason. They came out of a store, and they thought they had some drugs or some guns on them, and they shot both of them. One of them died at the scene. One of them dies like a week later in the hospital. They had no right to do that, so this is payback, man. Anything I saw and been through with the cops, you can't tell me it's a good cop."

Fourteen of the Latino and nine of the black boys in the study commented on the racial implications of criminalization. They all believed that, despite having differences on the streets with the other racial group, there exists a social order in which the dominant outcomes are not interracial conflict or racial solidarity; instead, the boys in this study found ways to avoid negative interactions with the other racial group, by following certain rules of avoidance and respect. Despite their close living and recreational proximity to one another, black and Latino boys, in comparison to intraracial conflicts, rarely had conflict with one another.

Whenever the boys in this study talked about racial solidarity, it was often linked to the struggle against criminalization and police brutality. Jordan's perspective is representative of the perspective held by the nine boys who became politically active: "I'm speaking towards the Black perspective, but I understand they treat the Mexicans the same way!

They treat the Mexicans the same way, the same way: they all affiliated with gangs. They feel any Mexicans are in gangs—you know what I'm saying? They mess with Mexicans all the same ways they discriminate Black people." Although each racial group may have experienced criminalization in unique ways, what I found with the boys in this study is that they believed that their experiences were very similar. This belief, in turn, generated a racial solidarity among boys who had been criminalized. They held a worldview that informed them that "Mexicans and Blacks are treated in the same way." This feeling of collective racialization facilitated the process by which nine of the forty boys in this study participated in formal political action against police brutality. Meetings and marches that the boys participated in were multiracial, including blacks, Latinos, and whites.

The process of being criminalized developed oppositional identities in all the boys in this study. Some enacted this opposition by committing "irrational" transgressions, such as "going dumb" or disobeying their probation officers. A few boys developed a deeper sense of dissent by participating in marches, protests, and meetings aimed at ending police brutality. While criminalization had many detrimental consequences for the boys, for many it also sparked a deep desire to know why they were targeted, and some developed a keen sense of dissent, often informal and occasionally more formal.

Prominent social movements scholar Pamela Oliver reminds us that, in the context of mass incarceration generated by the repression of the social movements of the mid-twentieth century, we have to pay attention to the new and unique forms of resistance and mobilization taking place among marginalized populations. She argues that among these populations dissent may also be expressed in crime: "There is individual dissent and collective crime, and both are common. The more repressive a system, the more dissent takes the form of individual, often anonymous, acts of resistance. . . . We need to ask how oppressed people can gain redress under conditions of extreme repression, and to understand the forms that resistance can take when the possibility of direct resistance is blocked."[21] In an environment where there were few formal avenues for expressing dissent toward a system, which the boys believed to be extremely repressive, they developed forms of resistance that they believed could change, even if only temporarily, the outcome of their treatment. The boys believed they had gained redress for the punitive social control they had encountered by adopting a subculture of resistance based on fooling the system and by committing crimes of resistance, which made no sense to the system but were fully recognizable to those who had been misrecognized and criminalized.

Paradoxically, punitive social control also created a deep self-awareness of the class position in which these young people found themselves. These boys all demonstrated a clear understanding of the process of punishment described in this book. In addition, their deviant and delinquent actions, except when they were drunk or high, served as an attempt to act in their own rational interests. Marginalized young people have agency and political awareness; they have a clear understanding of the system of punitive social control that impacts their daily lives. While some of what the boys told me was one-sided, full of half-truths, and with a clear bias and misrecognition of their social conditions and the intentions of most social control institutions to genuinely help them, these young people could clearly articulate the mechanisms by which they ended up marked and tracked into the criminal justice system. Their actions, subcultures, and worldviews were developed in direct opposition to punitive social control. This resistance carried the seeds of redemption, self-determination, resilience, and desistance. Embracing the positive aspects of this resistance, teaching young people how to use it to navigate in mainstream institutions, and granting less damaging consequences for young people who break the law are all challenges that we must take on if we are to change the trajectory of punitive social control.

In an era of mass incarceration, political mobilization among marginalized populations most affected by punitive social control is centered around unshackling handcuffs, prying open prison bars, and shaking iron cages off their backs. The social movements of the new millennium among the most marginalized classes have arrived, and they are centered on dismantling punitive social control. The ideology of this control is constantly contested and challenged by marginalized young people. Because ideology is always political, ideological change occurs in the everyday interactions that youth have with dominant forces. If policy makers, scholars, program workers, and activists are to find viable ways of working with those populations most affected by punitive social control, they will have to be willing to hand over some bolt cutters; they will have to be willing to take the "risk" of proposing and implementing policies and programs that provide more reintegration and less disintegration; they will have to be willing to join the movement to dismantle punitive social control and the criminalization that keeps it company.

We must eliminate the zero-tolerance policies that are rampant in schools, policing, and community centers. School-based police officers must be given limitations: schools don't allow music teachers to teach math, so why do they allow police officers to stand in for counselors, administrators, parents, or teachers? Police are trained to find and eliminate criminality; they are not trained to teach or to nurture. Therefore, neither police nor criminal justice practices should monopolize social control. The right arm of the state, the punishing arm, must be restrained and uncoupled from the left arm, the nurturing arm. We must find ways to eliminate the use of criminal justice metaphors and practices as a means of solving everyday social problems. Redistributing resources from criminal justice institutions back into nurturing institutions must become a priority. In addition, we must hold educational and criminal justice institutions accountable for violating young people's civil and human rights, not just when they shoot and kill someone—the end of the punitive death continuum—but at the beginning of the process, when they first tell third-grader that they have a prison cell waiting for him when he grows up or when they place handcuffs on a fifth-grader because he threw a spitball at the teacher. This process of social and physical death imposed through punitive social control begins at a young age for marginalized males of color. By the time my childhood friend JJ was killed by police at age twenty he had already been expelled from school, kicked out of his house, and granted a criminal record. Contesting the unjustness of his killing was futile because he had already been marked as social junk, deserving of severe punishment, even if meted out through lynching by bullet.

The killing of marginalized men of color by police or by those acting as vigilantes to secure their community, along with the process of punitive social control that follows them and other individuals like them from young ages, have created the impetus for those hypercriminalized, hypermarginalized classes that are often rendered as apolitical and unproductive by even their own communities to resist, to protest, to become politicized and override the draconian social order of punitive social control.

The experiences documented by these young men are reflected in the Trayvon Martin case, as well as the recent cases of Tamir Rice (twelve-year-old boy shot by a Cleveland police officer who mistook his toy air gun for a real firearm), Eric Garner (died after being placed in a chokehold by an NYPD officer), and Michael Brown (unarmed teen shot and killed by a police officer in Ferguson, Missouri). While the circumstances that undergird each case are quite different, the commonality that runs across them is the assumption of criminality and dangerousness that leads to the degradation of black and brown lives. The injustice that surrounds the aggressive and overpolicing of minority citizens along with the inequities in social control processes more broadly have led President Obama to sign an executive order that establishes the Task Force on 21st Century Policing, the purpose of which is to foster strong and collaborative community ties between law enforcement and the very communities they are sworn to protect. While there remains great debate about the salience of race and ethnicity in criminal justice decision making, one thing remains clear: black and brown people are disproportionately targeted, searched, arrested, and incarcerated. Moreover, they are two to three times more likely to have force used against them by law enforcement. These disparities require greater attention to the problem of race/ethnicity and how it disadvantages black and brown people in the criminal justice system.

NOTES

1. Rios 2011, 159.

2. Parts of this chapter were previously published in *Punished: Policing the Lives of Black and Latino Boys* (Rios 2011).

3. Becker 1963.

4. http://www.alternet.org/news-amp-politics/1-black-man-killed-every-28-hours-police-or-vigilantes-america-perpetually-war-its.

5. http://www.nytimes.com/2014/08/27/opinion/how-the-supreme-court-protects-bad-cops.html?_r=0.

6. See Patterson 1982.

7. Rodriguez 2006, 5.

8. Lipsitz 1998, 183.
9. Giroux 2009, 124.
10. See Romero 2001.
11. Kelley 1997, 53.
12. Anderson 1999, 10.
13. Payne 2008.
14. Castells 1997.
15. Quinney 1977.
16. Hagedorn 2008.
17. Padilla 1992.
18. Padilla 1992, 5.
19. Becker 1963.
20. Swidler 1986.
21. Oliver 2008, 13.

REFERENCES

Anderson, Elijah. 1999. *Code of the Street: Decency, Violence, and Moral Life of the Inner City*. New York: Norton.

Becker, Howard. 1963. *Outsiders: Studies in the Sociology of Deviance*. New York: Free Press.

Castells, Manuel. 1997. *The Power of Identity*. Oxford: Blackwell.

Giroux, Henry A. 2003. *Democracy beyond the Culture of Fear*. New York: Palgrave Macmillan.

———. 2009. *Youth in a Suspect Society: Democracy or Disposability?* New York: Palgrave Macmillan.

Hagedorn, John. 2008. *A World of Gangs: Armed Young Men and Gangsta Culture*. Minneapolis: University of Minnesota Press.

Kelley, Robin D. G. 1997. *Yo' Mama's Disfunktional! Fighting the Culture Wars in Urban America*. Boston: Beacon.

Lipsitz, George. 1998. *The Possessive Investment in Whiteness: How White People Profit from Identity Politics*. Philadelphia: Temple University Press.

Oliver, Pamela E. 2008. "Repression and Crime Control: Why Social Movement Scholars Should Pay Attention to Mass Incarceration as a Form of Repression." *Mobilization* 13 (1): 1–24.

Padilla, Felix. 1992. *The Gang as an American Enterprise*. New York: Rutgers University Press.

Patterson, Orlando. 1992. *Slavery and Social Death: A Comparative Study*. Cambridge, MA: Harvard University Press.

Payne, Yasser. 2008. "'Street Life' as a Site of Resiliency: How Street Life–Oriented Black Men Frame Opportunity in the United States." *Journal of Black Psychology* 34 (1): 3–31.

Quinney, Richard. 1977. *Class, State and Crime*. New York: Longman.

Rios, Victor M. 2011. *Punished: Policing the Lives of Black and Latino Boys*. New York: New York University Press.

Rodriguez, Dylan. 2006. *Forced Passages: Imprisoned Radical Intellectuals and the U.S. Prison Regime*. Minneapolis: University of Minnesota Press.

Romero, Mary. 2001. "State Violence and the Social and Legal Construction of Latino Criminality: From el Bandido to Gang Member." *Denver University Law Review* 78:1081–1118.

Swidler, Ann. 1986. "Culture in Action: Symbols and Strategies." *American Sociological Review* 51 (2): 273–86.

4

Threat, Danger, and Vulnerability

Trayvon Martin and Gwen Araujo

TOYA LIKE, LORI SEXTON, AND SAVANNAH PORTER

Recent scholarship on the intersections of race, ethnicity, class, and gender has pointed to their far-reaching influence on various phenomena related to crime and justice. Importantly, these works have moved criminological theory and research beyond simple comparisons across discrete categories, thus allowing for a more complex examination of the influence of interlocking inequalities on individuals' experiences with crime, victimization, and the justice system. We draw upon this growing body of literature to examine the influence of characteristics such as race, ethnicity, gender and sexual orientation, class, and age on individuals' perceptions of others as threatening or dangerous as well as their assessments of their own vulnerabilities to these perceived threats/ dangers. We do so through the examination of two seemingly unrelated cases that elucidate the role and importance of intersectionality in how conflicts unfold on the ground: the combative, and ultimately fatal, encounter between Trayvon Martin and George Zimmerman, and the brutal murder of Gwen Araujo, a young, transgender Latina woman. We use a variety of data sources, including news coverage and social commentary on the deaths and the events surrounding them, to more fully understand the context of these violent encounters and highlight the commonalities across these seemingly disparate cases.

In this chapter, we address the following research questions: (1) What role might race, gender, and class inequalities have played in the situations that Martin and Araujo (and the men who killed them) found themselves in? (2) Beyond this, how might these intersections have affected the course of events that led to their deaths? And (3) how might these intersections have affected perceptions of threat, danger, and vulnerability among the victims and perpetrators, and what role might these perceptions have played in the conflicts that unfolded? We utilize these cases as empirical windows through which the role of inter-sections between race/ethnicity, age, class, and gender in shaping the situational context of conflicts can be better understood. We do so in order to establish the groundwork for a tentative framework in the symbolic interactionist tradition that can help us to understand the impacts of intersectionality on violent encounters more generally.[1]

Social Status, Vulnerability, and Threat

Sociological theory and research have long emphasized that humans are more the product of our social environment than something rigidly predetermined by nature or biology. Indeed these works posit that the very essence of who we are—the *self*—is composed of a variety of inter-related, contextually informed identities that are performed or enacted, rather than the result of biological inclinations or psychological pre-dispositions. This view is grounded in symbolic interactionism, which suggests that "the self is not an object that has inherent meaning, but is a construct that is given meaning through an actor's choices, mediated by the relationships, situations, and cultures in which he or she is embed-ded."[2] From this perspective, the self is symbolically formed through social interactions with others and the broader structural conditions in which individuals find themselves.

Intimately related to this notion of the self as "symbolic, situationally constructed, and structured" are the constructs *identity* and *status*.[3] In essence, social interactions with others and structural conditions shape the process by which identity is constructed as well as the process by which we construct the identities of others.[4] Concomitant with con-structing the identities of others is the allocation of status value to these imputed identities. Individual characteristics such as race, class, gender, sexual orientation, and age carry with them values that position indi-viduals differentially in the social hierarchy; these values shift the focus from individual identities (whether claimed by oneself, or assigned by others) to statuses.[5] Importantly for our purposes in this chapter, scholars have noted that constructions of deviant identities are due in part to the reflected appraisals of significant others.[6] Moreover, others have pointed to the effects of broader society in shaping deviant status and identity,[7] which are often conferred to individuals through routine societal enactment of laws and normative rules that can be arbitrarily applied, especially to the socially and economically disadvantaged.[8]

Alongside the performance of identity and assessment of others' identities and statuses is the social construction of one's vulnerability to violence and perceptions of others as threatening or dangerous. Because identity reflects the intersection of numerous characteristics, it is likely to inform interpersonal interactions in myriad ways. In the following section, we review the extant literature on social constructions of gender, sexual orientation, race, ethnicity, and class, considering their individual and collective effects on perceptions of vulnerability and threat.

Constructing Vulnerability across Gender, Sexual Orientation, Race, Ethnicity, and Class

The idea that the self is socially constructed has perhaps been asserted most often by gender and feminist scholars. In their foundational article "Doing Gender," West and Zimmerman open with a simple statement that draws an unambiguous distinction between biology and identity: "In the beginning there was sex and there was gender."[9] While sex in its most basic explanation is anatomical, and thus is captured in the dichotomous terms "male" and "female," gender is authenticated on a social "stage" in which "actors" demonstrate masculinity and femininity.

In the United States, these constructs are often considered to be synonymous. For instance, we readily associate nurturing and socially cohesive behaviors (i.e., purported feminine characteristics) with being female, while dominance, aggression, and independence (i.e., ascribed masculine behaviors) are commonly linked to males. In this way, gender is socially produced and maintained in daily, routine activities and interactions that shape our social worlds, while gendered notions of sex are improperly and implicitly reified. Gender roles and norms are reproduced and maintained in the family, school, workplace, and various other institutions that structure day-to-day life.[10] While this is not to say that these roles and norms are not routinely challenged or restructured, such change is typically met with resistance and at times nullified via the existing structure of gender inequality. For instance,

Hollander demonstrated that women and girls are commonly characterized as being vulnerable to violence while their male counterparts are often depicted as invulnerable to it.[11] More recently, in their examination of African American youth's perception of violence, Cobbina, Like-Haislip, and Miller found that young men often perceived females as ineffectual and inept in their use of violence.[12] In explaining this depiction, Like-Haislip and Cobbina conclude that "when faced with the realities of female violence, young men sought to protect their masculine identities by minimizing or belittling female violence as irrational and ineffective, despite its volatile nature."[13] These findings are particularly important given the narrowing gender gap in violence, especially between African American males and females.[14] Consequently, violence is constructed as a masculine (and therefore male) behavior, and female participation in these acts is often disparaged, in an attempt to protect masculinity.

Embedded within this hierarchal system of gender inequality is heteronormativity, or the preference for and assumption of heterosexual orientation in our society. Like gender, heterosexuality is perceived as a natural byproduct of femininity and masculinity. As Schilt and Westbrook explain, heteronormativity is "the suite of cultural, legal, and institutional practices that maintain normative assumptions that there are two and *only two* genders, and that gender reflects biological sex, and that only sexual attraction between those 'opposite' genders is natural or acceptable."[15] Indeed, heteronormativity could not exist without fixed gender roles and norms.[16] Just as masculinity is aligned with status, power, and privilege in relation to femininity, so too is heterosexuality in relation to homosexuality. Consequently, the enactment of sexual identity is situated within this hierarchal framework that devalues femininity and homosexuality. This social construction of sexual identity, in turn, disadvantages nonheterosexual orientations including individuals who identify as gay, lesbian, bisexual, and/or transgender.[17] As aforementioned, "doing" masculinity is equated to dominant behaviors while "doing" femininity is made synonymous with submission. Individuals who defy or violate these normative standards of gender are placed at the margins. Consequently, acts of violence perpetrated against them go largely unnoticed and often unpunished and may too be a way of protecting masculinity. In fact, next to racial/ethnic identity, sexual orientation is the most common motivation for hate and bias crimes. These crimes, which are more often perpetrated against males, are typically violent in nature and occur in public settings.[18]

Race and ethnicity are also understood to be performed rather than innate. While few would argue against the biological attributes of race and ethnicity such as skin tone and other physical traits, most have recognized the social construction of racial identities in the United States. Racial and ethnic identities not only serve to organize individuals and/ or groups according to cultural backgrounds of shared ancestry, language, norms, and values, but also allow for relational distance between groups via social, economic, and political hierarchies. They become a basis for clustering groups along lines of status and privilege, essentially placing some in positions of advantage and power while concomitantly restricting others in parallel systems of disadvantage and oppression.[19]

Racial identities have historically and contemporarily been linked to crime and deviance. Whites are often depicted as vulnerable and susceptible to violence while nonwhites, especially African Americans, are readily associated with danger and violence.[20] Despite these perceptions, official data have consistently shown that the majority of individuals arrested for violent crimes are white. Between 1995 and 2010, for instance, whites constituted approximately 60 percent of violent crime arrestees on average. Still, more attention is paid to the disproportionate rate at which blacks are arrested for these offenses. This focus, however, ignores the fact that given their relative population sizes, it would take far more arrests of whites to produce disproportionality while, on the other hand, slight increases for blacks could easily produce the same result. Moreover, the disparate rate at which blacks are arrested for these offenses does not mitigate that whites make up the majority of violent crime arrestees or the possibility that arrest practices may in part be a reflection of broader societal depictions of blacks as dangerous and violent.[21] This criminalization or stereotypical view of blacks is extremely pervasive in American society, driven by media accounts that "systematically over-represent African Americans as criminal; portray Black males as particularly dangerous, and present information about Black suspects that assumes their guilt."[22] Though driven largely by these mass media accounts and rooted heavily in a system of racism and stereotyping of blacks, these depictions have real-life implications on perceptions of this group as crime-prone and violent, not only among the general public,[23] but also among professionals in the criminal justice system.[24]

Class, too, is argued to be enacted and performed by individuals and is negotiated and achieved via social interactions. Like the aforementioned characteristics, class is positioned within a hierarchal structure of unequal access to resources essential to achieving and maintaining status. As West and Fenstermaker note, "the accomplishment of class in everyday life rests on the presumption that everyone is endowed with equal opportunity, and therefore, the real differences in the outcomes we observe must result from individual differences in attributes like intelligence and character."[25] Consequently, class inequality is often masked in a system of meritocracy in the United States that disguises inequitable and limited access to educational and vocational opportunities that are foundational to the construction of class identity. The unequal distribution of these opportunities is eclipsed by institutional and social arrangements that equate wealth with hard work, ingenuity, and talent while poverty is associated with a lack of effort, skill, and initiative.[26] Poverty and/or lower class status then are viewed as behavioral outcomes, with little, if any, attention given to structural inequalities that produce and maintain distinctions between the haves and the have-nots. As was the case with gender and race, behavioral assumptions associated with class have coupled lower class status with criminality. The salience of class as an indicator of criminal threat is so potent that Hollander concludes that "being poor . . . is sufficient to be seen as dangerous," net of any other sociodemographic characteristics such as race, age, and gender.[27]

The extant research reviewed here emphasizes how gender, sexual orientation, race, and class are what individuals *do* as opposed to who or what they *are*. These behaviors—"doing" gender, "doing" heterosexuality, "doing" race, and "doing" class—are the result of cultural norms and expectations that are maintained and reinforced in social encounters. Success in negotiating and accomplishing these identities becomes the mechanism for "doing" difference and thus generating status, power, and privilege. Although each identity can be seen as separate and emerging from various aspects of the social structure and stratification within this structure, they are enacted and experienced simultaneously.[28] It is at the intersection of these identities that (dis)advantage is created, produced, and reinforced. The symbolic interactionist perspective posits that these interlocking inequalities affect the process by which identity is constructed and negotiated in social interactions, and thus the lens through which individuals view themselves and their social worlds.[29] Specifically, these intersections influence how individuals perceive themselves in the context of others, and notably their own vulnerability to danger, in addition to how they shape or perceive others as threatening or dangerous.

This assessment not only of danger but especially of one's own vulnerability to violence is probably best captured in the fear of crime literature. These works have consistently pointed to the influence of gender, race, class, and sexual orientation on fear of crime. For example, scholars have demonstrated that females are far more likely than their male counterparts to be fearful of crime. However, with the exception of rape and sexual assault, they are far less likely than males to be victims of violence. In explaining this phenomenon, researchers have shown that driving women's heightened level of fear is the undergirding ubiquitous fear of rape and sexual assault. As Stanko notes, "the reality of sexual violence is a core component of being female and is experienced in a variety of everyday, mundane situations."[30] Consequently, females' fear of burglary or robbery, for example, is the product of the "shadow of sexual assault" that looms in the background, as these crimes may be construed as a gateway to sexual violence.[31] In this sense, it is not the crime per se that drives fear, but rather individuals' assessment of their vulnerability to related violence. Another case in point is that older people (especially those fifty-five and older) are far less likely than younger people to be victims of violent crime, yet the elderly report much higher levels of fear compared to their younger counterparts.[32] It may be that older persons are not relying on official statistics to inform them of their risks but instead are evaluating their susceptibility to injury and importantly their (in)ability to withstand a violent attack when determining their level of fear of crime. Moreover, contemporary works in these areas show that assessments of risk for victimization (and inadvertently the perception of others as dangerous) are performed via an "intersectional lens" in that individuals make these evaluations based not on gender, age, race, or class but rather a combination of these. Hollander found that a combination of these characteristics is invoked when determining the threat of situations and others.[33] For example, although blacks are often associated with crime and dangerousness, it is the fear of *young black males*, in particular, that is pervasive among the white middle class; in this respect, race, age, and gender intersect to heighten fear and perceived threat.

In sum, this chapter examines the role of the interlocking inequalities of race, ethnicity, class, gender, and sexual orientation in shaping social interactions—especially those that are violent in nature. Informed by the symbolic interactionist perspective and various strands of social constructionism that stem from it, we utilize a rich set of data to make inferences about the role that intersectionalities may have played in two particular violent encounters. In keeping with the primary focus of this volume, we first draw on the fatal shooting of Trayvon Martin, underscoring the role of race, ethnicity, gender, and (perceived) class in his violent encounter with George Zimmerman. We then turn to a second, seemingly unrelated case—the beating and strangulation of Gwen Araujo—to demonstrate the utility of our framework in understanding violent encounters beyond the case of Trayvon Martin, emphasizing the role of race, ethnicity, gender, and sexual orientation in her death at the hands of multiple offenders. The commonality across these two violent encounters lies at the heart of our framework: the identities and statuses of the victim and perpetrators were central to both the unfolding of the encounters themselves, and public discourse that framed and made meaning of these encounters after the fact. These two high-profile cases, though starkly contrasting on the surface, elucidate the utility of symbolic interactionism within a social constructionist framework to understand how violent conflicts between individuals unfold on the ground.

Data and Method

Data

The data collection process involved collecting a wide range of news articles and pieces of social commentary on the murders of Trayvon Martin and Gwen Araujo. By doing this, we gained insight into both of the events that transpired as well as learned how the intersecting inequalities influenced public perception of fear and crime surrounding these events. The search strategy incorporated online databases including Google, Google News, and LexisNexis. Upon searching the listed databases, search terms began with the victim and perpetrator names in combination. Once this option was exhausted, a search was conducted using only the victim's name, followed by a search with only the perpetrator's name. This strategy was designed to collect data sources that would yield two types of data relevant to our analysis: the interactional context between victims and perpetrators during the violent encounters, and background information on the victims and perpetrators that would shed light on the intersectionalities that they individually embodied.

For the news articles, search results were limited to the fourteen national news outlets with the largest distributions and news sources local to the city where the murders occurred. The national news outlets included were ABC News, *Chicago Tribune*, CNN, *Forbes*, Fox News, *Huffington Post*, *Los Angeles Times*, MSNBC, *New York Times*, NPR, *Seattle Times*, *USA Today*, *Wall Street Journal*, and *Washington Post*. Local news sources included *Sanford Herald* and *Orlando Sentinel* (for the Trayvon Martin case), and *San Jose Mercury News*, *Oakland Tribune*, and *San Francisco Chronicle* (for the Gwen Araujo case). While searching for social commentaries, the same search terms were used, but results were not limited to the specific outlets named above. Blog posts, larger commentary websites, and nonprofit organization websites were also used in finding social commentaries on the Trayvon Martin and Gwen Araujo cases, as these sources included public perception and sentiment that can be the basis of the social construction of fear, threat, and vulnerability—all of which are essential to the present analysis.

The data collection process took approximately three months and a total of sixty-three articles (both news and social commentary) were determined to fit our collection criteria. The numbers of usable news sources and social commentaries were virtually equal using these parameters, totaling twenty-eight articles, ranging from 2002 to 2014, relevant to the Gwen Araujo case and thirty-five articles, ranging from 2012 to 2014, relevant to the Trayvon Martin case. Pulling articles from this range of dates allowed for a broad array of media and public perceptions of the Trayvon Martin and Gwen Araujo cases. This approach

TABLE 4.1. Summary of Sources by Case and Type

	Articles collected for Trayvon Martin case ($n = 35$)	Articles collected for Gwen Araujo case ($n = 28$)
Social commentary	14	15
National news	17	6
Local news	4	7

has both strengths and limitations. The extended time span for the articles about Gwen Araujo allows for a fuller dataset more comparable in size to that for the Trayvon Martin case, due to advancements in technology and a proliferation of news media and social commentary in more recent years. Conversely, this longer time span may render the data sources themselves less comparable to those for the Trayvon Martin case, as it allows for a longer period for reflection, analysis, and remembrance of the events surrounding Gwen's death.

It is important to note that it was much more difficult to find information on Gwen Araujo than on Trayvon Martin. The amount of material found on the Trayvon Martin case was overwhelming given how recently the incident occurred and the technological advancements that have occurred since the death of Gwen Araujo. However, upon reviewing the available articles on the Martin/Zimmerman case, we determined that much of the information was repetitive. The opposite was true with the Gwen Araujo case. The first search conducted on Araujo and her perpetrators was through the Google News database. The search yielded only three sources. A regular Google search showed more promise; however, many of the articles were redundant. The bulk of information gathered on the Araujo case was local and compressed via LexisNexis. Despite these limitations, we believe that the data gleaned on both incidents allow us to assess the importance of interlocking inequalities on the violent encounters in these notable, high-profile cases.

Analytic Strategy

We employ a qualitative analytical strategy in assessing the aforementioned data by conducting a thorough, systematic content analysis of the media accounts on the nature and circumstances of these violent encounters. As Zhang and Wildemuth note, "qualitative content analysis goes beyond merely counting words or extracting objective content from texts to examine meanings, themes, and patterns that may be manifest or latent in a particular text."[34] Specifically, we draw upon these accounts to understand the process by which the social construction of others as threatening and dangerous occurs. We also assess the process by which others perceive themselves as vulnerable to such threats and danger and how their assessments of their own vulnerabilities might shape their behavior. The processes by which race, gender, class, and sexual orientation help to shape such perceptions are also emphasized in our analytical approach.

While qualitative analyses of this nature often entail the use of inductive coding whereby the data are categorized or organized across emergent themes or patterns found in the accounts, we instead employed a deductive approach. This strategy involved coding the data in ways consistent with the symbolic interaction perspective described above. This provided a basis to either validate or expand upon these conceptual frameworks for understanding the role of intersecting inequalities on violent interpersonal conflicts.

Interlocking Inequalities in the Death of Trayvon Martin

Trayvon Martin was a seventeen-year-old African American male who was born and raised in Miami, Florida. Trayvon's mother, Sybrina Fulton, and father, Tracy Martin, separated in 1999.[35] As a teenager, Trayvon performed average in school. His junior year of high school, Trayvon's mother transferred him to Dr. Michael M. Krop High School, a magnet school in the suburbs of Miami-Dade County Public Schools. Trayvon was suspended three times upon transferring.[36] After the third suspension, Trayvon's father took him back to Twin Lakes, a middle-class neighborhood in Sanford, Florida, "to disconnect and get his priorities straight."[37]

George Zimmerman was a thirty-year-old mixed-race Hispanic. His father was Caucasian and his mother was Peruvian. George identified himself as Hispanic on voter registration reports. He was raised in Manassas, Virginia, and later relocated to Florida after his high school graduation.[38] After moving, George started a job at an insurance agency in Lake Mary.[39] In 2007, George married Shellie Dean; a few years later, they moved into the Retreat at Twin Lakes. It was here George became "a self-appointed neighborhood watchman."

On February 26, 2012, video surveillance captured Trayvon Martin leaving a nearby 7-Eleven convenience store at 6:34 PM, where he bought an iced tea and a pack of Skittles. At approximately 7:11 PM, George Zimmerman called the police department to report a "suspicious guy" in a hoodie walking in the Twin Lakes neighborhood. The police instructed George to stay in his vehicle. At 7:13 PM, George parked his SUV and claimed that the suspect, Trayvon, began running. At this point, George exited his vehicle and chased after Trayvon. An altercation between George and Trayvon took place. Moments later, police were dispatched to the scene where they found Trayvon shot in the chest and George "bleeding from the nose and back of the head."[40] George claimed that he "killed the teen in self-defense after a scuffle."[41]

Perception of the Victim: Threat, Danger, and Vulnerability

The perceived victim in this encounter depends heavily on the way in which it is depicted in media reports. Given that this incident ended in Trayvon's death, he is more frequently described as the victim in these accounts. When viewed as the victim, Trayvon was commonly portrayed as an "unarmed" teen, possessing only a soft drink and candy when he was "racially profiled" and "attacked" by George.[42] The emphasis on Trayvon being unarmed was often coupled with comments regarding the nonthreatening items he had in his possession at the time of his death as a way of demonstrating his impotence in the encounter. For example, in an article from a news broadcast in central Florida, it was emphasized that "police said they found a bag of Skittles and a can of iced tea on Martin, but no weapons."[43] In another by an Orlando, Florida, news affiliate, the following description was provided: "the unarmed 17-year-old was walking to his father's home in Sanford with snacks when he was had a confrontation with George Zimmerman that ended his life."[44] The purpose of these depictions is arguably to eviscerate any notion that Trayvon presented a viable threat to George and was therefore culpable in his death. As one reporter penned, "Trayvon had a bag of Skittles and a can of iced tea. Zimmerman had a 9 millimeter handgun."[45] Similarly, Martin family attorney Benjamin Crump was quoted as stating, "Zimmerman, an adult, had a gun. Trayvon Martin, a 17-year-old, had Skittles. No way you can say self-defense."[46] Importantly, this depiction advertently served as a precursor to the stance that Trayvon was racially profiled by Zimmerman.

Commentators on this encounter readily pointed to the role of the profiling of young black males in the United States as the underlying reason for which Zimmerman viewed Trayvon as "suspicious" and pursued him even after being instructed not to do so by the police.[47] Trayvon's race, gender, and perceived class were socially constructed as threatening and dangerous by Zimmerman according to some. His race, age, gender, and even clothing (hoodie) are commonly mentioned in media accounts that echoed this sentiment. Blow posited that this case singularly "reignited a furor about vigilante justice, racial-profiling and equitable treatment under the law, and it has stirred the pot of racial strife."[48] Indeed, some have situated this fatal encounter in the long-standing history of the criminalization of blacks dating back to slavery and the Jim Crow era of America, which set the foundation for contemporary disparate treatment of blacks in general and targeting of young black males in particular.[49]

Media correspondents have suggested that Trayvon's death has become "symbolic" of the criminalization and concomitant devaluation of the lives of young black males in America.[50] In his essay on this phenomena, Mullins lamented that "black people—and black men in particular—are still viewed and judged as though we were all one person, with one mind, and that we either are criminals or are about to become criminals."[51] The normalization of their inequitable treatment has, in turn, set the stage for potentially hostile encounters between young black males and those in positions of authority. As Walker noted, "by now it's cliché that parents of black young men often school them on how to act in certain neighborhoods or when approached by the police,"[52] given their underlying fear that not following these rules of engagement could result in their arrests, physical injury, or, worse still, their deaths. The common practice of identifying young African American males as dangerous and threatening as the landscape under which the Martin/Zimmerman incident unfolded was prolific in media accounts regardless of their particular story slant (e.g., details about Trayvon and George's lives; public sentiment following the verdict). For example, Tobar reported on the sentiment held by commentators and authors such as Lisa Bloom who argued that "Zimmerman misread the situation because he was prejudiced and was fixated on black youths in his neighborhood."[53] Similarly, Botelho and Yan included the following excerpt from a statement provided by the NAACP following George's acquittal: "The most fundamental of civil rights—the right to life—was violated the night George Zimmerman *stalked* and then took the life of Trayvon Martin."[54]

These descriptions of Trayvon and his death were paralleled to contrasting depictions of George Zimmerman as the victim in this incident. This depiction of George is often situated in accounts of the "rash of burglaries" occurring in his "gated" neighborhood in the year prior to his encounter with Trayvon. George's neighborhood reportedly experienced several burglaries, which were largely attributed to young black males. In response to the incidents, George's neighborhood association formed a watch group, for which he served as leader. During his patrols as watch captain George carried a nine-millimeter handgun.[55] Arguably, these reports depict George as an individual "fighting against a failed system" in which law enforcement is rendered ineffective in controlling crime, forcing citizens to defend themselves from threats of victimization.[56] Media references to his community and the purported offenders preying upon it are prominent when George is portrayed in this light. The adjective "gated" was typically used to describe his neighborhood and likely to infer its middle-class status, and this depiction was juxtaposed to reports of it being overrun by outsiders—young black males—who were committing brazen acts of burglary. Take in the following incidents reported in an article published by Reuters:

> One morning in July 2011, a black teenager walked up to Zimmerman's front porch and stole a bicycle. . . . A police report was taken, though the bicycle was not recovered. But it was the August incursion into the home of Olivia Bertalan that really troubled the neighborhood, particularly Zimmerman. . . . Bertalan was at home with her infant son while her husband, Michael, was at work. She watched from a downstairs window,

she said, as two black men repeatedly rang her doorbell and then entered through a sliding door at the back of the home.[57]

These descriptions provide a contextual backdrop for George's position that his actions were taken in self-defense. Indeed, the reports typically point out that George was not initially arrested by the police following the shooting of Trayvon Martin because they believed his claims of self-defense. His arrest occurred only following public pressure, largely from the African American community, and upon his subsequent acquittal George's attorney was quoted as saying, "George Zimmerman was never guilty of anything except firing the gun in self-defense."[58] These statements elucidate the view that George's actions were not the basis of racial bias but were instead the result of his fear of being victimized—again.

To further augment George's claim of self-defense and to refute the counterargument that he racially profiled Trayvon, some commentators readily pointed to his own identity as a minority. His Hispanic heritage is identified in these articles, as his mother is reported as a Peruvian immigrant.[59] Furthermore, biographical accounts of his childhood often suggested that George grew up in a family that promoted diversity. Reportedly, his mother led a "growing Catholic Hispanic enclave" within the church the family attended, and his grandmother, who lived with his family, frequently "cared for two African American girls who ate their meals at the Zimmerman household and went back and forth to school each day with the Zimmerman children."[60] As an adult, George is purported to have opened an insurance agency in which he partnered with a black friend.[61] Consequently, following his acquittal of Trayvon's murder, his attorney Don West was reported saying, "the prosecution of George Zimmerman was a disgrace . . . I am thrilled that this jury kept this tragedy from becoming a travesty."[62] Another attorney, Mark O'Hara, directly refuted the notion that George profiled Trayvon, stating "his history was not as a racist."[63]

Perception of the Perpetrator: Threat, Danger, and Vulnerability

While the varying position of Trayvon or George as the perpetrator in their encounter was less prevalent, these media accounts provide valuable insight into the ongoing debate of how these interactions unfold and the role of danger, threat, and vulnerability in seemingly routine encounters. Despite the more prevalent view of Trayvon as the victim, some held that he actually instigated the conflict that resulted in his death. In such accounts Trayvon was suggested to have "pounced" on and to have "attacked" George. These reports often emphasize the injuries George sustained in the encounter, including his reported nose fracture and head contusions.[64]

These claims are further buttressed by depictions that cast shadows on Trayvon's character. For example, Botelho reported that Trayvon was in the Sanford community "after being suspended for the third time" from his high school in Miami.[65] Others critiqued Trayvon's appearance. For instance, news analyst Bill O'Reilly reportedly stated that if he was not wearing a hoodie he probably would not have been killed. Similarly, former talk show host Geraldo Rivera purportedly blamed Trayvon's appearance, stating he was "dressed in thug wear."[66] These caricatures of Trayvon inadvertently portray him as culpable in his demise, in that the way in which he carried himself or dressed made him responsible for George's perceptions of Trayvon as dangerous.

On the other hand, others point to George as the aggressor in their fatal encounter. In these reports he is commonly depicted as an over-zealous, wannabe cop who overreacted and committed an unjustified act of murder. In a report by Philip Caulfied for the *New York Daily News* Trayvon's father argued that George "made a rush to judgment to judge Trayvon as criminal, as suspicious . . . he got out of that car. He put Trayvon in that position."[67] George's unsuccessful attempts at becoming a law enforcement officer and his self-appointment as leader of his neighborhood watch group are commonly pointed out in these reports.[68] Moreover, this depiction suggests that George's prejudice against young black males was masked by the broader, ubiquitous nature of racial inequality inherent to laws such as Stand Your Ground.

These accounts place the onus on laws such as Stand Your Ground, which can escalate disagreements into deadly conflicts. Critics argue that such statutes encourage gun ownership among citizens who may misread or act abruptly in interactions with others they perceive as threatening. On these laws, Debrabander commented, "when we fail to grasp all of the facts of the situation such as the real intentions of a perceived attacker, this may lead us to react with excessive and unjust force."[69] These laws then become the "shaky ground" on which individuals claim self-defense following what some perceive to be very costly rash judgments.[70]

The above media accounts clearly emphasize the role of race, ethnicity, gender, and perceived class on the violent encounter between Trayvon and George. The intersections of these identities and statuses likely became symbolic cues of threat and vulnerability and thus shaped the interactions that unfolded between the two that resulted in Trayvon's death and disparate views regarding George's culpability. In building upon this point, we turn to another high-profile case—that of Gwen Araujo—to further demonstrate the role of intersectionalities on perceptions of threat and vulnerability in shaping violent encounters.

Interlocking Inequalities in the Death of Gwen Araujo

Gwen Araujo, who was born Edward Araujo, Jr. to parents Sylvia Guerrero and Edward Araujo, was a seventeen-year-old Latina transwoman who lived in Newark, California. Although Gwen was born biologically male, she had identified and presented as female since at least age fourteen, when she came out to her parents as transgender.[71] Although Gwen's parents struggled with accepting her as female, her mother conveyed a message of unconditional love on the day Gwen came out to her: "Whether you're a man or a woman, I'm going to love you."[72] Despite this, Sylvia Guerrero acknowledged, "We didn't go to the mall the next day and buy girl clothes."[73] Thus, as Gwen initiated her transition at the young age of fourteen, she did so largely on her own. She adopted her female name (in homage to singer Gwen Stefani), grew her hair out, and began wearing makeup and women's clothes. Not coincidentally, it was also around this age that Gwen began to run into trouble in school, eventually dropping out of high school because of the taunting and ridicule she suffered as a result of her gender presentation.[74]

At the time of Gwen's murder, the four perpetrators were only slightly older than she was. Jason Cazares, Michael Magidson, and José Merél, all twenty-two, and Jaron Nabors, nineteen, became friends with Gwen in the summer of 2002. The group spent much of their time at the Meréls' house in a working-class neighborhood of Newark.[75] During that summer, while spending time as part of the larger group, Gwen also dated both Michael and José.[76] On October 3, 2002, she attended a house party at the residence of Jose Merél's older brother, Paul Merél.[77] The four men began talking about Gwen and their sexual encounters with her, speculating about her biological sex. They instructed Nichole Brown, Paul's girlfriend at the time, to take Gwen into the bathroom and inspect her genitals for definitive proof of Gwen's biological sex.[78] Nichole complied, sticking her hand up Gwen's miniskirt to feel for her genitals. Upon discovering that Gwen had a penis, Nichole screamed, causing Michael to wrestle Gwen to the ground, where he proceeded to pull Gwen's underwear aside to confirm, and then placed Gwen in a headlock upon seeing her genitals.[79] Nichole then reported seeing Michael punch and choke Gwen.[80]

After this José hit Gwen in the head with a can of food and then over the head with a frying pan.[81] She was later "tied up and carried into the garage to stop blood from getting on the carpet."[82] Michael then tied a rope around Gwen's neck while Jason admitted to hitting Gwen in the head with a shovel.[83] Gwen's reported last words were pleas for mercy, "Please, don't I have a family?"[84] Once Gwen was dead, the men threw her body into the back of Michael's pickup truck and drove 120 miles to the Sierra Nevada foothills in El Dorado County, where they buried her in a shallow grave, and then stopped for McDonald's on the way home.[85] Gwen was missing for more than two weeks before Jaron confessed to the police and her body was discovered.[86]

Perception of the Victim: Threat, Danger, and Vulnerability

Perhaps even more important than Gwen's own sexual orientation, however, are her perpetrators' assumptions of what her biological sex meant for *their* sexual orientation. According to the logic of heteronormativity, Gwen's biological sex (male) rendered any sexual attraction or behavior on behalf of her (also male) perpetrators indicative of homosexuality. Gwen's female identity and presentation notwithstanding—because they certainly did not stand in any prominent place in the sequence of events that led to her death—the biological reality of the situation was the reality that was attended to by those involved in the encounter. These simple assumptions, likely made subconsciously and implicitly in the span of less than a second, were informed and structured by systems of heteronormativity that presume a natural and complementary fit between women/femininity and men/masculinity, and systems of misogyny that place the former below the latter. Heteronormativity is closely intertwined with misogyny, inasmuch as it functions as a way of "maintaining the gender hierarchy that subordinates women to men."[87] It is through the lens of heteronormativity that we can understand the ways in which the stigma surrounding homosexuality is largely the stigma of sexism; in men, homosexuality is viewed as feminine and therefore less than. In this way, sexual orientation and gender are intimately linked from a symbolic interactionist standpoint, not just for Gwen, but also for her perpetrators, whose very masculinity was threatened by their sudden realization that they had engaged in sexual activity with a "man."

Taking into account the particular intersection of sexual orientation and gender that Gwen embodied, set against the backdrop of heteronormativity and misogyny, it is easy to surmise how these statuses may have affected perceptions of threat, danger, and vulnerability in the encounter leading to her death. Gwen's status as a young woman who was not out as transgender, and was openly living as a woman, resulted in a situation in which her perpetrators originally had accurate knowledge of her gender, but inaccurate knowledge of her biological sex. Gwen, like many other young transgender women, likely knew that hiding her biological sex would put her at risk of physical harm if it were to be revealed. Nonetheless, she went to great lengths to avoid disclosing her biological sex, taking such measures as claiming to be menstruating and insisting on having only anal sex, even throughout multiple sexual encounters with her perpetrators.[88] And the moment at which the information finally came to light proved fateful. Although Gwen's victimization may have been the direct result of her biological sex, the context surrounding the interpretation of her sex and its implications—real or imagined—for gender and sexual orientation is crucial to understanding the events that unfolded. As Schilt and Westbrook note, the challenge that transgender people pose to heteronormativity is particularly acute in sexual situations like the one Gwen found herself in that night, as these are interactional contexts deeply rooted in and largely structured by the performance of both gender and sexual orientation.[89]

Perception of the Perpetrator: Threat, Danger, and Vulnerability

The perceived threat that Gwen posed to the four men who murdered her has not been disputed. According to news reports and court documents (both witness testimony and legal arguments), when Gwen's biological sex was revealed to her perpetrators, they reacted—predictably—with shock. The most common account of the events leading to Gwen's death describes an emotional response that was a lethal blend of "anger and rage and shock and revulsion," to quote one of the perpetrators' defense attorneys.[90] It was argued in court, for instance, " 'The three accused are ordinary human beings . . . with all the goodness, strength and weaknesses of ordinary people. . . . They're not bad kids.'"[91] Being "ordinary human beings," the logic follows that the revelation that a female sexual partner was biologically male (and by implication, not an ordinary human being) would be experienced as a threat. One defense attorney went so far as to explain that his client's "ego was shattered" upon learning the truth about Gwen's genitalia,[92] while another employed an analogy in which the perpetrators "became as lobsters in a boiling pot; caught in the caldron of events and emotions . . . [that] no one can escape."[93]

Over the course of two plea bargains, two trials, and one hung jury, defense attorneys repeatedly relied upon this interpretation of events, utilizing what is known as the "trans panic defense"—a variant of the "gay panic defense" used successfully in numerous criminal cases before. The trans panic defense is employed as a justification for a violent response in the wake of a revelation that a sexual partner (or even a person simply making sexual advances) is biologically male despite presenting as female. It is premised upon the notion that unknowingly engaging in sexual activity with a member of one's own sex is grounds for "panic," and therefore a justification for violent response. Implicit in the trans panic defense is an understanding of threat, vulnerability, and dangerousness that has little to do with physical safety—at least on the part of the victim. Buttressed by heteronormative thinking that equates homosexuality with diminished masculinity and therefore weakness, the trans panic defense posits that the disclosure of Gwen's biological sex presented a threat to the manhood of the perpetrators, rendering them vulnerable to the dangerousness of Gwen's biology and all that it implied. According to this defense, in response to the perceived threats to their masculinity, the perpetrators read Gwen as dangerous. This rendered them vulnerable (in terms of masculinity), prompting them to lash out violently. Their violent response can be viewed as simultaneously serving two purposes: effectively neutralizing the threat and reasserting their masculinity through the show of violent force, a "masculine-coded act."[94] Whether the trans panic defense is an accurate characterization of the motives and interpretations of the perpetrators, the defense strategy in and of itself signals the powerful cultural pervasiveness of assumptions about intersections between gender and sexual orientation, and their bearing on perceived threat, vulnerability, and dangerousness.

Discussion

At first glance, the deaths of Trayvon Martin and Gwen Araujo have little in common. Trayvon, a young, black man, was fatally shot by a stranger—a white Hispanic man thirteen years his senior—walking down the street in a gated community. Gwen, a young Latina transwoman, was beaten and killed inside a private residence by four young men with whom she had been friends for some time. To more fully understand the incidents as they unfolded on the ground, and the cultural and sociopolitical contexts in which they are situated, we have used news media sources concerning victims and perpetrators of both incidents to examine the role that intersectionalities may have played in the violent encounters that left two young people dead. Our analyses reveal striking similarity with regard to the potential for threat—be it the threat to physical safety imputed by George Zimmerman or the threatened masculinity of Gwen's perpetrators—to result in perceptions of dangerousness and vulnerability that set in motion violent, even fatal, chains of events. Set against vastly different cultural backdrops—heteronormativity and misogyny in the case of Gwen, and an ethos of racial malaise in the death of Trayvon—these intersections proved dangerous, even as the statuses that composed them and the contexts in which they were situated differed starkly. In this discussion, we compare and contrast the role that intersectionalities played in perceptions of threat, danger, and vulnerability for the encounters that ultimately took Gwen and Trayvon's lives by tracing the initial assumptions of dangerousness and assessments of threat versus the reality of dangerousness and threat that was later revealed.

In understanding the context of Gwen's death, gender, biological sex, and sexual orientation are paramount. Gwen's gender proved to be something of a catch-22; the very same feminine characteristics that belied her "dangerousness" eventually rendered her vulnerable, thus leading to her murder. Throughout her encounters with the four men who ultimately took her life, Gwen presented as female and was known to them accordingly. When perceived as female, Gwen posed no threat to the men; she was viewed as a "regular" young woman, a friend and occasional sexual partner who was not dangerous in the least. In fact, not only did their friendship with Gwen allow their tenuous grasp on masculinity to remain unthreatened, their engagement in casual sex with Gwen may even have bolstered it. It was not until her biological sex was revealed that Gwen suddenly became a threat, rendering her perpetrators vulnerable to assaults on their masculinity and heterosexuality. As a young woman, Gwen was not threatening in the least—not to the physical safety of the men who killed her, nor to their masculinity. As a *transgender* woman, however, Gwen was so dangerous that she presented a threat to be dealt with immediately, violently, and with finality. Given this complex scenario of performed and presumed gender, concealed biological sex, and a startling revelation of the perceived mismatch between the two, Gwen's perceived dangerousness and the attendant threat that she posed to her perpetrators shifted markedly over the course of her relationship with them. The danger that Gwen posed lay not in her gender, but specifically at the nexus among her gender, biological sex, and presumed sexual orientation. Thus, the intersectionality that ultimately led to Gwen's death was not immediately visible—it lurked below the surface, concealed by an attractive woman with long hair, a pretty face, and a miniskirt.

This script is flipped when considering the death of Trayvon Martin; gone are the initial assumptions of safety and perceptions of non-threat. In the encounter that led to his death, it likely took less than a second for Trayvon to be read as dangerous by George Zimmerman. The image of Trayvon—a young, black male, donning the now iconic hoodie—walking at night in a gated community immediately registered as threatening to George. The intersections embodied by this image—of race, gender, age, and social status—coalesced into an immediate representation of threat. That Trayvon was unarmed, carrying only an iced tea and a bag of candy, did not factor into George's initial assessments of threat, dangerousness, and vulnerability. In this sense, Trayvon was assumed to be dangerous, despite the fact that he likely presented little to no threat to George's safety or the safety of the neighborhood. He was simply a young man walking back to his parents' home after purchasing a snack. Unlike Gwen's concealed intersectionalities—which rendered her dangerous only once they were revealed—Trayvon's intersectionalities were front and center on the night of his death. Unfortunately, the statuses Trayvon embodied and the clothing that he donned signaled a dangerousness that was not really there and consequently did not stop them from leading to his death.

Through an analysis of news media accounts of Trayvon and Gwen's deaths, we are able to see the cultural construction of the narratives of the incidents as they unfolded on the ground. We gain insight into the chain of events, the motivations of the actors, and the larger context in which the events are situated. The use of news media reports to analyze the role that intersectionalities played in these incidents is not without limitation, however. A primary concern is the uneven reporting on the deaths of Trayvon and Gwen. Gwen's murder made national headlines in 2002, but the news coverage of her death and the attendant trials paled in comparison to the media frenzy surrounding Trayvon's death ten years later. This differential can actually serve to strengthen our analysis of the role of intersectionality in violent encounters, however. In the twenty-four-hour news cycle world in which we live, media representations both reflect and help constitute cultural realities. The disparity in news coverage of Gwen and Trayvon's deaths—as well as the qualitative differences in the tenor and content of the coverage—can shed light on the cultural milieus in which these violent incidents unfolded.

Some have noted that Gwen's death was largely overlooked by the media, especially as compared to the high-profile murder of Matthew Shepard four years earlier. Matthew was a young, white gay man who was murdered in rural Wyoming by two strangers whom he met at a bar. Like Gwen's murder, the incident was largely regarded as a hate crime by the popular media, although no hate crime charges were pursued. Unlike Gwen, however, Matthew was an easy and sympathetic target for the mainstream media to latch onto. At age twenty-one, Matthew appeared much younger than he was, and looked like the prototypical, all-American boy next door; it was frequently remarked by the news media that he could have been "anyone's son." Gwen, by contrast, was not so easily described by the media, let alone offered forth as a relatable victim. News coverage vacillated between referring to Gwen as a man and a woman, and pronoun use was similarly noncommittal. That Gwen had dropped out of school, used alcohol and drugs, engaged in promiscuous sex with the perpetrators, and concealed her "true" identity were emphasized in many news reports, rendering Gwen a victim who could easily be seen as less than pure. Trayvon's death, in contrast, was covered widely and passionately by the news media long after the incident occurred. News coverage began with reports of the encounter between Trayvon and George, but later gave way to content that varied from a social movement outcry against the murder of young black men like Trayvon around the country, to detailed coverage of the trial that broadened in focus to encompass key witnesses like Rachel Jeantel, to follow-ups on George Zimmerman's life even once he had been acquitted. As described in the findings above, Trayvon's death was taken by many to be symbolic of the criminalization and devaluation of the lives of young black men across the nation—while Gwen's death was viewed largely as an unfortunate incident that happened to one particular young person under very idiosyncratic circumstances, and was not likely to resonate with the general public.

While we use these two very different cases to exemplify the role of intersecting inequalities in violent encounters and the conversations that help make meaning of them, symbolic interactionism provides a powerful framework for understanding the role of intersecting inequality on assessments of threat, danger, and vulnerability more generally as well. For instance, this framework could shed light on the deaths of unarmed yet somehow "threatening" black males at the hands of law enforcement officers that have garnered widespread media, public, and policy attention as of late. The examples are, unfortunately, myriad: the

2014 strangulation of Eric Garner in New York, the shooting death of Michael Brown in Ferguson, Missouri, less than a month later, and the shooting of twelve-year-old Tamir Rice in Cleveland, Ohio, in November of the same year.

Violent encounters that are even less empirically similar to Trayvon Martin's death—and which received far less media attention—could also be analyzed. Take, for instance, Dionte Greene: a young, gay black man who was murdered in his own car in Kansas City, Missouri. Dionte's intersectionalities not only contributed to his death, but did so in ways that we will never quite comprehend—since these same intersectionalities all but guaranteed that his death went virtually unnoticed in a city where black men are killed every day, and the murder of a gay man in the black community is something best not discussed. Dionte's murder barely received any press coverage—even locally—until the *Guardian* picked up the story more than a month later in a piece titled "Black, Gay and Shot Dead in His Own Car: This Is Another Missouri Killing We Should Talk About."[95] The *Guardian* piece explicitly addressed the role of intersectionality in not only Dionte's murder, but also the lack of media coverage. The author notes that "justice vanishes too often with cases that force police departments and even the most progressive communities to consider victims who lived at the intersection of multiple sexual and gender identities—the complex people who are at a much higher risk of facing hate-motivated violence, or even perpetrating it."[96]

Just as justice "vanishes too often" when dealing with intersecting inequalities, so too does understanding. Taken together, the cases of Trayvon Martin and Gwen Araujo and the media coverage that surrounds them provide a lens through which we can view the role of intersectionality in violent conflicts. The culmination of the different intersecting statuses of both victims and perpetrators resulted in perceptions of threat, danger, and vulnerability in different ways and for different reasons. Informed by vastly different cultural, sociopolitical, and legal contexts, that both of these encounters ended the same way—with a young person dead and a lack of consensus on the culpability of those who took their lives—speaks to the patterned nature of intersecting inequalities, despite different empirical manifestations, that has clear applicability across diverse cases.

NOTES

1. Also see Decoster, and Heimer 2006.
2. Fine 1993, 78.
3. Ibid., 77.
4. Weigert 1986.
5. Berger et al. 1977; Ridgeway 1991.
6. Matsueda 1992; Heimer and Matsueda 1994; Bartusch and Matsueda 1996; Kaufman and Johnson 2004.
7. Lemert 1951.
8. Becker 1963; Goode and Ben-Yehuda 1994.
9. West and Zimmerman 1987, 125.
10. Ibid.; West and Fenstermaker 1995; Schilt and Westbrook 2009, 458; Hagan 1989.
11. Hollander 2001, 101.
12. Cobbina, Like-Haislip, and Miller 2010.
13. Like-Haislip and Cobbina, forthcoming.
14. See Lauritsen and White 2001.
15. Schilt and Westbrook 2009, 441.
16. Messerschmidt 2012.
17. West and Fenstermaker 1995; Schilt and Westbrook 2009, 458.
18. Sandholtz, Langston, and Planty 2013.
19. Hattery and Smith 2007.
20. Miller, Like, and Levin 2006; Hollander 2001, 101.
21. Young 2006.
22. Oliver 2003, 15.
23. Ibid.
24. Young 2006.
25. West and Fenstermaker 1995, 28.
26. Ibid.
27. Hollander 2001, 101.
28. West and Fenstermaker 1995.
29. Decoster and Heimer 2006; also see Messerschmidt 2012.
30. Stanko 1995, 50.
31. See Warr 1985; Stanko 1995; Wesley and Gaarder 2004.
32. Ferraro 1995.
33. Hollander 2001, 101.
34. Zhang and Wildemuth 2005, 1.
35. Burch and Isensee 2012.
36. Burnside and Hamacher 2012.
37. CBS Miami 2012.
38. Francescani 2012.
39. Ibid.

40. Ibid.

41. Dahl 2012.

42. Arvin 2014; Alvarez and Buckley 2013; Botelho and Yan 2013; Botelho 2012.

43. WFTV 2012.

44. Eiland 2013.

45. Blow 2012.

46. WFTV 2012.

47. Alvarez and Buckley 2013; Botelho and Yan 2013; Blow 2012; Botelho 2012; Francescani 2012.

48. Blow 2012.

49. Harper 2014.

50. See Arvin 2014; Gamboa 2012.

51. Mullins 2014.

52. Walker 2014.

53. Tobar 2014.

54. Botelho and Yan 2013.

55. Francescani 2012.

56. See Miller, Like, and Levin 2006.

57. Francescani 2012.

58. Alvarez and Buckley 2013.

59. Francescani 2012.

60. Ibid.

61. Ibid.

62. Alvarez and Buckley 2013.

63. Ibid.

64. CNN Library 2014; Alvarez and Buckley 2013; Blow 2012; Botelho 2012; Schapiro 2012.

65. Botelho 2012.

66. Jonsson 2012.

67. Caulfied 2012.

68. CNN Library 2014; McLendon 2014; Botelho and Yan 2013; Francescani 2012; Harper 2014.

69. Debrabander 2014.

70. See Walker 2014.

71. Megino 2012; St. John and Lee 2002.

72. Ritter 2002.

73. Economides 2006.

74. Ritter 2002.

75. Locke 2004.

76. Ibid.

77. Murphy 2002.

78. St. John 2004.

79. St. John and Lee 2002.

80. Ibid.
81. Lee 2006.
82. Locke 2004.
83. Ibid.
84. Dignan 2004.
85. Ibid.
86. Murphy 2002.
87. Cameron and Kulick 2003, 45.
88. Wronge 2005a.
89. Schilt and Westbrook 2009, 458.
90. Hoge 2004.
91. Wronge 2005a.
92. Wronge 2005b.
93. Wronge 2005a.
94. Schilt and Westbrook 2009, 458.
95. Stafford 2014.
96. Ibid.

REFERENCES

Alvarez, L., and C. Buckley. 2013. "Zimmerman Is Acquitted in Trayvon Martin Killing." *New York Times*. http://www.nytimes.com/2013/07/14/us/george-zimmerman-verdict-trayvon-martin.html?pagewanted=alland_r=0.

Arvin, C. 2014. "Clicktivism' Moves Civil Rights Forward in a New Generation." *New Pittsburgh Courier*. http://newpittsburghcourieronline.com/2014/03/24/clicktivism-moves-civil-rights-forward-in-a-new-generation/.

Bartusch, D. J., and R. L. Matsueda. 1996. "Gender, Reflected Appraisals, and Labeling: A Cross-Group Test of Interactionist Theory of Delinquency." *Social Forces* 75 (1): 145–77.

Becker, H. S. 1963. *Outsiders*. New York: Simon & Schuster.

Berger, J. M., H. Fisek, R. Z. Norman, and M. Zelditch. 1977. *Status Characteristics and Social Interaction*. New York: Elsevier.

Blow, C. 2012. "The Curious Case of Trayvon Martin." *New York Times*. http://www.nytimes.com/2012/03/17/opinion/blow-the-curious-case-of-trayvon-martin.html.

Botelho, G. 2012. "What Happened the Night Trayvon Martin Died." CNN. http://www.cnn.com/2012/05/18/justice/florida-teen-shooting-details/.

Botelho, G., and H. Yan. 2013. "George Zimmerman Found Not Guilty of Murder in Trayvon Martin's Death." CNN. http://www.cnn.com/2013/07/13/justice/zimmerman-trial/.

Burch, A., and L. Isensee. 2012. "Trayvon Martin: A Typical Teen Who Loved Video Games, Looked Forward to Prom." *Miami Herald*. http://www.miamiherald.com/2012/03/22/2708960/trayvon-martin-a-typical-teen.html.

Burnside, J., and B. Hamacher. 2012. "Trayvon Martin School Suspensions Revealed." NBC 6 South Florida. http://www.nbcmiami.com/news/Trayvon-Martin -Suspended-From-School-Three-Times-Report-144403305.html.

Cameron, D., and D. Kulick. 2003. *Language and Sexuality.* Cambridge: Cambridge University Press.

Caulfied, P. 2012. "'What Kind of God?' Do You Serve, Killer?" *New York Daily News.* http://www.lexisnexis.com.proxy.library.umkc.edu/lnacui2api/api/version1/getDoc Cui?oc=00240andhnsd=fandhgn=tandlni=5653-8CR1-JBKB-V4RBandhns=tand perma=trueandhv=tandhl=tandcsi=270944%2C270077%2C11059%2C8411and secondRedirectIndicator=true.

CBS Miami. 2012. "Parents Seek Justice for Unarmed Son's Killing." http://miami .cbslocal.com/2012/03/10/parents-seek-justice-for-unarmed-sons-killing/.

CNN Library. 2014. "Trayvon Martin Shooting Fast Facts." CNN. http://www.cnn.com/ 2013/06/05/us/trayvon-martin-shooting-fast-facts/.

Cobbina, J., T. Like-Haislip, and J. Miller. 2010. "Gang Fights versus Cat Fights: Urban Young Men's Gendered Narrative of Violence." *Deviant Behavior* 31 (7): 569–624.

Dahl, J. 2012. "Trayvon Martin Shooting: A Timeline of Events." CBS News. http:// www.cbsnews.com/news/trayvon-martin-shooting-a-timeline-of events/.

Debrabander, F. 2014. "Locke and Load: The Fatal Error of the 'Stand Your Ground' Philosophy." *New York Times.* http://opinionator.blogs.nytimes.com/2014/02/23/ locke-and-load-the-fatal-error-of-the-stand-your-ground-philosophy/?_php= trueand_type=blogsand_r=0.

Decoster, S., and K. Heimer. 2006. "Crime at the Intersections: Race, Class, Gender, and Violent Offending." In *Many Colors of Crime: Inequalities of Race, Ethnicity, and Crime in America, edited by* R. D. Peterson, L. J. Krivo, and J. Hagan, 138–57. New York: New York University Press.

Dignan, J. 2004. "Hung Jury in Araujo Muder." *Gay City News.* http://gaycitynews.com/ gcn_326/hungjuryinaraujo.html.

Economides, E. 2006. "Gwen Araujo's Story Fills Actor with Sense of Purpose." *Inside Bay Area.* http://www.lexisnexis.com.proxy.library.umkc.edu/lnacui2api/api/ version1/getDocCui?oc=00240andhnsd=fandhgn=tandlni=4K5S-3N50-TXCN-.

Eiland, T. 2013. "Vigils Planned on 2-Year Anniversary of Trayvon Martin's Death." WESH.com Orlando. http://www.wesh.com/trayvon-martin-extended-coverage/ vigils-planned-on-2year-anniversary-of-trayvon-martins-death/24678316#!Bd069.

Ferraro, K. F. 1995. *Fear of Crime: Interpreting Victimization Risk.* Albany: State University of New York Press.

Fine, G. A. 1993. "The Sad Demise, Mysterious Disappearance, and Glorious Triumph of Symbolic Interactionism." *Annual Review of Sociology* 19:61–87.

Francescani, C. 2012. "George Zimmerman: Prelude to a Shooting." Reuters. http:// www.reuters.com/article/2012/04/25/us-usa-florida-shooting-zimmerman -idUSBRE83O18H20120425.

Gamboa, S. 2012. "Florida Shooter's Race a Complicated Matter." Associated Press.

http://web.archive.org/web/20120406122016/http://hosted.ap.org/dynamic/
stories/U/US_NEIGHBORHOOD_WATCH_WHITE_OR_HISPANIC?SITE=
APandSECTION=HOMEandTEMPLATE=DEFAULT.

Goode, E., and N. Ben-Yehuda. 1994. "Moral Panics: Culture, Politics, and Social Construction." *Annual Review of Sociology* 20:149–71.

Hagan, J. 1989. "A Power-Control Theory of Gender and Delinquency." In *Criminological Theory: Past to Present*, edited by F. Cullen and R. Agnew, 254–64. Los Angeles: Roxbury.

Harlow, C. W. 2005. *Hate Crime Reported by Victims and Police*. Washington, DC: U.S. Department of Justice, Office of Justice Programs, Bureau of Justice Statistics.

Harper, L. 2014. "The Criminality of Blackness." *Huffington Post*, March 25. http://www.huffingtonpost.com/lisa-sharon-harper/the-criminality-of-blackness_b_5021863.html.

Hattery, A. J., and E. Smith. 2007. *African American Families*. Thousand Oaks, CA: Sage.

Heimer, K., and R. L. Matsueda. 1994. "Role-Taking, Role Commitment, and Delinquency: A Theory of Differential Social Control." *American Sociological Review* 59 (3): 365–90.

Hoge, P. 2004. "Hayward/Defense Attorney Calls Transgender Victim Guilty of 'Deception and Betrayal.'" *SF Gate*. http://sfgate.com/cgi-bin/article.cgi?f=/c/a/2004/04/16/BAG3H666781.DTL.

Hollander, J. 2001. "Vulnerability and Dangerousness: The Construction of Gender through Conversation about Violence." *Gender & Society* 15:83–109.

Jonsson, P. 2012. "Geraldo Rivera (Again) Says Trayvon Martin's 'Thug Wear' Got Him Profiled." *Christian Science Monitor*. http://www.lexisnexis.com.proxy.library.umkc.edu/lnacui2api/api/version1/getDocCui?oc=00240andhnsd=fandhgn=tandlni=55PB-19W1-JC8H-M2NWandhns=tandperma=trueandhv=tandhl=tandcsi=270944%2C270077%2C11059%2C8411andsecondRedirectIndicator=true.

Kaufman, J. M., and C. Johnson. 2004. "Stigmatized Individuals and the Process of Identity." *Sociological Quarterly* 45 (4): 807–33.

Lauritsen, J. L., and N. A. White. 2001. "Putting Violence in Its Place: The Influence of Race, Ethnicity, Gender, and Place on Risk for Violence." *Criminology & Public Policy* 1 (1): 37–60.

Lee, H. 2006. "Three Sentenced to Prison in Araujo Slaying." *SF Gate*. http://www.sfgate.com/news/article/Three-sentenced-to-prison-in-Araujo-slaying-2542846.php.

Lemert, E. M. 1951. *Social Pathology*. New York: McGraw-Hill.

Like-Haislip, T. Z., and J. Cobbina. Forthcoming. "Emotional Girls and Rational Boys: Gendered Discussions of Violence among African American Adolescents." *Crime & Delinquency*.

Locke, M. 2004. "Case of Slain Transgender Teen Could Go to Jury This Week." *U-T San Diego*. http://legacy.utsandiego.com/news/state/20040601-0012-ca-transgenderkilling.html.

Matsueda, R. L. 1992. "Reflected Appraisals, Parental Labeling, and Delinquency: Specifying a Symbolic Interactionist Theory." *American Journal of Sociology* 97 (6): 1577–1611.

McLendon, G. 2014. "Trayvon Martin's Mother, Panel Talk Race Issues at UR." *Democrat and Chronicle*. http://www.democratandchronicle.com/story/news/2014/03/21/ur-panel-explores-race-issues/6725125/.

Megino, N. 2012. "Remembering Slain Transgender Teen Gwen Araujo. *Newark Patch*. http://newark.patch.com/groups/goodnews/p/remembering-slain-transgender-teen-gwen-araujo.

Messerschmidt, J. W. 2012. *Gender, Heterosexuality, and Youth Violence: The Struggle for Recognition*. Lanham, MD: Rowman & Littlefield.

Miller, J., T. Z. Like, and P. Levin. 2006. "The Caucasian Evasion: Victims, Exceptions and Defenders of the Faith." In *Images of Color/Images of Crime*, 3rd ed., edited by C. R. Mann, M. Zatz, and N. Rodriguez, 111–27. Los Angeles: Roxbury.

Mullins, D. 2014. "Personal Essay: 'Invisible Man' in the Age of Trayvon and Jordan." *Aljazeera America*. http://america.aljazeera.com/articles/2014/3/1/personal-essay-theinvisiblemanintheageoftrayvonandjordan.html.

Murphy, D. 2002. "3 Are Charged in Death of Man Who Dressed Like a Woman." *New York Times*. http://www.nytimes.com/2002/10/19/us/3-are-charged-in-death-of-man-who-dressed-like-a-woman.html.

Oliver, M. B. 2003. "African American Men as 'Criminal and Dangerous': Implications of Media Portrayals of Crime on 'Criminalization' of African American Men." *Journal of African American Studies* 7 (2): 3–18.

Ridgeway, C. 1991. "The Social Construction of Status Value: Gender and Other Nominal Characteristics." *Social Forces* 70 (2): 367–86.

Ritter, J. 2002. "Slaying of Transgender Boy Haunts City." *USA Today*. http://usatoday30.usatoday.com/news/nation/2002-10-20-hatecrime_x.htm.

Sandholtz, N., L. Langston, and M. Planty. 2013. *Hate Crime Victimization, 2003–2011*. Washington, DC: U.S. Department of Justice, Office of Justice Programs, Bureau of Justice Statistics.

Schapiro, R. 2012. "Trayvon Injuries Hand Scraped Before Shot Fired at 'Intermediate' Range: Reports." *Daily News*. http://www.lexisnexis.com.proxy.library.umkc.edu/lnacui2api/api/version1/getDocCui?oc=00240andhnsd=fandhgn=tandlni=55NF-W3Y1-DY2D-J2XHandhns=tandperma=trueandhv=tandhl=tandcsi=270944%2C270077%2C11059%2C8411andsecondRedirectIndicator=true.

Schilt, K., and L. Westbrook. 2009. "Doing Gender, Doing Heteronormativity: 'Gender Normals,' Transgender People, and the Social Maintenance of Heterosexuality." *Gender & Society* 23 (4): 441–58.

Stafford, Z. 2014. "Black, Gay and Shot Dead in His Own Car: This Is Another Missouri Killing We Should Talk About." *Guardian*. http://www.theguardian.com/commentisfree/2014/dec/02/-sp-missouri-killing-dionte-greene.

Stanko, E. A. 1995. "Women, Crime, and Fear." *Annals of the American Academy of Political and Social Science* 539:46–58.

St. John, K. 2004. "Hayward/Witness Tells How She Learned Transgender Teen Was Male." *SF Gate*. http://www.sfgate.com/bayarea/article/HAYWARD-Witness-tells -how-she-learned-2765958.php.

St. John, K., and Lee, H. 2002. "Slain Newark Teen Balanced Between Two Worlds/3 Charged in Death of Youth Who Was Living His Dream as a Female." *SF Gate*. http://www.sfgate.com/bayarea/article/Slain-Newark-teen-balanced-between-two -worlds-3-2782669.php.

Tobar, H. 2014. "Lisa Bloom's 'Suspicious Nation' Dips into Trayvon Martin Case." *Los Angeles Times*. http://www.latimes.com/books/jacketcopy/la-ca-jc-lisa-bloom -20140302,0,1301510.story#axzz2x0ujb7RF.

Walker, T. 2014. "Trayvon and Jordan: Why Knowing Their Names Hurts." *Huffington Post*. http://www.huffingtonpost.com/tricia-elam-walker/trayvon-and-jordan-why -he_b_4856317.html.

Warr, M. 1985. "Fear of Rape among Urban Women." *Social Problems* 32 (3): 238–50.

Weigert, A. J. 1986. "The Social Production of Identity: Metatheoretical Foundations." *Sociological Quarterly* 27 (2): 165–83.

Wesley, J. K., and E. Gaarder. 2004. "The Gendered 'Nature' of the Urban Outdoors: Women Negotiating Fear of Violence." *Gender & Society* 18 (5): 645–63.

West, C., and S. Fenstermaker. 1995. "Doing Difference." *Gender & Society* 9 (1): 8–37.

West, C., and D. Zimmerman. 1987. "Doing Gender." *Gender & Society* 1 (2): 125–26.

WFTV. 2012. "Neighborhood Watch Leader Who Fatally Shot Teen Not Arrested; Family Files Suit." http://www.wftv.com/news/news/family-teen-fatally-shot -neighborhood-watch-leader/nLNq9/.

Wronge, Y. 2005a. "Defendants Portrayed as Ordinary Men Shocked into Violent Rage." *San Jose Mercury News*. http://www.lexisnexis.com.proxy.library.umkc.edu/ lnacui2api/api/version1/getDocCui?oc=00240andhnsd=fandhgn=tandlni=4GYM -WYS0-01JV-91FHandhns=tandperma=trueandhv=tandhl=tandcsi=270944%2 C270077%2C11059%2C8411andsecondRedirectIndicator=true.

Wronge, Y. 2005b. "Slain Transgender Youth Allegedly Lied to Defendants to Get Sex." *San Jose Mercury News*. http://www.lexisnexis.com.proxy.library.umkc.edu/ lnacui2api/api/version1/getDocCui?oc=00240andhnsd=fandhgn=tandlni=4H0H -P0X0-01JV-92JSandhns=tandperma=trueandhv=tandhl=tandcsi=270944%2 C270077%2C11059%2C8411andsecondRedirectIndicator=true.

Young, V. 2006. "Demythologizing the 'Criminalblackman': The Carnival Mirror." In *Many Colors of Crime: Inequalities of Race, Ethnicity, and Crime in America*, edited by R. D. Peterson, L. J. Krivo, and J. Hagan, 54–66. New York: New York University Press.

Zhang, Y., and B. Wildemuth. 2005. "Qualitative Analysis of Content." *Analysis* 1 (2): 1–12.

PART II

Where Do You Stand?

5

Go Ahead and Shoot—The Law Might Have Your Back

History, Race, Implicit Bias, and Justice in Florida's
Stand Your Ground Law

KATHERYN RUSSELL-BROWN

This chapter examines the evolution of Florida's Stand Your Ground law and the crucible of thorny issues it raises in light of the George Zimmerman / Trayvon Martin case. The case sits at the crossroads of history, race, fear, and criminal justice. While other cases have raised similar issues, this case is critical because of its application of Florida's Stand Your Ground law. The 2005 law offers a new window into how race impacts the application of self-defense law. A critical race theory approach is used to analyze how the Stand Your Ground law reinforces the mainstream narrative of race and crime. This analysis underscores the value of using historical and empirical research to understand and investigate the evolution of the law, the application of the law, and the question of whether the law is just. The goal of this approach is to challenge the "doctrinal orthodoxy concerning race and law."[1]

This chapter has six sections. The first section provides the historical background on the law of self-defense and use of deadly force. The second section looks at Florida law prior to the adoption of Stand Your Ground. The third section describes the carefully orchestrated plan to enact Stand Your Ground legislation. The fourth section details how the new law altered the landscape of self-defense and the use of deadly force in Florida. The fifth section reviews the empirical literature on the law's impact. This discussion includes a look at the impact of race in Stand Your Ground cases, how the law has spurred legislation in over half of all states, and recent changes to the Florida law. The sixth and final section identifies and critiques key sociological questions raised by the enactment and application of Stand Your Ground. The questions raised include how race impacts the perception of "reasonable fear" and what role implicit bias has in actions based on these perceptions. This part also examines the social impact of Stand Your Ground's racially disparate outcomes. The discussion concludes with a consideration of the distinction between law and justice and why this matters.

Stand Your Ground and the Zimmerman Case: A Note

There has been some debate as to whether the Zimmerman case invoked Florida's Stand Your Ground law. Zimmerman's defense attorney, Mark O'Mara, has argued that the case did not involve Stand Your Ground because Zimmerman did not request an immunity hearing.[2] However, other factors matter in a determination of whether a case is properly classified under Stand Your Ground. One factor is whether the case incorporated the language of the Stand Your Ground law. The jury instructions at Zimmerman's trial included wording from the Stand Your Ground statute and used the term "stand your ground."[3] Another factor is whether the Stand Your Ground law had an impact on the outcome of the case. Members of Zimmerman's jury stated that they discussed Stand Your Ground during their deliberations.[4] Furthermore, and most critically, in compliance with Stand Your Ground law, Sanford, Florida, police failed to gather and secure key evidence following Martin's death. Zimmerman was briefly questioned, was not arrested, and was allowed to go home the night of the killing. Zimmerman's lawyers made a strategic decision not to request immunity. However, the Stand Your Ground law remained at the center the case.

Self-Defense and Deadly Force: A Look Back

Twenty-first-century American law on the use of deadly force to defend oneself emerged from opposing legal philosophies.[5] The first perspective draws from the English common-law view that human life is sacred and should be protected whenever possible. According to this approach, the law should encourage people to respect life and discourage vigilante justice. In line with this view, under English common law, a person was required to retreat "to the wall" before he or she could kill another person in self-defense. The core rationale for this perspective is the value of human life, including the life of a person who is attacking another person.[6] Furthermore, it was believed that private citizens should not be allowed to "take capital revenge" against one another.[7]

Homicides were viewed as public wrongs, and courts imposed the retreat rule to ensure that the right to defend oneself was not mistaken for the right to kill another person. In addition, the common-law approach was based on the assumption that the state is the best arbiter of conflict between individuals.[8] It was believed that the retreat rule would lead to a decline in the murder rate—as personal disputes would be handled in court and not on the street. It would also operate as a "powerful means to produce a society of civility."[9] However, many states were not persuaded that the English common-law rule of retreat should apply. Only a minority of states have adopted the rule of retreat.

The second approach is "no retreat." In the face of threatened violence, an individual should be allowed to stay put—to stand his or her ground and fight back against an attacker. In the 1800s, the "no-retreat" approach was particularly attractive to frontier states, which viewed retreat as a sign of cowardice. *Erwin v. State*, an 1876 case decided by the Ohio Supreme Court, represents this perspective. The court declined to use the retreat rule and overturned the defendant's conviction. It stated, "[A] true man, who is without fault, is not obliged to fly from an assailant who, by violence or surprise, maliciously seeks to take his life or do him enormous bodily harm."[10] In *Brown v. United States* (1921), the U.S. Supreme Court addressed the retreat rule. The murder case involved a victim who had a knife and a defendant who had a gun. The Court ruled that retreat is not always required. Instead, it is a factor for the court to consider when evaluating a self-defense claim. Many people viewed the rule of retreat as an outdated legal carryover from the common law. Today the majority of states do not require retreat before the use of deadly force.

The Castle Doctrine has served as a middle ground for these opposing viewpoints on when deadly force is appropriate to defend oneself. According to the Castle Doctrine, people who are faced with deadly force in their home can respond with deadly force. They do not have to retreat, run away, or try to get to a safe place. As early as 1895, courts made reference to the Castle Doctrine. In *Beard v. United States*, a case involving a man who claimed he killed another man in self-defense, the

U.S. Supreme Court stated that a person who was where he had a lawful right to be and who did not provoke an assault "is not obliged to retreat, but may stand his ground" and defend himself.[11] In a later case, Judge Benjamin Cardozo explicitly refers to "dwelling" in his discussion of when a person has to retreat before using deadly force. In *People v. Tomlins* (1914) Judge Cardozo commented that a "man assailed in his own dwelling" does not have to retreat. "He may stand his ground and resist the attack. He is under no duty to take to the fields, and the highways, a fugitive from his own home."[12] The Castle Doctrine allows a person to respond to an attack in her home with lethal force. This exception to the rule of retreat recognizes the sanctity of one's home and a person's right to protect the place where she lives. Over time, the Castle Doctrine has been extended to include one's workplace.[13]

The above discussion outlines the two basic legal approaches to self-defense and the use of deadly force. Over the decades, states have been divided over whether someone must attempt to get to a place of safety before resorting to deadly force. The differing philosophies on when lethal force should be permissible to defend oneself are rooted in beliefs about whether it is best to have the law or individuals resolve disputes, and the value of human life.

Florida before Stand Your Ground

Before it passed Stand Your Ground legislation in 2005, Florida was a retreat state. Florida was one of the states that followed the English common law and sought balance between the right of self-defense and the goal of protecting life. Deadly force was permissible in few instances. A person had a duty to retreat, if possible, before using lethal force: "[A] person under attack [has] 'to retreat to the wall or ditch' before taking a life."[14] Florida's self-defense statute did not impose a duty to retreat—the retreat rule became law through the Florida state courts. Prior to Stand Your Ground, Florida also required that the person using force prove reasonable fear.[15] It had to be established that it was reasonable to believe that force was required to "prevent imminent death or great bodily harm to himself . . . or another."[16] The one exception to the retreat rule was if the person threatened was at her home or in her workplace. Florida recognized the Castle Doctrine, which was first referenced in an 1892 case.[17] Like the rule of retreat, the Castle Doctrine was implemented through the Florida judiciary and was never codified into state legislation.[18]

Over the decades, the retreat rule took several legal turns as the Florida courts addressed how broadly it should apply. The range of issues considered by the courts included whether the Castle Doctrine applied to attacks between two house occupants, whether it applied when the victim and attacker were employees at the same workplace, whether it applied to houseguests, and whether it extended to one's car.[19] Prior to Stand Your Ground, self-defense was an affirmative defense. If the defendant was able to meet the requirements of a self-defense claim, reasonable fear and retreat, he or she might avoid a conviction. A jury decided whether the defendant had a reasonable belief that deadly force was necessary. In its evaluation, the jury was required to take into consideration both subjective and objective factors—whether the defendant believed he or she was in fear *and* whether a reasonable person would have been in fear.[20]

On the Road to Stand Your Ground

On April 26, 2005, Florida governor Jeb Bush signed the Protection of Persons/Use of Force bill—commonly known as Stand Your Ground—into law. The legislation took effect on October 1, 2005. At Governor Bush's side was Marion Hammer, the former president of the National Rifle Association (NRA). Hammer's presence symbolized the long-standing and close working relationship between Florida's Republicans and the gun rights lobby. In the mid-1970s, when the NRA became increasingly concerned that Florida would pass stricter gun control laws, it formed the Unified Sportsmen of Florida. The new group positioned an NRA representative within the state, to combat a "burst of gun control measures being filed by northerners who had moved to South Florida."[21] In 1978, Hammer became a full-time lobbyist for the Unified Sportsmen of Florida and the NRA's chief Florida lobbyist. She worked to increase the rights of gun owners, and in 1987 she was behind a successful effort to enact "right to carry" firearms legislation in Florida. This law made it easier for residents to legally carry concealed weapons in public.

Hammer and her colleagues continued to advocate for increased rights for gun owners. The James Workman case was used to argue for new legislation on self-defense. Workman's use of deadly force against Rodney Cox was offered as proof that expanded gun rights were necessary to protect innocent victims of crime. In 2004, as a result of the severe damage done to their Pensacola home by Hurricane Ivan, the Workmans slept in an RV in their driveway, approximately twenty feet from their house. During the night, Workman's wife called 911, when she saw someone approaching their house. She told her husband and he left the trailer with his gun to confront the man, Rodney Cox. Workman fired a warning shot, the pair scuffled, and Workman fired again, this time killing Cox. The State Attorney's Office conducted a review of the case, which lasted less than three months. Following the review, no homicide charges were filed against Workman. The case sparked outrage among the conservative right, and it became a symbol of the law's failure to protect law-abiding gun owners. Florida state senator Durell Peaden commented, "You're entitled to protect your castle. . . . Why should you have to hire a lawyer to say, 'This guy is innocent?'"[22] Although the case facts were drastically different than those reported throughout the press, the NRA used the case to argue that the law and courts were biased against gun owners.[23]

The NRA's response to the Workman case was swift and certain. It enlisted the support of two Florida legislators, Senator Peaden and Representative Dennis Baxley. The aim was to draft legislation that would achieve two goals. The first objective was to ensure that gun owners who used their weapons in self-defense would not be brought into the criminal justice system. Legal immunity would be made available to protect gun owners from criminal charges. The second objective was to ensure that if a gun owner did face criminal charges for using deadly force, the law would presume that his actions were legally justified.

Senator Peaden sponsored the Protection of Persons/Use of Force bill in the Florida Senate, and Representative Baxley argued for the law in the state's House of Representatives. Hammer lobbied across the state for the bill, which she repeatedly referred to as the Castle Doctrine—improperly implying that it was an extension of the existing Castle Doctrine.[24] The NRA placed its considerable financial weight behind the proposed law, spending thousands of dollars on advertising and donating thousands of dollars to Jeb Bush's 2002 gubernatorial campaign, individual Florida legislators, and the Florida Republican Party Committee.[25] Supporters argued that Stand Your Ground would deter criminals because they would fear being harmed by armed citizens. Furthermore, they argued, the bill was needed to protect potential victims of crime. Hammer stated that this was because the "courts have manipulated the law into a position where the law favors criminals rather than victims and law abiding citizens."[26]

Stand Your Ground faced vigorous opposition. Some police agencies, law enforcement officers, and police chiefs argued that it would give too much power to inexperienced gun owners and encourage vigilante justice. John Timoney, Miami's police chief, argued that the bill would encourage "people to possibly use deadly physical force where it shouldn't be used." The president of the Florida Prosecuting Attorneys Association stated that the Stand Your Ground bill would protect people who use force when they do not need to use it. Victims' advocacy groups warned that the new law would lead to more crime.[27] Gun control groups cautioned that the law would create a new class of innocent crime victims. Arthur Hayhoe, the director of the Florida Coalition to Stop Gun Violence, labeled Stand Your Ground a "jihad against public safety." He argued that the public would interpret passage of the law as sending the message, "I don't have to retreat."[28] The Brady Campaign, which promotes gun control legislation, expressed concern that tourists visiting Florida would be unaware of the law and vulnerable to acts of vigilantism.

On March 23, 2005, the Stand Your Ground bill was passed by a unanimous, thirty-nine to zero, vote in the Florida Senate. The Senate floor debates indicate there was some confusion about how broadly the law would apply. Some senators argued that the bill would allow anyone to use deadly force against someone walking down the street whom they perceived to be a threat. The bill's sponsor, Senator Peaden, responded, "You have to be in the confines of the dwelling. . . . You can't just shoot anybody on the street and drag 'em in."[29] Following the Senate's vote, on April 5, 2005, the Florida House of Representatives passed Stand Your Ground by a ninety-four to twenty vote. The next section looks at how the new law shifted the legal landscape of self-defense in Florida.

Stand Your Ground: New Rules

Florida's Stand Your Ground rewrote the law on self-defense and use of deadly force (see the appendix). It changed the law in five key areas. First, Stand Your Ground removed all geographical limits on the use of deadly force. It abolished the Castle Doctrine and replaced it with a new rule—you may stand your ground wherever you are, you do not have to retreat. The new law allows Floridians to stand their ground anywhere they have a lawful right to be. The effect of this change was to make the entire state of Florida one's "castle." In this way, Stand Your Ground gives new meaning to the expression "at home in the world." With the passage of Stand Your Ground legislation, Florida went from being a "retreat" state to a "no-retreat" state.[30]

Second, the new law creates a "presumption of reasonableness."[31] Under Stand Your Ground, if a person who has been charged with unlawful use of force says that she reasonably believed that she needed to use deadly force, the burden is on the prosecutor to disprove the claim. The presumption that the defendant's actions were reasonable gives her an initial advantage.

When the Castle Doctrine was in effect, someone claiming self-defense would be evaluated using an objective standard. The defendant's actions would be compared with the actions of a "reasonable person." If the court determined that the defendant's response was reasonable— those actions that would be expected under the circumstances—then his use of force would be justifiable. However, the new law eliminated this requirement. Stand Your Ground does not require that the defendant's actions were the actions of a reasonable person. Stand Your Ground requires that the defendant's actions were reasonable to *him*. In effect, this subjective standard creates a "presumption of fear."[32] The defendant has to establish that he was afraid and feared that he was being confronted with unlawful deadly force.

Allowing courts to use a subjective standard is problematic because whether someone causes another person to be fearful may or may not be reasonable. Whether a person is perceived as threatening involves a mix of legal and nonlegal factors. The use of a subjective standard to define fear provides legal cover to apply perceptions based on stereotypes about race, gender, and socioeconomic status. Prior to Stand Your

Ground, a defendant's claim that she acted in self-defense was an affirmative defense that was decided at trial.[33] The defendant was required to prove to the court that she had to use lethal force to protect herself from serious harm. Stand Your Ground creates a high bar for the prosecution — by requiring that it disprove the defendant's claims that her actions were reasonable.[34]

Third, the language of Stand Your Ground changes the requirements as to whether the victim has to be faced with actual deadly force and whether the threat has to be imminent. The new law potentially allows a person to use deadly force even when she is not faced with deadly force. For instance, so long as the person who uses deadly force believes there was an unlawful and forced entry, her use of lethal force may be permissible.[35] Furthermore, Stand Your Ground allows for the use of lethal force even when the victim does not face an immediate threat.[36] This is a remarkably odd outcome given the U.S. Supreme Court's decision in *Tennessee v. Garner* (1985), where the Court held that a police department policy that allowed officers to shoot nonviolent fleeing felons was unconstitutional.

Fourth, Stand Your Ground gives criminal and civil immunity to anyone who is justified in using lethal force in self-defense. This is a broad grant of immunity, one that bars legal actions, such as a wrongful death lawsuit. The one exception to immunity is if the deadly force is used against a law enforcement officer.

Fifth, Stand Your Ground law gives police officers the power to determine whether there was a justifiable use of deadly force. Police officers who arrive on the scene following an incident determine whether they should make an arrest or allow the person who used deadly force to go home. Stand Your Ground gives police officers the final authority to decide whether a shooting was justified or unjustified — a determination typically left to the court system. In this way, Stand Your Ground allows police officers to act as proxies for judges and juries.[37]

As these changes make clear, the passage of Florida's Stand Your Ground law represents a fundamental change in the law of self-defense and deadly force. The 2005 law expands the circumstances in which a person can use lethal force to protect himself. With this expansion, Stand Your Ground moves self-defense from being an issue of courtroom justice to an issue of street justice. The law works to create a hybrid track of justice—between traditional law and vigilante justice. This transformative legal shift runs contrary to the common-law approach, which holds that criminal law matters are best mediated by the justice system, not lay individuals. Florida's Stand Your Ground law rode to passage on a wave of promises including deterrence and increased public safety. The next section examines whether the empirical data confirm the predictions made by Stand Your Ground supporters and evaluates the costs associated with its passage.

Stand Your Ground in Action (Post-2005)

Several of the concerns raised by opponents of Stand Your Ground have come to pass. Crime data and empirical research show that after Stand Your Ground became law there was a threefold increase in the rate of justifiable homicides in Florida.[38] This coincided with an increase in the number of requests for concealed gun permits. Five years before Stand Your Ground was passed in Florida, there was an average of twelve justifiable killings each year; since the law's passage, there has been an average of thirty-six. Supporters of Stand Your Ground argued that the law would deter crime. Opponents of the legislation have pointed to the racial impact of the law. The research, detailed below, indicates that Stand Your Ground has been disproportionately available to whites who have claimed self-defense.

A Look at the Cases

The *Tampa Bay Times* newspaper has collected data on over two hundred Stand Your Ground cases, from 2005 to 2013. The newspaper's detailed interactive website includes case factors, such as the race and gender of the victim and accuser, county where the crime took place, whether the case involved a fatal or nonfatal encounter, and the outcome of the case.[39] The findings outlined in figure 5.1 are notable. First, in more than two-thirds of the cases, the person who used deadly force was not punished. In 35 percent of the cases the accuser was not charged or the charges were dismissed by the prosecutor. In 23 percent of the cases the judge granted the accuser immunity, and in the remaining 10 percent of cases the accuser was acquitted. Second, in 32 percent of the

Case outcomes

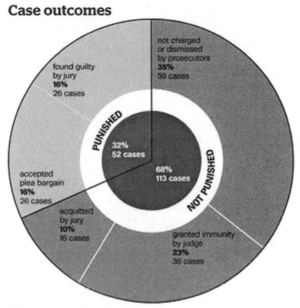

Weapon comparison

The law has freed killers even though most of their victims
were unarmed.

Figure 5.1. Case outcomes. Source: Darla Cameron, *Tampa
Bay Times.*

cases the accuser received punishment for her actions and she either
accepted a plea bargain (16 percent) or was found guilty by a jury (16
percent). Third, in 70 percent of the cases involving a fatality, the victim
was unarmed. Fourth, in 63 percent of the cases that resulted in a fatality the accuser used a gun. The chart graphically illustrates the sizeable
gap between Stand Your Ground cases that result in punishment and
those where no punishment is imposed.[40]

Table 5.1 provides insight on how race impacts the outcome in Stand
Your Ground cases where someone was killed. The table reports several

TABLE 5.1. Florida Stand Your Ground Cases Involving Fatalities, 2005–13

	Justifiable use of force (killer acquitted)	Conviction (killer convicted)	% of cases overall
White accuser/white victim	34	26	52
White accuser/black victim	6	1	6
White accuser/Hispanic victim	4	1	4
Black accuser/white victim	4	3	6
Black accuser/black victim	18	8	22
Black accuser/Hispanic victim	1	0	<1
Hispanic accuser/white victim	2	3	4
Hispanic accuser/black victim	3	0	2
Hispanic accuser/Hispanic victim	2	0	2
	74	42	

Source: *Tampa Bay Times*, December 20, 2013.

interesting findings. First, the majority of Stand Your Ground cases involve a white accuser and a white victim (52 percent). Second, whites accused of unlawful use of deadly force were much more likely to prevail if their victim was African American. In 57 percent of the cases involving white accusers and white victims, the accuser's use of force was found to be justifiable. This compares with 86 percent of the cases involving a white accuser and a black victim. Third, in 69 percent of the cases involving blacks who used deadly force against other blacks, the force was found to be justifiable. The same finding holds true for Hispanic accusers. In all three cases involving a Hispanic accuser who had a black victim, there was a finding of justifiable force. Fourth, in 75 percent of the cases where the person killed was black, the killing was found to be justifiable. In only 55 percent of the cases involving a white victim was the death ruled justifiable. Overall defendants who used Stand Your Ground were more likely to be successful if their victim was black. This finding, that the race of the victim impacts the outcome of a case, is in accord with long-standing empirical research. Most notably the Baldus Study, cited by the U.S. Supreme Court in *McCleskey v. Kemp*

(1987), demonstrated that the victim's race was a significant predictor of whether a capital defendant would receive the death penalty.

Warning Shots

The case of Marissa Alexander brought the issue of the appropriate punishment for warning shots into the national spotlight. Alexander, whose estranged husband had threatened to assault her, fired a warning shot at him. No one was injured. Alexander was charged with three counts of aggravated assault with a deadly weapon. She was convicted under a mandatory-minimum law and sentenced to twenty years in prison. In April 2014, the Florida legislature passed a bill that expanded Stand Your Ground to include warning shots. However, the warning shot bill, which was strongly backed by the NRA and Florida Carry, creates more opportunities for people to use guns without facing legal consequences.

The warning shot bill also included a lesser-known amendment that will likely have a far-reaching impact on the availability of information about Stand Your Ground cases. The bill allows for the removal of records—expungement—in cases where the charges have been dropped or the accuser is acquitted and found to have used justifiable force. This provision would make it more difficult for researchers and reporters to gather data on Stand Your Ground cases and empirically evaluate its impact, racial and otherwise.[41] It would also make it more likely that concerns about bias raised by marginalized racial groups would go unheeded.[42]

Florida Governor's Task Force on Citizen Safety and Protection

In 2012, months after the national and international outcry following the Martin case, Florida governor Rick Scott established a task force to review the self-defense sections of the Florida statutes (chapter 776) and their implementation. The nineteen-member Task Force on Citizen Safety and Protection comprised primarily supporters of the Stand Your Ground law. The group's recommendations acted as an endorsement for Stand Your Ground. The Task Force's nine recommendations did little to address the concerns raised about the law's breadth, application, and racial impact. The recommendations include increasing the self-defense training for police officers, lawyers, and judges; examining standards for neighborhood watch associations; reviewing Florida's ten-twenty-life law; and considering the funding of research that examines the effect of race and gender on how Stand Your Ground is applied.[43] Two members of the Task Force filed separate recommendations and argued for more substantial changes to the law.[44] These members also emphasized the need to eliminate the legal presumptions that favor the killer and the need to address the racial consequences of Stand Your Ground.

Stand Your Ground across the Nation

Following in Florida's footsteps, more than thirty states have adopted some version of Stand Your Ground laws, through either legislation or the courts. A mix of social, political, and economic factors has made Stand Your Ground laws appealing throughout the country, from the heartland to border states. The NRA joined forces with the American Legislative Exchange Council (ALEC), a conservative legislative group. Marion Hammer presented Florida's Stand Your Ground law to ALEC's Criminal Justice Task Force. The NRA and ALEC worked together to fund and promote the adoption of Stand Your Ground laws across the fifty states. These lobbyists were able to capitalize on the widespread fear of terrorism, evoked by the September 11, 2001, attacks.[45] Furthermore, and more insidiously, they were able to take advantage of the race-based fears prompted by the images of looting and crime following Hurricane Katrina in 2005. Surveys indicate that during that time period, people felt more vulnerable and less safe.[46]

Empirical studies on the impact of Stand Your Ground laws in states beyond Florida have found patterns that match those found in Florida. John Roman's research for the Urban Institute offers a particularly compelling look at the difference in magnitude between justifiable homicides in Stand Your Ground states compared with non–Stand Your Ground states.[47] Roman's findings are based on more than fifty thousand cases from the FBI's Supplementary Homicide Report, from 2005 to 2010. The data show that 2.57 percent of these homicide cases were found to be legally justified.

The racial patterns that emerge in cases involving justifiable homicide are revealing as well. Roman found that 56 percent of the homicides involved a white offender and a white victim, 4 percent involved a white offender and a black victim, 43 percent involved a black offender and black victim, and 9 percent involved a black offender and white victim.[48] The analysis further demonstrates that in Stand Your Ground states, white-on-black homicides were the killings that were most likely to be found justified (11.4 percent). This contrasts with black-on-white homicides, which were the killings that were least likely to be found justified (1.2 percent).[49]

Roman also analyzed a subset of cases with fact patterns similar to the Zimmerman case. The data included 2,631 cases where there was a male victim, a male shooter, no previous relationship between the victim and shooter, and the use of a firearm. Roman found significant racial disparities in how these cases were decided in Stand Your Ground states. In white-on-black homicide cases, the shooting was determined to be justified in 44 percent of the cases, compared with 11 percent for black-on-white homicide cases.

Other studies also support the concerns raised by opponents to Stand Your Ground laws. Overall states with enhanced self-defense laws (such as Stand Your Ground) experienced an increase in violence. For instance, Chandler McClellan and Erdal Tekin's research found that states with Stand Your Ground laws experienced an increase in the number of firearm-related homicides of white men.[50] In addition, Mark Hoekstra and Cheng Cheng's study found that homicides increased as the costs associated with the use of deadly force declined.[51] The bottom line of the various studies of the racial impact of Stand Your Ground in Florida and beyond is that it is both easier for whites to successfully use Stand Your Ground laws and more difficult for blacks to successfully use Stand Your Ground laws. Furthermore, when the victim is white, Stand Your Ground is less likely to be a successful defense.

Other Things Considered: Guns, Fear, and Justice

Stand Your Ground law, its history, its current application, and its future, raises a number of intertwined issues. This section argues that in order to make sociolegal sense of Stand Your Ground cases such as George Zimmerman's, we must examine the historical relationship between the law and African Americans and how the law has been utilized to respond to racialized threats. This history marks a clear pathway to current criminal laws, such as Stand Your Ground. As well, understanding Stand Your Ground requires acknowledging historically rooted stereotypes about African Americans. Contemporary and past images consistently present African Americans as deviant, aggressive, and criminal. These images drive our perceptions of which groups are to be feared, who is fearful, the appropriate responses to fear, and whether that fear is justified under the law. This leads to a consideration of whether Stand Your Ground laws can be both legal and just.

Race and Gun Control

The history of how law has been used as an instrument of racial exclusion and control was one of the salient issues following Trayvon Martin's killing. Some questioned whether the impetus for Stand Your Ground laws and other laws that expand the rights of gun owners was a desire to control and regulate African Americans through a form of legalized vigilantism. Specifically, the concern was that the gun rights lobby plays on white fear of black crime, and by doing so engages in a kind of racial profiling. In response to these claims, NRA President David Keene stated that it is the people who seek to limit gun use who have a racist history: "When you go back in history, the initial wave of [gun laws] was instituted after the Civil War to deny blacks the ability to defend themselves."[52] While Keene's remark regarding the post–Civil War time period is factually accurate, it does not tell the whole story.[53] A more accurate assessment requires a consideration of what happened prior to the Civil War.

In an attempt to quell slave insurrections, laws were adopted that made it illegal for slaves to keep or carry arms. These laws were part of the slave codes. Slave codes were antebellum laws that regulated and monitored the movements of African slaves in America. The laws prescribed the rules of daily living for slaves. This included regulations stating how many slaves could travel together at one time, when religious worship was permissible, and prohibitions against learning to read or write. Overall, slaves were subject to a system of criminal laws and punishments that were different in nature and kind to the laws that applied to whites. The slave codes prohibited slaves from carrying guns and other weapons.

Slaves found with weapons were subject to lashings. The slave codes were enforced by slave patrols, the first uniquely American form of policing.[54] Slave patrollers had the authority to stop and search slaves and whip those who did not have written permission to be away from their plantation. Patrollers raided slave cabins to search for runaways, evidence of literacy (e.g., books, paper), and guns. Notably laws banning blacks from possessing guns were not limited to the states that had slavery. Free states also had laws that prohibited free blacks from carrying arms.[55]

Laws prohibiting blacks from carrying guns were temporarily suspended during the Civil War. However, immediately after the Civil War, laws known as the black codes were enacted to disarm blacks. The black codes were the postslavery version of the slave codes. A Mississippi 1865 law stated that "no freedman, free negro or mulatto" could "keep or carry firearms of any kind," unless he had a license issued by the police.[56] A black person found with arms could be subject to a fine or jail. These harsh laws and their punishment were not enough for some whites. To ensure that these laws were not just "on the books," groups of vigilante whites, antecedents of the Ku Klux Klan, went on night rides to terrorize blacks, ransack their homes, and seize any weapons they found.[57]

Throughout its history, the NRA's platform on guns has been tied explicitly or implicitly to race. The NRA was formed in 1871, just after the Civil War. The organization's mission was to "promote and encourage rifle shooting on a scientific basis."[58] The NRA did not always promote the expansion of gun rights. For instance, in the 1920s, the NRA helped draft the Uniform Firearms Act. This law was a response to the prevalence of urban gun violence, which was associated with immigrants. The model legislation was designed to restrict who could carry concealed firearms in public. Under the Uniform Firearms Act, only "suitable" persons with "proper reason" could be granted a gun license. Disfavored groups such as racial minorities and immigrants were most likely to be deemed unsuitable and therefore ineligible for gun licenses. Most states adopted this legislation. A notorious example concerning the definition of "suitable" involves Martin Luther King, Jr. In 1956, following the firebombing of his home, King's application for a gun permit was denied.[59]

A fuller review of the NRA's history shows that in earlier periods it promoted gun control. In more contemporary times it has supported the expansion of gun rights. Keene's comments overlook how gun laws, which today are written in race-neutral language, are often successful because they are viewed as a way to manage African Americans. Furthermore, his comments do not address the disparate racial impact of gun laws, such as Stand Your Ground. National surveys consistently show a huge racial split between the percentage of blacks and whites who support Stand Your Ground laws. A 2013 Quinnipiac University national poll found that 57 percent of whites approve of Stand Your Ground laws, compared with 57 percent of blacks who disapprove of the law.

Reasonable Fear and the Criminalblackman

The Stand Your Ground law does something remarkable.[60] Under the law, a person who says he feared for his life can use that fear to justify his killing of the person he feared—regardless of whether there is objective proof that he should have been fearful. The bottom line is that Stand Your Ground enables a subjective assessment of fear to be used to exculpate a killer. As discussed above, the Florida law adopts a presumption of reasonable fear in self-defense cases. If the person who used force believed that his life was being threatened, his use of deadly force is presumed to be reasonable. This presumption gives legal weight to the perceptions of the person who says he was threatened with lethal force. If a law gives weight to a subjective assessment of fear—as Stand Your Ground does—it should also take into consideration how fear is calculated. Specifically it should evaluate the factors that impact perceptions of fear. The latter piece is missing from Stand Your Ground laws and their application by the courts. Under Stand Your Ground, a person's subjective perception of threat can determine whether his use of force was justifiable. At the same time, however, the basis of that fear is not subjected to rigorous legal scrutiny or put into any empirical perspective.

This absence is particularly critical when we consider the widespread images and stereotypes about race and crime.[61] Race matters in perceptions of violence and fear of crime. Across the social sciences, including sociology, criminology, psychology, and economics, research shows a long-standing and persistent stereotype of African Americans as criminal. In a group of studies that used video simulations to examine how people responded to perceived threats, psychologists found that people were more likely to "shoot" armed black targets more quickly than armed white targets. They were also more likely to shoot unarmed black targets than unarmed white targets. The researchers determined that the relationship between perceptions and images of race and crime is "bidirectional"—the relationship works in two ways. One, for most people the idea of crime brings to mind images of black faces, *and* two, images of black faces bring to mind thoughts of crime.[62]

Racial associations have clear relevance to criminal cases, particularly those involving self-defense claims. A growing body of empirical research explores implicit bias and unconscious racial bias. These biases are of particular importance given that they tend to be strong, though not necessarily intentional. Furthermore, implicit biases tend to work to the disadvantage of stigmatized groups. L. Song Richardson and Phillip Goff use the term "suspicion heuristic" to describe the psychological process through which many people link blackness with criminality.[63] Their work describes the mental shortcuts that lead people to see blacks as deviant and how these views scan impact *behavior*. These racial associations are most likely to be acted upon in situations where a person has little time to think—such as a situation where a person believes she is being confronted with deadly force. All told, the mental shortcuts that are used to calculate suspicion places those who most often fit the criminal stereotype—African Americans—at a higher rate of death or serious bodily harm. This reality is borne out by the statistics on who benefits from Stand Your Ground. As discussed above, self-defense cases with a white victim are the ones where the use of deadly force is least likely to be found justifiable.

George Zimmerman, in his phone conversation with the 911 dispatcher, made overt connections between race and criminality. His comments included, "We've had some break-ins in my neighborhood and there's a real suspicious guy"; "This guy looks like he's up to no good, or he's on drugs or something"; "He's a Black male"; and "They always get away." Notably, Zimmerman's comments offer no objective proof of criminal activity. He did not see Martin engage in any unlawful behavior. Martin's black body within the gated community was enough to trigger Zimmerman's suspicion that Martin was a criminal. This is a textbook example of the "suspicion heuristic" that Richardson and Goff describe. We have seen this "Black equals criminal threat" equation played out in other high-profile criminal cases including Bernhard Goetz's subway shooting of four black men in 1984 and Rodney King's beating by Los Angeles police in 1991.

The trouble with the dominant and widely held stereotype that links blackness with criminality is that it leaves little room for the reality that the overwhelming majority of African Americans do not engage in criminal offending. The negative racial images combined with statistics on the disproportionate rate of crime by blacks have been used to argue that fear of blacks, and of black men in particular, is reasonable and justified. The glaring flaw with this view is that it allows the criminal activity of some blacks to be treated as the criminal activity of all blacks. This "some equals all" formula is a false conflation. At core it is an argument for "statistical discrimination" that has great costs for the justice system in particular and society at large.[64] This "reasonable fear" argument has been used to justify the disparate racial impact of Stand Your Ground laws.

Stand Your Ground laws allow for a subjective evaluation of "reasonable fear." Given this, these laws should be required to take into account the impact of race-based biases and stereotypes. How individuals evaluate who and what is interpreted as a criminal threat impacts individual actions. The empirical research shows that racial associations work in ways that stigmatize blacks and show that people are more likely to perceive blacks as a threat. In turn, they are more likely to respond violently to blacks. Courts hearing Stand Your Ground claims should have to evaluate the effect of implicit racial bias. This could be done either through expert testimony or special jury instructions.[65]

Law v. Justice

Race-based critiques of the criminal justice system are not new. For decades, scholars have identified laws and legal practices that have created stark racial disproportionality within the justice system, including the war on drugs, racial profiling by law enforcement, mandatory-minimum sentences, felony disenfranchisement, and mass incarceration.[66] Stand Your Ground laws fit within the larger structure of the criminal justice system, which consists of the police, courts, and corrections. Stand Your Ground law is particularly ripe for critique because the self-defense law reaches across the continuum of the justice system—from prearrest to sentencing. Furthermore, it involves issues of life and death. At core, the law raises questions about societal evaluations of race, ethics, and criminal law.

Patricia Williams's analysis of the difference between the words *lex* and *jus* provides a useful starting point for this discussion.[67] Williams observes that lex, the root of the word "legal," refers to society's written laws and codes, such as statutes and judicial decisions. Jus, the root of the word "justice," differs greatly in meaning from lex. Jus embodies the ethical and abstract dimensions of law. These conceptions include rationales for particular rules or punishments (e.g., deterrence). Williams argues that a viable, legitimate, and ethical justice system mandates the existence of both law *and* justice. Williams states, "The word of law . . . is a subcategory of the underlying social motives and beliefs from which it is born. It is the technical embodiment of attempts to order society according to a consensus of ideals. When society loses sight of those ideals and grants obeisance to words alone, law becomes sterile and formalistic; *lex* is applied without *jus* and is therefore unjust. The result is compliance with the letter of the law, but not the spirit."[68] A look at Stand Your Ground through Williams's law versus justice framework indicates that Stand Your Ground is more law than justice. The language of the Stand Your Ground law offers a front narrative. This is what Williams refers to as lex. For instance, when we look at the wording of the Florida statute, there is no indication that the law will favor or disfavor particular victims or defendants. It simply details the state's legal rules for the use of deadly force in self-defense cases. However, as discussed in the previous section, the history, evolution, and rationale of a law tell as much about it as its codified expression. The application of Stand Your Ground law provides a back narrative. This is what Williams refers to as jus. The back narrative reveals the law's ethical dimensions—how it applies in the real world. In the case of Stand Your Ground, the empirical evidence compellingly shows that the law has been applied in a racially skewed manner. Self-defense cases with black victims are much more likely to be found "justifiable force" than self-defense cases with white victims. Furthermore, given the research findings on racial stereotypes and fear of crime, the racially disparate application of Stand Your Ground was predictable. Analyzed together, the front and back narratives of a law allow us to assess whether the arc of a particular law bends toward or away from justice. The background on Florida's Stand Your Ground law, including the rationale behind the law, the push to enact the law, and how the law has been applied, raises a serious question: there is ample evidence that the Stand Your Ground law causes social harm.

The social and racial harm of Stand Your Ground laws reaches beyond the people who are directly harmed—as users or victims of deadly force. A self-defense law that consistently works to the disadvantage of African Americans operates as a kind of legal macroaggression.[69] Macroaggressions are aggravated forms of microaggressions. The term "microaggression" has been used to describe racial assaults that are "subtle, stunning . . . non-verbal . . . 'put-downs' of Blacks by Whites."[70] Macroaggressions are microaggressions that operate on a larger, socio-legal scale. One of the macroaggressions in the Zimmerman case was the fact that the Stand Your Ground law required so little action by law enforcement. After being questioned by police, Zimmerman was allowed to return home the same night he killed Trayvon Martin, with no criminal charges pending against him. Another macroaggression was the fact that it took the special prosecutor more than forty days after Martin's death to arrest and charge Zimmerman with murder. These legal failures were perceived by many people as a racial assault by the justice system. They triggered a groundswell of protests across the country and abroad.[71]

Summary

Florida's Stand Your Ground law has altered the national landscape of self-defense law. In over thirty states, people who believe they have been threatened with force can now stand their ground far beyond their home or place of business. Under the law, a person who uses deadly force in response to a perceived threat is given a presumption of reasonableness. The research on Stand Your Ground clearly demonstrates that the law has a racial impact. A person who uses force to protect herself from someone black is much more likely to be found legally justified than a person who uses force to protect himself from someone white. The bottom line is that under Stand Your Ground black life has less value than white life. In fact, Florida's Stand Your Ground law and its progeny are deeply tied to race, law, and history. A look at the development of firearms legislation shows that a series of laws, during and after slavery, were adopted to keep guns out of the hands of African Americans. These movements are linked to contemporary images that link blackness with crime. Studies indicate that these racialized representations have real-life consequences, making it objectively more likely that someone would shoot a black person than a white person. The Stand Your Ground law supports these race-based fears with its subjective presumption of reasonableness. It does not require consideration of how implicit or unconscious racial bias impacts perceptions of fear. As a result, the law imposes a severe social cost. The law's failure to acknowledge our racial blind spots itself causes harm. For many, Stand Your Ground deepens an already existing distrust of the law. The analysis of Stand Your Ground leads to the conclusion that adherence to the letter of the law, without an eye toward justice, is by its very definition unjust.

Appendix

Florida Stand Your Ground Legislation

Stand Your Ground amended two sections of the Florida Criminal Code, §776.012 and §776.031, and created two new sections, §776.013 and §776.032. These are the core legislative sections of Stand Your Ground law. There are statutes included under the Justifiable Use of Force chapter of the Florida Statutes.

§ 776.012 *Use of force in defense of person.* A person is justified in using force, except deadly force, against another when and to the extent that the person reasonably believes that such conduct is necessary to defend himself or herself or another against the other's imminent use of unlawful force. However, a person is justified in the use of deadly force and does not have a duty to retreat if:

(1) He or she reasonably believes that such force is necessary to prevent imminent death or great bodily harm to himself or herself or another or to prevent the imminent commission of a forcible felony; or
(2) Under those circumstances permitted pursuant to § 776.013.

§ 776.013 Home protection; use of deadly force; presumption of fear of death or great bodily harm.

(1) A person is presumed to have held a reasonable fear of imminent peril of death or great bodily harm to himself or herself or another when using defensive force that is intended or likely to cause death or great bodily harm to another if:
  (a) The person against whom the defensive force was used was in the process of unlawfully and forcefully entering, or had unlawfully and forcibly entered, a dwelling, residence, or occupied vehicle, or if that person had removed or was attempting to remove another against that person's will from the dwelling, residence, or occupied vehicle; and
  (b) The person who uses defensive force knew or had reason to believe that an unlawful and forcible entry or unlawful and forcible act was occurring or had occurred.
(2) The presumption set forth in subsection (1) does not apply if:
  (a) The person against whom the defensive force is used has the right to be in or is a lawful resident of the dwelling, residence, or vehicle, such as an owner, lessee, or titleholder, and there is not an injunction for protection from domestic violence or a written pretrial supervision order of no contact against that person; or
  (b) The person or persons sought to be removed is a child or grandchild, or is otherwise in the lawful custody or under the lawful guardianship of, the person against whom the defensive force is used; or

(c) The person who uses defensive force is engaged in an unlawful activity or is using the dwelling, residence, or occupied vehicle to further an unlawful activity; or

(d) The person against whom the defensive force is used is a law enforcement officer, as defined in s. 943.10(14), who enters or attempts to enter a dwelling, residence, or vehicle in the performance of his or her official duties and the officer identified himself or herself in accordance with any applicable law or the person using force knew or reasonably should have known that the person entering or attempting to enter was a law enforcement officer.

(3) A person who is not engaged in an unlawful activity and who is attacked in any other place where he or she has a right to be has no duty to retreat and has the right to stand his or her ground and meet force with force, including deadly force if he or she reasonably believes it is necessary to do so to prevent death or great bodily harm to himself or herself or another or to prevent the commission of a forcible felony.

(4) A person who unlawfully and by force enters or attempts to enter a person's dwelling, residence, or occupied vehicle is presumed to be doing so with the intent to commit an unlawful act involving force or violence.

(5) As used in this section, the term:

(a) "Dwelling" means a building or conveyance of any kind, including any attached porch, whether the building or conveyance is temporary or permanent, mobile or immobile, which has a roof over it, including a tent, and is designed to be occupied by people lodging therein at night.

(b) "Residence" means a dwelling in which a person resides either temporarily or permanently or is visiting as an invited guest.

(c) "Vehicle" means a conveyance of any kind, whether or not motorized, which is designed to transport people or property.

§ 776.031 Use of force in defense of others.
A person is justified in the use of force, except deadly force, against another when and to the extent that the person reasonably believes that such conduct is necessary to prevent or terminate the other's trespass

on, or other tortious or criminal interference with, either real property other than a dwelling or personal property, lawfully in his or her possession or in the possession of another who is a member of his or her immediate family or household or of a person whose property he or she has a legal duty to protect. However, the person is justified in the use of deadly force only if he or she reasonably believes that such force is necessary to prevent the imminent commission of a forcible felony. A person does not have a duty to retreat if the person is in a place where he or she has a right to be.

§ 776.032 Immunity from criminal prosecution and civil action for justifiable use of force.

(1) A person who uses force as permitted in § 776.012, § 776.013, or § 776.031 is justified in using such force and is immune from criminal prosecution and civil action for the use of such force, unless the person against whom force was used is a law enforcement officer, as defined in § 943.10(14), who was acting in the performance of his or her official duties and the officer identified himself or herself in accordance with any applicable law or the person using force knew or reasonably should have known that the person was a law enforcement officer. As used in this subsection, the term "criminal prosecution" includes arresting, detaining in custody, and charging or prosecuting the defendant.

(2) A law enforcement agency may use standard procedures for investigating the use of force as described in subsection (1), but the agency may not arrest the person for using force unless it determines that there is probable cause that the force that was used was unlawful.

(3) The court shall award reasonable attorney's fees, court costs, compensation for loss of income, and all expenses incurred by the defendant in defense of any civil action brought by a plaintiff if the court finds that the defendant is immune from prosecution as provided in subsection (1).

NOTES

1. Obasogie 2013.
2. O'Mara 2014.
3. Circuit Judge Debra Nelson's jury instructions included the following language: "If George Zimmerman was not engaged in an unlawful activity and was attacked in any place where he had a right to be, he had no duty to retreat and had the right to stand his ground and meet force with force, including deadly force if he reasonably believed that it was necessary to do so to prevent death or great bodily harm to himself or another or to prevent the commission of a forcible felony." http://media.cmgdigital .com/shared/news/documents/2013/07/12/Zimmerman_Final_Jury_Instructions.pdf.
4. One of the jurors stated that the jury acquitted Zimmerman based on the trial evidence and "because of the heat of the moment and the Stand Your Ground." See Caputo 2013.
5. Sullivan 2013.
6. Zbrzeznj 2012.
7. Beale 1903, 568, 574.
8. Bobo 2008.
9. Ibid., 343.
10. *Erwin v. State*, 29 Ohio St. 185, 199–200 (1876).
11. *Beard v. U.S.*, 158 U.S. 550, 564 (1895).
12. *People v. Tomlins*, 107 NE 496 (1914).
13. Catalfamo 2007.
14. Lave 2013, 832.
15. Fla. Stat. §776.012 (2004).
16. Ibid.
17. Catalfamo 2007, 512.
18. Zbrzeznj 2012, 241.
19. Catalfamo 2007, 511–23; National Black Law Students Association Judicial Advocacy Team 2012.
20. Zbrzeznj 2012, 245–47.
21. Lave 2013, 836.
22. Montgomery 2012.
23. Ibid.
24. Roig-Franzia 2012.
25. Lave 2013, 837–38.
26. Goodman 2005.
27. Block 2012; Israel 2012.
28. Goodman 2005.
29. Flatow 2013.
30. Fla. Stat. § 776.013(3).
31. Jansen and Nugent-Borakove 2007, 5.
32. Ibid.; Sullivan 2013, 4.
33. Lave 2013, 834.

34. Zbrzeznj 2012, 254–55.

35. Ibid.; Jansen and Nugent-Borakove 2007, 7.

36. Fla. Stat. § 776.013(1)(a).

37. Fla. Stat. § 776.032.

38. Fisher and Eggen 2012.

39. Davis 2014.

40. Hundley, Martin, and Humburg 2012.

41. Strupp 2014.

42. Obasogie 2013.

43. Task Force on Citizen Safety and Protection 2013, 5–8.

44. Ibid., 33–41.

45. Fisher and Eggen 2012.

46. Jansen and Nugent-Borakove 2007.

47. Roman 2013.

48. These findings are similar to those reported in Table 5.1, with one notable difference. In Table 5.1 the number of fatalities involving a black accuser and white victim (seven) is the same as the number for fatalities involving a white accuser and black victim. What is different is the number of cases where the shooting was deemed a justifiable use of force.

49. Roman 2013, 6.

50. McClellan and Tekin 2012.

51. Hoekstra and Cheng 2012.

52. Winkler 2013.

53. Cobb 2013.

54. Russell-Brown 2009, 40–41.

55. Russell 1913. Some commentators have addressed the link between slave patrols and neighborhood watch programs. See, e.g., Asim 2014; Hartmann 2013.

56. Cottrol 1994, 344–45.

57. Emberton 2013.

58. National Rifle Association, http://www.nrahq.org/history.asp.

59. Winkler 2013.

60. Russell-Brown 2009, 14.

61. Lee 2013.

62. Eberhardt et al., 2004.

63. Richardson and Goff 2012, 295.

64. Armour 1994.

65. Richardson and Goff 2012, 325–26.

66. Mauer 2006; Alexander 2010.

67. Williams 1987.

68. Ibid., 132–33.

69. Russell-Brown 2009.

70. Ibid., 25; Vega 2014.

71. Lawson 2013.

REFERENCES

Alexander, M. 2010. *The New Jim Crow: Mass Incarceration in the Age of Colorblindness*. New York: New Press.

Armour, Jody. 1994. "Race Ipsa Loquitor: Of Reasonable Racists, Intelligent Bayesians, and Involuntary Negrophobes." *Stanford Law Review* 46:781.

Asim, Jabari. 2014. "Shooting Negroes." *Crisis Magazine*, 12–21.

Beale, Joseph. 1903. "Retreat from a Murderous Assault." *Harvard Law Review* 16 (8): 568.

Beard v. United States, 158 U.S. 550 (1895).

Block, Melissa. 2012. "A History of 'Stand Your Ground' Law in Florida" (interview with David Ovalle). National Public Radio, March 20, 2012.

Bobo, Jason. 2008. "Following the Trend: Alabama Abandons the Duty to Retreat and Encourages Citizens to Stand Their Ground." *Cumberland Law Review* 38:339.

Brown v. United States, 256 U.S. 335 (1921).

Caputo, Marc. 2013. "Juror: We Talked Stand Your Ground Before Not-Guilty Verdict." *Miami Herald*, July 18.

Catalfamo, Christine. 2007. "Stand Your Ground: Florida's Castle Doctrine for the Twenty-First Century." *Rutgers Journal of Law and Public Policy* 4:504.

Cobb, Jelani. 2013. "Perceived Threats." *New Yorker*, July 29.

Cottrol, Robert, ed. 1994. *Gun Control and the Constitution: Sources and Explorations on the Second Amendment*. New York: Routledge.

Davis, Chris. 2014. "Florida's Stand Your Ground Law." *Tampa Bay Times*. http://www .tampabay.com/stand-your-ground-law.

Eberhardt, Jennifer, Phillip Attiba Goff, Valerie Purdie, and Paul Davies. 2004. "Seeing Black: Race, Crime and Visual Processing." *Journal of Personality and Social Psychology* 87 (6): 876–93.

Emberton, Carole. 2013. *Beyond Redemption: Race, Violence and the American South after the Civil War*. Chicago: University of Chicago Press.

Erwin v. State, 29 Ohio St. 185 (1876).

Fisher, Marc, and Dan Eggen. 2012. "Stand Your Ground Laws Coincide with Jump in Justifiable-Homicide Cases." *Washington Post*, April 7.

Flatow, Nicole. 2013. "Former Florida Senator: I Regret My Vote for Stand Your Ground More Than Any Other." ThinkProgress, July 31, 2013. http://thinkprogress .org/justice/2013/07/31/2389171/florida-legislators-passed-stand-your-ground -amidst-confusion-about-scope-of-the-law.

Goodman, Amy. 2005. "Florida Lawmakers Expand Law to Kill in Self Defense" (interview with Marion Hammer and Arthur Hayhoe). Democracy Now, April 5. http://www.democracynow.org/2005/4/6/florida_lawmakers_expand_law_to_ kill.

Hartmann, Thom. 2013. "Zimmerman Verdict: The Slave Patrol Is Alive and Well in Florida." *Daily Take*, July 15. http://www.truth-out.org/opinion/item/17573 -zimmerman-verdict-the-slave-patrol-is-alive-and-well-in-florida#.

Hoekstra, Mark, and Cheng Cheng. 2012. "Does Strengthening Self-Defense Law Deter

Crime or Escalate Violence? Evidence from Expansions to Castle Doctrine." *Journal of Human Resources* 48 (3): 821–54.

Hundley, Kris, Susan Martin, and Connie Humburg. 2012. "Florida 'Stand Your Ground' Law Yields Some Shocking Outcomes Depending on How Law Is Applied." *Tampa Bay Times*, June 1. http://www.tampabay.com/news/publicsafety/crime/florida-stand-your-ground-law-yields-some-shocking-outcomes-depending-on/1233133.

Israel, Josh. 2012. "Opponents of Florida's 'Stand Your Ground' Law Predicted 'Racially Motivated Killings.'" DemocraticUnderground, March 23. http://www.democratic underground.com/1002459977.

Jansen, Steven, and M. Elaine Nugent-Borakove. 2007. "Expansions to the Castle Doctrine: Implications for Policy and Practice." Alexandria, VA: National District Attorneys Association.

Jonsson, Patrik. 2013. "Racial Bias and 'Stand Your Ground' Laws: What the Data Show." *Christian Science Monitor*, August 6.

Lave, Tamara Rice. 2013. "Shoot to Kill: A Critical Look at Stand Your Ground Laws." *University of Miami Law Review* 67:827.

Lawson, Tamara. 2013. "A Fresh Cut in an Old Wound—A Critical Analysis of the Trayvon Martin Killing." *University of Florida Journal of Law and Public Policy* 23:271.

Lee, Cynthia. 2013. "Making Race Salient: Trayvon Martin and Implicit Bias in a Not Yet Post-Racial Society." *North Carolina Law Review* 91:1555.

Mauer, M. 2006. *Race to Incarcerate*. New York: New Press.

McClellan, Chandler, and Erdal Tekin. 2012. "Stand Your Ground Laws and Homicides." Discussion Paper 6705, July. Bonn: Institute for the Study of Labor.

Montgomery, Ben. 2012. "Florida's 'Stand Your Ground' Law Was Born of 2004 Case, but Story Has Been Distorted." *Tampa Bay Times*, April 14.

National Black Law Students Association Judicial Advocacy Team. 2012. "'Stand Your Ground': History, Development, and Significance of the Trayvon Martin Case." White paper, September 20. http://nblsa.org/wp-content/uploads/2014/06/NBLSA_Stand_Your_Ground_White_Paper.pdf.

Obasogie, Osagie. 2013. "Foreword: Critical Race Theory and Empirical Methods." *UC Irvine Law Review* 3:183.

O'Mara, Mark. 2014. "It's Not about 'Stand Your Ground' It's about Race." CNN Opinion, February 19.

People v. Tomlins, 107 N.E. 496 (1914).

Richardson, L. Song, and Phillip Attiba Goff. 2012. "Self Defense and the Suspicion Heuristic." *Iowa Law Review* 98:293.

Roig-Franzia, Manuel. 2012. "Fla. Gun Law to Expand Leeway for Self-Defense." *Washington Post*, April 26.

Roman, John. 2013. "Race, Justifiable Homicide, and Stand Your Ground Laws: Analysis of FBI Supplementary Homicide Report Data." Washington, DC: Urban Institute.

Russell, John Henderson. 1913. *The Free Negro in Virginia: 1619–1865*. Baltimore: Johns Hopkins University Press.

Russell-Brown, Katheryn. 2009. *The Color of Crime*. New York: New York University Press.

Strupp, Joe. 2014. "Florida Journalists: Stand Your Ground Changes Will Hurt Reporting." Media Matters for America Blog, March 21. http://mediamatters.org/blog/2014/03/21/florida-journalists-stand-your-ground-changes-w/198563.

Sullivan, Ronald. 2013. "Stand Your Ground Laws: Civil Rights and Public Safety Implications of the Expanded Use of Deadly Force." October 29. Testimony prepared for the Committee of the Judiciary, Subcommittee on the Constitution, Civil Rights, and Human Rights, U.S. Senate.

Task Force on Citizen Safety and Protection. 2013. "Report of the Governor's Task Force on Citizen Safety and Protection." February 21. http://www.flgov.com/wp-content/uploads/2013/02/Citizen-Safety-and-Protection-Task-Force-Report-FINAL.pdf.

Tennessee v. Garner, 471 U.S. 1 (1985).

Vega, Tanzina. 2014. "Students See Many Slights as Racial 'Microaggressions.'" *New York Times*, March 21.

Williams, Patricia. 1987. "Spirit-Murdering the Messenger: The Discourse of Finger-pointing as the Law's Response to Racism." *University of Miami Law Review* 42:127.

Winkler, Adam. 2013. "Gun Control Is 'Racist'? The NRA Would Know." *New Republic*, February 4.

Zbrzeznj, Lydia. 2012. "Florida's Controversial Gun Policy: Liberally Permitting Citizens to Arm Themselves and Broadly Recognizing the Right to Act in Self-Defense." *Florida Coastal Law Review* 13:231.

6

The Dangers of Racialized Perceptions and Thinking by Law Enforcement

DAVID A. HARRIS

At the intersection of race and criminal justice, the trial of George Zimmerman for killing seventeen-year-old Trayvon Martin became the most widely discussed case of 2013. Trayvon Martin left his father's house in a gated Florida community to walk to a nearby convenience store.[1] As he returned home with candy and a container of iced tea, he encountered Zimmerman, another resident of the community who, that night, carried a gun. Zimmerman had unfulfilled ambitions to become a police officer; on that night he patrolled as a member of a volunteer neighborhood watch group. Zimmerman suspected Martin, a young black male in a hooded sweatshirt, of criminal activity. He alerted police via a 911 call; the operator said the police would respond and instructed Zimmerman to remain in his vehicle. Zimmerman disobeyed these instruction and confronted Martin. Accounts of what happened next vary, but afterward Martin lay dead, shot by Zimmerman.

The trial of Zimmerman focused increased attention on Florida's Stand Your Ground (SYG) law, which allows a person to use deadly force in any public place in which that person is lawfully present, when the person reasonably believes that deadly force is necessary to defend against a threat of death or grave injury.[2] The SYG law had already achieved great notoriety both inside and outside of Florida before the Zimmerman case.[3] But the death of Martin—a young African American man—at the hands of Zimmerman seemed to bring out racialized perceptions and reasoning at every step. Public debate centered on questions of racial profiling, and the threat posed by an unknown young black man (as opposed to how people would have perceived an unknown young white man).[4] Largely unnoticed in this discussion was the question of how implicit racial perceptions and biases may have affected not just the actions of Zimmerman, but also the actions of law enforcement. In the initial phase of the case, prior to any national media exposure, police in Sanford, the small town in which the shooting took place, did not arrest Zimmerman, saying that the SYG law prohibited this.[5] Amid charges that the police may not have investigated fully or fairly, the authorities brought in a special prosecutor from outside the county, to renew the investigation and make charging decisions.[6]

The trial that followed resulted in the acquittal of Zimmerman, ending the case.[7] But it left unresolved the questions that this chapter will explore: How do SYG laws contribute to the racialization of perception and thinking by law enforcement? What negative effects occur in the criminal justice system because of how SYG laws interact with race? And how might unconscious bias play a role in these issues?

What we know now about SYG laws, nearly ten years after Florida created the first one, should give us pause. The empirical evidence that has emerged over the past several years shows that Florida's SYG law, and similar laws enacted in most states across the United States, have serious flaws. At best, these laws do not accomplish what proponents promised. At worst, they may increase deadly violence, with a distinct racial inflection.

Beyond these deficiencies, SYG laws also expose and underline the importance of implicit bias: racial biases that operate unconsciously in everyone. In fact, SYG laws may allow these biases to operate freely; policing and law enforcement decisions may become racialized. Assumptions about race and criminality may lead officers into mistakes with consequential negative impacts by skewing officers' views about the actions and intentions of people they encounter because of those citizen's racial or ethnic characteristics. When influenced by implicit bias, law enforcement perceptions of the potential culpability of individual people can cause officers to focus on the wrong people, and to take actions they might not otherwise.

As deeply entrenched as this problem may seem, solutions do exist. As Cynthia Lee's work teaches, instead of acting as if police (or anyone else, for that matter) could become blind to race or ethnicity, the racial aspects of these situations need to be discussed openly and acknowledged.[8] This will present a challenge to law enforcement, but with the

United States becoming more demographically diverse every year,[9] police effectiveness and public safety depends upon it.

What SYG Laws Say and What We Know about How They Function

Modern SYG laws appeared in the American legal system only recently. They come against the background of centuries of Anglo-American law on homicide and self-defense. The law of homicide prohibits the unlawful killings of human beings; it seeks to prevent death and to avoid bloodshed. The law has never obligated an innocent person under deadly attack to simply endure violence without striking back, however. A person suffering unlawful aggression has the right to self-defense: she may respond to force with the amount of force necessary to protect herself. If under attack with deadly force, she may respond in kind.[10] A killing in which the innocent person under attack kills her attacker constitutes a homicide, but an excused one, as long as the survivor had a reasonable belief that her life was in imminent danger.[11]

Self-defense law has always contained an important caveat. If the person under attack *knows* that she can avoid the danger to herself by retreating—*escaping in complete safety, without risking further danger to herself*—she must retreat.[12] The "rule of retreat" served the same interest as the law against homicide: avoid unnecessary bloodshed or death—even the death of the unjustified attacker—unless there was no way to escape the attacker's aggression. Preservation of human life remained the ultimate goal, even in a situation of justified self-defense. The rule of retreat applied everywhere, *except the home of the person under attack.* This exception to the rule of retreat, known as the Castle Doctrine,[13] made sense: the home served as the ultimate place of safety. Thus a victim of aggression did not have to attempt to retreat from the attacker in her own home; she could stand and fight.

SYG laws make a fundamental change in homicide and self-defense law: they abolish the rule of retreat. SYG laws abolish the rule of retreat *in any place the person defending herself has a right to be.* Put another way, SYG laws apply the no retreat rule that has always applied in the home to any public place. The person under unjustified attack need not retreat from the aggressor, even if she *knows* that she can escape in complete safety; she can stand her ground and use deadly force if she faces deadly force. In a self-defense case arising in a state with an SYG law, the person who kills her attacker would not have to prove that she had no means of escaping the deadly force of the attacker. Instead, she need only prove that she had a reasonable fear of death or deadly injury, and that she killed in a place in which she had a right to be.

In Florida's SYG statute, this core idea appears front and center: a person with a reasonable fear of deadly force can use deadly force without having to retreat in any place the person has a right to be.[14] The law goes further: it grants criminal and civil immunity to the person claiming an SYG defense. When the facts reveal an SYG situation—i.e., one person who killed another makes a reasonable claim that she did so in self-defense—police may not arrest, detain, charge, or prosecute the person. Police and prosecutors may investigate the killing using "standard procedures," but they cannot arrest the person unless the law enforcement agency "determines that there is probable cause that the force that was used was unlawful."[15] Should the police or prosecutors choose to pursue charges anyway, the person is entitled to a pretrial hearing in which a judge decides whether the defendant should have received SYG immunity.[16]

Florida's enactment of the first SYG law, in 2005, led to a wave of change across the United States. According to professor Tamara Lawson of St. Thomas University School of Law, as of 2014, thirty-four states had SYG provisions that allowed any innocent person under attack to use deadly force in public, with no duty to retreat. Nine of the thirty-four states have SYG provisions created by court decisions, not legislation.[17] (These numbers do not include states that have a no retreat rule only for the home; as explained above, virtually all states have always had this traditional rule.)

Viewing SYG laws in the abstract, one might make some predictions about how these statutes would work in practice. SYG laws lower the potential costs and consequences of using deadly violence in self-defense; economists would likely predict that this lower cost should lead more people to use deadly force in self-defense. But proponents of SYG laws did not expect this, at least according to their statements advocating for new SYG laws. First, proponents said, crime would decrease, especially the most violent crime, and especially homicides, because criminals would know that law-abiding citizens would have greater freedom to use deadly force when threatened. Advocates also said that SYG laws like Florida's would protect good citizens by creating immunity from the flood of civil lawsuits brought by felons shot by citizens defending themselves. The net effect would be *not more, but less* crime and deadly violence, especially killings, and much less frivolous legal action by criminals who belonged in jail.[18]

Of course, forces other than these arguments by vocal proponents may also explain the passage of SYG laws. While no evidence exists of a racialized *purpose* for SYG laws, racialized fears of crime may have promoted passage of them. For some years, researchers have known that fear of crime by white people may have much to do with fear of black people generally. According to Ashley Kuhn and Jodi Lane of the University of Florida, there exists "an association between ethnocentric attitudes and fear of crime, where negative attitudes about people of other races in one's community are associated with more fear. . . . In urban environments, whites and minorities assumed that criminals were young minority males. . . . Women, regardless of race, saw young minority males as 'a dangerous class.'"[19] Similarly, Professor Wesley Skogan of Northwestern University has said that both prejudice against and residential proximity to blacks correlate with fear of crime in whites.[20] Thus even with no explicit causal connection, the existence of racialized fears of crime would make passing SYG laws easier.

SYG laws began to appear in 2005, starting with Florida's law. With the passage of almost ten years, researchers now have some data they can use to study the laws' effects. The first empirical evaluations cast doubt on the assumptions of SYG advocates. (As for the prevention of frivolous lawsuits, there seems to have been little evidence of the alleged torrent of legal actions in the first place; researchers have not pursued the subject.)

The first thing researchers have tested empirically focuses on the central promise of the SYG laws: that the right to use deadly force without retreat outside the home will make us safer from serious crime, especially homicide. In their article "Does Strengthening Self-Defense Law Deter Crime or Escalate Violence? Evidence from Expansions to Castle Doctrine,"[21] Texas A&M University researchers Cheng Cheng and Mark Hoekstra tested these assertions. They examined data on crime and homicide patterns from 2000 to 2010. They utilized data from states that passed an SYG law in that period, and compared violent crimes and homicides before and after passage of the SYG laws. In addition, they used data from other states that did not pass SYG laws during the same period. From these data, Cheng and Hoekstra made comparisons of SYG states and non-SYG states, both before and after passage of these laws in the states that passed them; they also compared states in the same geographic regions. The results did not support the arguments of the proponents of SYG laws. As for violent crimes—defined in the study to include burglary, robbery, and aggravated assault—Cheng and Hoekstra found that SYG laws did not deter these crimes. They report that "we find no evidence of deterrence effects" for any of these crimes.[22] But they did find one very noticeable change. In SYG states, they saw more homicides—defined in the study as murders and non-negligent manslaughters—*after* the passage of these laws. SYG laws, they said, "increase homicides by a statistically significant 8 percent," which means an additional six hundred homicides per year across all states that have enacted SYG laws. The direction of the effect should surprise anyone who agreed with the idea that SYG laws would make us safer; the strength of the effect—a full 8 percent—should alarm anyone who values the sanctity of life.

As with any good science, we look for whether other researchers can replicate the results of studies—especially early ones. Cheng and Hoekstra's results find support in another 2012 paper, by Chandler McClellan and Erdal Tekin of Georgia State University.[23] Using a different data source and a different methodology than Cheng and Hoekstra, McClellan and Tekin report similar results: "Stand Your Ground laws are associated with a significant increase in homicides." They say their results "are robust to a number of specifications and unlikely to be driven entirely by the killings of assailants."[24] The results obtained by McClellan and Tekin bear strong resemblance to those of Cheng and Hoekstra: "our findings raise serious doubts against the argument that Stand Your Ground laws make America safer."[25]

Beyond this evidence of foundational problems, empirical work on SYG laws now reveals that they have a disparate racial impact. In his study "Race, Justifiable Homicide, and Stand Your Ground Laws: Analysis of FBI Supplementary Homicide Report Data,"[26] John Roman of the Justice Policy Center of the Urban Institute examined SYG data to determine whether "justifiable homicides differ by the race of the victim and offender" and whether certain "fact patterns of homicides increase racial disparities." Roman aimed to "analyze objective national data that could measure the presence of racial disparities in rulings of justifiable homicides."[27] Roman's analysis shows, first, that states with SYG laws "have statistically significantly higher rates of justifiable homicide than non-SYG states."[28] Introducing race into the analysis produces startling results. Roman writes that "controlling for all other attributes, the odds a white on black homicide is found justified is 281 percent greater than the odds a white on black homicide is found justified."[29] And for cases that exhibit particular facts, SYG laws "worsen the disparity." Specifically, in cases that feature (1) a single victim, (2) a single shooter, (3) a male victim and a male shooter, (4) a victim and a shooter who are strangers to each other, and (5) the use of a gun, the presence of an SYG law increases the disparities between cases in which a white kills a black victim, and cases in which a black kills a white victim.

Thus the fears of those who believe that SYG laws have increased deadly violence seem justified by the empirical evidence. Perhaps more disturbing, SYG laws seem to have a disparate racial impact. If racial effects creep into the actions of those who defend themselves under SYG laws, we need to ask whether we might also see racial effects on police behavior.

Unconscious Bias in Policing and Law Enforcement: How It Operates and Its Impact

Racial bias in policing and law enforcement can have a significant impact on the actions police take: on which people end up on the receiving end of those actions, and on what those actions are. But before taking on the question of what impact the racialization of police actions might have, we must first understand where and how it arises.

Even in today's world, discussion of racial bias in an institution, or an allegation that a particular person has engaged in racist behavior, prompts us to look for a specific type of racist conduct or speech. We look for people who use racial epithets when they speak. Or perhaps we think of people who insists, "I'm not prejudiced, but everyone knows it's just a fact that _____ (fill in the name of a racial or ethnic group under discussion) are responsible for most of the _____ (add social problem of choice)."

Certainly, some people hold these beliefs and attitudes, and in some contexts they may even predominate. But the problem of racialized attitudes in just about every sector of American society, including law enforcement, is actually both larger and far more subtle. The racism we see today in our society, and in turn in our law enforcement agencies, almost never manifests itself in old-school, blatant bigotry. Rather, what we see is unconscious racism: in the words of the psychology literature, implicit bias. The great majority of Americans, both inside and outside law enforcement, hold conscious beliefs that prize equality and fairness. According to these beliefs, we should treat everyone equally, because all people deserve justice and fair dealing from others and from their government. But empirical studies have uncovered something different. It turns out that almost every person possess an intricate web of unconscious biases in favor of particular groups and against others. These biases may sit in direct opposition to our conscious egalitarian beliefs. Although we have no awareness that these implicit biases exist and operate within us, they can actually override our conscious beliefs about race. This may cause us to act in ways we might not otherwise toward minorities, without any idea that this is happening.

The best-known evidence of implicit bias comes from the implicit association test, or IAT, a test anyone can take online.[30] The IAT measures our mental associations between racially identifiable words or partial photographs of faces (the lowest part of the forehead, the eyes, the nose, and the space between the nose and mouth), and positive or negative words. The viewer sits at a computer and hits a key to associate a white face with a positive word (e.g., good, flower, smile) or a black face with a negative word (bad, hostile, fight). In the next part of the test, the instructions are reversed: the viewer must hit the key when she sees a white face with a negative word, or a black face with a positive word. As the viewer does the task, the computer measures the speed with which the viewer hits the key, down to tiny fractions of seconds. The computer then compares the reaction speed of the viewer to tasks congruent with stereotypes (associating white names or faces with positive words, or associating black names or faces with negative words) with the reaction speed for tasks *not* congruent with stereotypes (associating black names or faces with positive words, or associating white names or faces with negative words). The results often shock those who believe that they possess strictly egalitarian values. Almost always, people respond more quickly to stereotype-congruent tasks than stereotype-noncongruent tasks. Viewers make more rapid choices when associating white faces with positive words than negative words; they also respond faster when associating black faces with negative words than positive ones. Most people find it measurably more difficult (i.e., react more slowly) to associate black faces and positive words than to associate white faces and positive words; they have less difficulty (i.e., react more quickly) associating black faces with negative ideas than white faces with positive ideas. The researchers called these differences in associative capacities implicit biases, and they have found these biases in favor of whites in 75 percent of all of the fourteen million persons who had taken the test through 2013,[31] *including almost 40 percent of black test takers.*[32] All of those who showed implicit bias for whites and against blacks carry a set of racial biases that may impact their thoughts and actions, and these biases remain hidden, even from them.

It is when implicit biases combine with heuristics in our unconscious thinking that race-infected thinking and action can occur. Nobel Prize–winning psychologists Amos Tversky and Daniel Kahneman have described heuristics as rules of thumb that allow human beings to transform complicated, difficult decisions into much easier, almost automatic evaluations of information.[33] People use heuristics unconsciously and rapidly; they constitute fast and efficient ways of thinking. Using heuristics often gets things right; they are "frequently accurate" and achieve these results without using "valuable cognitive resources."[34] But because people resort to heuristics when faced with difficult judgments and a lack of time to gather information, they also "produce systemic errors of judgment that predictably recur in certain situations."[35] Psychologists call these heuristic-based errors of judgment *biases.* Furthermore, people usually do not consciously control these heuristic-based processes; indeed, they do not even know they are at work.[36] Our conscious minds and beliefs *can* override these rapid solutions; nevertheless, we usually adopt them unquestioningly, without even knowing they are there. This makes heuristic-based errors "difficult to eliminate or even recognize."[37] Human beings can live with some of this; indeed, they need it in order to survive, because of the immense drain on cognitive resources it would take to fully consider each decision. But when these heuristics concern race and suspicion of criminality or violence, dangerously negative results can follow.

The evidence of implicit biases linking blacks with negative concepts in the minds of the great majority of people gives rise to a particular heuristic: it associates blacks with crime and danger. The psychologist Phillip Atiba Goff and co-author L. Song Richardson call the rule of thumb that associates blacks with crime and danger "the suspicion heuristic."[38] Any person in a situation of uncertainty will have difficulty predicting when he or she might face the danger of a violent crime, especially so when encountering a stranger. Walking down a city street at night toward an unknown person allows precious little time to gather and process facts or evidence. To cope with this situation, people "will make their judgments of [potential] criminality quickly, based on small slices of behavior, under highly stressful circumstances."[39] The suspicion heuristic comes into play immediately and unconsciously; implicit negative associations with blacks swing into action. This dovetails with considerable research that shows that our society equates blacks with violent street crime; our mental images—what we might call stereotypes—feature blacks as criminal thugs engaged in crime.[40] For example, the work of Birt Duncan showed that mildly aggressive behavior performed by an African American person is seen as more threatening than the identical behavior performed by whites.[41] Research by H. Andrew Sagar and Janet Ward Schofield of the University of Pittsburgh reinforced Duncan's findings.[42] Sagar and Schofield presented subjects with drawings and verbal accounts of two-person interactions—for example, two boys bumping into each other. The subjects perceived the actor as meaner and more threatening if the actor was portrayed as African American than if the actor was portrayed as white. And this perception held true for both African American and white subjects in the study.

This produces predictable results. The suspicion heuristic biases the judgments people make when they encounter blacks, without the individuals knowing that this is happening, and even if they hold conscious egalitarian beliefs. Whites, and even some blacks, will tend to think black people they encounter are potential criminals who pose a danger.

Worse, the unconscious use of the suspicion heuristic can lead beyond thoughts, to actions. According to Goff and Richardson, the suspicion heuristic can "influence behaviors as well" as perceptions, and "can result in people acting more aggressively than they might otherwise," all "without any conscious awareness that one is behaving this way."[43]

It is hard to overstate the combined potential impact of implicit bias against blacks and the suspicion heuristic on the use of SYG laws. The mere existence of SYG laws lowers the potential cost of engaging in deadly violence; one can use deadly force in any public place, even when avoiding violence is possible, and still use the SYG defense to argue that the jury should not convict. Implicit bias against blacks, especially the aspect of seeing blacks not just negatively but also as likely to be violent or dangerous, increases the likelihood that people with weapons will shoot them; the armed parties are just more likely to feel fear, and therefore to shoot. And when the victim is black, members of juries—also infected with the same implicit bias—are more likely to understand and sympathize with the shooter, because they will more likely feel that the (black) victim posed a real danger.

The Consequences: How Police and the Public May Pay a Price for Unconscious Racial Bias

Unconscious racial bias in law enforcement can play out in many ways. In the Trayvon Martin case, beyond the effects that race may have had on the jury's verdict and public perception and reaction to the case, racial stereotypes and implicit biases may have seeped into the investigative process, and into the charging decision that initially allowed George Zimmerman to walk away without charges. We have other examples of how racialized unconscious bias may enter into law enforcement decision making. And when this happens, the consequences can be strongly negative—even deadly. Thus we might expect implicit bias to affect the work of police and prosecutors under an SYG law.

Police training always includes the handling, use, and deployment of firearms. This training usually includes instruction on when officers may properly resort to the use of deadly force. This decision to shoot, which may occur in a split second, can have life-and-death consequences, and introducing racialized police thinking into the mix can have catastrophic results. Thus researchers have tried to understand whether race plays any role in decision making on whether or not to shoot at a suspect.

Social psychologist Joshua Correll has played a leading role in this field of study. In "The Police Officer's Dilemma: Using Ethnicity to Disambiguate Potentially Threatening Individuals,"[44] Correll and his colleagues showed subjects a "simplistic videogame" in which they would see a man, either black or white, in a public place. The man would be holding an object: sometimes a gun, or sometimes an innocuous item such as a cell phone, wallet, or soda can. Participants were told to shoot or not shoot by pressing individual buttons, and researchers measured their accuracy (did the subject shoot an armed or unarmed man?) and their response speed. The results: "Both in speed and accuracy, the decision to fire on an *armed* target was facilitated when that target was African American, whereas the decision not to shoot an *unarmed* target was facilitated when that target was white."[45] Correll and his colleagues called this the Shooter Bias, and they noted that their results squared with those of other researchers. They explained that the Shooter Bias occurs because "a target's ethnicity, though technically irrelevant to the decision task at hand, somehow interferes with participants' ability to react appropriately to the object in the target's hand."[46] According to the authors, "The decision to shoot may be influenced by a target person's ethnicity. . . . Participants showed a bias to shoot African American targets more rapidly and/or more frequently than White targets. The implications of this bias are clear and disturbing. Even more worrisome is the suggestion that mere knowledge of the cultural stereotype, which depicts African Americans as violent, may produce Shooter Bias, and that even African Americans demonstrate the bias."[47] The authors also point out that the Shooter Bias "does not seem to simply reflect [overt] prejudice toward African Americans, and there is reason to believe the effect is present simply as a function of stereotypic associations that exist in our culture."[48]

In a follow-up paper, titled "Across the Thin Blue Line: Police Officers and Racial Bias in the Decision to Shoot,"[49] Correll and his colleagues tested ideomotor effects: situations in which implicit associations influence behavior, without any awareness by the subjects. (Richardson and Goff say that this influence of implicit associations on behavior

"happens either too quickly to be controlled," or is "motivated by unconscious processes.")[50] Might ideomotor effects influence police officers'
decisions on whether to shoot or not? Correll et al. presented both civilians and police officers with visual scenarios: photographs, each showing one man, either black or white (evenly divided in the sample), in
realistic poses in public places (parks, shopping malls, and the like) with
an object in hand. The object varied: sometimes the person had a gun,
sometimes a cell phone or a wallet. The researchers asked the civilian
and police officer subjects to use two buttons connected to a computer
system—one labeled "shoot" and the other "don't shoot"—when they
decided whether or not to "fire" based on what they saw. This allowed
testing of two possibilities. First, the civilian and police officer subjects
might shoot more unarmed black suspects than unarmed white suspects. Second, the subjects could just be faster to shoot armed black
suspect than armed white suspects.

The results of the experiment revealed that racial bias does, in fact,
creep into the crucial shoot/don't shoot decision. The responses of
both civilian and police officer subjects indicated a similar level of bias
regarding the speed of decision making. Both civilian and police officer subjects made accurate decisions to shoot more quickly when they
faced armed black suspects than when they faced armed white suspects.
But a difference emerged between police and civilians with regard to
the accuracy of those decisions. With a white target holding the object,
civilians were less accurate than police in deciding whether or not to
shoot. In the words of Correll and colleagues, the police were "less 'trigger happy'" than civilians.[51]

The research of Correll and his colleagues has profound implications.
First, more unarmed blacks will die in confrontations with police than
unarmed whites, because blacks would be perceived as more dangerous and crime prone than whites. But, just as importantly, civilian and
police officer subjects shot armed black suspects more quickly than they
shot armed white suspects. That is, both the civilian and police officer subjects perceived danger more quickly with the armed blacks than
the armed whites. This may mean a gain in officer safety in situations
involving black armed suspects. But we should not ignore the lurking negative trade-off. Since they were slower to shoot at armed white
suspects, evidently because they did not perceive danger from them as

quickly, police officers could face greater danger from armed whites. This underestimation of danger from whites—perhaps a slower perception of danger from whites puts it more accurately—means that armed white suspects would have a greater opportunity to kill or injure.

The research by Correll and his colleagues may also help to answer a related, important question: can training make a difference in how we respond to and deal with our implicit biases? When it came to shooting at black and white suspects, there were differences between civilians and police officers. The civilian subjects of the experiment shot more unarmed black suspects than unarmed white suspects. With police officers, who unlike civilians had received training in whether or not to shoot, a different pattern emerged. Officers had a greater ability to "inhibit a racial bias in favor of shooting [unarmed black suspects]."[52] This shows "that training can reduce automatic racial biases in some cases." And when Correll et al. extended appropriate training to civilians, those civilians "showed a significant decrease in racial bias."[53]

Correll's work has important implications for the safety of both civilians and police officers, especially under SYG laws. If racialized perceptions intrude into such a delicate and potentially catastrophic decision as whether or not to shoot at someone, we will have more unarmed blacks shot than unarmed whites, at least by civilians. This would have major implications for states with SYG laws, which lower the cost of using deadly force, and thus make it more likely that civilians will use deadly force. In the bargain, racialized unconscious bias may make police officers more vulnerable to attack by armed white assailants, because the officers are slower to recognize the danger they may face from whites than from blacks.

Circling Back: George Zimmerman and the Killing of Trayvon Martin

We can't know for certain whether race played a role in any particular case, and this goes for the initial decision of Sanford, Florida, law enforcement not to charge George Zimmerman. It may have been that the police and prosecutors would have come to the same decisions under Florida's SYG law, even with a white victim and a black shooter. But in light of what we know about how implicit racial bias works and the forms it takes in our society, it seems naïve to believe that race *could not* have played a role. Indeed, we should expect to see law enforcement outcomes influenced by the pervasive racial bias that exists; willfully insisting on "colorblindness" or other such comforting clichés constitutes wishful thinking, and nothing more. It would in fact be startling if SYG laws did not produce disparate impacts on African Americans, as John Roman's work shows that it does. Proponents of SYG laws must take ownership of this reality, as well as the other empirical evidence of an increase in deadly violence brought on by these laws.

Understood in the most basic way, Florida's SYG law and others like it make it more likely that people will resort to deadly force. These laws lessen the potential cost of using deadly force, by supplying a defense in many more cases of the use of deadly force. The Florida law goes further, supplying both criminal and civil immunity. And the empirical evidence seems to show that more deadly violence is exactly what results. The research on unconscious racial bias, and especially on the fact that most Americans see African Americans as more violence prone and dangerous—that is, more threatening—make the course of events early in the Zimmerman case—insufficient police questioning, Zimmerman released, more investigation, and no charges—not so surprising.

When race creeps in to decision making in the criminal justice system—that is, when policing, prosecution, or even jury decisions become racialized—damage can occur, and justice may go unserved. Whether this happens overtly, due to conscious bigotry, or invisibly, through unconscious bias, does not change the fact of the damage caused, or its lasting and consequential nature. The racialization of criminal justice can only corrode the ideals and institutions that hold us together as a people. And none of us can afford that, no matter what racial, ethnic, or other group we think we belong to. We are all Americans, and our Constitution and our laws that promise dignity, fairness, and equal treatment must protect all of us—or they protect none of us.

NOTES

1. Barry et al. 2012, A1.
2. 2013 Fla. Stat. Title XLVI, Crimes, Ch. 776, Sec. 776.013.
3. See, e.g., Bhasin 2011; Campbell 2011.
4. See, e.g., Chasmar 2013 (Martin's father, appearing on the *Today* show, stating,

"Was he racially profiled? I think that, if Trayvon had been white, this wouldn't have never happened so, obviously, race has played some type of role."); NeJame 2012 (criminal defense attorney states his opinion that "however, with the evidence that has emerged . . . proof of a racial motive concerning the shooting seems wholly lacking."), available at http://www.cnn.com/2012/05/30/opinion/nejame-zimmerman-racial-profiling/.

5. Barry et al. 2012.

6. Ibid.

7. Alvarez and Buckley 2013.

8. Lee 2013.

9. See, e.g., U.S. Census Bureau 2015 (by 2050, no clear racial or ethnic majority will exist in the United States); Passel and Cohn 2008 (by 2050, nearly 20 percent of all Americans will be foreign-born); Burns, Barton, and Kerby 2012 ("The U.S. workforce is undoubtedly becoming more diverse. . . . The proportion of people of color participating in the workforce will only increase as the United States becomes a more racially and ethnically diverse country").

10. See, e.g., *U.S. v. Peterson*, 483 F.2d 1222 (U.S. Ct. Apps., D.C. Cir., 1973) (quoting Blackstone's teaching that "all homicide . . . amounts to murder, unless . . . *excused* on the account of accident or self-preservation . . .").

11. Ibid.

12. Ibid. ("Within the common law of self-defense there developed the rule of 'retreat to the wall,' which ordinarily forbade the use of deadly force by one to whom an avenue for safe retreat was open. . . . The doctrine of retreat was never intended to enhance the risk to the innocent; . . . on the contrary, [the person attacked] could stand his ground and use deadly force otherwise appropriate if the alternative were perilous . . .").

13. Ibid. ("It is well settled that one who through no fault of his own is attacked in his home is under no duty to retreat therefrom," calling this rule the "castle exception").

14. 2013 Fla. Stat. Title XLVI, Crimes, Ch. 776, Sec. 776.013.

15. 2013 Fla. Stat. Title XLVI, Crimes, Ch. 776, Sec. 776.032.

16. Ibid.

17. Lawson 2014.

18. McClellan and Tekin 2012, 4.

19. Kuhn and Lane 2014.

20. Skogan 1995.

21. Hoekstra and Cheng 2012.

22. Ibid., 4.

23. McClellan and Tekin 2012.

24. Ibid.

25. Ibid.

26. Roman 2013.

27. Ibid., 1.

28. Ibid., 7.

29. Ibid., 9.

30. The Implicit Association Test is probably best understood by visiting the website for Project Implicit at Harvard, https://implicit.harvard.edu/implicit/index.jsp, and taking one or more of the many available IATs available on the site. See also Bananji and Greenwald 2013, a general audience book about the IAT by two of the creators of the test. See also Lee 2013.

31. Bananji and Greenwald 2013, 47.

32. Henneberger 2013.

33. Tversky and Kahneman 1974.

34. Richardson and Goff 2012.

35. Ibid., 298.

36. Ibid.

37. Ibid., 301.

38. Ibid., 297.

39. Ibid., 310.

40. Eberhardt et al. 2004, 876 ("The stereotype of Black Americans as violent and criminal has been documented by social psychologists for almost 60 years"); Trawalter et al. 2008, 1322 ("There is overwhelming evidence that young Black men are stereotyped as violent, criminal, and dangerous . . . both implicitly as well as explicitly") (citations omitted).

41. Duncan 1976, 591.

42. Sagar and Schofield 1980.

43. Richardson and Goff 2012, 305.

44. Correll et al. 2002.

45. Ibid., 1325, emphasis added.

46. Ibid.

47. Ibid., 1327.

48. Ibid., 1328.

49. Correll et al. 2007.

50. Richardson and Goff 2012, 305.

51. Correll et al. 2007, 1020.

52. Ibid.

53. Ibid. But see Richardson and Goff 2012, 306 (noting some counterproof from the work of one of the authors finding that "the degree to which officers associated Blacks with apes predicted both the degree to which they misperceived black children as adults and justified violence against them").

REFERENCES

Alvarez, Lisette, and Cara Buckley. 2013. "Zimmerman Is Acquitted in Trayvon Martin Killing." *New York Times*, July 13. http://www.nytimes.com/2013/07/14/us/george-zimmerman-verdict-trayvon-martin.html?pagewanted=alland_r=0.

Bananji, Mahrzarin, and Anthony Greenwald. 2013. *Blind Spot: Hidden Biases of Good People*. New York: Delacorte Press.

Barry, Dan, et al. 2012. "In the Eye of a Firestorm: In Florida, an Intersection of Tragedy, Race and Outrage." *New York Times*, April 2, A1.

Bhasin, Sabina. "'Stand Your Ground' Defense Coming Up in at Least Two More Collier Cases." *Naples Daily News*, December 11. www.naplesnews.com/news/2011/dec/11/saavedra-orr-burton-collier-stand-your-ground-law/.

Burns, Crosby, Kimberly Barton, and Sophia Kerby. 2012. "The State of Diversity in Today's Workforce." Washington, DC: Center for American Progress. http://www.americanprogress.org/issues/labor/report/2012/07/12/11938/the-state-of-diversity-in-todays-workforce/.

Campbell, Alexia. 2011. "More Hope to Use 'Stand Your Ground' Law to Gain Freedom." *Sun Sentinel*, September 12. http://articles.sun-sentinel.com/2011-09-12/news/fl-boat-shooting-defense-20110912_1_murder-charges-michael-monahan-controversial-state-law.

Chasmar, Jessica. 2013. "Trayvon Martin's Father: My Son Was Racially Profiled." *Washington Times*, July 18. http://p.washingtontimes.com/news/2013/jul/18/trayvon-martins-father-my-son-was-racially-profile/.

Correll, Joshua, Bernd Wittenbrink, Bernadette Park, and Charles M. Judd. 2002. "The Police Officer's Dilemma: Using Ethnicity to Disambiguate Potentially Threatening Individuals." *Journal of Personality and Social Psychology* 83:1314–29.

Correll, Joshua, Bernd Wittenbrink, Bernadette Park, Charles M. Judd, Tracie Keesee, and Melody S. Sadler. 2007. "Across the Thin Blue Line: Police Officers and Racial Bias in the Decision to Shoot." *Journal of Personality and Social Psychology* 92:1006–23.

Duncan, Birt L. 1976. "Differential Social Perception and Attribution of Intergroup Violence: Testing the Lower Limits of Stereotyping of Blacks." *Journal of Personality and Social Psychology* 34:590–98.

Eberhardt, Jennifer L., et al. 2004. "Seeing Black: Race, Crime, and Visual Processing." *Journal of Personality and Social Psychology* 87:876–93.

Henneberger, Melinda. 2013. "Beware the 'Mindbugs' That Infect You with Prejudices." *Washington Post*, February 8. http://www.washingtonpost.com/blogs/she-the-people/wp/2013/02/07/out-damned-spot-the-mindbugs-of-bias-that-sneak-into-our-brains/.

Hoekstra, Mark, and Cheng Cheng. 2012. "Does Strengthening Self-Defense Law Deter Crime or Escalate Violence? Evidence from Expansions to Castle Doctrine." *Journal of Human Resources* 48 (3): 821–54.

Kuhn, Ashley, and Jodi Lane. 2014. "Racial Socialization, Fear, and Expected Reactions to a Suspicious Person." http://scholarship.law.ufl.edu/cgi/viewcontent.cgi?article=1003andcontext=csrrr_events.

Lawson, Tamara F. 2014. "Stand Your Ground Laws: 50 State Table." Unpublished manuscript, March 15.

Lee, Cynthia. 2013. "Making Race Salient: Trayvon Martin and Implicit Bias in a Not Yet Post-Racial Society." *North Carolina Law Review* 91:1555–1612.

McClellan, Chandler, and Erdal Tekin. 2012. "Stand Your Ground Laws and Homicides." Discussion Paper 6705, July. Bonn: Institute for the Study of Labor.

NeJame, Mark. 2012. "Trayvon Martin Shooting Wasn't a Case of Racial Profiling." CNN Opinion, May 30. http://www.cnn.com/2012/05/30/opinion/nejame-zimmerman-racial-profiling/.

Passel, Jeffrey S., and D'Vera Cohn. 2008. "U.S. Population Projections: 2005–2050." Washington, DC: Pew Research Center.

Richardson, L. Song, and Phillip Atiba Goff. 2012. "Self-Defense and the Suspicion Heuristic." *Iowa Law Review* 98:293–332.

Roman, John. 2013. "Race, Justifiable Homicide, and Stand Your Ground Laws: Analysis of FBI Supplementary Homicide Report Data." Washington, DC: Urban Institute.

Sagar, H. A., and J. W. Schofield. 1980. "Racial and Behavioral Cues in Black and White Children's Perceptions of Ambiguously Aggressive Acts." *Journal of Personality and Social Psychology* 39:590–98.

Skogan, Wesley G. 1995. "Crime and the Racial Fears of White Americans." *Annals of the American Academy of Political and Social Science* 593:53–71.

Trawalter, Sophie, et al. 2008. "Attending to Threat: Race-Based Patterns of Selective Attention." *Journal of Experimental Social Psychology* 44:1322–27.

Tversky, Amos, and Daniel Kahneman. 1974. "Judgment under Uncertainty: Heuristics and Biases." *Science* 185 (4157): 1124–31.

U.S. Census Bureau. 2015. "U.S. Population Projections." http://www.census.gov/population/www/projections/summarytables.html.

U.S. v. Peterson, 483 F.2d 1222 (U.S. Ct. Apps., D.C. Cir. 1973).

7

The Acquittal of George Zimmerman

*Race and Judges' Perceptions about the Accuracy of
Not Guilty Verdicts*

AMY FARRELL, PATRICIA Y. WARREN, DEVON JOHNSON,
JORDYN L. ROSARIO, AND DANIEL GIVELBER

"George Zimmerman, the neighborhood watch volunteer who fatally shot Trayvon Martin, an unarmed black teenager . . . was found not guilty late Saturday night of second-degree murder. He was also acquitted of manslaughter, a lesser charge. After three weeks of testimony, the six-woman jury rejected the prosecution's contention that Mr. Zimmerman had deliberately pursued Mr. Martin because he assumed the hoodie-clad teenager was a criminal and instigated the fight that led to his death."[1]

The Zimmerman verdict raises important questions about the role of race in determining case outcomes. Many of those disappointed with the verdict believe racial bias was the driving mechanism behind Zimmerman's acquittal. While numerous empirical studies have found that a defendant's race affects the types of legal outcomes she or he receives,[2] others have found that when relevant legal factors are taken into account, a defendant's race does not matter.[3] In a quest to further understand the complexity of race and case outcomes, some scholars have also explored the interactive role of defendant and victim race and found that when defendants of color commit crimes against white victims, they are punished more harshly.[4] Regardless of how individual cases are resolved, the problem of race and the potential for racial bias in jury decision making requires attention. In this chapter, we explore these issues by examining how the racial and ethnic background of defendants and victims may influence jury and judicial decision making using data from the National Center for State Courts Study.[5]

Understanding Acquittals in Context

In general, judges in criminal cases tell jurors that they must presume that the accused are not guilty of the crimes charged. They also tell jurors that prosecutors are required to provide evidence to convince them beyond all reasonable doubt that the defendants are guilty. If the state (i.e., the prosecutor) succeeds in doing so, then juries are instructed to convict. If the state fails to eliminate reasonable doubt about guilt, then juries must acquit. A not guilty verdict says something definitive about the evidence that the state introduced—that it was insufficient to eliminate all reasonable doubt about guilt from the minds of the jurors. But acquittals do not address, or answer, the question of whether defendants are *factually innocent*. All we know is that the juries were not persuaded by the prosecution to believe that the defendants committed the crimes charged.

Although juries are designed to ensure that the innocent are protected to the greatest extent humanly possible, this arrangement results in what has been aptly termed *adjudicatory asymmetry*, the belief that guilt is based on a factual conclusion concerning the defendant's behavior whereas an acquittal reflects only an absence of proof.[6] We know (or believe we know) that the convicted are guilty of the crime because the evidence has eliminated every reasonable doubt. We do not know that the acquitted are innocent; the not guilty verdict may be a product of the government's very high burden of proof in a criminal case, the jury's failure to follow instructions, the failure of a key witness to testify as expected, a jury's dislike of the law involved, or a distrust of the state's witnesses. Any of these reasons may result in reasonable doubt about guilt, and that doubt exonerates.

Because it is not an affirmative declaration of innocence, an acquittal does not preclude the state or others from showing that the defendant committed the crime in question under a different standard of proof (e.g., the preponderance of the evidence test used in civil cases). For example, in one of the most famous criminal prosecutions of the last quarter century, the acquittal of O. J. Simpson of murder in a criminal trial did not preclude a different jury, in a civil suit brought by the victim's families, from finding that it was more probable than not that he committed murder.[7] Nor does the acquittal necessarily preclude a judge from giving Simpson a longer sentence than would otherwise be appropriate if he is convicted of a different crime.[8] Finally, should Simpson ever be charged with even more crimes, the state may be able to introduce evidence of the murders of Nicole Simpson and Ronald Goldman to demonstrate a pattern of criminal behavior. In his case, at least, prosecutors, courts, and many people in the public do not believe that his acquittal meant he was innocent.

Acquittals are essentially invisible. We know very little about why juries or judges conclude that defendants are not guilty. Since the vast majority of research concerning those accused of crime is based upon sentencing or prison data, we also know little about those who are found not guilty. In practice, most prosecutors, defense counsel, and judges encounter the acquitted infrequently. If we combine criminal cases resolved through guilty pleas (the overwhelming majority) with the relatively few cases resolved by verdicts after trial, we find that an acquittal occurs approximately once in every one hundred cases. For example, according to the Bureau of Justice Statistics data, only 3 percent of all criminal cases were actually resolved through trials in which judges or juries rendered verdicts of guilt or innocence.[9] Of the small proportion of cases that did go to trial, approximately one-third resulted in acquittals. Thus, although acquittals represented only a tiny fraction of criminal dispositions, they represented a much larger proportion of those rare cases that did go to trial. Given these statistics, it is perhaps not surprising that acquittals have remained relatively unexamined by social scientists, legal scholars, and policy makers. Rather, they are treated as random events, "signifying nothing" about the actual guilt or innocence of those prosecuted for crime.

The collective indifference to acquittals, except in high-profile cases, reverberates beyond the injustice of ignoring the possibility that a jury acquittal signals innocence. If we do not know *why* the jury acquits, we can ignore the possibility that innocents are charged and prosecuted fully. An acquittal can be (and typically is) treated as a *failure* by the police, the prosecutor, the jury, or any combination of those entities to do their respective jobs appropriately rather than as the successful exoneration of the innocent. We can ignore claims that plea bargaining may force the innocent to falsely admit guilt simply to avoid the draconian penalty attached to the conviction of certain crimes. If we ignore acquittals—if we accept that "defendants are acquitted for many reasons, the least likely being innocence"[10]—we reduce criminal justice outcomes to extremely accurate, if sometimes harsh, convictions and very inaccurate, if sometimes emotionally understandable, acquittals.

What we do know about acquittals comes essentially from three sources: (1) a study of nearly four thousand mid-twentieth-century criminal jury trials by University of Chicago law professors Harry Kalven and Hans Zeisel,[11] which is considered the seminal study of judge-jury decision making, and a handful of studies conducted to attempt to replicate its conclusions; (2) depictions of acquittals in popular culture; and (3) anecdotes. Anecdotes and media presentations focus upon the counterintuitive; "guilty man acquitted" and "innocent man convicted" stories are more interesting than trials in which juries arrive at correct verdicts. They tell us little about the frequency or nature of trials in which the jury produced accurate results.

The American Jury, published in 1966, contained an analysis of the results of a survey conducted in the mid-1950s. Kalven and Zeisel asked hundreds of judges to assess jury verdicts in terms of how the judges would have decided the cases. They found that judges agreed with the jury verdicts in 78 percent of all cases; when they disagreed, juries were far more likely to acquit when the judges would have convicted (19 percent of all cases) than they were to convict when the judges would have acquitted (3 percent of all cases). Judges and juries agreed that acquittals were appropriate in only 14 percent of all cases. Sir William Blackstone insisted, "The law holds that it is better that ten guilty escape, than that one innocent suffer."[12]

Importantly, Kalven and Zeisel's findings demonstrated that juries were more acquittal-prone than judges because of evidentiary difficulty. That is, when evidence in criminal cases is difficult to decipher, juries believe they are "liberated" to consider nonevidentiary factors in resolving the questions of fact. More simply put, close cases "liberated" the jurors to consider values, and this consideration frequently resulted in juries acquitting when the judges would have convicted.[13] As Kalven and Zeisel have argued, "The jury yields to sentiment in the apparent process of resolving doubts as to evidence. The jury, therefore, is able to conduct its revolt from the law within the etiquette of resolving issues of fact."[14] Apparently, judges were immune from the influence of sentiment. Kalven and Zeisel's liberation hypothesis has largely guided our understanding and interpretation of jury decision making and has arguably shaped the direction and scope of social science research on juries.[15]

The representation of trials and their outcomes in popular culture resonates with Kalven and Zeisel's finding that jurors embrace sentiment when jurors acquit those whom judges would have convicted. Courtroom scenes and trials are so common in movies, television, and literature that a majority of our experience with criminal adjudication and our expectations of it come from things we see or read as opposed to our direct experiences.[16] Although the representation of trials and their outcomes in the American media is not static, little attention has been paid to the experiences of defendants who are acquitted of crimes.[17] Unlike real life, where the facts are contested, in fictional accounts the viewer or reader is generally let in on the truth through flashbacks to the events in question. Heroic lawyer characters, either defense lawyers fighting tirelessly for their (possibly) wrongfully accused clients or prosecutors upholding the values and wisdom of the state, then represent the truth that as audience members we already understand.[18] Rarely do fictional judges or juries return verdicts that contradict this truth, comforting the public that through the aggressive presentation of the defense and prosecution cases, the legal process arrives at the correct result.

Anecdotes suggest that actual trials are lessons in civics, and acquittals are the price society pays for taking so seriously the obligation that the government has to be able to demonstrate guilt convincingly in open court. No criminal case in the past quarter century has captured the public attention as much as the O. J. Simpson murder trial, a case in which the verdict is almost universally perceived as historically inaccurate. As one commentator characterized it, criminal adjudication is an administrative process, with trials operating as the occasional adjudicatory hearing designed to ensure that the government is administering fairly.[19]

Race and Acquittals

Little is known about the role of race, of defendant, victim, or court actors, in explaining acquittals. Applying Kalven and Zeisel's hypothesis that close cases result in juries being liberated to embrace values, some commentators have found that defendant race (an extralegal factor if ever there was one) has its greatest role in those cases that are close on evidence.[20] Research by Givelber and Farrell using the same data analyzed in the current study found no support for this proposition as an explanation of jury behavior. When judges believed that the case was close on the evidence, they found juries were as likely to acquit as to convict. Race of defendant was also not relevant to predicting jury acquittal in cases that were close on the evidence. When the defendants were black and the judges viewed the evidence as evenly balanced, juries acquitted roughly half of the time. Similarly, when the defendants were of other races and the evidence was evenly balanced, juries acquitted roughly half of the time. They conclude that even if cases that the judges considered close on the evidence open the door for juries to consider values (a proposition the authors debate), the race of the defendants was not considered as a value affecting the outcome of their deliberations.[21] To date there has been limited attention devoted toward understanding the direct role of victim race or the interactive role between defendant and victim race in predicting acquittals or explaining the perceived accuracy of such acquittals. Research on punishment severity, however, suggests defendants of color are treated most harshly when they are sentenced for crimes against white victims.[22]

The racial composition of juries has also been suggested as a potential explanation of jury verdicts. A good deal of social science research has been devoted to understanding how individual and group demographic characteristics of jurors and juries, such as race, gender, and age composition, affect jury decision making. While racial groups appear to differ in their assessment of the criminal justice system, empirical research finds individual juror demographic characteristics to be only weakly associated with criminal jury verdicts,[23] though there is a consistent line of research suggesting an interaction between juror and defendant race with juror leniency toward defendants with similar characteristics as jury members.[24] In addition, the composition of more racially mixed juries has been found to alter juror interactions and decision making, mainly in the direction of increased leniency for black defendants.[25] Despite a relatively large body of research on the effect of racial composition of juries, few studies have directly examined the relationship between judge and jury agreement across juries with variable levels of nonwhite group representation.[26]

The Present Study

The acquittal of George Zimmerman raises important questions about the accuracy and legitimacy of juries returning not guilty verdicts. Historically the public has been concerned about not guilty verdicts in high-profile cases. Such acquittals raise questions about the legitimacy of the criminal justice system and trust in jury decision making. Because acquittals are rare and little research has examined them in depth, high-profile acquittals shape the public understanding of acquittals. While the public forms opinions about the criminal justice system based on high-profile criminal trials, these cases and their outcomes are often departures from routine criminal cases, even for serious violent crimes. As described above, there are many reasons to suspect that race is a factor in how the public perceives the accuracy and justness of acquittals.

In the current study, we examine acquittals in two ways. First we explore the factors that predict a jury acquitting compared to convicting. Second, we examine the circumstances in which judges indicate disagreement with a jury's finding of not guilty and assess whether judges' perceptions about the accuracy and legitimacy of not guilty verdicts differ in cases involving nonwhite defendants, victims, and jurors. Based on the limited research on acquittals we predict that (1) acquittals will be less likely when the defendant is black, (2) defendant and victim race will affect judge satisfaction with jury decisions to acquit, and (3) juror race will affect judge satisfaction with the case outcomes.

Data and Method

The data used to answer these questions were originally collected and analyzed by the National Center for State Courts (NCSC) as part of a study on hung juries.[27] The dataset is unique because it includes responses from judges, jurors, and attorneys participating in criminal trials in four different courts in the United States. The NCSC collected information on noncapital felony trials from trial courts in the Central Criminal Division of the Los Angeles County Superior Court,

California; the Maricopa County Superior Court (Phoenix), Arizona; the Bronx County Supreme Court, New York; and the Superior Court of the District of Columbia between 2000 and 2001.[28] The data include case information about the nature of the charges, demographic information on the offender and victim, trial evidence and procedures, and final verdict. In addition to case information collected by court personnel, questionnaires were administered to the judge who presided in each of the sampled cases and the prosecution and defense attorneys to elicit information about their perceptions of the case proceedings and outcomes. Individual jurors in each case completed questionnaires about their perceptions of the evidence and testimony, the deliberation process, and their individual voting during the deliberation process. The original dataset includes responses from 3,497 jurors serving on 382 separate criminal cases.

To understand the relationship between defendant and victim race and the likelihood of acquittal, we utilize a dichotomous measure of case outcome where an acquittal is coded as 1 and a conviction 0.[29] In each case, judges were also asked to indicate whether or not they would have acquitted or convicted the defendant had the case been a bench trial. We compare the predictors of real jury acquittals and hypothetical judge acquittals to test our first hypothesis that juries are less likely acquit defendants who are black.

In a second set of models we examine judges' perceptions of the accuracy of the jury verdict. Judge satisfaction is measured on a scale from 1 (not at all satisfied) to 7 (very satisfied). These analyses help us identify situations where acquittals are perceived by the presiding judge as more or less accurate. It is important to note that the measure of judges' perception is not a definitive test of the true correctness of an acquittal, but rather provides a sense of judge satisfaction or dissatisfaction with the jury's verdict after the judge has heard all the evidence in the case. These models allow us to test our second hypothesis that judges are more likely to agree with jury acquittals when the defendant is white.

In the final set of models, we utilize the measure of judge satisfaction with the jury decision to examine variation in judge satisfaction with acquittals compared to convictions across juries with more white members compared to juries with more black and Hispanic members.

We include a number of measures that affect juror decision making and may also affect judges' perceptions of the accuracy of those decisions across all our analyses. The strength of the evidence presented at trial is arguably one of the most important predictors of jury decision making.[30] We include a subjective measure of the strength of the evidence based on the trial judge's assessment of the evidence in each case (measured on a scale where 1 indicates the judge believes the evidence favors the prosecution and 7 indicates the evidence favors the defense). Previous research suggests that jurors were less likely to convict in cases where the penalties are more severe.[31] While statistics on potential penalties are not available in the present data, we utilize other measures of severity such as the type of charge (a dichotomous variable indicating whether the crime involved a personal victimization)[32] and the number of charges.

Key variables are included to measure the impact of defendant and victim race. Defendant race is measured as a dummy code indicating the defendant is white, black, Hispanic, or another race. Similarly, victim race is measured as a dummy code indicating the victim is white, black, Hispanic, or another race. Analysis that examines the interaction of defendant and victim race is limited in these data as only 170 of the 328 cases analyzed here include a charge of personal victimization. Defendant gender is measured as 0 if the defendant is female and 1 if the defendant is male.[33]

Additional controls are included for the characteristics of the setting where each trial took place. We measured court location with dummy variables for LA County, Maricopa County, the Bronx, or Washington, DC. We also include measures for the proportion of the jury that is white, black, Hispanic, or other races. Table 7.1 presents the descriptive statistics for all measures.

Logistic regression models are estimated to predict the effect of defendant and victim race on acquittals and the likelihood that a judge would have acquitted had the case been a bench trial. Marginal means are employed to illustrate the variation in means of judge satisfaction with jury acquittals compared to convictions, controlling for covariates. Marginal means for acquittals and convictions are plotted to illustrate variation in judge satisfaction with the jury verdict.

Findings

Mirroring national data, acquittals are relatively rare events in the NCSC data. Table 7.1 demonstrates that approximately 30 percent of the criminal trials analyzed resulted in a jury acquittal. Interestingly, judges are less likely than jurors to acquit a defendant. On average, judges indicate they would acquit the defendant had the case been a bench trial in 17 percent of the cases. Logistic regression was employed to estimate the effect of defendant race on the likelihood of either real jury acquittals or hypothetical judge acquittals. As illustrated in table 7.2, defendant race does not predict either jury acquittals or hypothetical judge acquittals. Juries are more likely to acquit defendants with private representation. Not surprisingly, both juries and judges are more likely to acquit when the evidence favored the defense (i.e., when the prosecutors and defense are close on evidence).

TABLE 7.1. Descriptive Statistics ($N = 328$)

	Mean/%	SD	Min	Max
Acquittal	30%			
Judge would acquit	17%			
Judge satisfaction	5.58	1.86	1	7
LA	20%			
Maricopa	26%			
Bronx	29%			
DC	25%			
Victim	52%			
Defendant male	92%			
White defendant	11%			
Black defendant	55%			
Hispanic defendant	28%			
Other defendant	7%			
Private representation	18%			
Close on evidence	3.15	1.50	1	7
% jury white	44.15	30.73	0	100
% jury black	27.43	26.25	0	100
% jury Hispanic	23.36	23.19	0	100

TABLE 7.2. Likelihood of Acquittal ($N = 328$)

	Jury acquits Odds ratio	Judge would acquit Odds ratio
LA	0.34**	0.68
Maricopa	0.27**	2.39
Bronx	0.48	0.48
Victim	0.79	0.39**
Black defendant	0.93	0.40
Hispanic defendant	1.51	1.04
Other race defendant	1.48	1.45
Close on evidence	1.91***	4.03***
Private representation	2.06**	0.94
% jury black	0.99	1.01
% jury Hispanic	0.99	1.01
R^2	.20	.32

** $p < .05$; *** $p < .01$

Table 7.3 demonstrates that race of the defendant similarly does not predict acquittal when we examine only those cases that involve a personal victimization. Victim race, however, does predict jury verdicts. Jury acquittals are less likely when victims are black. Victim race has no influence on the likelihood that judges will acquit. On first blush these findings seems counter to the belief that juries undervalue harm committed against black and Hispanic people. As a line of research on racial disparities in criminal justice system processing suggests, the interaction between defendant race and victim race likely explains this pattern.[34] In this sample, white and Hispanic victims were victimized by defendants of many different races; for example, of the relatively small number of white victims included in this sample, 25 percent of these victims were victimized by white defendants, 20 percent by Hispanic defendants, 48 percent by black defendants, and 8 percent by persons of other races. Black victims in this sample were almost entirely victimized by black defendants (94 percent of black victims victimized by black defendant). There are also important differences across sites that may explain the patterns we identify regarding acquittals and victim race. Ultimately a larger and more diverse sample of cases is needed to

TABLE 7.3. Likelihood of Acquittal—Personal Victimization Only ($N = 170$)

	Jury acquits Odds ratio	Judge would acquit Odds ratio
LA	0.18**	0.08
Maricopa	0.29	0.94
Bronx	0.55	0.11
Black defendant	6.58	3.61
Hispanic defendant	2.58	1.98
Other race defendant	8.38	16.97
Victim black	−2.02**	0.24
Victim Hispanic	1.05	2.05
Victim other race	0.49	0.46
Close on evidence	2.44***	5.05***
Private representation	4.62**	0.89
% jury black	0.97*	1.01
% jury Hispanic	0.99	1.01
R^2	.29	.33

* $p < .1$; ** $p < .05$; *** $p < .01$

TABLE 7.4. Judge Satisfaction with Case Outcomes by Defendant Race

	Defendant white B (SE)	Defendant black B (SE)	Defendant Hispanic B (SE)
LA	−5.56 (6.04)	−0.33 (0.94)	−0.76 (2.29)
Maricopa	−15.19 (8.08)*	1.95 (1.12)*	−0.71 (2.67)
Bronx	1.66 (5.11)	−1.94 (1.02)*	−5.14 (2.27)**
Close on evidence	0.36 (0.35)	0.26 (0.14)*	0.33 (0.16)**
Private representation	0.15 (1.79)	1.19 (0.89)	0.49 (1.47)
% jury black	−0.44 (0.16)**	0.02 (0.02)	0.01 (0.04)
% jury Hispanic	0.00 (0.04)	0.04 (0.02)	0.01 (0.03)
Acquittal	0.58 (1.80)	−1.61 (0.64)**	0.62 (1.20)
R^2	.45	.12	.19

* $p < .1$; ** $p < .05$

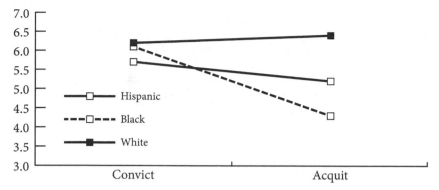

Figure 7.1. Estimated marginal means of judge satisfaction with verdict by defendant race.

more fully understand the direct and interactive influence of victim and defendant race on case outcomes.

Although defendant race does not predict whether or not a defendant was acquitted, the findings displayed in table 7.4 demonstrate that defendant race significantly affects judges' perceptions of the accuracy of acquittals. Overall judges are less satisfied with the verdict of a criminal case when a jury acquits. The estimated marginal mean of judge satisfaction with an acquittal controlling for court site, representation, and whether or not the case involved personal victimization was 4.7. When the jury convicted the defendant, judge satisfaction with the verdict rose to 5.9, a statistically significant increase from judge satisfaction when the defendant was acquitted.

Stark differences in judge satisfaction with jury acquittals emerge when we consider the race of the defendant. As illustrated in figure 7.1, unlike the overall trend where judges are dissatisfied with acquittals, judges are more satisfied with jury verdicts when white defendants are acquitted (6.4 marginal mean of satisfaction) compared to when white defendants are convicted (6.2 marginal mean of satisfaction). Conversely, judges are less satisfied with jury verdicts when black defendants are acquitted (4.3 marginal mean of satisfaction) compared to convicted (6.1 marginal mean of satisfaction). There is no statistical difference between judge satisfaction when Hispanic defendants are acquitted compared to convicted.

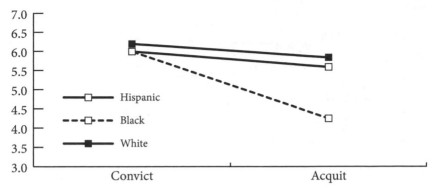

Figure 7.2. Estimated marginal means of judge satisfaction with verdict by victim race.

To determine how victim race affects judge evaluation of jury verdicts we must first confine the analysis to a smaller subset of cases involving personal victimization ($n = 170$). As illustrated in figure 7.2, judges are less satisfied when juries acquit in cases involving victims of all racial groups. Interestingly, judges are the most dissatisfied with acquittals in cases involving black victims. It is important to note that there was little interracial victimization in the data analyzed here. Most cases involving black victims also involve black suspects, making it difficult to disentangle the influence of race in judgments about the accuracy of acquittals. These findings raise important questions about the perceived accuracy of acquittals but do not shed sufficient light on how perceptions about the accuracy of jury decisions vary when victims and suspects are from different racial groups.

Jury race has a modest influence on judge dissatisfaction case outcomes. As illustrated in table 7.4, judges in the NCSC data are less satisfied with jury decisions, regardless of acquittal or conviction, when a greater proportion of the jury is black. The relationship between juror race and judge dissatisfaction with the jury's decision is strongest and statistically significant in those cases where the defendant is white. In these cases, the judge is increasingly dissatisfied with the jury decision as the proportion of black jury members increases. While previous analyses suggest that judges are most dissatisfied when juries acquit black defendants, these findings suggest our perceptions about the accuracy of criminal trials may be further racialized through perceptions about the decisions of juries with larger numbers of black jurors.

Discussion

There are two important conclusions that can be drawn from the current research. First, understanding the salience of race and ethnicity in the acquittal decision is a complex undertaking. Although the popular rhetoric is to point specific blame on racial bias and discrimination, the story is more complicated and requires more specific scholarly attention. It is the case that while the race of both the defendant and victim was salient in the Zimmerman trial, in the current study the defendant race does not affect the likelihood of a jury acquittal. In routine criminal cases, roughly equal proportions of white defendants are acquitted of crimes in comparison to black defendants, controlling for crime severity and other legally relevant factors. In addition, juries were less likely to acquit defendants when the victim was black. While this is an important finding, it is necessary to note that in this study, defendants and victims were most often from the same racial group. Therefore, we were limited in our ability to further explore these relationships.

Second, supported by the popular notion that acquittals are errors of justice, we found that judges are far less satisfied with the outcome of a criminal case when a jury acquits. These findings suggest that while race and/or ethnicity may not be influential in jury decision making, race is a significant determinant in judicial satisfaction with jury acquittals. That is, while judges are generally not satisfied when juries acquit, these effects are much stronger when the defendant is black, suggesting that judicial officials believe acquittals of black defendants are more likely to be errors of justice. These decisions are especially brought into question when acquittals are handed down by juries with larger proportions of black citizens. Such conclusions may be driven by cultural presumptions of black dangerousness and guilt. In their study, for example, Steffensmeier and colleagues found that judicial officials were more likely to view black men as dangerous, committed to street life, and less reformable than other offenders.[35] These stereotypical portrayals of black lives have often fostered fear of black citizens among the American populace.

It is also important to note that in a criminal justice system where acquittals are rare events, more research is needed to understand how acquittals occur and to what degree race of the victim and/or defendant affects jury decisions to acquit. Notably absent from the present analyses was an examination of how the legal process unfolds and how mixed race events might influence the decision to acquit. This is an important next step in scholarly research on acquittals because prior research suggests that racial bias in the criminal justice process is heightened in situations where the defendant is black and the victim is white. Because a majority of the crimes involving personal victimization in the NCSC data include victims and defendants of the same race, it is difficult to tease out whether racial differences in acquittals or judges' perceptions of acquittals of black victims are due to the fact that both defendants and victims are black. We are unable to determine whether judges recognize that black lives matter and are therefore less satisfied when juries acquit in cases where a black person has been victimized or, conversely, whether judges believe black defendants are more likely to be guilty and therefore are most satisfied when black defendants are convicted, regardless of the race of their victim.

When questions of racial injustice arise, we look to scholarly research to help us understand whether or not the system is to blame, but social science is inherently limited in its ability to determine whether any one verdict is just or accurate. The legitimacy of an acquittal is called into question particularly when it is part of a complex pattern of racial disparities woven throughout the criminal justice process. As a result, acquittals may represent a public "last straw," the coup de grâce in an unjust legal process. Serious attention to and inquiry into acquittals is needed in order to address questions about the legitimacy of the criminal justice process.

While the founding principles of American justice rest on assumptions of equality and fairness under the law, the persistence of racial and ethnic disparities in both crime and punishment decisions continue to raise important questions about the equality and impartiality of the justice system. High-profile cases such as the trial and acquittal of George Zimmerman and the recent grand jury decisions not to indict Darren Wilson, the police officer who fatally shot Michael Brown in Ferguson, Missouri, or any of the police officers involved in the physical altercation that led to the death of Eric Garner in Staten Island, New York, bring the process and the legitimacy of American justice into question. While no individual scholarly attempt can fully capture the multidimensional elements that give rise to racial and ethnic disparities and what many perceive as criminal *in*justice, it is important to highlight (and address) the role of racial and ethnic bias in decision making in order to foster a process of justice that is free from bias, and to increase trust in the system among all Americans, but particularly minorities. This can be accomplished with the help of ongoing scholarly efforts that seek to identify and remedy racial and ethnic bias where it may occur.

NOTES

1. Alvarez and Buckley 2013.

2. Steffensmeier and Demuth 2000; Mustard 2001. See also Levine 2000. For more comprehensive reviews of the literature on race and dispositional decisions in the criminal justice system, see Walker, Spohn, and DeLone 2004; Zatz 1987; Cole 2000.

3. Devine et al. 2009; Myers and Talarico 1987; and Wilbanks 1987.

4. Baldus, Pulaski, and Woodworth 1983. See also Field 1979, who found that jurors are more likely to convict black defendants in rape cases involving white victims, and Lynch and Haney 2000, who found in mock jury trials that white jurors were more likely to sentence black defendants to death compared to white defendants.

5. Parts of this chapter were previously published in Givelber and Farrell 2012.

6. Stith 1990.

7. Ayres 1997.

8. Freiss 2008. Simpson was sentenced to between nine and thirty-three years for an armed robbery he committed in Las Vegas in 2008.

9. Kyckelhal and Cohen 2008.

10. Ibid.

11. Kalven and Zeisel 1966.

12. Blackstone 1908, 358.

13. Kalven and Zeisel 1966, 165.

14. Ibid., 165n4.

15. Hans and Vidmar 1991.

16. Surette 1992. One study using interviews with over four hundred jurors about their experiences serving as jurors and their impressions of courts revealed that jurors who frequently watched courtroom dramas were more influenced by the shows than by their direct experiences as jurors in real courts (Podlas 2006).

17. Papke 1999; Rafter 2000.

18. Rafter 2000.

19. Lynch 1998.

20. Baldus, Pulaski, and Woodworth 1983.

21. Givelber and Farrell 2012.

22. Baldus, Pulaski, and Woodworth 1983.

23. King 1993.

24. Chadee 1996.

25. Sommers 2006 found that experimental jurors deliberating on a case involving a black defendant shared more information and were more lenient toward black defendants than were all-white juries.

26. Using the same data analyzed here, Eisenberg et al. 2005 examined the relationship between racial composition of juries and judge-and-jury conviction levels, finding weak but significant relationships between the percentage of the jury that is black and judge convictions in cases where juries would acquit, though these findings did not consistently survive more sophisticated multivariate analyses.

27. Hannaford-Agor et al. 2002.

28. Sites were originally chosen based on convenience and access, with some attention to sites with concerns about the problem of hung juries. See Hannaford-Agor et al. 2002 for a detailed description of the study design, sampling, and survey response rates.

29. Thirty-five cases where the jury was hung and no verdict was rendered were excluded from the analysis. Not surprisingly, judges are extremely dissatisfied with hung juries. An additional 19 cases were excluded due to missing data in the dependent variable. The final dataset analyzed here includes 328 cases.

30. Devine et al. 2009.

31. Barnett 1985.

32. Personal victimization includes cases of murder, attempted murder, manslaughter, rape, robbery, assault, and child abuse.

33. Defendant gender is excluded from final analyses as a small proportion of all defendants (approximately 8 percent) are female.

34. See Myers 1979; LaFree 1980; Radelet 1981.

35. Steffensmeier, Ulmer, and Kramer 1998.

REFERENCES

Alvarez, Lizette, and Cara Buckley. 2013. "Zimmerman Is Acquitted in Trayvon Martin Killing." *New York Times*, July 13, 2013.

Ayres, B. Drummond. 1997. "Civil Jury Finds Simpson Liable in Pair of Killings." *New York Times*, February 5.

Baldus, David., C. Pulaski, and G. Woodworth. 1983. "Comparative Review of Death Sentences: An Empirical Study of the Georgia Experience." *Journal of Criminal Law and Criminology* 74:661–753.

Barnett, A. 1985. Some Distribution Patterns for the Georgia Death Sentence. *University of California at Davis Law Review* 18:1327–74.

Blackstone, William. 1908. *Commentaries on the Laws of England: Book of the Fourth, 1765–69*. Philadelphia: J.B. Lippincott.

Chadee, Derek. 1996. "Race, Trial Evidence and Jury Decision Making." *Caribbean Journal of Criminology and Social Psychology* 1:59–86.

Cole, David. 2000. *No Equal Justice: Race, and Class in the American Criminal Justice System*. New York: New Press.

Devine, Dennis, Jennifer Buddenbaum, Stephanie Houp, Nathan Studebaker, and D. Stolle. 2009. "Strength of Evidence, Extraordinary Influence and the Liberation Hypothesis: Data from the Field." *Law and Human Behavior* 32 (3): 136–48.

Eisenberg, Theodore, Paula Hannaford-Agor, Valerie Hans, Nicole Waters, G. Thomas Munsterman, Stewart J. Schwab, and Martin T. Wells. 2005. "Judge-Jury Agreement in Criminal Cases: A Partial Replication of Kalven and Zeisel's 'The American Jury.'" *Empirical Legal Studies* 2 (1): 171–206. http://ssrn.com/abstract=593941. Accessed September 15, 2006.

Field, Herbert. 1979. "Rape, Trials and Jurors' Decisions: A Psycholegal Analysis of the Effects of Victim, Defendant and Case Characteristics." *Law and Human Behavior* 3:261–84.

Freiss, Steve. 2008. "After Apologies, Simpson Is Sentenced to at Least 9 Years for Armed Robbery." *New York Times*, December 6.

Givelber, Daniel, and Amy Farrell. 2012. *Not Guilty: Are the Acquitted Really Innocent*. New York: New York University Press.

Hannaford-Agor, Paula, Valerie Hans, Nicole Mott, and G. Thomas Munstermann. 2002. *Are Hung Juries a Problem? Evaluation of Hung Juries in Bronx County, New York, Los Angeles County, California, Maricopa County, Arizona and Washington, D.C., 2000–2002*. Ann Arbor, MI: Inter-University Consortium for Political and Social Research.

Hans, Valerie, and N. Vidmar. 1991. "'The American Jury' at Twenty Five Years." *Law and Social Inquiry* 16:323–50.

Kalven, Harry, Jr., and Hans Zeisel. 1966. *The American Jury*. Boston: Little, Brown.

———. 1971. *The American Jury*. Chicago: University of Chicago Press.

King, Nancy. 1993. "Postconviction Review of Jury Discrimination: Measuring the Effects of Juror Race on Jury Decisions." *Michigan Law Review* 92:63–130.

Kyckelhal, Tracey, and Thomas Cohen. 2008. *Felony Defendants in Large Urban Counties, 2004*. Washington, DC: Bureau of Justice Statistics.

LaFree, G. D. 1980. "The Effects of Sexual Stratification by Race on Official Reactions to Rape." *American Sociological Review* 45:842–54.

Levine, James P. 2000. "The Impact of Racial Demography on Jury Verdicts in Routine Criminal Cases, the System." In *Black and White: Exploring the Connections Between Race, Crime and Justice*, edited by Michael W. Markowitz and Delores D. Jones-Brown, 153–71. New York: Praeger.

Lynch, Gerard E. 1998. "Our Administrative System of Criminal Justice." *Fordham Law Review* 2117:2124–29.

Lynch, Michael, and Craig Haney. 2000. "Discrimination and Instructional Comprehension: Guided Discretion, Racial Bias and the Death Penalty." *Law and Human Behavior* 24:337–58.

Mustard, David B. 2001. "Racial, Ethnic and Gender Disparities in Sentencing: Evidence from the U.S. Federal Courts." *Journal of Law and Economics* 44:285–314.

Myers, Martha. 1979. "Offended Parties and Official Reactions: Victims and the Sentencing of Criminal Defendants." *Sociological Quarterly* 4:529–40.

Myers, Martha, and Susette Talarico. 1987. *The Social Contexts of Criminal Sentencing.* New York: Springer.

Papke, David R. 1999. "Conventional Wisdom: The Courtroom Trial in Popular Culture." *Marquette Law Review* 82 (3): 471.

Podlas, Kimberlianne. 2006. "'The CSI Effect': Exposing the Media Myth." *Fordham Intellectual Property, Media & Entertainment Law Journal* 16:429–65.

Radelet, Michael. 1981. "Racial Characteristics and the Imposition of the Death Penalty." *American Sociological Review* 46:918–27.

Rafter, Nicole. 2000. *Shots in the Mirror: Crime Films and Society.* Oxford: Oxford University Press.

Sommers, Samuel R. 2006. "On Racial Diversity and Group Decision Making: Identifying Multiple Effects of Racial Composition on Jury Deliberations." *Journal of Personality and Social Psychology* 90:597–612.

Steffensmeier, Darrell, Jeffery Ulmer, and John Kramer. 1998. "The Interaction of Race, Gender, and Age in Criminal Sentencing: The Punishment Cost of Being Young Black, and Male." *Criminology* 36:763–97.

Steffensmeier, D., and S. Demuth. 2000. "Ethnicity and Sentencing Outcomes in the U.S. Federal Courts: Who Is Punished More Harshly?" *American Sociological Review* 65:705–29.

Stith, Kate. 1990. "The Risk of Legal Error in Criminal Cases: Some Consequences in the Asymmetry in the Right to Appeal." *University of Chicago Law Review* 57:1–61.

Surette, R. 1992. *Media, Crime, and Criminal Justice: Images and Realities.* Pacific Grove, CA: Brooks/Cole.

Walker, Samuel, Cassia Spohn, and Miriam DeLone. 2004. *The Color of Justice Race, Ethnicity, and Crime in America.* 3rd ed. Belmont, CA: Wadsworth/Thomson.

Wilbanks, William. 1987. "The Myth of a Racist Criminal Justice System." *Journal of Contemporary Criminal Justice* 3:88–93.

Zatz, Marjorie. 1987. "The Changing Forms of Racial/Ethnic Biases in Sentencing." *Journal of Research in Crime and Delinquency* 24 (1): 69–92.

8

Up to No Good

The Context of Adolescent Discrimination in Neighborhoods

BRYAN L. SYKES, ALEX R. PIQUERO, JASON GIOVIANO,
AND NICOLAS PITTMAN

Criminal victimization is not random and occurs in a variety of social contexts. The associated risk of victimization depends on the daily activities (employment, leisure, etc.) that place prospective victims on an intersectional path with offenders.[1] As one attempts to complete those daily activities, the probability of criminal victimization increases with the existence of a likely offender, the presence of a suitable target, and the absence of a capable guardian, commonly referred to as the routine activities perspective.[2]

In recent years, an increasing number of African American adolescents and young adults have experienced victimization of the deadliest kinds such that these cases have been spotlighted nationally. In February 2012, Trayvon Martin was shot and killed by George Zimmerman while returning home from a convenience store. During the 911 call, Zimmerman indicated that "the neighborhood had some break-ins" and that "there's a real suspicious guy [Martin]" who looked like he was up to no good or on drugs because he was "looking at all the houses."[3] While a number of political leaders, community activists, and television pundits have made claims of racial bias and animus in each case, little is known about how often, under what conditions, and in what contexts discrimination is experienced by African American adolescents transitioning to adulthood, and how neighborhood characteristics may prime youth for experiencing what we would call "stereotype threat," that is, "the risk of confirming, as self-characteristic, a negative stereotype about one's group."[4]

This chapter investigates how perceptions of neighborhood safety are related to discrimination experienced by young men. We argue that local burglaries in the Sanford, Florida, area placed Martin in a position to experience increased scrutiny by neighborhood watch members, and that Martin's encounter with Zimmerman fits the classic definition of stereotype threat. By treating current and past discriminatory experiences as a means of priming that is necessary for stereotype threat, criminological aspects of the neighborhood accentuated and reinforced (mis)perceptions of wrongdoing for Zimmerman. To understand how this could occur, we begin by reviewing the literature on racial and stereotype threat theory to show how neighborhood context can shape fear of crime and engender discriminatory forms of policing and surveillance.

Racial and Stereotype Threat Theory

Since sociologists Herbert Blumer and Hubert Blalock developed group threat theory—which posits that the inclusion and ascension of minority groups in social, economic, and political life threatens the majority group's control over the distribution of resources and power they seek to preserve[5]—a number of studies have theoretically and empirically investigated how prejudice operates against minorities in a variety of sociopolitical contexts. Some research has shown that racial threat by subordinate groups has produced prejudicial and discriminatory use of crime control policies,[6] school discipline,[7] felon disenfranchisement legislation,[8] punishment attitudes,[9] the death penalty,[10] and lynchings.[11] Racial threat—often measured as an increasing percentage of nonwhites in a city, county, or state—has also been found to increase negative attitudes toward minorities,[12] particularly African Americans.[13]

While racial threat occurs in specific geographical contexts, stereotype threat is known to exist in a number of different testing and employment environments for different racial, gender, and age groups. Stereotype threat, a situation in which a person is, or feels to be, at risk of confirming a negative stereotype related to his or her social group, has a negative impact on the performance of blacks,[14] other minorities,[15] and girls in stereotypically male-dominated fields like math and science, in both Western and non-Western contexts.[16] In fact, stereotype threat is so pervasive that even children between the ages of six and ten suffer its consequences.[17] As well, unconscious racial stereotypes have been found to influence justice decision makers' perceptions of culpability and punishment.[18]

Stereotype threat is thought to operate through three separate and interrelated mechanisms: physiological stress that serves to impair prefrontal brain processing, the tendency to actively monitor performance, and subsequent self-regulation efforts to suppress negative thoughts and emotions.[19] It could be that both Zimmerman and Martin suffered from any one or all of these conditions depending on the situational context wherein the dynamic interaction unfolded. Furthermore, cognitive impairment due to stereotypes also "spill over" into other areas of functioning. For instance, stereotype threat has been linked with unfavorable mental health outcomes. Williams and Mohammed assert that the perception of discrimination associated with being stereotyped can lead to increased stress, as well as anxiety and depression.[20] The spillover from experiences of stereotype threat is known to decrease self-control and increase aggression,[21] two factors that likely served to amplify the tension between Martin and Zimmerman following Zimmerman's decision to engage Martin on the basis of his unfounded suspicions. Thus, it is likely that both Zimmerman and Martin experienced opposite forms of stereotype threat that are rooted in the monitoring of performance (Zimmerman) and the inability to suppress negative thoughts and emotions (Martin).

It is unknown whether stereotype threat, among children and adolescents, exists in different neighborhood contexts. The increased scrutiny and surveillance of Martin may have increased his risk of experiencing stereotype threat. Indeed, Ragsdale argues that surveillance is "a socio-cognitive process whereby members of a dominant group, motivated by suspicion, fear, anxiety, or prior conditioning, monitor members of non-dominant groups' language, emotional expression, and behavior."[22] Consistent with Ragsdale's definition, the transcript of Zimmerman's 911 call stresses his fear and anxiety that Martin may burglarize homes in the area given prior neighborhood crimes, and Zimmerman focuses his impromptu and extraneous comments on Martin's expressional and behavioral attributes despite Martin not attempting to enter any homes prior to the 911 call. Research shows that being the target of prejudice affects self-control because the stigma induced depletes the ego of the person targeted.[23] The stigma attached to being surveilled in one's own neighborhood may constitute the priming necessary to induce the stereotype threat stimulus Martin experienced. Yet, little is known about the prevalence of stigma and discrimination within different types of neighborhoods. To understand why residential context matters as a possible prime for stereotype threat, we turn to scholarship on neighborhood composition and crime.

Neighborhood Composition and Fear of Crime

Much research finds that racially segregated, nonwhite neighborhoods have higher crime rates than white communities.[24] In addition, racial isolation pervades many urban areas,[25] resulting in high levels of poverty, depression, stress, and negative health outcomes among residents.[26] The social and health consequences of racial segregation contribute to perceptions of powerlessness, mistrust, and local neighborhood detachment.[27] Fear of crime among whites exacerbates racial segregation by ensuring that their residential proximity to blacks and Hispanics is kept at a distance.[28] High residential instability in combination with low population density predisposes these areas to disorganization, as residents are dispersed over large distances and less likely to develop the community norms, goals, and values necessary to combat disorder.[29]

Yet, neighborhoods that are more racially heterogeneous may also suffer from misperceptions about crime. Skogan contends that individual perceptions of crime, even in neighborhoods experiencing periods of significant decline, are not always consistent with actual levels of offending.[30] This finding holds useful explanatory power at both the individual and community levels, as the fear of crime influences both the frequency and quality of interactions between neighbors. These interactions facilitate social bonds between neighbors that have been shown to affect levels of collective efficacy within neighborhoods.[31]

Fear of neighbors, however, undermines a neighborhood's capacity to solve problems of crime and disorder, paralyzing and plunging residential areas into further isolation and decay. Past work has attempted to elucidate how fear and crime simultaneously operate. Baba and Austin examined perceptions of crime and social interactions among neighbors, and contend that when fear is low, community involvement reaches its apex.[32] However, when fear of crime rises, participation within a neighborhood and its activities declines until crime reaches its peak. This pattern may seem strange upon first glance; however, the relationship is likely attributable to low-crime communities consisting of high percentages of individuals with heavy involvement in neighborhood life, implying that participation in crime-centered organizations may simply be one of many areas of involvement for highly attached residents.

Seminole County, Florida, is approximately 12 percent black, whereas the Sanford neighborhood, where Martin was killed, is 31 percent black.[33] Neighborhood context—and perceptions of neighborhood crime and disorder—shape local beliefs about victimization and social institutions. Such conceptions about the ecological conditions of one's neighborhood and its social structures determine expectations about interpersonal interactions and how residents perceive and enforce standard operating rules about crime, disorder, and victimization. Past work documents how race relations, social control, and policing converge to accentuate and exacerbate perceptions of neighborhood crime and race.

In a very important study, Quillian and Pager used survey data from Chicago, Seattle, and Baltimore to examine the relationship between neighborhood racial composition and resident perceptions of neighborhood crime, and found that the greater the percentage of young black men in a neighborhood, the higher the perceptions were regarding the level of neighborhood crime.[34] Also, their results suggest that the negative effect of the percentage of blacks was stronger for whites than blacks.[35] Consistent with these findings, Oliver and Mendelberg show that in metropolitan areas with greater concentrations of African Americans, whites exhibit significantly more negative stereotypes about blacks, with "whites' negative racial attitudes increasing with higher percentages of blacks [in the area]."[36]

Such perceptions of disorder are strongly influenced by the racial, ethnic, and socioeconomic structure of the neighborhood. Sampson and Raudenbush show that at the neighborhood level, black presence, violent crime, and poverty have positive and significant effects on perceptions of total, physical, and social disorder, while at the person level, blacks are less likely to perceive any of the three disorders.[37] However, as the percentage of blacks in the block group increases, Latino respondents perceived much more disorder than whites.[38] The cultural stereotypes and implicit bias associated with race often means that markers of disadvantage are inextricably and cognitively linked in the minds of many Americans,[39] with the imputation of individual disreputability being conflated with neighborhoods composed of stigmatized minorities.[40]

Moreover, interpersonal contact across racial groups matters for understanding collective bonds and social trust within communities. Marschall and Stolle examine how context, social interaction, and interracial experiences influence perceptions of trust and find that neighborhood context matters, but that the effects vary.[41] Specifically, whites in low-status contexts—defined by both the education levels of residents and respondents' perceptions of neighborhood problems—are less likely to trust others; however, for blacks, informal socializing is more important for trust in heterogeneous neighborhoods where the opportunities and incidence of interracial interactions are greater.[42] Thus, perceptions of risk depend on both neighborhood context and race. In the Zimmerman-Martin case, the perception of neighborhood break-ins may have directly or indirectly contributed to the lack of trust exhibited by Zimmerman.

In addition, community-based theories (social disorganization, urban disadvantage/deprivation, community development and spatial diffusion) may be useful in understanding variability in racial profiling at the local level.[43] Research on policing has been at the forefront of documenting how neighborhood characteristics influence officer perceptions and their behavior.[44] In a two-department study, Werthman and Piliavin found that officers defined certain geographic areas as suspicious places: "past experience leads them [officers] to conclude that more crimes are committed in the poorer sections of town than in the wealthier areas, that Negroes are more likely to cause public disturbances than Whites, and that adolescents in certain areas are a greater source of trouble than other categories of the citizenry."[45] This process, known as "ecological contamination," refers to the manner in which "the socioeconomic character of [an] area in which the police encounter [a] suspect may attach to the individual suspect, independent of the suspect's personal characteristics or behavior."[46] Additional research by Smith using police-citizen observation data showed that police behaved differently in different neighborhood contexts, concluding that the "propensity of police to exercise coercive authority is not influenced by the race of the individual suspect per se but rather the racial composition of the area in which the encounter occurs."[47] In one recent and methodologically advanced study, Terrill and Reisig used systematic social observation data from a study of police in Indianapolis, Indiana, and St. Petersburg, Florida, to examine how neighborhood context influenced the level of force police used during encounters with suspects, finding that, net of a host of factors, officers used higher levels of force in disadvantaged neighborhoods as well as in neighborhood characterized by high homicide rates.[48] And perhaps even more interesting, Terrill and Reisig found that inclusion of both concentrated disadvantage and the homicide rate rendered a previously significant minority effect on level of force insignificant,[49] and concluded that "minority suspects are more likely to be recipients of higher levels of police force because they are disproportionately encountered in disadvantaged and high-crime neighborhoods."[50] Several other studies have reached the similar conclusion that police behavior varies greatly across ecological contexts.[51] Thus, the geographic location of police call for service and/or interaction helps to condition how they may perceive suspects and/or incidents and, in turn, influence their behavior.[52] It is possible that Zimmerman's neighborhood watch position imbued him with a pseudo-policing persona that emboldened him to defy actual law enforcement by pursuing Martin when he was instructed to disengage.

Importantly, Stewart and colleagues studied a similar issue within a different social context and reached opposite conclusions.[53] They examined whether perceptions of racially biased policing against black teens is due to neighborhood racial composition, net of many other factors, and found that African American youth were most often discriminated against by police in predominantly white neighborhoods, especially those white neighborhoods that were experiencing growth in black population. However, it is unknown how neighborhood quality and safety matter for understanding experiences of discrimination that may extend beyond the police force.

Current Focus

As our review has shown, research on stereotype threat operates in controlled testing environments, but at the same time there is virtually no research examining how neighborhood context matters in the production of stereotype threat among adolescents. Given the importance of the adolescent period across multiply important life domains, such as education, social skills, delinquency, and employment, consideration of stereotype perceptions is important for understanding where those perceptions originate, how they influence interpersonal and vicarious interactions, and the kinds of opportunities they may create or inhibit. We investigate how neighborhood safety—based on perceptions about neighborhood crime—is associated with perceptional discrimination among adolescents. We hypothesize that nonwhite adolescents will report greater levels of discrimination in less safe neighborhoods because of elevated surveillance.[54]

Experiences with Neighborhood Safety and Racial Prejudice

We use data from the 2011–12 National Survey of Children's Health (NSCH) to investigate adolescent perspectives on, and experiences with, neighborhood safety and racial prejudice. NSCH data are collected by the National Opinion Research Center at the University of Chicago on behalf of the Centers for Disease Control and Prevention. The NSCH randomly sampled (cell phone and landline) telephone numbers to locate households with children aged birth to seventeen, and within each household one child was randomly selected to be the subject of an interview. The researchers asked the same demographic and health questions of all children; however, because children experience the social world at different stages of development, specific questions were asked about early (for those aged birth to five) and middle to adolescent (ages six to seventeen) childhood. Parents were asked about family functioning, parental health, neighborhood/community characteristics, health coverage, and other demographic information. Each interview lasted, on average, about twenty-seven minutes, and data were collected between February 28, 2011, and June 25, 2012. Over 95,600 child-level interviews were completed, with the number of interviews ranging from over 1,800 to 2,200 per state. When weighted, NSCH results represent the noninstitutionalized social experiences and familial conditions of all minors in the United States and within each state. Our weighted analysis focuses on adolescent (fourteen to seventeen years old) discriminatory experiences within specific ecological contexts.

Table 8.1 displays the operationalization and coding of measures in our study. The central variables in our study are racial differences in exposure to, and frequency of, discrimination among adolescents by neighborhood crime designations. Past research shows that social institutions, neighborhood disorder, and social cohesion are relevant to residential stability and crime reduction.[55] Therefore, we construct five distinct measures of social and neighborhood background to include as controls. Social institutions include scaled measures of whether the neighborhood has sidewalks, playgrounds, recreational centers, and libraries. Neighborhood disorder is the count of whether litter, dilapidated housing, and broken windows are present in the neighborhood.

TABLE 8.1. Descriptive Statistics of Variables and Measures for Adolescents 14–17, NSCH 2012

Variable	Measure	Coding	Mean	SD
Neighborhood safe	Parent feels the adolescent is safe in their community or neighborhood	Y = 1, N = 0	0.88	0.32
Discriminated against	Adolescent was treated or judged unfairly because of his/her race/ethnicity	Y = 1, N = 0	0.07	0.26
Often discriminated against	Adolescent was often treated or judged unfairly because of his/her race/ethnicity	Y = 1, N = 0	0.25	0.43
Social institutions ($\alpha = .64$)	Count of social institutions (sidewalks, playgrounds, rec centers, and libraries) in community	0 = low, 4 = high	3.16	1.12
Neighborhood disorder ($\alpha = .59$)	Count of neighborhood disorders (litter, dilapidated housing, and broken windows)	0 = low, 3 = high	0.40	0.76
Social cohesion ($\alpha = .82$)	Count of social cohesion (people help each other out, residents watch each other's kids, adults trust each other, and people count on one another)	0 = low, 4 = high	3.47	1.11

(continued)

TABLE 8.1 (*continued*)

Variable	Measure	Coding	Mean	SD
Self-control (α = .69)	Count of adolescent self-control measures (does not stay calm when faced with a challenge, bullies others, argues with adults, is a bother to parents, is difficult to care for, and angers parents)	0 = high, 6 = low	1.70	1.61
Concentrated disadvantage (α = .72)	Count of adverse childhood experiences (parental incarceration, witness domestic violence, living in poverty, living in a single-parent household, having unmet medical needs, being on welfare, receiving food stamps, and receiving reduced price lunches)	0 = low; 9 = high	1.51	1.86
NH-white	Adolescent is non-Hispanic white (baseline)	Y = 1, N = 0	0.57	0.50
NH-black	Adolescent is non-Hispanic black	Y = 1, N = 0	0.15	0.35
Hispanic	Adolescent is Hispanic	Y = 1, N = 0	0.19	0.40
NH-other	Adolescent is non-Hispanic other	Y = 1, N = 0	0.09	0.28
LT HS education	Mother has less than high school education (baseline)	Y = 1, N = 0	0.13	0.34
HS diploma	Mother has high school diploma	Y = 1, N = 0	0.24	0.43
Some college or more	Mother has some college education or more	Y = 1, N = 0	0.63	0.48
Age	Age of adolescent	# of years	15.5	1.11
Male	Adolescent is male	Y = 1, N = 0	0.51	0.50
Employed full-time	At least one adult in household was employed 50 out of 52 weeks in past 12 months	Y = 1, N = 0	0.85	0.36

Source: Authors' calculations of National Survey of Children Health (NSCH) data. Weighted $N = 16{,}837{,}733$.

Social cohesion measures the connectedness of residents through their ability to help each other, watch each other's kids, trust one another, and count on each other. Self-control measures include how well the adolescent can control his or her behavior and the ease/difficulty parents report in caring for the child. Concentrated disadvantage contains nine measures of adverse childhood experiences that include parental incarceration, witnessing domestic violence, living in poverty, living in a single-parent household, having unmet medical needs, being on welfare, receiving food stamps, and receiving reduced price lunches.[56]

In addition, measures of social background reflect, to varying degrees, the social inequality in contemporary America. According to NSCH data, almost 8 percent of children have experienced the incarceration of a parent, more than double the percentage observed in other studies.[57] Rapid changes in family life, data collection, and social policy may partially explain discrepant estimates of parental incarceration in population and survey data.[58] Nevertheless, other markers of disadvantage—living in poverty and in single-parent households, receipt of welfare and reduced-cost lunches, and having unmet medical needs— also point to a significant fraction of children facing hardships that may influence the likelihood of experiencing prejudice and discrimination in contemporary America, particularly at an age and during an era when social status may matter more for successful transition into adulthood.

Method

We employ two different methods to investigate the relationship between neighborhood safety and discrimination. First, we fit multiple neighborhood-specific probit models to estimate the likelihood that nonwhite adolescents experience discrimination. We report marginal effects, which express the rate of change in the dependent variable (i.e., the predicted probability) relative to a unit change in an independent variable.[59] All models are evaluated at their mean values.

Because selection into specific neighborhoods is not random, we use propensity score matching methods to reduce the bias associated with observable social background characteristics. The propensity score is the conditional probability of living in an unsafe neighborhood given a set of demographic, social background, and labor market covariates that predict adolescent discrimination experiences and that are potential confounders in the association between neighborhood quality and prejudice. The method balances social background characteristics of adolescents living in safe and unsafe neighborhoods (the treatment and control groups, respectively) to ensure that any differences in experiencing discrimination between adolescents are not due to significant, pretreatment differences in factors that predict residing in a particular neighborhood.[60] We use a kernel matching algorithm, where the kernel function and bandwidth transform the distance of the propensity score so that closer control cases receive greater weight in the matching process than cases further away.

Results

Table 8.1 presents the weighted sample means and deviations of measures in our study. Approximately 88 percent of parents think their neighborhood is safe. Among young adults, 7 percent experienced discrimination due to their race or ethnicity, and among them, one out of four experienced discrimination often. On average, a little over three social institutions can be found in neighborhoods, and disorder is relatively low in these data. Respondents indicate that their communities are deeply cohesive, and adolescents tend to display higher self-control (as evinced by lower values on the self-control measures). Like neighborhood disorder, concentrated disadvantage is relatively low, indicating few adverse childhood experiences. The sample of adolescents is 57 percent white, 15 percent black, 19 percent Hispanic, and 9 percent of another race. Most of the youth reside in highly advantaged households, with 63 percent of their parents having some college education.

Our investigation into the association between neighborhood safety and adolescent experiences of prejudice begins by focusing on national estimates. Figure 8.1 displays the percentage of adolescents who have ever experienced prejudice, by neighborhood safety status and race. Overall, in neighborhoods that are unsafe, one out of eight adolescents reports that he or she has experienced discrimination (the first bar in the chart). Yet, youth who reside in safe residential areas experience lower levels of discrimination, with 7 percent stating that they have been the target of racial/ethnic prejudice.

The overall percentage of teens encountering prejudice conceals tremendous racial inequality, in part because of both differential selection into safe/unsafe neighborhoods and the likelihood of perceiving and/ or experiencing bias based on race. Approximately one in twenty white youth in unsafe neighborhoods experiences racial prejudice, and in safe

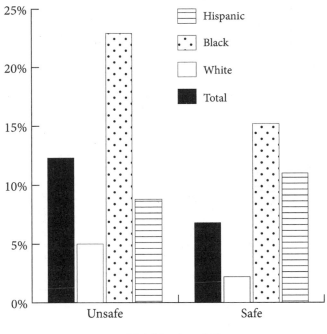

Figure 8.1. Percentage of adolescents who have ever experienced discrimination, by race and neighborhood type. Source: Authors' calculations from National Survey of Children's Health (NSCH) data. All estimates are nationally weighted.

areas this figure is around one in fifty (the second bar in the chart). For nonwhite youth, the social experience is very different. Roughly one in four African American teens reports experiencing prejudice in unsafe neighborhoods (the third bar in the chart). Blacks who perceive their residential areas to be safer are significantly less likely to experience racial prejudice, compared to blacks in unsafe areas; however, their likelihood of racial discrimination is much higher than that for both whites and Hispanics regardless of perceptions about neighborhood quality.

The Latino percentages are particularly vexing (the fourth bar in the chart). In unsafe neighborhoods, nearly 9 percent of Hispanic adolescents encounter discrimination, far lower than the figure for African Americans. This finding may be consistent with the "Latino Paradox": that "Hispanic Americans do better on a wide range of social

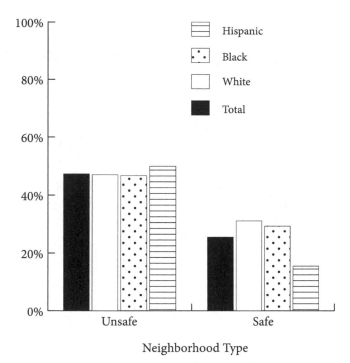

Figure 8.2. Percentage of adolescents who frequently experience discrimination, conditional on having experienced any discrimination, by race and neighborhood type. Source: Authors' calculations from National Survey of Children's Health (NSCH) data. All estimates are nationally weighted.

indicators—including propensity to violence—than one would expect given their socioeconomic disadvantages."[61] Yet, Hispanic youth who view their residential areas as safe are 25 percent more likely to experience prejudice than Latinos in unsafe neighborhoods. Differences in discriminatory mechanisms and social conditions, or recent growth in the Latino population, may explain higher levels of prejudice Hispanic youth encounter in safe neighborhoods. This particular finding requires much more scrutiny.

While perceptions of neighborhood safety matter for situating adolescent perceptions of prejudice within a particular spatial context, the frequency of experiencing prejudicial treatment may also vary by perceptions of residential quality, as displayed in figure 8.2. Among adolescents who have experienced racial bias and live in unsafe neighborhoods, nearly one in two has been a frequent victim of discriminatory treatment. This estimate declines to roughly one in four when the residential area is considered safe. While the percentages of youth who frequently experience prejudice are relatively similar across racial groups in unsafe neighborhoods, the adolescents living in safe communities experience significantly lower levels of frequent discrimination. Among youth who have experienced racial prejudice in safe neighborhoods, roughly 31 percent of white, 29 percent of black, and 16 percent of Hispanic adolescents were frequently exposed to racial discrimination.

Research shows that young black men report the highest levels of investigatory stops among policing agents.[62] Because this volume is concerned with the Zimmerman-Martin interaction that was the result of an investigatory stop, we restrict subsequent analyses to adolescent males to explore how neighborhood type and experiences of discrimination may reflect the highly gendered nature of racialized surveillance. Thus, we estimate the likelihood that black and Hispanic boys experience prejudice in both safe and unsafe residential areas after controlling for the rich set of indicators listed in table 8.1, including neighborhood disorder, social institutions, social cohesion, and self-control. Table 8.2 shows the marginal changes in the probability of a male adolescent ever experiencing prejudice by neighborhood safety status.

Race matters in understanding the risk of experiencing discrimination in various neighborhood contexts. Among adolescents in unsafe neighborhoods, black boys are over 19 percentage points more likely

TABLE 8.2. The Marginal Changes in the Probability of Adolescent Males Ever Experiencing Discrimination by Race and Neighborhood Type

	Ever discriminated against		Discriminated against frequently	
	Unsafe	Safe	Unsafe	Safe
Black	19.4***	8.8***	13.7**	−2.7
Hispanic	10.5*	8.3***	2.2	−4.5**

$* p < .05; ** p < .01; *** p < .001$ (two-tailed tests)

Source: Authors' calculation from a (probit) probability model that estimates the likelihood of an adolescent ever experiencing discrimination or being discriminated against frequently, after accounting for community institutions, neighborhood disorder, social cohesion, concentrated disadvantage, self-control, and social background characteristics listed in table 8.1. Whites are the reference group. All estimates are marginal effects, and measures are evaluated at their mean values. Estimates are also adjusted for unobserved differences between states using state fixed effects, and the standard errors are clustered on states to account for correlated adolescent responses within the same geographic space.

than white boys to have experienced some form of racial/ethnic discrimination. Hispanics, too, are significantly more likely than whites to report experiencing prejudice. These racial differences hold in safe neighborhoods; however, our findings indicate that levels of discrimination black and Hispanic youth face in safe residential areas are remarkably similar in comparison to whites.

The frequency of racial discrimination youth experience varies by neighborhood type. In unsafe communities, black boys are almost 14 percentage points more likely to repeatedly encounter prejudice than white boys, whereas this association was not observed for Hispanics. However, in safe residential areas, Hispanics were significantly less likely than whites to frequently experience discrimination, whereas there is no measureable difference between white and black youth in the frequency of their prejudicial treatment.

It is possible that the associations reported in table 8.2 are largely driven by selection into both neighborhood type and particular discriminatory encounters. Because we are interested in understanding how residential context may have mattered in structuring stereotype threat, table 8.3 presents unmatched and matched estimates of ever experiencing discrimination, and the frequency of such experiences, by neighborhood type for adolescent males controlling for race. Unmatched estimates indicate that living in a safe neighborhood reduces an adolescent male's likelihood of encountering racial prejudice by 9.2 percentage points. However, selection into residential neighborhoods explains 37

TABLE 8.3. Matched and Unmatched Estimates of Neighborhood Safety on the Likelihood of Experiencing Discrimination among Adolescent Males

	Ever discriminated against			Discriminated against frequently		
	Safe	Unsafe	Difference	Safe	Unsafe	Difference
Unmatched	.056	.148	−.092***	.243	.366	−.123***
Matched	.056	.113	−.058***	.243	.299	−.056**

** $p < .01$; *** $p < .001$ (two-tailed tests)

Source: Authors' calculation from a propensity score matching model that estimates the effect of neighborhood type on the likelihood of an adolescent ever experiencing discrimination or being discriminated against frequently. All models control for race, community institutions, neighborhood disorder, social cohesion, concentrated disadvantage, self-control, and social background characteristics listed in table 8.1. Given that the distributional form for experiencing discrimination in particular neighborhoods is unknown, the standard errors of these estimates have been bootstrapped 500 times to obtain a more precise measure of the finite sampling approximations associated with adolescent discrimination in community context.

TABLE 8.4. Matched Estimates of Neighborhood Safety on the Likelihood of Experiencing Discrimination among Adolescent Males by Race

	Ever discriminated against			Discriminated against frequently		
	Safe	Unsafe	Difference	Safe	Unsafe	Difference
Black	.157	.172	−.015	.290	.346	−.056
Hispanic	.047	.123	−.075***	.239	.292	−.053**

** $p < .01$; *** $p < .001$ (two-tailed tests)

Source: Authors' calculation from a propensity score matching model that estimates the effect of neighborhood type on the likelihood of an adolescent ever experiencing discrimination or being discriminated against frequently. All models control for community institutions, neighborhood disorder, social cohesion, concentrated disadvantage, self-control, and social background characteristics listed in table 8.1. Given that the distributional form for experiencing discrimination in particular neighborhoods is unknown, the standard errors of these estimates have been bootstrapped 500 times to obtain a more precise measure of the finite sampling approximations associated with adolescent discrimination in community context.

percent of this finding, as the matched sample estimate lowers the association to 5.8 percent. A similar finding is observed for the frequently encountering racial prejudice, although the selection bias grows to 55 percent.

Last, to discern how youth of color experience discrimination in safe and unsafe residential areas after accounting for neighborhood selectivity, we ran race-specific, propensity score models. Table 8.4 displays race-specific, matched estimates of neighborhood quality on the likelihood of experiencing racial prejudice. Although the percentage differences are the same for blacks and Hispanics, we find that neighborhood context does not matter for explaining the discriminatory experiences of young, black males. For Hispanics, however, residing in safe neighborhoods lowers their chances of both experiencing and frequently encountering racial prejudice. This finding is an artifact of how observed selection bias reported in table 8.3 distorts the complex relationship among race, place, and discrimination.

Conclusions and Implications

In 1899, W.E.B. Du Bois published an essay wherein he postulated four causes of what he called "negro crime" in the South: a convict-lease system, where the state uses inmates as laborers for revenue generation; the attitudes of courts, which produce a double standard of justice; the increasing lawlessness of mobs who use lynching and vigilante justice in lieu of a legitimate trial; and the color line, the use of race to segregate all domains of social life.[63] The death of Trayvon Martin by George Zimmerman, as well as Zimmerman's subsequent acquittal, highlights this peculiarly Du Boisian basis of racial justice. The circumstances surrounding the death of Martin that evening raise a number of sociological questions about surveillance, neighborhood crime, and stereotype threat.

Past work on neighborhood composition and perceptions of crime as well as research on surveillance and police interactions indicate that nonwhites are more likely to be perceived as dangerous, are less likely to be trusted, and are at an increased risk for having force used against them, particularly in disadvantaged neighborhoods. Our work may explain how a routine neighborhood watch beat led to the death of a residential minor who had not committed any crime. The social ecology of an area (Sanford, Florida) as well as the relentless monitoring and pursuit of Martin by Zimmerman may have converged to prime Martin in a stereotype threat framework. Because minorities are aware of their status and are stigmatized within educational, residential, and employment environments, stereotype threat presents a real and dangerous problem for people of color in both safe and unsafe residential areas.

Using a large national database, our work shows that nearly one in fourteen adolescents experiences some form of racial discrimination in his or her neighborhood, and that among those who have experienced prejudice, one in four encounters such bias frequently. One of the key and perhaps unexpected findings from our work concerns the lack of a statistically distinguishable effect on experiences of discrimination among black male adolescents. This lack of a difference between neighborhoods suggests that young black adolescents in safe as well as unsafe neighborhoods share similar perceptions of discrimination. Perhaps, then, among this specific demographic (young, black, males) their perceptions are drawn independent of neighborhood conditions—or at least the conditions measured in this study. Given that our work is among the first to study these specific questions and relationships, it is generally unknown whether the discriminatory processes young (black) men experience are the result of different sources of prejudice within particular contexts that are independent of neighborhood quality or arise from their own life experiences and/or those of their parents and/

or friends. Recent research shows that investigatory police stops are disproportionately experienced by young black men, and that these stops are associated with increased perceptions of discrimination among people of color.[64] Understanding the potentially wide range of inputs into these discriminatory experiences among adolescents is an important question worthy of future investigation.

Moreover, although the data do not contain information regarding the sources or types of discrimination experienced by adolescents, which is a noted limitation, it could be that adolescents encounter racial bias from peers and adults in a variety of contexts. Future research should explore when, where, how, and by whom youth are exposed to discrimination. Untangling the processes by which young adults come into contact with racial stigma is of great importance as they prepare to transition to adulthood and interact with diverse individuals of all races and ages.

Ultimately it is important to investigate how bias and discrimination are experienced by young adults in different social environments, particularly if adolescents are at risk of validating perceived stereotypes. Past work, for instance, shows that stereotype threat can operate in academic settings,[65] criminal interrogations,[66] and athletic competitions.[67] Neighborhood context may be another domain where stereotype threat exists if the actions and behavior of either individual comports with a negative stereotype about his race. It is also especially important to better unpack the differences across race/ethnicity, which were pronounced among both blacks and Hispanics—but with some differences according to the type of residential community. It would also be useful to consider these issues across gender, as minority men and women may have different perceptions regarding discrimination.

The educational system often provides youth, particularly those from backgrounds of disadvantage, with early experiences of both discrimination and formal social control that may serve to instill and reinforce stereotypes discussed above.[68] Additional research focused on the short- and long-term implications of these experiences is needed to better understand the full extent of the issues addressed in this chapter.

Going forward, we hope that our initial foray into understanding the prevalence and intensity of stereotype-reinforcing discrimination across both context and race/ethnicity serves to heighten awareness of this issue as an important area of criminological scholarship. As well, we hope that issues related to selection, which are pronounced in the neighborhood literature, are attuned to and dealt with in the best manner possible. Our findings clearly show that this is a particularly important aspect of understanding the full picture with respect to racial/ethnic differences in stereotype discrimination.

NOTES

1. Hindelang, Gottfredson, and Garofalo 1978.
2. Cohen and Felson 1979.
3. MotherJones 2012, 1.
4. Steele and Aronson 1995, 797.
5. Blumer 1958; Blalock 1967.
6. Western 2006; Eitle, D'Alessio, and Stolzenberg 2002; Jacobs and Carmichael 2001; Wacquant 2001.
7. Welch and Payne 2010.
8. Behrens, Uggen, and Manza 2003.
9. Alexander 2010; King and Wheelock 2007; Baumer, Messner, and Rosenfeld 2003.
10. Carmichael, Jacobs, and Kent 2005.
11. Tolnay, Deane, and Beck 1996; Tolnay and Beck 1995.
12. Quillian 1995; 1996.
13. Taylor 1998.
14. Steele and Aronson 1995; Steele 1997.
15. Aronson and Salinas 2001; Kang and Chasteen 2009.
16. Aronson, Quinn, and Spencer 1998; Picho and Stephens 2012.
17. McKown and Weinstein 2003.
18. Graham and Lowery 2004.
19. Schmader, Johns, and Forbes 2008.
20. Williams and Mohammed 2009.
21. Inzlicht and Kang 2010.
22. Ragsdale 2000, 33.
23. Inzlicht, McKay, and Aronson 2006.
24. Krivo and Peterson 1996, 2000; Krivo et al. 1998; Peterson and Krivo 1993; Shihadeh and Flynn 1996.
25. Massey and Denton 1989; 1993; Massey 1990; Massey, Condran, and Denton 1987.
26. Massey 1996; Ross 2000; Ross and Mirowsky 2001; Aneshensel and Sucoff 1996.
27. Geis and Ross 1988; Ross, Mirowsky, and Pribesh 2001; Woldoff 2002; Warner and Rountree 1997.

28. Skogan 1995; Chiricos, McEntire, and Gertz 2001; Emerson, Chai, and Yancey 2001; Taylor and Covington 1993.

29. Crutchfield, Geerkin, and Gove 1982; Sampson, Raudenbush, and Earls 1997; Sampson 2012.

30. Skogan 1986.

31. Sampson, Raudenbush, and Earls 1997.

32. Baba and Austin 1991.

33. U.S. Census Bureau 2010a; 2010b.

34. Quillian and Pager 2001.

35. Ibid., 718.

36. Oliver and Mendelberg 2000, 574.

37. Sampson and Raudenbush 2004.

38. Sampson and Raudenbush 2004.

39. Bobo and Massagli 2001; Banaji 2002; Loury 2002.

40. Hagan 1994; Sampson and Raudenbush 2004.

41. Marschall and Stolle 2004.

42. Marschall and Stolle 2004.

43. Parker et al. 2004.

44. See Novak and Chamlin 2012; Petrocelli, Piquero, and Smith 2003.

45. Werthman and Piliavin 1967, 75.

46. Terrill and Reisig 2003, 295.

47. Smith 1986, 332.

48. Terrill and Reisig 2003.

49. Ibid., 304.

50. Ibid., 306.

51. Cf. MacDonald and Stokes 2006; MacDonald et al. 2007.

52. See also Herbert 1998, 358.

53. Stewart et al. 2009.

54. Goffman 2014.

55. Peterson, Krivo, and Harris 2000; Patillo 1998; Sampson, Raudenbush, and Earls 1997; Wilson 1987; Wilson and Kelling 1982.

56. While several alphas may be somewhat less than ideal, alpha is a lower bound of reliability (in that it underestimates the true reliability; see Carmines and Zeller 1979). As well, past research has created indices from survey questions with values as low as .48 (Turney and Wildeman 2013, 975), but several studies routinely report alpha levels around .69 (King and Wheelock 2007, 1262; Turney and Wildeman 2013, 973–75).

57. Pettit, Sykes, and Western 2009; Wildeman 2009.

58. Sykes and Pettit 2014.

59. Long 1997; Powers and Xie 2000.

60. Rosenbaum and Rubin 1983; 1984.

61. Sampson 2008, 29.

62. Epp, Maynard-Moody, and Haider-Markel 2014, 67.

63. Du Bois [1899] 2011.
64. Epp, Maynard-Moody, and Haider-Markel 2014.
65. Steele and Aronson 1995.
66. Najdowski 2011.
67. Stone et al. 1999.
68. Wald and Losen 2003.

REFERENCES

Alexander, Michelle. 2010. *The New Jim Crow: Mass Incarceration in the Age of Color-blindness.* New York: New Press.

Aneshensel, Carol, and Clea Sucoff. 1996. "The Neighborhood Context of Adolescent Mental Health." *Journal of Health and Social Behavior* 37:293–310.

Aronson, Joshua, Dianne Quinn, and Steven Spencer. 1998. "Stereotype Threat and the Academic Underperformance of Minorities and Women." In *Prejudice: The Target's Perspective*, edited by J. K. Swim and C. Stangor, 83–103. San Diego, CA: Academic Press.

Aronson, Joshua, and Moises Salinas. 2001. "Stereotype Threat, Attributional Ambiguity, and Latino Underperformance." Unpublished manuscript, University of Texas at Austin.

Baba, Yoko, and Mark D. Austin. 1991. "Investigation of a Curvilinear Relationship: Perceived Neighborhood Safety and Social Interaction." *Sociological Focus* 24 (1): 45–59.

Banaji, Mahzarin R. 2002. "Social Psychology of Stereotypes." In *International Encyclopedia of the Social and Behavioral Sciences*, edited by Neil J. Smelser and Paul B. Baltes, 15100–104. Oxford: Elsevier.

Baumer, Eric, Steven Messner, and Richard Rosenfeld. 2003. "Explaining Spatial Variation in Support for Capital Punishment: A Multilevel Analysis." *American Journal of Sociology* 108:844–75.

Behrens, Angela, Chris Uggen, and Jeff Manza. 2003. "Ballot Manipulation and the 'Menace of Negro Domination': Racial Threat and Felon Disenfranchisement in the United States, 1850–2002." *American Journal of Sociology* 109:559–605.

Blalock, Hubert M. 1967. *Toward a Theory of Minority-Group Relations.* New York: John Wiley.

Blumer, Herbert. 1958. "Race Prejudice as a Sense of Group Position." *Pacific Sociological Review* 1:3–7.

Bobo, Lawrence, and Michael Massagli. 2001. "Stereotyping and Urban Inequality." In *Urban Inequality: Evidence from Four Cities*, edited by Alice O'Connor, Charles Tilly, and Lawrence Bobo, 89–162. New York: Russell Sage Foundation.

Carmichael, Jason, David Jacobs, and Stephanie Kent. 2005. "Vigilantism, Current Racial Threat, and Death Sentences." *American Sociological Review* 70 (4): 656–77.

Carmines, E. G., and R. A. Zeller. 1979. *Reliability and Validity Assessment.* Thousand Oaks, CA: Sage.

Chiricos, Ted, Ranee McEntire, and Marc Gertz. 2001. "Perceived Racial and Ethnic Composition of Neighborhood and Perceived Risk of Crime." *Social Problems* 48:322–40.

Cohen, Lawrence E., and Marcus Felson. 1979. "Social Change and Crime Rate Trends: A Routine Activities Approach." *American Sociological Review* 44:588–608.

Crutchfield, Robert D., Michael R. Geerkin, and Walter E. Gove. 1982. "Crime Rate and Social Integration." *Criminology* 20 (3/4): 467–78.

Du Bois, W.E.B. (1899) 2011. "The Negro and Crime." In *The Sociological Souls of Black Folk: Essays by W.E.B. Du Bois*, edited by Robert Wortham, 103–7. Lanham, MD: Lexington.

Eitle, David, Stewart D'Alessio, and Lisa Stolzenberg. 2002. "Racial Threat and Social Control: A Test of the Political, Economic and Threat of Black Crime Hypothesis." *Social Forces* 81 (2): 557–76.

Emerson, Michael, Karen Chai, and George Yancey. 2001. "Does Race Matter in Residential Segregation? Exploring the Preferences of White Americans." *American Sociological Review* 66:922–35.

Epp, Charles, Steven Maynard-Moody, and Donald Haider-Markel. 2014. *Pulled Over: How Police Stops Define Race and Citizenship*. Chicago: University of Chicago Press.

Fox, James Allen. 2000. "Demographics and U.S. Homicide." In *The Crime Drop in America*, edited by Alfred Blumstein and Joel Wallman, 288–317. New York: Cambridge University Press.

Geis, Karlyn, and Catherine Ross. 1988. "A New Look at Urban Alienation: The Effect of Neighborhood Disorder on Perceived Powerlessness." *Social Psychology Quarterly* 61:232–46.

Goffman, Alice. 2014. *On the Run: Fugitive Life in an American City*. Chicago: University of Chicago Press.

Graham, Sandra, and Brian Lowery. 2004. "Priming Unconscious Racial Stereotypes about Adolescent Offenders." *Law and Human Behavior* 28:483–504.

Hagan, John. 1994. *Crime and Disrepute*. Thousand Oaks, CA: Pine Forge.

Herbert, Steve. 1998. "Police Subculture Revisited." *Criminology* 36:343–69.

Hindelang, Michael J., Michael R. Gottfredson, and James Garofalo. 1978. *Victims of Personal Crime: An Empirical Foundation for a Theory of Personal Victimization*. Cambridge, MA: Ballinger.

Inzlicht, Michael, and Sonia K. Kang. 2010. "Stereotype Threat Spillover: How Coping with Threats to Social Identity Affects, Aggression, Eating, Decision Making, and Attention." *Journal of Personality and Social Psychology* 99 (3): 467–81.

Inzlicht, Michael, Linda McKay, and Joshua Aronson. 2006. "Stigma as Ego Depletion: How Being the Target of Prejudice Affects Self-Control." *Psychological Science* 17 (3): 262–69.

Jacobs, David, and Jason Carmichael. 2001. "The Politics of Punishment across Time and Space. A Pooled Time-Series Analysis of Imprisonment Rates." *Social Forces* 80:61–91.

Kang, Sonia, and Allison Chasteen. 2009. "The Moderating Role of Age-Group Identification and Perceived Threat on Stereotype Threat among Older Adults." *International Journal of Aging and Human Development* 69 (3): 201–20.

King, Ryan, and Darren Wheelock. 2007. "Group Threat and Social Control: Race Perceptions of Minorities and the Desire to Punish." *Social Forces* 85 (3): 1255–80.

Krivo, Lauren, and Ruth Peterson. 1996. "Extremely Disadvantaged Neighborhoods and Urban Crime." *Social Forces* 75:619–48.

———. 2000. "The Structural Context of Homicide: Accounting for Racial Differences in Process." *American Sociological Review* 65:547–59.

Krivo, Lauren, Ruth Peterson, Helen Rizzo, and John Reynolds. 1998. "Race, Segregation, and the Concentration of Disadvantage: 1980–1990." *Social Problems* 45:61–80.

Lewis, Valerie A., Michael O. Emerson, and Stephen L. Klineberg. 2011. "Who We'll Live With: Neighborhood Racial Composition Preferences of Whites, Blacks and Latinos." *Social Forces* 89 (4): 1385–1408.

Long, J. Scott. 1997. *Regression Models for Categorical and Limited Dependent Variables.* Thousand Oaks, CA: Sage.

Loury, Glenn. 2002. *The Anatomy of Racial Inequality.* Cambridge, MA: Harvard University Press.

MacDonald, John M., and Robert J. Stokes. 2006. "Race, Social Capital, and Trust in the Police." *Urban Affairs Review* 41:358–75.

MacDonald, John M., Robert J. Stokes, Greg Ridgeway, and K. Jack Riley. 2007. "Race, Neighborhood Context, and Perceptions of Injustice by the Police in Cincinnati." *Urban Studies* 44:2567–85.

Marschall, Mellisa J., and Dietlind Stolle. 2004. "Race and the City: Neighborhood Context and the Development of Generalized Trust." *Political Behavior* 26:125–53.

Massey, Douglas. 1990. "American Apartheid: Segregation and the Making of the Underclass." *American Journal of Sociology* 96:329–57.

———. 1996. "The Age of Extremes: Concentrated Affluence and Poverty in the Twenty-First Century." *Demography* 33:395–412.

Massey, Douglas, Gretchen Condran, and Nancy Denton. 1987. "The Effect of Residential Segregation on Black Social and Economic Well-Being." *Social Forces* 66:29–56.

Massey, Douglas, and Nancy Denton. 1989. "Hypersegregation in U.S. Metropolitan Areas: Black and Hispanic Segregation along Five Dimensions." *Demography* 26:373–93.

———. 1993. *American Apartheid: Segregation and the Making of the Underclass.* Cambridge, MA: Harvard University Press.

McKown, Clark, and Rhonda Weinstein. 2003. "The Development and Consequences of Stereotype Consciousness in Middle Childhood." *Child Development* 74 (2): 498–515.

MotherJones. 2012. "Transcript of George Zimmerman's Call to the Police." http://www.motherjones.com/documents/326700-full-transcript-zimmerman. Retrieved August 20, 2014.

Najdowski, Cynthia. 2011. "Stereotype Threat in Criminal Interrogations: Why Innocent Black Suspects Are at Risk for Confessing Falsely." *Psychology, Public Policy, and Law* 17 (4): 562–91.

Novak, Kenneth, and Mitchell Chamlin. 2012. "Racial Threat, Suspicion, and Police Behavior: The Impact of Race and Place in Traffic Enforcement." *Crime & Delinquency* 58:275–300.

Oliver, J. Eric, and Tali Mendelberg. 2000. "Reconsidering the Environmental Determinants of Racial Attitudes." *American Journal of Political Science* 44:574–89.

Parker, Karen F., John M. MacDonald, Geoffrey P. Alpert, Michael R. Smith, and Alex R. Piquero. 2004. "A Contextual Study of Racial Profiling: Assessing the Theoretical Rationale for the Study of Racial Profiling at the Local Level." *American Behavioral Scientist* 47:943–62.

Patillo, Mary. 1998. "Sweet Mothers and Gangbangers: Managing Crime in a Black Middle-Class Neighborhood." *Social Forces* 76:747–74.

Peterson, Ruth, and Lauren Krivo. 1993. "Racial Segregation and Black Urban Homicide." *Social Forces* 71:1001–26.

Peterson, Ruth D., Lauren J. Krivo, and Mark A. Harris. 2000. "Disadvantage and Neighborhood Violent Crime: Do Local Institutions Matter?" *Journal of Research in Crime and Delinquency* 37 (1): 31–63.

Petrocelli, Matthew, Alex R. Piquero, and Michael R. Smith. 2003. "Conflict Theory and Racial Profiling: An Empirical Analysis of Police Traffic Stop Data." *Journal of Criminal Justice* 31:1–11.

Pettit, Becky, Bryan Sykes, and Bruce Western. 2009. "Technical Report on Revised Population Estimates and NLSY 79 Analysis Tables for the Pew Public Safety and Mobility Project." Cambridge, MA: Harvard University.

Picho, Katherine, and Jason Stephens. 2012. "Culture, Context and Stereotype Threat: A Comparative Analysis of Young Ugandan Women in Coed and Single-Sex Schools." *Journal of Educational Research* 105 (1): 52–63.

Powers, Daniel, and Yu Xie. 2000. *Statistical Methods for Categorical Data Analysis.* San Diego, CA: Academic Press.

Quillian, Lincoln. 1993. "Migration Patterns and the Growth of High-Poverty Neighborhoods, 1970–1990." *American Journal of Sociology* 105:1–37.

———. 1995. "Prejudice as a Response to Perceived Group Threat: Population Composition and Anti-immigrant and Racial Prejudice in Europe." *American Sociological Review* 60:586–611.

———. 1996. "Group Threat and Regional Change in Attitudes toward African Americans." *American Journal of Sociology* 102:816–60.

Quillian, Lincoln, and Devah Pager. 2001. "Black Neighbors, Higher Crime? The Role of Racial Stereotypes in Evaluations of Neighborhood Crime." *American Journal of Sociology* 107:717–67.

Ragsdale, Brian. 2000. "Surveillance of African American Men and Its Possible Effect on Social, Emotional, and Psychological Functioning." *Journal of African American Men* 5 (1): 33–42.

Rosenbaum, Paul, and Donald Rubin. 1983. "The Central Role of the Propensity Score in Observational Studies for Causal Effects." *Biometrika* 70:41–55.

———. 1984. "Reducing Bias in Observational Studies Using Subclassification on the Propensity Score." *Journal of the American Statistical Association* 79:516–24.

Ross, Catherine. 2000. "Neighborhood Disadvantage and Adult Depression." *Journal of Health and Social Behavior* 41:177–87.

Ross, Catherine, and John Mirowsky. 2001. "Neighborhood Disadvantage, Disorder, and Health." *Journal of Health and Social Behavior* 42:258–76.

Ross, Catherine, John Mirowsky, and Shana Pribesh. 2001. "Powerlessness and the Amplification of Threat: Neighborhood Disadvantage, Disorder, and Mistrust." *American Sociological Review* 66:568–91.

Sampson, Robert J. 2008. "Rethinking Crime and Immigration." *Contexts* 7 (1): 28–33.

———. 2012. *Great American City: Chicago and the Enduring Neighborhood Effect.* Chicago: University of Chicago Press.

Sampson, Robert J., and Stephen W. Raudenbush. 2004. "Seeing Disorder: Neighborhood Stigma and the Social Construction of 'Broken Windows.'" *Social Psychology Quarterly* 67:319–42.

Sampson, Robert J., Stephen W. Raudenbush, and Felton Earls. 1997. "Neighborhoods and Violent Crime: A Multilevel Study of Collective Efficacy." *Science* 277 (5328): 918–24.

Schmader, Toni, Michael Johns, and Chad Forbes. 2008. "An integrated Process Model of Stereotype Threat Effects on Performance." *Psychological Review* 115 (2): 336–56.

Shihadeh, Edward, and Nicole Flynn. 1996. "Segregation and Crime: The Effect of Black Social Isolation on the Rates of Black Urban Violence." *Social Forces* 74:1325–52.

Skogan, Wesley. 1986. "Fear of Crime and Neighborhood Change." In *Communities and Crime,* edited by A. J. Reiss Jr. and Michael Tonry, 203–30. Chicago: University of Chicago Press.

———. 1995. "Crime and the Racial Fears of White Americans." *Annals of the American Academy of Political and Social Science* 539:59–71.

Smith, Douglas A. 1986. "The Neighborhood Context of Police Behavior." In *Communities and Crime,* edited by A. J. Reiss Jr. and Michael Tonry, 313–41. Chicago: University of Chicago Press.

Steele, Claude. 1997. "A Threat in the Air: How Stereotypes Shape Intellectual Identity and Performance." *American Psychologist* 52:613–29.

Steele, Claude, and Joshua Aronson. 1995. "Stereotype Threat and the Intellectual Test Performance of African-Americans." *Journal of Personality and Social Psychology* 68:797–811.

Stewart, Eric A., Eric P. Baumer, Rod K. Brunson, and Ronald L. Simons. 2009. "Neighborhood Racial Context and Perceptions of Police-Based Racial Discrimination among Black Youth." *Criminology* 47:847–87.

Stone, Jeff, Christian Lynch, Mike Sjomeling, and John Darley. 1999. "Stereotype Threat Effects on Black and White Athletic Performance." *Journal of Personality and Social Psychology* 77 (6): 1213–27.

Sykes, Bryan, and Becky Pettit. 2014. "Mass Incarceration, Family Complexity, and the Reproduction of Childhood Disadvantage." *Annals of the American Academy of Political and Social Science* 654:127–49.

Taylor, Marylee C. 1998. "How White Attitudes Vary with the Racial Composition of Local Populations: Numbers Count." *American Sociological Review* 63:512–35.

Taylor, Ralph, and Jeanette Covington. 1993. "Community Structural Change and Fear of Crime." *Social Problems* 40:374–97.

Terrill, William, and Michael D. Reisig. 2003. "Neighborhood Context and Police Use of Force." *Journal of Research in Crime and Delinquency* 40:291–321.

Tolnay, Stewart E., and E. M. Beck. 1995. *A Festival of Violence: An Analysis of Southern Lynchings, 1882–1930.* Champaign: University of Illinois Press.

Tolnay, Stewart E., Glenn Deane, and E. M. Beck. 1996. "Vicarious Violence: Spatial Effects in Southern Lynching, 1890–1919." *American Journal of Sociology* 102: 788–815.

Turney, Kristen, and Christopher Wildeman. 2013. "Redefining Relationships: Explaining the Countervailing Consequences of Parental Incarceration for Parenting." *American Sociological Review* 78 (6): 949–79.

U.S. Census Bureau. 2010a. "Sanford (City), Florida." http://quickfacts.census.gov/qfd/states/12/1263650.html. Accessed August 7, 2014.

———. 2010b. "Seminole County, Florida." http://quickfacts.census.gov/qfd/states/12/12117.html. Accessed August 7, 2014.

Wacquant, Loic. 2001. "Deadly Symbiosis: When Ghetto and Prison Meet and Mesh." *Punishment & Society* 3 (1): 95–134.

Wald, Johanna, and Daniel J. Losen. 2003. "Defining and Redirecting a School-to-Prison Pipeline." *New Directions for Youth Development* 99:9–15.

Warner, Barbara, and Pamela Rountree. 1997. "Local Social Ties in a Community and Crime Model: Questioning the Systemic Nature of Informal Social Control." *Social Problems* 44:520–36.

Welch, Kelly, and Allison Payne. 2010. "Racial Threat and Punitive School Discipline." *Social Problems* 57 (1): 25–48.

Werthman, Carl, and Irving Piliavin. 1967. "Gang Members and the Police." In *The Police: Six Sociological Essays*, edited by D. Bordua, 56–98. New York: John Wiley.

Wildeman, Christopher. 2009. "Parental Imprisonment and the Concentration of Childhood Disadvantage." *Demography* 46 (2): 265–80.

Williams, David R., and Selina A. Mohammed. 2009. "Discrimination and Racial Disparities in Health: Evidence and Needed Research." *Journal of Behavioral Medicine* 32:20–47.

Wilson, James Q., and George Kelling. 1982. "Broken Windows: The Police and Neighborhood Safety." *Atlantic*, March, 29–38.

Wilson, William Julius. 1987. *The Truly Disadvantaged: The Inner City, the Underclass and Public Policy.* Chicago: University of Chicago Press.

Woldoff, Rachel. 2002. "The Effects of Local Stressors on Neighborhood Attachment." *Social Forces* 81:87–116.

PART III

Which Voices Count?

9

From *Simpson* to *Zimmerman*

Examining the Effects of Race, Class, and Gender in the Failed Prosecution of Two Highly Publicized, Racially Divisive Cases

DELORES JONES-BROWN AND HENRY F. FRADELLA

Everybody talks about justice, but it is those who have known it the least who believe in it the most.
—Derrick Bell

In her 1998 book, *The Color of Crime: Racial Hoaxes, White Fear, Black Protectionism, Police Harassment, and Other Macroaggressions*, Katheryn Russell-Brown includes a chapter titled "Are We Still Talking about O.J.?" The chapter begins with a post-acquittal conversation that goes as follows:

> WHITE FEMALE: How can you say you agree with the verdict when you believe O.J. killed them? Anyway, the case wasn't about race.
> BLACK FEMALE: There was reasonable doubt. Race matters.
> WHITE FEMALE: The jury's verdict makes a mockery of the justice system.
> BLACK FEMALE: How come you weren't this upset after the first Rodney King trial in Simi Valley, or for that matter after the acquittal of Claus von Bulow?
> WHITE FEMALE: Those cases were different. Isn't domestic violence important to you?
> BLACK FEMALE: Of course. Are you saying that if I agree with the verdict that I support domestic violence?
> WHITE FEMALE: I give up![1]

One might imagine a similar conversation in the wake of the Zimmerman acquittal but with the racial roles reversed:

BLACK MALE OR FEMALE: How can you say you agree with the verdict when you know that Zimmerman stalked and killed him? This case is about racial profiling.

WHITE MALE OR FEMALE: There was reasonable doubt. Race doesn't matter.

BLACK MALE OR FEMALE: The jury's verdict makes a mockery of the justice system.

WHITE MALE OR FEMALE: How come you weren't this upset after the O. J. Simpson trial; or for that matter the acquittal of Michael Jackson?

BLACK MALE OR FEMALE: Those cases were different. In those cases there really was reasonable doubt. Isn't racial profiling important to you?

WHITE MALE OR FEMALE: Maybe, if it really exists. Are you saying that if I agree with the verdict then I support racial profiling?

BLACK MALE OR FEMALE: Well do you?

These conversations expose the "fallacy of objectivity"[2] that surrounds mainstream thinking about the American criminal justice process. They reveal, instead, a long and deep-seated racial divide over what constitutes justice and whether the American justice system has ever embodied it. This divide affects perceptions about the system, its processes, those who are processed through it, and those on whose behalf the system is expected to operate.[3] These questions become most acute in cases where victims and defendants are of different races, though there are moments or cases during which there seems to be some measure of racial consensus.[4] The downside of these moments of consensus is that they create an expectation that this sense of agreement will carry forward into the future. When it does not, that is, when the next racially divisive case arises, and the populace cannot agree on what constitutes a just outcome, the consensus-building process must begin anew, amid racial frustrations, stereotypes, fear, and expectations that are nearly four centuries old.[5]

For many blacks, the death of Trayvon Martin and the acquittal of George Zimmerman represent a pattern of racial victimization that they know all too well. Older blacks can point to America's history of lynching and the acquittals of white defendants for killing civil rights workers, returning servicemen, and even children,[6] as evidence that the American justice system is not colorblind. Younger blacks can point to police stops and multiple cases of police shootings that do not result in conviction and that involve white officers killing unarmed black men,[7] as proof of both fatal racial profiling and the failure of the American justice system to safeguard their right to liberty or to life.[8] Legal scholars point to the U.S. Supreme Court's sanctioning of the "out of place"[9] doctrine and racially tinged terminology, like "high crime area," in cases like *Illinois v. Wardlow* as valid means to assess "reasonable" suspicion,[10] as indicative of the Court's tacit or overt support of a system that is by no means colorblind.[11]

Social science has contributed significantly to a tendency to see black men as criminal and potentially dangerous. The inclusion of racial categories in official crime statistics, emphasis on racial disproportionality in crime, particularly crimes of violence, and empirical studies that compare blacks to whites using proportional rates of arrest, conviction, and incarceration serve to reinforce racial stereotypes and deny individual agency and responsibility to members of racial and ethnic groups.[12] Thorsten Sellin was one of the first mainstream criminologists to acknowledge this social fact and its reinforcement through media.[13] In his award-winning 2010 book, *The Condemnation of Blackness: Race, Crime and the Making of Modern Urban America*, historian Khalil Gibran Muhammad reproduces the following 1928 quote from Sellin, which may help us understand the racial dynamics of Trayvon Martin's death, George Zimmerman's acquittal, and the divided public reaction to both:

We [whites] are prone to judge ourselves by our best traits and strangers by their worst. In the case of the Negro, stranger in our midst, all beliefs prejudicial to him aid in intensifying the feeling of racial antipathy engendered by his color and his social status. The colored criminal does not as a rule enjoy the racial anonymity which cloaks the offenses of individuals of the white race. The press is almost certain to brand him, and the more revolting his crime proves to be the more likely it is that his race will be advertised. In setting the hall-mark of his color upon him, his individuality is in a sense submerged, and instead of a mere thief, robber, or murderer, he becomes a representative of his race, which in its turn is made to suffer for his sins.[14]

These words by Sellin capture what we refer to today as *racial profiling*, a sociological phenomenon that has been studied intensely since the legal scholarship of David A. Harris challenged the use of racial profiles in the early 1990s.[15] Muhammad's astute dissection of Sellin's quote provides a powerful lens through which to examine what we will call the Martin/Zimmerman *trilogy*—that is, (1) the death/killing, (2) the prosecution/acquittal, and (3) the public reaction. According to Muhammad, "Sellin's 'we,' linked to the notion of the Negro as a 'stranger in our midst,' marked not only his whiteness but also and more importantly, his position within a dominant racialized community with the power to define those outside it . . . crime itself was not the core issue. Rather, the problem was racial criminalization: the stigmatization of crime as 'black' *and* the masking of crime among whites as individual failure."[16] Muhammad notes, further, that, "the practice of linking crime to Blacks, as a racial group, but not whites, . . . reinforced and reproduced racial inequality" and that the concept of black criminality served as a kind of "ideological currency" that benefited whites, even or especially white criminals.[17]

By this logic, in interracial offending cases, there is an embedded set of racial assumptions that must be confronted en route to achieving a final outcome. In cases where the defendant is black and the victim is white, the guilt of the defendant is a foregone conclusion and the prevailing assumption is that the victim did not deserve criminal harm.[18] By contrast, in white-on-black crimes, the black *victim* enters the case cloaked in a presumption of criminality of which prosecutors must be mindful and both willing and capable of working to remove—that is, there is an initial assumption that the black victim did "something wrong" that warranted the treatment he or she received. Conversely by the mere fact of their whiteness, white defendants are shielded by an especially strong presumption of innocence that prosecutors must work especially hard to contradict.[19] Numerous jury studies and social psychological experiments confirm the contemporary salience of these claims, finding that juries are willing to convict black defendants on lesser evidence than that needed to convict whites.[20]

In this chapter we examine the complex ways in which race and, to a lesser extent, class and gender matter in the prosecution of interracial offending cases and demonstrate that the *social distance* between the courtroom workgroup and certain defendants, victims, witnesses, and even other courtroom actors can have a profound influence on how each "sees" and decides these cases.[21] At the end of the chapter, we demonstrate that this distance not only affects the different ways in which court actors see these cases, but even extends to scholars who study these topics, including the authors of this chapter. We begin our analysis by examining another highly publicized interracial offending case—the Rodney King beating—to set the framework for our subsequent discussion.

Lessons from the Rodney King Beating Case

The federal conviction of Los Angeles police officers for violating the civil rights of Rodney King during a vicious 1991 videotaped beating stood in strong contrast to the state court acquittal that led to multiple days of violent rioting that caused physical injury to many and resulted in roughly a billion dollars in property damage. Throughout the riots, many white Americans were incredulous, confused, or outright angry that the state court acquittals had engendered this kind of reaction and saw the reaction as illegitimate. Even one of the accused police officers was recorded in a television interview saying he was looking forward to "putting the incident behind" him, once he had been acquitted at the state level. The LAPD and the white Los Angeles community were not prepared for the reaction that black and other racial/ethnic minority residents had to what they saw as clear injustice.[22] Their white counterparts had been convinced that the whole matter would be over since the system had "done its job." The negative racialized perceptions of the protesters, held mostly though not exclusively by whites, served only to confirm that there are entrenched racial stereotypes about blackness and criminality that consistently stymie any progression the nation might make toward colorblindness.[23]

Highly publicized cases where victims and offenders are of different races continuously present opportunities to reassess the racial climate of the nation but often have disappointing results.[24] Unlike the prosecution of Simpson or Zimmerman, the trial for the King beating included a videotape, which, when viewed around the world, brought an international chorus of condemnation. Yet, the jurors in mostly white, mostly affluent, Ventura County saw matters differently. They accepted the defense position that King had brought the beating on himself by continuing to move when the officers attempted to subdue him—that the brutal beating was a legitimate outcome of his efforts to resist arrest.[25]

The Ventura County jury's acceptance of the LAPD's actions as an appropriate means to enforce the law reflects a palpable social distance between the jurors as triers of fact and Rodney King as a plausible *victim* of criminal conduct. They accepted the police version of the facts, likely because they could more easily identify with the officers and their purported protective role in civil society, than they could with King or his behavior on the videotape. Both their race and their class distanced them from feeling remorse for ruling that police can violently restrain civilians for alleged traffic violations, probably because they could not ever see themselves as potentially being that civilian. Both King's behavior on the videotape and the police description of it were likely consistent with stereotypes that the jurors themselves held of crime *perpetrators*.[26]

Having been cast by the defense in the role of perpetrator, rather than victim, to a jury with a similar worldview of people like him made it impossible to secure an assault conviction against King's assailants. To be asked by the prosecution to side with King against sworn police officers created more cognitive dissonance than the jurors were willing or perhaps capable of working through.[27] Though the prosecution anticipated that the change of venue from Los Angeles County, where the incident occurred, to Ventura County, where the trial took place, would pose some problems, an outright acquittal of all officers for all charges was beyond the scope of what much of the public thought was possible.[28] The residents in that county, no doubt, had had a lifetime of indoctrination that police officers are tasked with protecting and serving members of their group. It was possible for jurors to envision the police coming to their aid in the future, and perhaps even in defense against someone like Rodney King. Thus, despite the graphic video-tape or—once reinterpreted by the defense—*because of* the graphic videotape, there is little wonder that the Simi Valley jury returned a not guilty verdict.

There is also the question of whether the racial and gender identity of the prosecutor impacted the state court results. Social psychology suggests that the Simi Valley jurors could more easily identify with the white police officers than they could with the black male prosecutor, Terry White. The work of Stanford University social psychologist Jennifer Eberhardt and her colleagues suggests that, like Rodney King, the jurors were more likely to see White as a potential criminal than as a credible representative of their interests.[29] His racial similarity to King, at best, overtly or implicitly suggested to the jury that he was biased against the officers and in favor of the victim; at worst, it suggested he was not as competent as the defense attorneys, who were white males.[30] By all accounts, the Simi Valley jury pool and the final jury (ten whites, one Asian, one Latino) were strongly pro-police—a profession historically (and in many contemporary settings still) dominated by white men.

That is not to say the Simi Valley pool was necessarily overtly racist. Research has consistently demonstrated that a majority of Americans maintain implicit biases against blacks.[31] Even 40 percent of African Americans demonstrate implicit pro-white biases.[32] The key to under-standing these implicit racial biases rests on understanding that they operate "below the level of conscious awareness" as a function of what social psychology calls the *suspicion heuristic*.[33] This concept "explains how non-conscious processes can lead to systematic and predict-able errors in judgments of criminality—and influence subsequent behaviors—regardless of conscious racial attitudes."[34]

Why We Are Still Talking about O.J.

For many African Americans, the 1995 acquittal of Orenthal James (O. J.) Simpson, who is black, for the deaths of his former wife Nicole Brown Simpson and her friend Ronald Goldman, who were both white, represented an anomaly that they had never seen or heard of in their lifetime.[35] For more than three centuries, convictions—even convictions known to be wrongful—had been customary in the courts of both the North and South when black defendants were accused of killing white victims.[36] The expectation of conviction was bidirectional, meaning that it was held by blacks and whites alike. Not only were blacks likely to be convicted in such cases, they were also more likely than their white counterparts to be exposed to the death penalty in relation to such convictions.[37] The acquittal of Simpson shocked the nation with perhaps the same intensity as the Simi Valley verdict three years earlier, but this time it was the black defendant who walked free.

Media clips and opinion polls exposed the significant racial divide in the public's reaction to the Simpson jury's verdict. Postverdict polls showed that beliefs about Simpson's guilt were divided along both race and class lines. In all, 70 percent of whites (or roughly 139 million) believed that Simpson was guilty of the killings, but only 30 percent of blacks (or roughly 10 million) held a similar belief.[38] Polls also indicated that 65 percent of high-income people (those earning more than $50,000 per year) thought Simpson was guilty, while 41 percent of low-income people (those making $7,500 or less annually) believed he was not guilty.[39] In reporting these results, Russell-Brown notes that the polls failed to present data from the opinions of other racial and ethnic groups and that they did not report findings on the interaction between race and class. Research repeatedly suggests that low income has become a powerful proxy for black racial identity.[40] The dichotomous presentation of race as black or white has had a long and torturous history in the United States.[41]

The events that were the subject of the Simpson acquittal had all the makings of a television drama. The two victims were killed while the Simpson children slept a short distance away. Simpson and his wife had divorced after a history of reported domestic abuse. Simpson was reportedly angry at Nicole the night of the slaying. And, though often referred to as her "friend," Ron Goldman was reportedly the new man in Nicole's life. O. J. Simpson was a wealthy celebrity—a former professional athlete turned businessman and actor. Nicole Brown had come from humble beginnings but continued to live in the Brentwood mansion after the divorce. Ronald Goldman was a waiter at a local restaurant. In many ways, the racial identities in the incident ran counter to class norms. The black defendant was rich, his alleged victims less so. What got lost in the racialized frenzy in the aftermath of the verdict was that it was possible to envision Simpson as the killer on a number of race-neutral grounds related to the couple's history of domestic violence.[42]

But, the Simpson and Brown marriage encapsulated centuries old racial taboos. It violated prohibitions against race mixing and fulfilled fears about sexual competition. Simpson was black and Brown was white. They had two biracial children. He was physically abusive. They had married when she was quite young and she was considered particularly attractive. Thus, for some members of the public, despite Simpson's celebrity status, the dynamic of their marriage (made public after her death) conjured up the image of beauty and the beast—the brutish "Negro" male corrupting the virtues of white womanhood. Based on these age-old taboos, her postmarriage relationship with Ron Goldman signaled a return to where she "belonged." In liberal California, none of these racial subtexts seemed particularly relevant until after the verdict, when the public critique of the trial and jury verdict would become, at times, explicitly racist.[43]

The "dream team" of defense attorneys was accused of "playing the race card" when a key prosecution witness, a white police detective, Mark Fuhrman, was discredited for having used and then denied using the N-word during his career. Ultimately, Johnnie Cochran, a famous black defense attorney,[44] presented closing arguments to a mostly black jury, which found the black defendant not guilty in a case that involved the killing of two white victims. As previously noted, according to polls, at least 139 million whites found this outcome unacceptable.[45] Rather than examine the many race-neutral reasons why the case was not successfully prosecuted,[46] many critics pointed to race as the key factor in what they saw as a wrongful acquittal. The subsequent wrongful death verdicts against Simpson by a mostly white civil jury and his later conviction and imprisonment for the robbery and kidnapping of a memorabilia dealer reinforced views that Simpson was a dangerous guilty offender who had gotten away with murder because the "race card" had been played in his trial.[47]

Critics of the not guilty verdict accused the mostly black, mostly female criminal jury of being incompetent and emotional, while the mostly white civil jury's wrongful death verdict, two years later, was viewed as correct, fair, and "professional."[48] The criminal trial jury had violated the suspicion heuristic and its ubiquitous implication that black males are presumptively guilty. Critics also accused Lance Ito, the Japanese American judge who presided over the criminal proceedings, of incompetently running the trial—especially with regard to having allowed race to become part of the evidentiary process.[49] In other words, to critics, the perceived social closeness of the judge and jury to the defendant (based on their shared nonwhite status) caused them to hijack justice and render a factually inaccurate decision. Both sexism and racism left the Simpson trial prosecutors open to criticism for having lost "the trial of the century."[50] Marcia Clark, a white woman, and Christopher Darden, a black man, were blamed by some for not doing an adequate job of presenting their case and controlling the courtroom against the "antics" of the racially mixed defense "dream team," led by prominent African American lawyer Johnnie Cochran.[51]

Parallels between the King and *Simpson* Cases and the *Zimmerman* Trial

In part, each of these cases reflects appropriate and inappropriate masculine roles—casting either defendants or victims in the role of "thug," a powerful tool for impeding empathy by distancing the individual from conventional norms.[52] In the Simpson case, the criminal trial jury rejects the prosecution's attempt to depict the former NFL player as an angry, abusive thug turned murderer. In discussing the potential role of "Black protectionism" in the Simpson acquittal, Katheryn Russell-Brown notes that one of the questions blacks ask when a well-known black person is charged with a crime is, "Would he risk everything he has (e.g., wealth, fame, material possessions) to commit this offense?"[53] Similarly, while polls showed that 139 million whites thought that Simpson was guilty, they also showed that 60 million whites thought that he was not.[54] Unlike Trayvon Martin or Rodney King, O. J. Simpson was able to overcome the suspicion heuristic in the minds of 82 million people (60 million whites and 22 million blacks).[55] Some would say he was able to do so because he was a rich celebrity, instead of a hooded teenager or an alleged drug-abusing traffic violator with a long criminal record.

As for the officers who beat Rodney King, their conviction in federal court after the initial acquittals in Simi Valley allowed the United States to save face in the international human rights arena by sending a message that civil rights violations will not be tolerated.[56] Though many attribute the convictions to the presence of more ethnic and racial minorities on the jury,[57] and indeed the racial composition of the jury may have played a role, it is equally plausible that the two juries saw a qualitative difference between accusing the officers of civil rights violations as compared to the "thuggish" crime of aggravated assault. The racially mixed federal jury, composed predominantly of men (eight men and four women), was able to reach a consensus that the police conduct on the videotape was below that which is acceptable under civil law and (masculine) standards of decency (i.e., King was beaten and stomped while he was on the ground) without all having to concede that the officers behaved like common street thugs. Some have also suggested that the federal verdict might well have been influenced by concerns that an acquittal would result in more rioting[58] —rioting that would be viewed by some as valid resistance to an unjust system and by others as illegal thuggery.

In the Martin/Zimmerman case, the thug imagery plays a significant role in the divergent social views about the justifiability of Trayvon Martin's death and the legal validity of George Zimmerman's prosecution. Whether Trayvon Martin or George Zimmerman was the thug became the hotly contested factual question on both the front stage and back stage of the decision to bring the prosecution or not, and in the end was a deciding factor in the jury's verdict.[59] To many whites reacting to the case, Martin's family had used (illegitimate) "strong arm" tactics to bring the case to trial in the first place.[60] Media accounts almost immediately raised the issue of the applicability of the Stand Your Ground law and seemed to automatically assume that the defense could be applied (only) *in favor* of Zimmerman, although it was Zimmerman who brought a gun to the encounter.[61] No "stand your ground" analysis was presented on behalf of Martin, though as will be discussed in detail later in this chapter, such an analysis was essential to *dis*proving that Zimmerman had acted in self-defense.

Like the defense in the state trial of the Rodney King beating, George Zimmerman's attorneys were able to successfully convince the jury that

Trayvon Martin brought about his own death by confronting their client. In some circles, it has been suggested that Martin would still be alive if he had simply submitted to questioning by Zimmerman—questioning that Zimmerman had no legal authority in which to engage.[62] The suggestion that Martin should have passively submitted to whatever course of action Zimmerman deemed appropriate, as he carried out his self-appointed role as neighborhood watchman, rubs raw the racial tensions between blacks and whites over the measure of liberty to which blacks are entitled.[63] Other chapters in this volume address the many contours of both legal and social disagreement over this terrain. Here we note that to white jurors, judges, defense attorneys, and even prosecutors, the suggestion that Martin "cooperate" with Zimmerman might seem "normal,"[64] thus creating confusion and resistance to evidence and legal instructions inconsistent with those thoughts (i.e., the normalcy of cooperation).

The suggestion requires Martin to assume a subordinate position in the encounter. An all-female jury might not fully recognize the ways in which such a suggestion runs counter to traditional masculine identity, let alone the hypermasculinity of which black males are so often accused.[65] It also reinforces existing notions of race and class dominance—that is, white dominance over blacks and middle-class dominance over perceived lesser classes. It suggests that in order to be safe, black males must be willing to give up a portion of their autonomy—an autonomy that is already constantly under attack by the actions of real police officers pursuing policies that subject them to constant surveillance and confrontation.[66] The media portrayal of photos of Martin and his father in gangster-like poses and attire, discussions of his school record, allegations of drug use, the father's status of living with a girlfriend, and his mother's status as a black single mother all feed into existing stereotypes of young black men as (potentially) criminal and (potentially) violent—stereotypes that are supported by a large body of social science research that uses strikingly similar variables to predict crime or risk for criminality.[67]

As with the Simi Valley jury, the jurors in State v. Zimmerman were predominantly white (five whites and one Latina). Their likely social distance from Martin, his family, and the state's key witness, Rachel Jeantel,[68] and their likely social closeness to the assertions raised by the defense, may have created a "zone of believability" for the defense version of the facts, through which the prosecution's case failed to penetrate. Given all that we know about racial bias and stereotyping,[69] during voir dire, each potential juror should have been asked by the prosecution whether he himself or she herself had a general fear of young black men. Instead, there were tremendous efforts to mask the racial dynamics of the case in favor of the supposed race-neutral dictates of the law. Though nearly twenty years have passed since the Simpson trial, we suggest that the push to see and present the Martin/Zimmerman encounter, prosecution, and trial as race-neutral may be tied to the racialized reaction to the Simpson acquittal and likely distorts the reality, whether overt or implicit, of how each part of the trilogy played out.

Justice Is in the Eye of the Beholder

While the Martin family prayed for justice in the Zimmerman trial,[70] there was substantial disagreement as to what that would look like. Those who saw that the primary courtroom decision makers were white accurately predicted that the result would be an acquittal. White males presented the case-in-chief for both sides. A white female judge presided over the trial and decided all issues of law. A predominantly white jury decided how that law applied to the facts as they determined them to be. In the *Simpson* case, Nicole Brown's race, gender, and beauty were factors that made her a sympathetic victim to the white public, but may have put social distance between her and the predominantly minority jury.[71] Similarly, although Trayvon Martin's youth should have made him a sympathetic victim, prevailing criminal stereotypes about young black men rendered his victim status suspect.[72]

In the court of public opinion, and maybe even among the trial jurors themselves, consistent with the suspicion heuristic, speculations included that instead of truly being a victim, perhaps Martin intended to rob Zimmerman, despite the fact that it was Zimmerman who set into motion the deadly chain of events and it was Zimmerman who had the gun.[73] To support Zimmerman's claim of self-defense, the trial judge permitted expert testimony that Zimmerman was incapable of fighting back against the younger, stronger Martin.[74] It is not clear whether this testimony was objected to by the prosecution or adequately rebutted by testimony from the state. Like the reinterpretation of the Rodney King beating video, the intent of the testimony was to cast George Zimmerman in the role of victim and Trayvon Martin in the role of perpetrator. This testimony should have been vigorously objected to, particularly since Zimmerman did not take the stand himself.

From our perspectives as criminologists and former trial attorneys, to allow Zimmerman to bolster his self-defense claim in this way, while simultaneously protecting his right against self-incrimination, seems unduly and impermissibly prejudicial against the deceased. Similarly, the arrogant and often demeaning cross-examination of Rachel Jeantel—one of the prosecution's primary witnesses—by the white male defense attorneys would likely not have played well in front of a more diverse trial jury and perhaps would have been guarded against more rigorously by a mixed-race and mixed-gender prosecution team.[75] The treatment of nineteen-year-old Jeantel on the stand and in social media following her testimony was indicative of the social distance between courtroom actors and the nonidyllic witnesses to street crime.[76] After testifying, Jeantel was called inarticulate, hostile, and thuggish,[77] and her social class was put on trial with little recognition that it was not her choice to be an "ear witness" to the events leading up to her friend's death.[78]

Similarly, views about justice in the Martin/Zimmerman trilogy and the *Simpson* trial outcome were rife with disagreement over the validity of addressing racial bias in the legal analysis of the cases. Like many who found the Zimmerman verdict acceptable, critics of the Simpson verdict insisted that the incident itself had nothing to do with race and that therefore race should not have been introduced into the trial.[79] But, exploring potential interest or bias on the part of a witness has always been a legitimate means of impeaching or testing his or her credibility. When interviewed about the *Simpson* trial, Attorney Frank Leidman commented to the *San Francisco Examiner* that Johnnie Cochran was ethically obligated to impeach Detective Mark Fuhrman on his racist beliefs, noting that it would have been malpractice not to. In Leidman's view, "It was extraordinarily ordinary. He impeached a witness for bias . . . it's done all the time."[80] It seems that when the basis of that bias may be racial prejudice, some members of the public see such exploration as unduly volatile or distracting and hence something to be avoided.[81]

Had George Zimmerman taken the stand in his own defense, he would have had to explain his statements in the 911 call that suggested that he thought Trayvon Martin was "suspicious" or "on drugs or something," although he had not personally observed Martin do anything illegal. He would have had to explain why he chose to get out of his vehicle to follow Martin on foot after being told by the dispatcher that the police did not "need" him "to do that." And most importantly he would have had to explain why he brought a gun to the encounter. The answers to all of these questions have racial overtones that cannot validly be denied. We suggest that the Simpson trial made it unpopular for judges to allow evidence of racial bias to be introduced in criminal trials unless a defendant is specifically charged with a hate crime (see, for example, the 1998 killing of James Byrd in Jasper, Texas). We also suggest that one reason for masking racial motivation in a case is the desire to minimize the possibility of riots/civil disturbances in the aftermath of the trial.

For many whites, because the verdict in the *Simpson* trial failed to fulfill their need for justice, this warranted a total overhaul of the California justice system.[82] Among others, calls for system reform after the Simpson verdict included allowing for conviction on less than a unanimous vote and a reduction in jury size.[83] Though profoundly disappointed by the verdict, the majority of those who disagreed with the Zimmerman acquittal did not call for mass reform of Florida courtroom procedures.[84] As will be discussed shortly, for those with political power, it appears that the system had functioned as designed.

At the time of the Zimmerman trial, a sea of evidence already showed that Florida's self-defense laws were consistently applied in racial and gender-biased ways that favored white defendants.[85] Interestingly, one of the two recommended system reforms proposed in the aftermath of the Simpson acquittal—smaller juries—had already been adopted by Florida in 1968, nearly thirty years before the fallout over the *Simpson* verdict. As will be discussed in the next section, though upheld by federal case law, smaller juries and nonunanimous verdicts have both been found to produce latent and overt race-, class-, and gender-biasing effects.[86]

Bias by Design?

Interracial offending/victimization cases have the ability to revive divides that were once authorized under formal law. The overt social distancing of blacks from whites in Florida can be found in two provisions of its 1885 state constitution:[87]

- Article VII, Section 12 mandated that "White and colored children shall not be taught in the same school."
- Article XVI, Section 24 barred miscegenation by providing, "All marriages between a white person and a negro, or between a white person and a person of negro descent to the fourth generation, inclusive, are hereby forever prohibited."

Florida also has the dubious distinction of having imposed the nation's first poll tax and mandating that those taxes be used to fund its segregated schools. Article VI, Section 8, which read, "The Legislature shall have power to make the payment of the capitation tax a prerequisite for voting," had an immediate and substantial impact on the voting rights of blacks. In the presidential election of 1888, a record 62 percent of black males voted;[88] four years later that figure had dropped to 11 percent.[89]

Similarly, in the midst of the African American civil rights movement, in 1968, the Florida constitution underwent a massive overhaul. With regard to trial by jury, Article I, Section 22, was drafted to read, "The right of trial by jury shall be secure to all and remain inviolate. The qualifications and the number of jurors, not fewer than six, shall be fixed by law."[90] Pursuant to this constitutional change, Florida Statutes Annotated § 913.10 states, "Twelve persons shall constitute a jury to try all capital cases, and six persons shall constitute a jury to try all other criminal cases." It strikes us as more than coincidental that the size of criminal juries began to shrink in Florida shortly after the federal passage of the Civil Rights Act of 1964 and only one year after the National Advisory Commission on Civil Disorders (also known as the Kerner Commission) decried racial inequalities in the United States.

The racial inequality in the application of Florida's so-called Stand Your Ground laws, addressed briefly later in this chapter and in substantial detail in an earlier chapter of this volume, suggests that Florida law is still haunted by its overtly racist past.[91] We speculate that since Florida enshrined other forms of racial discrimination into several provisions of its state constitution in the past, it is likely that the change in jury size was made in order to facilitate convictions, especially the conviction of accused blacks.[92] We would argue that despite his mixed-race identity, in the courtroom George Zimmerman was sufficiently white to escape the suspicion heuristic and the presumption of guilt that runs with both black defendants and black victims, particularly males.

In the 1969 decision *Williams v. Florida*, the U.S. Supreme Court upheld Florida's law authorizing the use of six-person trial juries. In subsequent cases, the Court made clear that six is the minimum jury size in state criminal trials that is acceptable under the U.S. Constitution because "the purpose and functioning of the jury in a criminal trial is seriously impaired, and to a constitutional degree, by a reduction in size to below six members."[93] If a six-person jury is used, the verdict in a criminal case must be unanimous. If, however, a larger jury is impaneled in a state criminal trial, the verdict need not be unanimous. The Court has upheld state court convictions by juries whose members voted for guilty verdicts by margins nine to three.[94]

At the time *Williams v. Florida* was decided, a number of states allowed smaller juries to adjudicate misdemeanors offenses, ostensibly for the purposes of efficiency and economy. But, by the late 1960s, only four other states had authorized juries of fewer than twelve members to adjudicate felony cases: Louisiana, South Carolina, Texas, and Utah.[95] When considered alongside the timing of these changes, the geography of these particular locales gives one pause to question whether something other than efficiency and economy drove the decisions to allow felony convictions with criminal juries composed of only six members. Four of these jurisdictions (Florida, Louisiana, South Carolina, and Texas) were members of the Confederate States of America. And although Utah was not a state at the time of the U.S. Civil War, it has an arguably unique history of racism stemming, in part, from the state's ties to the Mormon Church.[96] Up until 1978, the church's doctrine banned blacks from Mormon ministry, claiming that dark skin is a "mark which was set upon their fathers" as a curse for their "transgression"[97] and that "Negroes [are] not entitled to the full blessings of the Gospel."[98]

The decisions in *Williams* and cases in its progeny have been widely criticized by psychologists who critiqued the Court's misunderstanding of the social scientific evidence on jury size. As Arizona State University law professor Michael J. Saks pointed out shortly after *Williams* was decided, the Court "ignored what is obvious to every social scientist: that when sampling from heterogeneous populations, sample size determines how well minority groups in the population will be represented."[99] Saks subsequently conducted a series of controlled experiments and found that "the actual difference in minority representation on 12- and 6-member juries was even more pronounced than the sampling theory had suggested. Few researchers, Saks concluded, would consider this difference to be, in the words of the *Williams* Court, 'negligible.'"[100]

Although a handful of studies reported only minor differences in the jury deliberation processes and outcomes for juries of six versus juries of twelve,[101] other studies have found significant differences.[102] Smith and Saks conducted a review of the empirical literature on juries and concluded the following:[103]

- racial, ethnic, religious, and sexual minorities are represented in a smaller percentage of 6-person as compared to 12-person juries;
- larger juries deliberate longer than smaller juries;
- talking time is more evenly divided among members of smaller juries, allowing for less domination by a strong voice or two as compared with larger juries;
- members of larger juries more accurately recall evidence both during deliberation and in individual recall afterward;
- 12-person juries recall more probative information and rely on evaluative statements and nonprobative evidence less than six-person juries . . . ; and
- jurors report more satisfaction in the deliberation process with 12-person juries than with smaller ones.[104]

Research also demonstrates that hung juries—juries unable to reach a unanimous verdict—occur more frequently with twelve-person juries than with six-person juries.[105] For many, a hung jury in the Zimmerman trial would have been preferable to an outright acquittal. When these findings from empirical research on smaller juries are juxtaposed geographically and temporally against the abandoned use of twelve-person juries in felony cases, one must seriously consider the question of whether the change was motivated, at least in part, by a desire to secure easier convictions against black defendants and consequently served as a motivation for those who pressed for adopting smaller juries or accepting nonunanimous jury decisions in the aftermath of the Simpson acquittal.

Conclusion

In the study of criminal justice, we currently show a preference for the collection and presentation of seemingly objective data to help audiences better understand the structure and function of justice processes.[106] But these processes are embedded in historical and contemporary contexts that are all but objective and that impact the lives of some social groups in disproportionate and profoundly personal ways. Interracial offending/victimization cases repeatedly put notions of justice on trial, and except in the most extreme cases (e.g., the dragging death of James Byrd), justice system actors and observers of different races, class statuses, and genders fail to reach consensus on what constitutes sufficient evidence of criminal wrongdoing and by whom. Like the Simpson verdict, the Martin/Zimmerman trilogy presents us with yet another opportunity to reexamine the parameters and limitations of our quests toward social, racial, and criminal justice and to (re)mark the territory where these quests are in substantial need of growth and development.

NOTES

1. Russell-Brown 1998, 47.

2. See Way 1998, citing Rabinow and Sullivan 1979 criticizing the objective ideal in the social sciences.

3. See Cureton 2000.

4. For example, little, if any, racial differences were evident in public reaction to the conviction, sentencing, and execution of Lawrence Russell Brewer for murdering James Byrd and of Timothy McVeigh for bombing the Oklahoma City federal building.

5. Starting with the importation of African slaves to the American colonies. See, e.g., Davidson 1988; Browne-Marshall 2013.

6. See Jones-Brown, Frazier, and Brooks 2014.

7. While police misconduct is not limited to white officers, cases like the July 2014 choking death of Eric Garner by a police officer in New York City and the August

shooting of unarmed teenager, Michael Brown, by a police officer in Ferguson, Missouri, cause particular social upheaval given not only the long history of injustice against African Americans in the United States, but also the fact that black suspects are between four and five times more likely, per capita, to die from police use of lethal force than are white suspects. See, e.g., Burch 2011, Smith 2004.

8. See Jones-Brown 2009.

9. See, e.g., E. L. Johnson 1995; Morrow 2015; Wacquant 2005; Jones-Brown 2007.

10. *Illinois v. Wardlow* 2000.

11. Morrow 2015; Jones-Brown et al. 2013 showing that blacks make up 53 percent of stops made by police and 23 percent of the New York City population.

12. Rather than raw numbers that consistently show a greater number of white than black arrests for most violent and property crime. See, e.g., *Sourcebook of Criminal Justice Statistics* (Bureau of Justice Statistics 2011, Table 4.10).

13. Thorsten Sellin enjoyed a long career on the faculty at the University of Pennsylvania as a sociologist and penologist. He is credited with being one of the pioneers of scientific criminology.

14. Muhammad 2010, 2, quoting Sellin 1928, 52.

15. Harris 1999a; 1999b.

16. Muhammad 2010, 2–3, emphasis added.

17. Ibid., 3.

18. Historically the presumption of guilt against black defendants has been strongest when black men have been accused of sexual assault against white women. See Jones-Brown, Frazier, and Brooks 2014; Ogletree 2010.

19. See, e.g., Eberhardt et al. 2004.

20. See Levine 2000; Anwar, Bayer, and Hjalmarsson 2012. See also Sommers 2007 finding mixed results on this topic.

21. *Social distance* is a sociological concept (see Bogardus 1925) that "refers to the extent to which people experience a sense of familiarity (nearness and intimacy) or unfamiliarity (farness and difference) between themselves and people belonging to different social, ethnic, occupational, and religious groups from their own" (Hodgetts 2014, 1776). See also Goff, Steele, and Davies 2008.

22. Though members of other groups also saw the verdict as unjust, their social investment in beliefs about the legitimacy of the system and their stake in other social institutions shielded them from the level of betrayal experienced by blacks.

23. See, e.g., Tyler and Hou 2003; Hetey and Eberhardt 2014.

24. The Texas jury's decision in Lawrence Russell Brewer's trial for murdering James Byrd is a notable departure from the usual pattern.

25. Ironically, this same argument was used by law enforcement officials in July 2014 to justify the death of civilian Eric Garner in New York City. Garner was choked to death during an attempted arrest for allegedly illegally selling cigarettes. See Sneed 2014.

26. This suspicion heuristic associates young African American males in particular with a stereotype linked to dangerousness and violent criminality. See Goff, Steele, and Davies 2008; Eberhardt et al. 2004; Lee 2013; Richardson and Goff 2012.

27. Implicit bias has been defined as "unconscious biases against members of stigmatized groups" (http://www.biasproject.org/). See also Eberhardt et al. 2004.

28. As reported by Terry White to a meeting of the National Black Prosecutors Association, in La Jolla, California, 1992.

29. See Eberhardt et al. 2004.

30. See, e.g., Fiske et al. 2002; Weiner 2005.

31. Lane, Kang, and Banaji 2007; Nosek, Banaji, and Greenwald 2002; Gabbidon, Higgins, and Wilder-Bonner 2013.

32. Banaji and Greenwald 2013.

33. Richardson and Goff 2012, 317.

34. Richardson and Goff 2012, 293. This suspicion heuristic associates young African American males, in particular, with a stereotype linked to dangerousness and violent criminality. It is worth noting that the Martin/Zimmerman encounter did not involve split-second decision making and reveals the subjectivity of determining that actors or behaviors are ambiguous. See Eberhardt et al. 2004; Lee 2013; Goff, Steele, and Davies 2008; Richardson and Goff 2012.

35. Here the term "African American" is used to distinguish between blacks born in the United States with native-born bloodlines dating back at least two generations from blacks born outside the United States. The terms "black" and "African American" are used interchangeably within this chapter.

36. Statistics reported by the Innocence Project suggest that blacks are substantially more likely than others to be wrongfully convicted, representing 61 percent of the organization's exonerees between 1989 and 2013.

37. See, e.g., Baldus, Pulaski, and Woodworth 1983; Baldus et al. 1998; Paternoster 2013; Pierce and Radelet 2005. See also, Eberhardt et al. 2006, finding that even among black defendants, those with stereotypical black physical features stood a greater chance of being sentenced to death than those without such features.

38. Russell-Brown 1998, 50.

39. Ibid., 52, citing Taylor 1995.

40. Khare, Joseph, and Chaskin 2014; Sampson and Wilson 1995; Shapiro 2004; Shapiro, Meschede, and Osoro 2013.

41. See Davis 2001.

42. According to the U.S. Department of Justice, between 1998 and 2002, of the 3.5 million violent crimes committed against family members, 49 percent were committed against spouses, 84 percent of spouse abuse victims were females, 83 percent of spouse murderers were males, and 50 percent of offenders in state prison for spousal abuse had killed their victims (Durose et al. 2005).

43. This is in contrast to the Zimmerman case, where disagreement over whether he should be charged began immediately following the slaying, with strong opinions on both sides. See Jones-Brown 2012.

44. Johnnie Cochran became the lead attorney (replacing Robert Shapiro) of the group of lawyers defending O. J. Simpson. The group was dubbed the Dream Team because it included some of the world's leading attorneys—F. Lee Bailey, Alan

Dershowitz, and Robert Kardashian, among them. See, Jones-Brown, Frazier, and Brooks 2014.

45. Russell-Brown 1998.

46. For a discussion of such race-neutral reasons, see Bugliosi (1996). In contrast, one need only look at contemporary news to still see the lingering effects of the Simpson acquittal. A Fox News story titled "20 Years Later, the Real Verdict on O. J. Simpson" (Williams 2014) stated, "Black people were so angry with racist cops then, they didn't want to see anyone put on trial except the police" (para. 6). Washington 2014 and E. C. Johnson 1995 present other parts of the Simpson case legacy.

47. Williams 2014; Washington 2014.

48. Jones 1995.

49. Kaplan 1995; Sweeney 1995.

50. See Jones-Brown, Frazier, and Brooks 2014.

51. See note 44.

52. Once cast in the role of thug, the individual, whether perpetrator or victim, does not fit the standards on the "middle class measuring rod" (Cohen 1955) and consequently is subjected to an array of negative assumptions.

53. Russell-Brown 1998, 60.

54. Ibid., 52. See also, CNN/*Time Magazine* Poll 1995.

55. See Williams 2014 noting that fewer people believe that Simpson was not guilty and Washington 2014 presenting a different view.

56. A proposition for which there seemed to be general consensus.

57. Two blacks and one Latino in the federal prosecution compared to one Asian and one Hispanic in the state trial.

58. See Jones-Brown, Frazier, and Brooks 2014.

59. Markel 2013.

60. The Sanford, Florida, police department did not immediately arrest George Zimmerman after the shooting. Protests and an online petition by the activist organization Color of Change are credited with having pushed the police and subsequently the Florida State's Attorney Office to arrest Zimmerman and prosecute the case.

61. See Jones-Brown 2012.

62. MacDonald 2012.

63. See Browne-Marshall 2013 and the U.S. Supreme Court's decision in *Dred Scott v. Sandford* (1857), frequently cited for the proposition that blacks "had no rights which the white man was bond to respect." The Court's majority opinion expressly states that people of African ancestry "had no rights or privileges but such as those who held the power and the Government might choose to grant them." In an Internet posting, the author, who describes himself as an antiracist essayist, author, and educator, draws parallels between the Martin/Zimmerman incident and the ruling in Dred Scott (Wise 2012).

64. Especially to an all-female mostly white jury, Zimmerman's claim that he was playing the (masculine) role of community protector at the time of the encounter might be seen as particularly meritorious and reason to give him the benefit of the doubt.

65. See, e.g., Oliver 1998; Majors and Billison 1993; Garfield 2010; Goff, Steele, and Davies 2008.

66. Jones-Brown et al. 2013; Fratello, Rengifo, and Trone 2013; Stoudt, Fine, and Fox 2012.

67. Moynahan 1965; Sampson and Wilson 1995; Lonardo et al. 2011.

68. Video footage of the direct examination and cross-examination shows that Ms. Jeantel was not properly shielded by the prosecution from attack by the defense and that even the court stenographer reacted toward Ms. Jeantel in ways that were inappropriate. See HuffingtonPostLive 2013.

69. See especially Allport 1954; Eberhardt et al. 2004; Eberhardt et al. 2006; Goff et al. 2008.

70. Whitaker 2013.

71. Though the victim Nicole Brown Simpson and the majority of jurors were female, the fact that she was the second wife of O. J. Simpson following a divorce from his African American childhood sweetheart and mother of his first children may have prevented any expected gender empathy given that the female jurors were also black and likely to see the second marriage as a betrayal of the first.

72. Eberhardt et al. 2004; Goff et al. 2014.

73. See Jones-Brown 2012.

74. For a transcript of the testimony of Dennis Root, Zimmerman's expert on the use of force, see CNN 2013.

75. See McCain 2013.

76. See, e.g., Conley, O'Barr, and Lind 1979.

77. HuffingtonPostLive 2013.

78. See McCain 2013.

79. Jones 1995; Williams 2014; Washington 2014.

80. Armstrong 1995, D1, as cited in E. C. Johnson 1995.

81. Jones 1995.

82. See E. C. Johnson 1995; Jones 1995.

83. E. C. Johnson 1995. Though the banning of cameras from the courtroom was one of the immediate and most sought-after changes.

84. Though there have been many calls for the repeal of Stand Your Ground legislation.

85. Roman and Downey 2012.

86. Saks 1974; Saks and Marti 1997; Smith and Saks 2008; Devine et al. 2001.

87. After the U.S. Civil War, Florida made several unsuccessful attempts to enact a postreconstruction constitution. The state remained under "radical reconstruction"—in other words, federal military control—until 1868, when a new constitution was approved and civil control of Florida resumed. This so-called carpetbag constitution vested the governor with the power to appoint county officials, implemented a public school system, and established a state prison (HistoryEngine.com n.d.).

88. Women did not get the right to vote until the passing of the Nineteenth Amendment in 1920.

89. HistoryEngine.com n.d.

90. This represents a change from the 1885 version, where the number of jurors and unanimity had not been specified.

91. See HistoryEngine.com n.d.

92. See the landmark U.S. Supreme Court decision *Gideon v. Wainwright* 1963, implicating class bias in the Florida justice system as well.

93. *Ballew v. Georgia* 1978, 239.

94. *Johnson v. Louisiana* 1972.

95. Today, Florida, Louisiana, and Utah continue to allow juries of fewer than twelve people to adjudicate felony cases, as do Arizona, Connecticut, and Indiana (Strickland et al. 2014). South Carolina and Texas abandoned this approach and became two of the thirty-four U.S. states (and the District of Columbia) that currently require twelve-person juries in felony cases (Strickland et al. 2014). In addition, nineteen U.S. jurisdictions also require twelve-person juries in misdemeanor cases: Alabama, Arkansas, California, Delaware, the District of Columbia, Hawaii, Illinois, Maine, Maryland, New Hampshire, New Jersey, Pennsylvania, Puerto Rico, Rhode Island, South Dakota, Tennessee, Vermont, West Virginia, and Wisconsin (Strickland et al. 2014).

96. Bringhurst 1981; Eskridge 2011.

97. Book of Mormon, Alma 3:6.

98. Stewart and Berrett 1960, 46–47.

99. Saks 1974, 19.

100. As quoted in Miller 1998, 655–65.

101. E.g., Pabst 1973; Roper 1979.

102. E.g., Hastie, Penrod, and Pennington 1983; Saks and Marti 1997; Levine 2000; Anwar, Bayer, and Hjalmarsson 2012.

103. Smith and Saks 2008.

104. Neubauer and Fradella 2013, 337.

105. Hannaford-Agor et al. 2002; Kalven and Zeisel 1966.

106. See Way 1998 and Rabinow and Sullivan 1979, explaining the limits of interpretive social science.

REFERENCES

Allport, G. W. 1954. *The Nature of Prejudice*. Reading, MA: Addison-Wesley.

Anwar, S., P. Bayer, and R. Hjalmarsson. 2012. "The Impact of Jury Race in Criminal Trials." *Quarterly Journal of Economics*, 1–39. http://qje.oxfordjournals.org/content/early/2012/04/15/qje.qjs014.full.pdf.

Apodaca v. Oregon, 406 U.S. 404 (1972).

Armstrong, D. 1995. "O.J. Trial: A Case of Business as Usual." *San Francisco Examiner*, October 15, D1.

Baldus, D. C., C. Pulaski, and G. Woodworth. 1983. "Comparative Review of Death

Sentences: An Empirical Study of the Georgia Experience." *Journal of Criminal Law and Criminology* 74 (3): 661–753.

Baldus, D. C., G. Woodworth, D. Zukerman, N. A. Wiener, and B. Broffitt. 1998. "Race Discrimination and the Death Penalty in the Post-*Furman* Era: An Empirical and Legal Overview with Preliminary Findings from Philadelphia." *Cornell Law Review* 83:1638–1770.

Ballew v. Georgia, 435 U.S. 233 (1978).

Banaji, M. R., and A. G. Greenwald. 2013. *Blind Spot: Hidden Biases of Good People.* New York: Delacorte Press/Random House.

Bogardus, E. 1925. "Measuring Social Distance." *Journal of Applied Sociology* 9: 299–308.

Bringhurst, N. G. 1981. *Saints, Slaves, and Blacks: The Changing Place of Black People within Mormonism.* Westport, CT: Greenwood.

Browne-Marshall, G. B. 2013. *Race, Law and American Society: 1607 to Present.* 2nd ed. New York: Routledge.

Bugliosi, V. 1996. *Outrage: The Five Reasons Why O. J. Simpson Got Away with Murder.* New York: Norton.

Burch, A. M. 2011. "Arrest-Related Deaths, 2003–2009 Statistical Tables." Washington, DC: U.S. Department of Justice, Bureau of Justice Statistics. http://www.bjs.gov/content/pub/pdf/ard0309st.pdf.

Bureau of Justice Statistics. 2011. *Sourcebook of Criminal Justice Statistics.* http://www.albany.edu/sourcebook/tost_4.html#4_j.

Cadet, D. 2013. "Rachel Jeantel, Trayvon Martin Friend: Teen Was Trying to Escape George Zimmerman." *Huffington Post*, June 26. http://www.huffingtonpost.com/2013/06/26/rachel-jeantel-trayvon-martin_n_3505587.html.

CNN. 2013. "Transcripts: George Zimmerman Trial; 'Use of Force' Expert Testifies." July 10. http://transcripts.cnn.com/TRANSCRIPTS/1307/10/cnr.02.html.

CNN/*Time Magazine* Poll. 1995. "Races Disagree on Impact of Simpson Trial." October 6. http://www.cnn.com/US/OJ/daily/9510/10-06/poll_race/oj_poll_txt.html.

Cohen, A. 1955. *Delinquent Boys: The Culture of the Gang.* New York: Free Press.

Conley, J. M., W. M. O'Barr, and E. A. Lind. 1979. "The Power of Language: Presentational Style in the Courtroom." *Duke Law Journal* 1978 (6): 1375–99.

Cureton, S. 2000. "Determinants of Black-to-White Arrest Differentials: A Review of the Literature." In *The System in Black and White: Exploring the Connections between Race, Crime and Justice*, edited by M. Markowitz and D. Jones-Brown, 65–71. Westport, CT: Praeger.

Davidson, B. 1988. *The African Slave Trade.* Rev. ed. New York: Back Bay Books.

Davis, F. J. 2001. *Who Is Black? One Nation's Definition.* State College: Pennsylvania State University Press.

Devine, D. J., L. D. Clayton, B. B. Dunford, R. Seying, and J. Pryce. 2001. "Jury Decision Making: 45 Years of Empirical Research on Deliberating Groups." *Psychology, Public Policy and Law* 7:622–727.

Dred Scott v. Sandford, 60 U.S. 393 (1857).

Duncan v. Louisiana, 391 U.S. 145 1968).

Durose, M. R., C. W. Harlow, P. A. Langan, M. Motivans, R. R. Rantala, and E. L. Smith. 2005. "Family Violence Statistics, Including Statistics on Strangers and Acquaintances." NCJ 207846. Washington, DC: U.S. Department of Justice, Office of Justice Programs, Bureau of Justice Statistics.

Eberhardt, J. L., P. G. Davies, V. J. Purdie-Vaughns and S. L. Johnson. 2006. "Looking Deathworthy: Perceived Stereotypicality of Black Defendants Predicts Capital-Sentencing Outcomes." *Psychological Science* 17 (5): 383–86.

Eberhardt, J. L., P. A. Goff, V. J. Purdie, and P. G. Davies. 2004. "Seeing Black: Race, Crime, and Visual Processing." *Journal of Personality and Social Psychology* 87:876–93.

Eskridge, W. N., Jr. 2011. "Noah's Curse: How Religion Often Conflates Status, Belief, and Conduct to Resist Antidiscrimination Norms." *Georgia Law Review* 45:657–720.

Fiske, S. T., A. C. J. Cuddy, P. Glick, and J. Xu. 2002. "Model of (Often Mixed) Stereotype Content: Competence and Warmth Respectively Follow from Perceived Status and Competition." *Journal of Personality and Social Psychology* 82 (6): 878–902.

Fradella, H. F. 2013a. "Thoughts on the *State v. Zimmerman* Verdict." *Western Criminologist*, Fall, 5–8.

———. 2013b. "Thoughts on the *State v. Zimmerman* Verdict: Everything That's Right and Wrong with the U.S. Justice System." *iPinion Syndicate*, July 14. http://ipinion syndicate.com/thoughts-on-the-state-v-zimmerman-verdict-everything-thats-right -and-wrong-with-the-u-s-justice-system/.

Fratello, J., A. Rengifo, and J. Trone. 2013. *Coming of Age with Stop and Frisk: Experiences, Self-Perceptions, and Public Safety Implications.* New York: Center on Youth Justice, Vera Institute of Justice.

Gabbidon, S. L., G. E. Higgins, and K. M. Wilder-Bonner. 2013. "Black Supporters of Racial Profiling: A Demographic Profile." *Criminal Justice Policy Review* 24 (4): 422–40.

Garfield, G. 2010. *Through Our Eyes: African American Men's Experiences of Race, Gender and Violence.* New Brunswick, NJ: Rutgers University Press.

Gideon v. Wainwright, 372 U.S. 335 (1963).

Goff, P. A., J. L. Eberhardt, M. Williams, and M. C. Jackson. 2008. "Not Yet Human: Implicit Knowledge, Historical Dehumanization, and Contemporary Consequences." *Journal of Personality and Social Psychology* 94: 292–306.

Goff, P. A., M. C. Jackson, B. A. DiLeone, C. M. Culotta, and N. A. DiTomasso. 2014. "The Essence of Innocence: Consequences of Dehumanizing Black Children." *Journal of Personality and Social Psychology* 106 (4): 526–45.

Goff, P. A., C. M. Steele, and P. G. Davies. 2008. "The Space between Us: Stereotype Threat and Distance in Interracial Contexts." *Journal of Personality and Social Psychology* 94:91–107.

Hacker, A. 1992. *Two Nations: Separate, Hostile and Unequal.* New York: Ballantine Books.

Hannaford-Agor, P. L., V. P. Hans, N. L. Mott, and G. T. Munsterman. 2002. *Are Hung Juries a Problem?* Washington, DC: National Center for State Courts.

Harris, D. A. 1999a. "Driving While Black: Racial Profiling on our Nation's Highways." New York: American Civil Liberties Union. https://www.aclu.org/racial-justice/driving-while-black-racial-profiling-our-nations-highways.

———. 1999b. "The Stories, the Statistics, and the Law: Why 'Driving While Black' Matters." *Minnesota Law Review* 84:265–326.

Hastie, R., S. D. Penrod, and N. Pennington. 1983. *Inside the Jury.* Cambridge, MA: Harvard University Press.

Hetey, R. C., and J. L. Eberhardt. 2014. "Racial Disparities in Incarceration Increase Acceptance of Punitive Policies." *Psychological Science* 25:1949–54.

HistoryEngine.com. n.d. "Florida Becomes First Southern State to Propose a Poll Tax." http://historyengine.richmond.edu/episodes/view/1615.

Hodgetts, D. 2014. "Social Distance." In *Encyclopedia of Critical Psychology,* edited by T. Teo, 1776–78. New York: Springer.

HuffingtonPostLive. 2013. "Rachel Jeantel's Unorthodox Testimony Ridiculed. Hosted by Nancy Redd." July 10. http://jobs.aol.com/videos/job-interviews/rachel-jeantels-unorthodox-testimony-ridiculed/517852034/.

Illinois v. Wardlow, 528 U.S. 119 (2000).

Johnson, E. C. 1995. *Proposed Reforms to the Criminal Justice System as a Reaction to the* Simpson *Verdict.* San Francisco, CA: Public Law Research Institute.

Johnson, E. L. 1995. "A Menace to Society: The Use of Criminal Profiles and Its Effects on Black Males." *Howard Law Journal* 38:629–64.

Johnson v. Louisiana, 400 U.S. 356 (1972).

Jones, D. 1995. "What the Simpson Trial Means for American Justice." *Minorities in the Profession Section Newsletter* 6 (1).

Jones-Brown, D. 2007. "Forever the Symbolic Assailant: The More Things Change the More They Remain the Same: Reaction Essay." *Criminology and Public Policy* 6 (1): 103–22.

———. 2009. "The Right to Life? Policing, Race and Criminal Injustice." *Human Rights* 36 (2). http://www.americanbar.org/publications/human_rights_magazine_home/human_rights_vol36_2009/spring2009/the_right_to_life_policing_race_and_criminal_injustice.html.

———. 2012. "In a Colorblind Society, Did Trayvon Martin Have a Right to Stand His Ground?" *Crime Report: Viewpoints,* March 30. http://www.thecrimereport.org/viewpoints/2012-03-in-a-colorblind-society-did-trayvon-martin-have-a-ri.

Jones-Brown, D., B. Frazier, and M. Brooks. 2014. *African Americans and Criminal Justice: An Encyclopedia.* Santa Barbara, CA: Greenwood/ABC-CLIO.

Jones-Brown, D., B. Stoudt, B. Johnston, and K. Moran. 2013. *Stop, Question and Frisk Policing Practices in New York City: A Primer (Revised).* New York: John Jay College, Center on Race, Crime and Justice. www.stopandfriskinfo.com.

Kalven, H., and H. Zeisel. 1966. *The American Jury*. Boston, MA: Little, Brown.

Kaplan, D. A. 1995. "Disorder in the Court." *Newsweek*, October 16, 58.

Khare, A. T., M. L. Joseph, and R. J. Chaskin. 2014. "The Enduring Significance of Race in Mixed-Income Developments." *Urban Affairs Review* 50 (4): 1–30.

Lane, K. A., J. Kang, and M. R. Banaji. 2007. "Implicit Social Cognition and Law." *Annual Review of Law and Social Science* 3:427–51.

Lee, C. 2013. "Making Race Salient: Trayvon Martin and Implicit Bias in a Not Yet Post-Racial Society." *North Carolina Law Review* 91:1555–1612.

Levine, J. P. 2000. "The Impact of Racial Demography on Jury Verdicts in Routine Adjudication." In *The System in Black and White: Exploring the Connections between Race, Crime and Justice*, edited by M. Markowitz and D. Jones-Brown, 153–69. Westport, CT: Praeger.

Lonardo, R. A., W. A. Manning, P. C. Giordano, and M. A. Longmore. 2011. "Offending, Substance Use, and Cohabitation in Young Adulthood." *Social Forum* 25 (4): 787–803.

MacDonald, H. 2012. "Why Manipulate the Tragedy of Trayvon Martin?" *National Review Online*, March 25. http://www.nationalreview.com/corner/294357/why -manipulate-tragedy-trayvon-martin-heather-mac-donald.

Majors, R., and J. M. Billison. 1993. *Cool Pose: The Dilemmas of Black Manhood in America*. New York: Lexington Books.

Markel, D. 2013, July 13. "Zimmerman's Not Guilty." *PrawfsBlawg*. http://prawfsblawg .blogs.com/.

McCain, R. S. 2013. "The 'New School' on CNN: If Rachel Jeantel Is the Future of America, We're Completely Doomed." *American Spectator*, July 17. http://spectator .org/print/55220.

Miller, R. H. 1998. "Six of One Is Not a Dozen of the Other: A Reexamination of *Williams v. Florida* and the Size of State Criminal Juries." *University of Pennsylvania Law Review* 146:621–86.

Morrow, W. J. 2015. "Examining the Potential for Racial Disparities in Use of Force during NYPD Stop and Frisk Activities." Doctoral dissertation, Arizona State University, Phoenix.

Moynahan, D. P. 1965. *The Negro Family: The Case for National Action*. Washington, DC: Government Printing Office.

Muhammad, K. G. 2010. *The Condemnation of Blackness: Race, Crime and the Making of Modern Urban America*. Cambridge, MA: Harvard University Press.

Neubauer, D. W., and H. F. Fradella. 2013. *America's Courts and the Criminal Justice System*. 11th ed. Belmont, CA: Wadsworth/Cengage.

Nosek, B. A., M. R. Banaji, and A. G. Greenwald. 2002. "Harvesting Implicit Group Attitudes and Beliefs from a Demonstration Web Site." *Group Dynamics: Theory, Research, and Practice* 6 (1): 101–15.

Ogletree, C., Jr. 2010. *The Presumption of Guilt: The Arrest of Henry Louis Gates, Jr. and Race, Class and Crime in America*. London: Palgrave Macmillan.

Oliver, W. 1998. *The Violent Social World of Black Men*. San Francisco: Jossey-Bass.

Pabst, W. 1973. "What Do Six-Member Juries Really Save?" *Judicature* 57:6–11.

Paternoster, R. 2013. "Racial Disparity in the Case of Duane Edward Buck: A Final Report." http://www.documentcloud.org/documents/616699-duane-buck-final -signed-paternoster-report.html#document/p1/a95424.

Pierce, G., and M. Radelet. 2005. "The Impact of Legally Inappropriate Factors on Death Sentencing for California Homicides, 1990–1999." *Santa Clara Law Review* 46:1–47.

Rabinow, P., and W. Sullivan. 1979. *Interpretive Social Science.* Berkeley: University of California Press.

Richardson, L. S., and P. A. Goff. 2012. "Self-Defense and the Suspicion Heuristic." *Iowa Law Review* 98:293–336.

Roman, J., and M. Downey. 2012. "Stand Your Ground Laws and Miscarriages of Justice." *Urban Institute MetroTrends Blog.* http://blog.metrotrends.org/author/ mitchandjohn/.

Roper, R. 1979. "Jury Size: Impact on Verdict's Correctness." *American Politics Quarterly* 7:438–52.

Russell-Brown, K. K. 1998. *The Color of Crime: Racial Hoaxes, White Fear, Black Protectionism, Police Harassment, and Other Macroaggressions.* New York: New York University Press.

Saks, M. J. 1974. "Ignorance of Science Is No Excuse." *Trial* 10:1–20.

Saks, M. J., and M. W. Marti. 1997. "A Meta-Analysis of the Effects of Jury Size." *Law and Human Behavior* 21:451–67.

Sampson, R. J., and W. J. Wilson. 1995. "Toward a Theory of Race, Crime, and Urban Inequality." In *Crime and Inequality*, edited by J. Hagan and R. D. Peterson, 37–56. Stanford, CA: Stanford University Press.

Schraub, D. 2013. "Zimmerman's Not Guilty." *PrawfsBlawg*, July 14. http://prawfsblawg .blogs.com/prawfsblawg/2013/07/zimmermans-not-guilty.html#comments.

Sedlak, A., D. Finkelhor, H. Hammer, and D. Schultz. 2002. "National Estimates of Missing Children: An Overview." Washington, DC: U.S. Department of Justice, Office of Justice Programs, Office of Juvenile Justice and Delinquency Prevention.

Sellin, T. 1928. "The Negro Criminal: A Statistical Note." *Annals of the American Academy of Political and Social Science* 140:52–64.

Shapiro, T. M. 2004. *The Hidden Cost of Being African American: How Wealth Perpetuates Inequality.* New York: Oxford University Press.

Shapiro, T., T. Meschede, and S. Osoro. 2013. *The Roots of the Widening Racial Wealth Gap: Explaining the Black-White Economic Divide.* Waltham, MA: Institute on Assets and Social Policy.

Smith, A., and M. J. Saks. 2008. "The Case for Overturning *Williams v. Florida* and the Six-Person Jury: History, Law, and Empirical Evidence." *Florida Law Review* 60:441–70.

Smith, B. W. 2004. "Structural and Organizational Predictors of Homicide by Police." *Policing: An International Journal of Police Strategies and Management* 27:539–57.

Sneed, T. 2014. "Garner, Brown Decisions Spark Calls for Grand Jury Reform: Some

Say Recent Moves Not to Charge Cops in Civilian Deaths Stem from a Faulty Process." *U.S. News & World Report*, December 12. http://www.usnews.com/news/articles/2014/12/12/after-eric-garner-michael-brown-decisions-calls-for-grand-jury-reform.

Sommers, S. 2007. "Race and the Decision Making of Juries." *Legal and Criminological Psychology* 12:171–87.

Stewart, J. J., and W. E. Berrett. 1960. *Mormonism and the Negro*. Salt Lake City, UT: Bookmark.

Stoudt, B. G., M. Fine, and M. Fox. 2012. "Growing Up Policed in the Age of Aggressive Policing Policies." *New York Law School Law Review* 56:1331–70.

Strickland, S., R. Schauffler, R. LaFountain, and E. Holt, eds. 2014. *State Court Organization*. Williamsburg, VA: National Center for State Courts. www.ncsc.org/sco.

Sweeney, J. P. 1995. "Ito Inspires Bill Involving Judges' Kin." *San Diego Union-Tribune*, August 24, A4.

Taylor, H. 1995. "Public Belief in O. J. Simpson's Guilt or Innocence Varies Greatly Not Just in Race but Also with Age, Education and Income." Harris Poll 1995 #21. New York: Louis Harris & Associates. http://www.harrisinteractive.com/vault/Harris-Interactive-Poll-Research-PUBLIC-BELIEF-IN-OJ-SIMPSONS-GUILT-OR-INNOCENCE-VA-1995-03.pdf.

Tennessee v. Garner, 471 U.S. 1 (1985).

Tyler, T. R., and Y. J. Huo. 2003. "Procedural Justice, Legitimacy, and the Effective Rule of Law." *Crime and Justice* 30:283–357.

Wacquant, L. 2005. "Race as a Civil Felony." *International Social Science Journal* 57 (183): 127–42.

Washington, J. 2014. "A Black and White View of the O. J. Simpson Case 20 Years Later." *Huffington Post*, June 8. http://www.huffingtonpost.com/2014/06/08/oj-simpson-trial_n_5468851.html.

Way, N. 1998. *Everyday Courage: The Lives and Stories of Urban Teenagers*. New York: New York University Press.

Weiner, B. 2005. "Motivation from an Attribution Perspective and the Social Psychology and Perceived Competency." In *Handbook of Competence and Motivation*, edited by A. J. Elliott and C. S. Dweck, 73–84. New York: Guilford.

West, C. 1994. *Race Matters*. New York: Vintage.

Whitaker, M. 2013. "Trayvon Martin Family Prays for 'Peaceful Justice.'" MSNBC, July 10. http://www.msnbc.com/politicsnation/trayvon-martin-family-prays-peaceful-jus.

Williams, J. 2014. "20 Years Later, the Real Verdict on O. J. Simpson." FoxNews.com, June 12. http://www.foxnews.com/opinion/2014/06/12/20-years-later-real-verdict-on-oj-simpson/.

Wise, T. 2012. "Trayvon Martin, White America and the Return of *Dred Scott*." March 27. http://www.timwise.org/2012/03/trayvon-martin-white-america-and-the-return-of-dred-scott/.

10

Divided by Race

Differences in the Perception of Injustice

ISAAC UNAH AND VALERIE WRIGHT

Race is the elephant in the room in much of the social and political life of Americans. Its presence in mixed interpersonal interactions is often obvious. Outside of such interactions, however, we can still find race lurking silently underneath the façade of normalcy in national conversations about crime, social policy, and politics.[1] As the most visible sign of difference among U.S. residents, race is celebrated as a source of diversity, inclusion, and strength. Yet for many Americans, race remains a source of guarded discomfort, and even irritation for some. As a result, many Americans, especially those in the majority group, remain aversive about discussing and confronting race for fear of being labeled racist.[2] Occasionally, however, a racial incident erupts that shocks the conscience and raises so many questions that it becomes impossible to avoid a focused and frank discussion about race and its role in the perception of injustice in the United States.

The killing of Trayvon Martin by George Zimmerman on February 26, 2012, in a townhouse community in Sanford, Florida, is one such incident. Martin's killing and the subsequent controversies surrounding the arrest, trial, and acquittal of Zimmerman rekindled a national conversation about race and the perception of injustice in the criminal justice system. It was a salient criminological event that, for well over a year, garnered sustained national media attention, provoked commentary from President Barack Obama, and stimulated private discussions among people of all races. A Gallup poll conducted in the immediate aftermath of the shooting revealed that a majority of Americans (66 percent) were following news about the shooting somewhat closely or very closely.[3]

The Reverend Jesse Jackson has remarked that "injustice anywhere is injustice everywhere."[4] This pithy statement assumes the interrelatedness of official injustice in various American communities; it further assumes that injustice is a concept that moves in a straight line, that you know it when you see it, a phenomenon that once observed will be interpreted evenhandedly anywhere and everywhere by fair-minded individuals. To some extent, our work in this chapter challenges this popular assumption of evenhandedness in the perceptions of injustice. We seize upon the opportunity presented by this salient crime event to test the racial gradient thesis, which emphasizes a hierarchy in public perception of injustice among racial and ethnic groups.[5]

Are there strong racial differences in public perceptions of injustice in the American criminal justice system? Do these differences adhere to a racial gradient? If so, why? These are some of the central questions of concern for social scientists at this historical moment when color blindness is continually invoked as a social goal and a black president sits atop American government. These questions form the centerpiece of this chapter. In a justice system where an unelected jury makes decisions that can affect an individual's life course, addressing these questions is important because, as David Easton pointed out, diffuse public support is an essential ingredient that lends legitimacy to the actions of government and ensures the survival and strength of democratic institutions, including the U.S. criminal justice system.[6]

In addressing these questions of racial differences in opinion about injustice, we strive to make two important contributions to the literature on race and public opinion. First, we illustrate that public reaction to the delayed arrest of Zimmerman as well as to his acquittal for Martin's killing symbolizes a long-standing disequilibrium concerning racial differences in opinion toward the criminal justice system among blacks, Hispanics, and whites. Second, we expand the explanatory value of the racial gradient thesis by employing two waves of public opinion data gathered before and after a salient criminological event to explain not only the racial differences in opinion surrounding such events, but also why Hispanics are typically sandwiched somewhere in between blacks and whites in the perceptions of injustice. We find strong and consistent support for the racial gradient thesis.

Racial Gradient Thesis and Group Perceptions of Injustice

The racial gradient thesis constitutes a core component of comparative conflict theory.[7] Researchers have long pointed to conflict theory as a critical framework for explaining racial and ethnic differences and similarities in criminal justice policy and in individual-level behavior.[8] At its genesis, the conflict perspective emphasized standard political and sociological concepts: social class, group threat, powerlessness and pursuit of interests in modern plural societies.[9] It asserted that threats to existing social, political, and economic arrangements posed by disadvantaged groups can be used to explain why certain groups are more likely than others to have encounters with the justice system.[10]

Early emphasis was placed on people's social class status and their attachment to the economic structure.[11] Social scientists paid little attention to the effects of racial and ethnic cleavages on social organization. Following the Marxist tradition, many simply assumed that race and ethnicity were merely social forms that in time will be assimilated into larger social identities based upon class.[12] Given the overlap between social class and race, however, ascriptive group cleavages failed to dissipate. Rather, they gained in theoretical and practical importance as subsequent investigations on the conflict perspective turned to the salience of race in grounding group conflicts and explaining black/white differences in opinion on crime and justice issues.[13] There was, and still is, little scholarly emphasis on Hispanic perceptions.

More recent analyses have turned toward a notable component of conflict theory—the racial gradient thesis—which emphasizes a hierarchy or gradation of opinion among groups in an ongoing competition for control of economic, political, and social structures.[14] Its underlying premise is that differences of opinion based on race and ethnicity exist on important criminal justice policies and have serious policy ramifications.[15] The racial gradient thesis postulates that public opinion on criminal injustice follows an intensity level adhering to a black/Hispanic/white gradient, with blacks being most likely to perceive injustice, whites being least likely to perceive injustice, and Hispanics being sandwiched in between blacks and whites.[16] Sociologists such as Hagan, Shedd, and Payne have asserted that blacks and Hispanics perceive more injustice relative to whites because they have less social, political, and economic power.[17] These relative power differences have hindered their ability to influence crime policy and have produced racially segregated neighborhoods in which blacks and Hispanics are disproportionately the targets of police brutality, racial profiling, having their neighborhoods constantly patrolled, and having increased encounters with law enforcement.

What are the causal antecedents of this apparent hierarchy in the perception of injustice among racial and ethnic groups? One antecedent is the historical mistreatment of racial minorities by law enforcement. The weight of social science evidence provides incontrovertible testament that, as a group, blacks have suffered the brunt of racial inequities in government policy concerning arrest,[18] drug enforcement,[19] mass incarceration,[20] and the escalation of criminal charges and punishments.[21] This painful reality is perceived by minority groups, particularly African Americans, as unfair, and it contributes to a feeling of alienation and distrust of legal and criminal justice institutions. Minority groups also perceive the police, courts, and other criminal justice institutions as instruments of "the system," assembled primarily to guard, protect, and promote the interest of whites, while minimizing competition over valuable resources such as jobs and political power.[22] A review of the literature by Bobo and Johnson suggests that an increasing number of scholars view the justice system as deliberately biased and that it constitutes a loosely coordinated racial order designed to reassert social control over blacks and minimize their menace to society.[23]

Buttressing this rather bleak vision of the justice system is an analysis by Schneider and Ingram that suggests that law itself functions as a tool established by, and for the benefit of, the dominant group, whose members control the levers of economic and political power, which they use for subjugating and suppressing the interest of socially constructed minority populations.[24] Therefore, it stands to reason that, unlike minority groups, whites are more inclined to develop significantly more positive affinity toward the criminal justice system and its social agents whom they believe are protecting what is rightfully theirs.

Macro-level studies provide further support for this group threat argument by showing that, on balance, the size of the black population in a state or city is positively associated with increased spending on police,[25] police strength,[26] incarceration rates,[27] and the likelihood that state governors would use aggressive language to describe the crime situation during their state of the state addresses.[28] Thus, the treatment and consideration of disadvantaged groups by the justice system is largely determined by the levels of perceived threat posed by blacks relative to their proportion in the population.

At a certain level, it is easily ascertained that racial differences in opinion are not surprising because perceptions of injustice are a reflection of individual experiences and are very widespread in American society. Minorities, particularly African Americans, are more likely to perceive that inequities in education, health care, and employment exist and that these problems are rooted in prejudice, discrimination, and denial of opportunity by whites.[29] Whites, however, tend to think that discrimination is a thing of the past and view the apparent inequality experienced by blacks and other minorities as the result of low motivation and lack of effort.[30]

There has been little empirical attention given to Hispanic perceptions of injustice, compared to research on African Americans and Anglos, although as the Hispanic population continues to increase, this dynamic is bound to change. The reason for the scant attention to Hispanic perceptions is not because Hispanics are infrequent targets of mistreatment by courts and law enforcement personnel but because Hispanics occupy a "disadvantaged middle ground where they are a less comprehensive and intensive focus of criminalization efforts than African Americans."[31] We think this reduced intensity of focus is due in part to Hispanics' lighter skin tone, which elevates them to a more socially acceptable position in society, making their experiences not as bad as those of African Americans but not as good as those of whites. Supporting this perspective is a growing line of social science research that suggests that skin tone is an important criterion of social acceptance and a strong indicator of how individuals are treated in sociolegal and political processes.[32] According to Portes and Rumbaut, a "racial gradient continues to exist in U.S. culture so that the darker a person's skin, the greater is the social distance from dominant groups and the more difficult it is to make his or her personal qualifications count."[33] However, one study showed that the perception of injustice among Hispanics is a function of frequency of contact with the justice system.[34] In that study,

Carter concluded that Hispanics reported having a good attitude toward police but saw it diminish after more contact with the police. Thus, it is possible that the arc of the cumulative experiences of Hispanics with law could bring convergence to the perceptions of Hispanics and blacks.

Explaining Racial Hierarchy in Perceptions of Injustice

Reasonable citizens would not discount the fact that the indignities and painful experiences of slavery and both de jure and de facto segregations have taught black people and their descendants in America to be suspicious of government institutions and the rules under which they function. But even if accounts of slavery are considered too distant to matter in today's world, several more contemporary reasons support the claim that blacks have received the proverbial short end of the stick in the U.S. criminal justice system, making them most likely to express negative sentiments toward the system relative to other racial/ethnic groups. We review some of these reasons here.

TREATMENT BY THE POLICE

As a whole, research on public perceptions of law enforcement suggests that opinions are highly polarized by race. Recent public opinion studies indicate that racial groups have divergent views related to crime and the justice system's response to criminal activity.[35] Studies have consistently shown that, regarding their treatment by police, blacks are more likely than whites to report that they have personally experienced discrimination,[36] have been racially profiled,[37] and have had excessive force used against them.[38] Many of these studies focus on adult perceptions of police mistreatment.[39] However, some attention has also been given to the perceptions of youth. For instance, Hagan, Shedd, and Payne studied the responses of Chicago public school students in the ninth and tenth grades to a series of questions about nonnormative behavior and personal interactions with police.[40] They reported that African American youth are most likely to have negative encounters with police and the most pronounced negative perceptions of the justice system. Conversely, whites have the most positive experiences with police. Hispanic students perceived their experiences with police to be better than those of blacks, but less positive than the experiences of whites. This finding implies that comparative relativism is at work. In other words, explanations for variations in perception are not merely a reflection of individual beliefs but are rooted in a collective sense of a groups' racial/ethnic position relative to other groups. Such experiences may contribute to African Americans, particularly those living in areas with aggressive policing, being more inclined to resent law enforcement and associated institutions compared to whites and even Hispanics.

SEGREGATION AND RELATIVE DEPRIVATION

Another antecedent of the apparent racial hierarchy in perceptions of injustice is rooted in residential and neighborhood segregation and relative deprivation. Blacks are more likely than whites to live in inner-city, segregated neighborhoods plagued by urban blight and its associated problems of extreme poverty, homelessness, unemployment, and crime.[41] Neighborhood-level studies point to economic disadvantage as a factor that may contribute to group perceptions of injustice and resentment.[42] Sampson and Bartusch relied on multilevel modeling to find that an important source of racial variations in attitudes about the police stems from the different neighborhood context in which blacks and whites tend to reside.[43] While their results clearly support the racial gradient thesis regarding racially divergent views about the police, their results also suggest that the concentration of poverty among African Americans accounts for many of the differences in dissatisfaction with police and the justice system more generally. In an effort to advance this line of research, a subsequent study tested differences in perceptions of the police using a sample of whites and blacks who were situated in similar ecological context.[44] MacDonald et al. found that race remained a prominent predictor of perceptions of injustice by the police even when neighborhood context was controlled.[45]

FREQUENT CONTACT WITH AGENTS OF THE
CRIMINAL JUSTICE SYSTEM

Another reason that blacks are more likely than Hispanics, and Hispanics more likely than whites, to perceive injustice is that relative to white neighborhoods, black and Hispanic neighborhoods have higher levels of police surveillance and arrests.[46] This increased contact, either directly or vicariously, fosters a perception that the police and other agents of the criminal justice system are unfairly targeting minority communities. The dissatisfaction among blacks, for example, stems from distinct sources. On one hand, when residents who reside in predominately black neighborhoods call for police assistance, they are unlikely to believe that the police responded adequately or promptly to their requests for service.[47] On the other hand, when police do respond to calls for service, resources are overwhelmingly devoted to enforcement rather than protection and prevention.[48]

Furthermore, in recent years, researchers have analyzed the frequency of both personal and vicarious contacts with the justice system to test the racial gradient thesis.[49] Generally speaking, they found that blacks, followed by Hispanics, are more likely than whites to be arrested, prosecuted, and incarcerated. It is no wonder then that America's prisons and jails are disproportionately populated with black and Hispanic residents.[50] Beyond these findings, researchers have assessed whether perceptions of injustice are linked to direct and indirect experiences with incarceration. Buckler et al. found strong support for the racial gradient thesis among populations with and without a history of incarceration. In a sample of individuals without an incarceration record, African Americans followed by Hispanics were more likely than whites to perceive racially disparate court outcomes.[51] Among males with an incarceration record, a similar racial gradient was found. Thus, the perceptions of injustice remain and inexorably retain an adherence to a racial gradient even after incarceration experiences have been taken into account.

Salient Crime Events and Perceptions of Injustice

Across the American historical landscape, salient crime events along with personal experiences with the law and law enforcement significantly shape enduring social attitudes about the legal system. We define "salient crime events" as those that shock the conscience and garner national attention in intensity and duration through media scrutiny and analysis by reporters, members of the public, law enforcement, and political figures. Danilo Yanich points out that incidences of crime events and especially those that trigger racial injustice in the modern era are numerous and varied, and that their effects tended to be localized.[52]

But crime events are not all created equal. Salient crime events usually attract sufficient attention as to shape perceptions nationally and across the racial divide by stimulating discussion and evaluation that could not have materialized had the event not occurred.

In this section, we focus on the contributions of salient crime events such as the Trayvon Martin killing in our understanding of perceptions of crime and justice policy. What do we know about how perceptions of injustice are formed, changed, and ultimately racialized as a result of salient crime?

American citizens have the capacity to form sound judgments, empathize, and react appropriately when they perceive official behaviors as unjust. Much work on how perceptions of injustice are formed relies on the procedural justice framework. Research on procedural justice indicates that people tend to focus on the fairness of procedures employed by criminal justice officials when evaluating the services provided by government and deciding how much legitimacy to bestow upon its agents.[53] This research maintains that what matters most in structuring individual perceptions is not instrumental gains from an encounter with authority but the nature of that encounter and the manner in which individuals in positions of authority treat ordinary citizens under the circumstances.[54]

Once formed, perceptions of government institutions tend to endure and are difficult to change. Work by Warren and Farrell suggests that perceptions of police misconduct are formed through repeated media exposure that brings public awareness and focus upon wrongs such as racial profiling, police brutality, and inexcusable use of deadly force against unarmed civilians.[55] A lack of effort to increase police accountability through legislative action and institutional reforms involving personnel changes at the top of police organizational hierarchy can allow such perceptions to fester and harden, often becoming racialized. In most cases, it is only by shining a spotlight on official wrongdoing that behaviors such as the use of excessive force by police can be monitored and eventually changed.

Although racial divisions in public opinion are commonplace, serious empirical research is scant with regard to testing racial differences in opinion on salient crime events. One of the few exceptions came after the Rodney King incident. King, an African American construction worker, was severely beaten by several officers from the Los Angeles Police Department (LAPD) in 1992 following a high-speed car chase. Much of the incident was captured on videotape by an uninvolved onlooker. The beating was aired repeatedly and in dramatic fashion on national television. The footage drew tremendous public outrage and raised concerns about police brutality toward racial minorities, concerns that were exacerbated by the subsequent acquittal of the officers, sparking the Los Angeles race riots.[56] Throughout the media coverage of the incident, there was little effort on the part of LAPD leadership to hold the officers accountable.

Lasley studied the short-term racial differences in citizen attitudes toward the LAPD before and in the aftermath of the King incident.[57] Using a sample of 369 residents of South Central Los Angeles, she analyzed differences in perceptions regarding police fairness toward citizens. The results revealed that irrespective of race, the Rodney King beating and the acquittal of the officers did fundamental damage to citizens' trust of the police and legal system. Furthermore, negative perceptions of the police were strongest among African Americans, who, it turned out, also held these views significantly longer than any other racial/ethnic group. Thus, lasting perceptions of police are formed when citizens are convinced the police have repeatedly behaved badly, have ignored constitutional rights of citizens, and are culpable.

But are such effects confined to Los Angeles, or are they transferable to other parts of the country given the widespread media coverage of the incident? Kaminski and Jefferis provide a possible answer.[58] Their test of Easton's theory of diffuse versus specific support for political systems using a survey experiment involving Cincinnati, Ohio, residents indicates that a prominent crime event involving an intensely publicized violent arrest of an African American youth in Cincinnati had more influence on perceptions of the local police than did the Rodney King incident.[59] But Kaminski and Jefferis admit that a salient crime event at the national level can serve as an anchor upon which local critical crime events can be interpreted and internalized,[60] which supports Easton's suggestion that "repeated frustration" of citizens based on race, ethnicity, or creed can damage their reservoir of goodwill toward public officials.[61]

Another study focused on racial differences in perceptions regarding the treatment of a group of six African American high school boys known as the Jena Six. The teens were convicted on December 4, 2006, for beating Justin Barker, a white student at Jena High School in Jena, Louisiana. Many civil rights activists asserted that charging the boys with attempted second-degree murder was excessive and discriminatory. Goidel, Parent, and Mann examined racial differences in public opinion on the prosecution of the Jena Six and found that reactions to the prosecution of the boys were filtered by race.[62] Relative to whites, blacks were more likely to follow the story in the media and to believe race was a factor in the decision to prosecute. Such results indicate that blacks not only are more interested in the salient crime incidents that raise questions about race relations, but also are more likely to believe that race colors the way in which the incidents are handled by officials.

More recently, the Martin and Zimmerman incident captured the nation's attention and started an arc of massive media coverage of the killings of African Americans by white males or white police officers never witnessed before. Analysis using survey data collected shortly after the shooting demonstrated that blacks were more likely than whites to believe race was a factor in the shooting; however, the views of Hispanics were not statically different from those of whites.[63] The authors also assessed whether there was a racial divide in opinion about whether Zimmerman would have been arrested if Martin were white and found support for the racial gradient thesis. In addition, the Pew Research Center conducted a national survey of adults to gauge public opinion on the Zimmerman verdict.[64] The data illustrate that the American public was divided over Zimmerman's acquittal along racial lines. While nearly half (49 percent) of whites were satisfied with the verdict, only 5 percent of blacks were. Furthermore, over three-quarters of blacks (78 percent) believed that the case raises important issues of race, compared to just over a quarter (25 percent) of whites.

Hypotheses

Our research broadens the scope of the literature on perceptions of injustice by directing attention to public reactions regarding salient criminological events, in this case the arrest and acquittal of George Zimmerman. We contend that the racial divide in public reactions to Martin's shooting, the eventual arrest of Zimmerman, and the not guilty verdict reflect long-standing views on race and the administration of justice. Based upon our theoretical discussion above, we present and test the following hypotheses concerning the racial gradient thesis:

H_1: Blacks followed by Hispanics are more likely than whites to believe that George Zimmerman would have been arrested if Trayvon Martin had been a white victim.

H_2: Blacks followed by Hispanics are less likely than whites to report that the jury reached the correct verdict.

H_3: Blacks followed by Hispanics are more likely than whites to believe that the criminal justice system is biased against blacks.

Data and Analytic Strategy

To test our hypotheses, we relied on data from two national surveys of American adults. First, the *USA Today*/Gallup poll "Trayvon Martin Case" was conducted from April 2 to 6, 2012, roughly one month after the shooting of Trayvon Martin but before Zimmerman's arrest by Sanford police. In reaction to public protests surrounding the reluctance of Sanford police to arrest Zimmerman, the survey asked whether respondents thought Zimmerman would have been arrested if he had killed a white person. This question forms the basis of our first dependent variable to assess the gradience of opinion among blacks, Hispanics, and whites about injustice. The question taps into respondents' fundamental understandings and views about the American legal system concerning the documented problem of aggressive prosecution for white victims relative to black victims. Respondents' racial identity, political affiliation, employment status, church attendance, parental status of children under eighteen, income and educational levels, and demographic characteristics were also queried in the survey. In addition, respondents were asked how closely they were following events surrounding the shooting in the media.

Second, we examined public opinion after the not guilty verdict was handed down. For that analysis, we turn to the Gallup News Service poll "George Zimmerman Verdict Reaction," conducted July 16, 2013, soon after the Zimmerman verdict. The poll asked several questions not included in the previous survey, such as, "From what you know about the case, do you think the verdict was right or wrong?" Respondents were also asked, "Do you think the American justice system is biased against black people?" These two questions form the crux of our analysis of opinion about injustice in the justice system, and we rely on them as dependent variables to test our second and third hypotheses.

Variable Coding

DEPENDENT VARIABLES

Based upon the discussion above, there are three dependent variables. The first is a dummy variable indicating whether Zimmerman would have been arrested if he shot a white person (coded yes = 1, no = 0). The second concerns postverdict reactions and asks whether respondents thought the verdict was correct (yes = 1, no = 0). The third regards whether respondents thought the justice system is biased against blacks (yes = 1, no = 0).

INDEPENDENT VARIABLES

Our analysis is limited to responses provided by black, Hispanic, and white respondents. We coded responses indicating membership in these racial and ethnic groups into dummy variables, with whites serving as the comparison category throughout. Gender was coded as male (1) or female (0). Political ideology was rated on a 5-point scale ranging from extremely liberal (–2) to moderate (0) to extremely conservative (+2).[65] Also included are two measures of social class status: income and educational level. Reported monthly family income was represented as less than $2,000 (1), $2,001 to $3,999 (2), $4,000 to $7,499 (3), $7,500 to $14,999 (4), and $15,000 or higher (5). Educational level was measured as high school graduate or less (1), some college (2), college graduate (3), and postgraduate education (4). Age was scored on a range representing 18 to 29 (1), 30 to 49 (2), 50 to 64 (3), and 65 or older (4). Marital status was coded as currently married (1) or unmarried (including widowed or divorce) (0). We controlled for frequency of church attendance, coded as never (1), seldom (2), about once a week (3), almost every week (4), and at least once a week (5). Respondents with children under the age of eighteen were coded 1, those without were coded 0. We controlled for regional differences in perceptions of injustice with a dummy variable (southerners = 1, non-southerners = 0). Finally, we took note of how closely respondents were following events of Martin's killing: not at all closely (1), not too closely (2), somewhat closely (3), very closely (4). Because of concerns about possibly losing too much information due to responses indicating nonattitudes,[66] linear multiple imputation was used to replace "don't know" responses for two questions that are susceptible to social desirability concerns: income and whether Zimmerman would have been arrested if he had shot a white person.

The descriptive statistics of the variables are reported in table 10.1. The samples roughly mirror the population of Anglos, Hispanics, and African Americans in the United States. Whites constitute the majority (roughly 77 percent) of the respondents. Hispanics are approximately 13 percent, and African Americans represent about 12 percent.

TABLE 10.1. Descriptive Statistics of the Variables

	Gallup poll, April 2012		Gallup poll, July 2013	
	n	Percentage	*n*	Percentage
Dependent variables				
Zimmerman arrested if he shot a white person (yes = 1)	1,273	42.3		
Zimmerman jury reached correct/just verdict (yes = 1)			1,379	54.3
Justice system biased against blacks (yes = 1)			824	32.4
Independent and control variables				
African American	350	11.7	252	9.9
Hispanic	382	12.7	268	10.5
White	2,961	77.3	2,014	79.3
Age				
18–29	620	20.6	337	13.3
30–49	1,019	33.9	669	26.3
50–64	773	25.7	802	31.6
65+	557	18.5	733	28.8

TABLE 10.1 (*continued*)

	Gallup poll, April 2012		Gallup poll, July 2013	
	n	Percentage	*n*	Percentage
Sex				
Males	1,535	51.1	1,272	50.1
Females	1,471	48.9	1,269	49.9
Married	1,573	52.7	1,333	52.5
Adult with children under 18	1,104	36.7	673	26.5
Education				
High school or less	1,225	40.8	633	24.9
Some college	838	27.9	785	30.9
College graduate	505	16.8	590	23.2
Postgraduate	402	13.4	481	18.9
Monthly income				
Less than $2,000	663	22.0	489	19.2
$2,000–$4,999	874	29.2	659	25.9
$5,000–$7,499	897	29.9	787	31.0
$7,500+	411	13.7	607	23.9
Job				
Full-time	1,521	50.6	1,229	48.4
Part-time	417	13.9	301	11.8
Unemployed	1,069	35.5		
Church attendance				
Never	606	20.2	541	21.3
Seldom	762	25.3	589	23.2
About once a month	329	11.0	298	11.7
Almost every week	241	8.0 .	212	8.3
At least once a week	1,027	34.2	842	33.1
Ideology				
Very liberal	145	4.8	120	4.7
Liberal	493	16.4	469	18.5
Moderate	1,179	39.2	1,021	40.2
Conservative	925	30.8	725	28.5
Very conservative	265	8.8	206	8.1
South	1,017	33.8	840	33.1
Non-South	1,989	66.2	1,701	66.9

There are more male respondents in the surveys (roughly 51 percent) than female (about 49 percent). Overall the surveys indicate that 42.3 percent of Americans thought Zimmerman would have been arrested sooner had he shot and killed a white person. Following the verdict, a majority of Americans (54.3 percent) reported that the not guilty verdict was correct. Only 32.4 percent of Americans thought that the justice system was biased against African Americans.

How Blacks, Hispanics, and Whites Perceive Criminal Injustice

Analysis of Gallup surveys on the Martin killing and Zimmerman's acquittal indicate that Americans are highly polarized along racial lines in their responses to nearly every aspect of the case and in their perceptions of how citizens are treated in the criminal justice system. Within that polarization, an interesting story of racial gradience emerges from the data. African Americans are by far the most skeptical of the actions and claims of the Sanford Police Department and of the jury's verdict. They are also most likely to agree that the justice system overall is biased against them. In each of these attitudinal dimensions, Hispanics are lodged between blacks and whites, providing strong support for the racial gradient thesis.

Figure 10.1 provides the racial and ethnic breakdown in the perception of injustice by blacks, Hispanics, and whites. Panel A addresses the question of whether the police would have arrested Zimmerman if Martin had been white. The proportion of African Americans who think the police would have done so is quite high (73.8 percent), and is almost double the proportion of whites (37.5 percent). Hispanic respondents fall in the middle. with 44.4 percent of them reporting that the decision would have been different if Martin had been white.

A similar trend emerges in panel B. While only 13.5 percent of African Americans reported that the jury made the correct decision in the Zimmerman verdict, more than 61 percent of whites think that the verdict is justified, with Hispanics registering in the middle. In panel C, the focus turns to opinion of the criminal justice system overall and its treatment of African Americans. Although only 28 percent of white respondents feel the system is biased against African Americans, 70 percent of African Americans point a finger at the criminal justice system

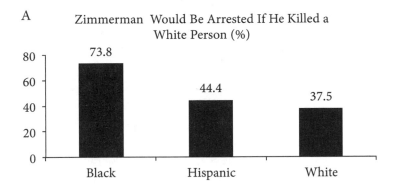

A   Zimmerman Would Be Arrested If He Killed a
White Person (%)

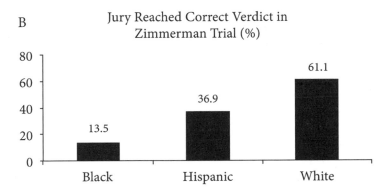

B   Jury Reached Correct Verdict in
Zimmerman Trial (%)

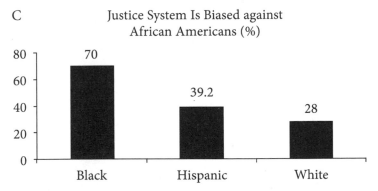

C   Justice System Is Biased against
African Americans (%)

Figure 10.1. Racial and ethnic breakdown of perception of injustice.

as being biased against their racial group. Once again, Hispanics registered in the middle, with 39.2 percent of them saying the system is biased against African Americans. Thus far, we have reported only associational analysis, which does not control for potentially confounding factors. To build greater rigor into our analyses and to construct a causal explanation of the gradient of public opinion among blacks, Hispanics, and whites, we estimate a series of logistic regression models consistent with the dichotomous dependent variables.

Table 10.2 reports two models estimated to test the racial gradient thesis directly. Model 1 features only the racial and ethnic group variables, with whites as the comparison category. This model explains 4 percent

TABLE 10.2. Testing Racial Gradient Thesis across Perceptions of Injustice in the Trayvon Martin Shooting

	Model 1		Model 2	
Variable	β (SE)	Odds ratio	β (SE)	Odds ratio
Black	1.54** (.10)	4.69	1.39** (.21)	4.05
Hispanic	.23** (.05)	1.26	.40* (.19)	1.49
Age			.03 (.06)	1.02
Children under 18			.12 (.13)	1.12
Church attendance			−.04 (.04)	.96
Educational level			.02 (.05)	1.02
Employed full-time			.08 (.13)	1.08
Employed part-time			.09 (.17)	1.09
Sex (male = 1)			−.56** (.11)	.57
Ideology			−.47** (.06)	.63
Income level			−.07 (.05)	.93
Married			.02 (.12)	1.02
South			−.14 (.11)	.87
Follow news of Trayvon shooting			.35** (.06)	1.42
Constant	−.51** (.07)		−.96** (.29)	.38
Sample n	2,910		2,783	
Pseudo-R^2	.04		.11	

Note: Entries are logistic regression estimates. Sample is restricted to blacks, Hispanics, and whites. Dependent variable for both models is whether Zimmerman would have been arrested if he had killed a white person.
* $p < .05$; ** $p < .01$ (all one-tailed tests)

of the variance and lends some credence to the racial gradient thesis. For African Americans compared to whites, the statistical odds are 4.69 times higher that Zimmerman would have been arrested if Trayvon Martin had been white, all else being equal. Using the divide-by-four rule,[67] we can convert the odds ratio into a probability score for a more straightforward interpretation of the effect.[68] Doing so, the probability is 38.5 percent higher that Zimmerman would have been arrested by Sanford police without delay had he killed a white seventeen-year-old male. For Hispanics compared to whites, the odds are 1.26 times higher that Zimmerman would have been arrested had Martin been white.

Model 2 includes the control variables and provides similarly strong support for the racial gradient thesis. Compared to whites, black respondents are significantly more likely to believe that Zimmerman would have been arrested had he killed a white person. The odds ratio is 4.05, representing a probability of 35 percent. The Hispanic variable is also statistically significant ($p < .05$), although the strength of the impact is not as high as that of blacks, lending additional support to our hypothesis. For Hispanics, the odds are 1.49 times higher that Zimmerman would have been arrested if Martin were white. The strong improvement in the explanatory power of the full model is noteworthy. The pseudo-R^2 values more than doubled in size, giving us greater confidence in the findings. Along with the race and ethnicity variables, three other independent variables also register statistically significant effects. For men, the odds are 43 percent lower that Zimmerman would have been arrested. Political conservatives are also less likely to think that Zimmerman would have been arrested if Martin were white, whereas political liberals are more inclined to think that Zimmerman would have been arrested had he shot a white person. Finally, individuals who closely follow the news of Martin's shooting are significantly more likely to report that Zimmerman would have been arrested if Martin were white.

In table 10.3, we turn our attention to the controversy surrounding Zimmerman's verdict. Here we report analysis for perceptions of the verdict as either correct or not and for perceptions of bias by the criminal justice system in its treatment of black people. Once again, we find strong and consistent support for the racial gradient thesis. Model 3 includes the race and ethnicity variables only. Using whites as the

TABLE 10.3. Testing the Racial Gradient Thesis across Perceptions of Injustice in the Zimmerman Trial

Variable	Model 3 (just verdict) β (SE)	Odds ratio	Model 4 (just verdict) β (SE)	Odds ratio	Model 5 (justice system biased against blacks) β (SE)	Odds ratio	Model 6 (justice system biased against blacks) β (SE)	Odds ratio
Black	−2.30** (.24)	.10	−2.18** (.27)	.11	1.89** (.19)	6.64	1.43** (.22)	4.17
Hispanic	−1.10** (.20)	.33	.80** (.24)	.45	.58** (.21)	1.79	.49* (.24)	1.64
Age			.15* (.07)	1.17			−.06 (.08)	.94
Children under 18			−.15 (.15)	.86			−.21 (.17)	.81
Church attendance			.04 (.04)	1.04			−.04 (.04)	.96
Educational level			.15* (.06)	1.16			.26** (.07)	1.30
Employed full-time			−.06 (.16)	.94			−.48** (.18)	.62
Employed part-time			.18 (.23)	1.19			−.11 (.23)	.89
Sex (male = 1)			.75** (.12)	2.11			.10 (.14)	1.10
Ideology			.62** (.07)	1.86			−.48** (.08)	.62
Income level			.27** (.06)	1.31			.02 (.06)	1.02
Married			.25 (.14)	1.28			−.50** (.15)	.61
South			.30* (.13)	1.35			−.03 (.15)	.97
Follow news of Trayvon shooting			−.08 (.07)	.93			.30** (.08)	1.35
Zimmerman verdict							−1.26** (.15)	.28
Constant			−1.55** (.33)	.21			−.96* (.40)	.38
Sample *n*	2,354		2,249		2,231		2,138	
Pseudo-*R²*	.09		.20		.08		.22	

Note: All entries are logistic regression estimates with robust standard errors. The dependent variable for models 3 and 4 is whether the jury reached the correct verdict in George Zimmerman's killing of Trayvon Martin (yes = 1; no = 0). Dependent variable in models 5 and 6 is whether the justice system is biased against blacks (yes = 1; no = 0). Samples are restricted to blacks, Hispanics, and whites.
* $p < .05$; ** $p < .01$ (all one-tailed tests)

comparison category, the model shows an explanatory capacity of 9 percent. Both the black and Hispanic variables are statistically significant and show negative coefficients as expected. Compared to whites, blacks and Hispanics are more inclined to think that the Zimmerman verdict was unjust. The odds are 90 percent lower that blacks think the verdict was justified compared to whites. For Hispanics, the odds are 67 percent lower compared to whites. A similar outcome is revealed in model 4, which includes all the control variables. The direction and effect size of the race and ethnicity variables remain consistent and robust. Congruent with the racial gradient thesis, the strength of the effect for blacks is significantly less than that of Hispanics, which is less than that of whites.

Of all the control variables in model 4, sex and ideology have the strongest effects on how Americans perceive the verdict. Men are more likely to view the verdict as correct compared to women. Political conservatives also believe strongly that the verdict is correct, with an odds ratio of 1.86. In addition, older Americans, those who are well educated, higher income earners, and southerners are all more likely to report that the Zimmerman's acquittal was justified. Notably, the explanatory capacity of this model doubles to 20 percent over the null.

The next set of analyses report the perceptions of blacks, Hispanics, and whites concerning whether the criminal justice system is biased toward African Americans. Once again, the analysis demonstrates strong support for the racial gradient thesis. Model 5 includes only race and ethnicity and explains 8 percent of the variance. The odds are 6.64 times higher that blacks view the criminal justice system as biased against black people compared to the odds that whites view the criminal justice system in this light. For Hispanics the variable is also statistically significant, but the effect is not as high as the effect for blacks. Overall, blacks have the most pessimistic view of the justice system. Specifically, blacks followed by Hispanics are most likely to perceive bias in the justice system. In model 6, we include all the control variables along with perceptions of the Zimmerman verdict. There is a 14 percent increase in the explanatory capacity of the model. As with previous models, blacks are significantly more likely to think that the justice system is biased against them. The effect of the coefficient is very strong and relatively resilient, with relative odds 4.17 times higher that blacks would perceive the justice system as biased compared to whites.

The coefficient for Hispanics is also statistically significant but somewhat smaller in value. Not surprisingly, individuals who think Zimmerman's verdict was correct are 72 percent less likely to report that the justice system is biased against blacks compared to those who think the verdict was incorrect. Along these lines, Americans working full-time, conservatives, and married individuals are also less likely to think that the justice system is biased against blacks. Individuals who are highly educated and those who closely followed the news of Martin's shooting are more likely to internalize a belief that the justice system is biased toward blacks.

Concluding Remarks

We set out to test the racial gradient thesis using the perceptions of Americans toward the Trayvon Martin killing by George Zimmerman, along with perceptions of the trial disposition and attitude toward the justice system. All of our hypotheses were confirmed, suggesting that intergroup conflict remains an important dimension of the American experiment. Blacks more than Hispanics, and Hispanics more than whites are significantly more likely to report that Zimmerman would have been arrested had he killed a white person, more likely to report that the criminal justice system is biased against blacks, and more likely to feel that the Zimmerman verdict was unjust.

Overall, our findings raise important questions about why Hispanic perceptions of injustice are continually sandwiched between black and white perceptions when examining evaluative assessments of salient criminological events. It is a complex issue, but we think that part of the answer takes us back to the comparative conflict perspective, specifically the idea of relative group position. In comparing blacks and Hispanics, there are certainly many social and economic similarities, but one important difference stands out that helps explain the trend we find. There is no question that blacks have endured a much longer and more fractious history with authorities in the United States than have Hispanics. In that sense, black people have a more crystallized sense of relative group position than do Hispanics in their perceptions of governmental actions and involuntary encounters with authorities. Therefore, when significant criminological events occur that further racialize crime, black people, unlike Hispanics who have been treated less badly, have that long history to tap into to inform their perceptions and reactions to injustice.

In order to promote legitimacy of the criminal justice system, American society cannot afford to write off the sentiments of blacks and Hispanics, the two largest groups of racial and ethnic minorities, if our democracy is to remain strong and stable. Around the world, public support for governmental activity is an essential ingredient for the survival and strength of democratic institutions, including the U.S. criminal justice system. For individuals working within these institutions, an abundance of diffuse public support is a powerful marker of institutional legitimacy and goodwill from which these governmental actors can draw "psychic income" and comfort for the decisions that they make. Former U.S. Supreme Court Justice Felix Frankfurter acknowledged the importance of public support for the courts when he stated in *Baker v. Carr* (1962) that the authority of the court system "ultimately rests on sustained public confidence in its moral sanctions."[69] We end on a cautionary note. Although the reservoir of goodwill that Americans possess toward the criminal justice system is substantial and resilient, it is not unlimited and can be seriously imperiled through repeated episodes of injustice by law enforcement, especially when these injustices are racialized.

NOTES

1. Edsall and Edsall 1990; Kinder and Sanders 1996; Schuman, Steeh, and Bobo 1985.

2. Gaertner and Dovidio 1986.

3. Gabbidon and Jordan 2013, 6.

4. Reverend Jesse Jackson, rephrasing a remark by Dr. Martin Luther King, Jr. in his "Letter from Birmingham Jail," that "injustice anywhere is a threat to justice everywhere." http://www.web.stanford.edu.

5. Weitzer and Tuch 2004; Hagan, Shedd, and Payne 2005; Gabbidon and Jordan 2013.

6. Easton 1965.

7. Key 1949; Blumer 1958; Blalock 1967; Chambliss and Seidman 1971.

8. Hagan and Albonetti 1982.

9. Blumer 1958; Key 1949; Blalock 1967.

10. Turk 1969.

11. Chambliss and Seidman 1971.
12. Bonacich 1980.
13. Hawkins 1987; Henderson et al. 1997; Hochschild 1995; Sigelman and Welch 1991.
14. Hagan, Shedd, and Payne 2005; Weitzer and Tuck 2004.
15. Cochran and Chamlin 2006.
16. Hagan, Shedd, and Payne 2005; Gabbidon and Jordan 2013.
17. Hagan, Shedd, and Payne 2005.
18. Tonry 1999.
19. Beckett, Nyrop, and Pfingst 2006.
20. Clear 2007; Unah and Coggins 2013.
21. Hagan and Albonetti 1982; Radelet and Pierce 1985; Unah 2011.
22. Giles and Evans 1986; Weitzer and Tuch 1999.
23. Bobo and Johnson 2004; see also King and Smith 2005.
24. Schneider and Ingram 1993.
25. Jackson and Carroll 1981.
26. Kent and Carmichael 2014; Kent and Jacobs 2005.
27. Jacobs and Carmichael 2001; Jacobs and Helms 1996; Yates and Fording 2005.
28. Unah and Coggins 2013.
29. Schuman, Steeh, and Bobo 1985.
30. Bobo and Kluegel 1997; Sigelman and Welch 1991.
31. Hagan, Shedd, and Payne 2005, 384.
32. Eberhardt et al. 2006; Terkildsen 1993; Portes and Rumbaut 2001.
33. Portes and Rumbaut 2001, 47.
34. Carter 1985.
35. Peffley and Hurwitz 2010.
36. Weitzer and Tuch 1999.
37. Lundman and Kaufman 2006; Weitzer and Tuch 2002.
38. Flanagan and Vaughn 1996.
39. Stewart et al. 2009; Weitzer and Tuch 2004; 2006.
40. Hagan, Shedd, and Payne 2005.
41. Sampson and Bartusch 1998; Anderson 1990; Wilson 1987.
42. Sampson and Bartusch 1998; Sampson and Lauritsen 1997.
43. Sampson and Bartusch 1998.
44. MacDonald et al. 2007.
45. Ibid.
46. Liska 1992.
47. Anderson 1990.
48. Ibid.
49. Buckler et al. 2011; Cole 1999.
50. Useem and Piehl 2008; Western 2006.
51. Buckler et al. 2011.

52. Yanich 2004.

53. Tyler 1990.

54. Tyler 1988; Tyler and Fagan 2008.

55. Warren and Farrell 2009.

56. The King beating lasted eighty-one seconds and included fifty-six blows (Riley 1992), and yet the officers were acquitted of using excessive force. The verdict led to three days of violent rioting, resulting in sixty deaths, more than sixteen hundred arrests, and almost a billion dollars in property damage (Hansen 1992).

57. Lasley 1994.

58. Kaminski and Jefferis 1998.

59. Easton 1965.

60. Kaminski and Jefferis 1998.

61. Easton 1965.

62. Goidel, Parent, and Mann 2011.

63. Gabbidon and Jordan 2013.

64. Dimock and Dohetry 2013.

65. There were 103 respondents (3 percent) who refused to answer the ideology question. Because the number is relatively small, we assigned these respondents to the moderate (neutral) category. Analyses both with and without this assignment were substantively equivalent.

66. Converse 1964.

67. Gelman and Hill 2007, 82.

68. The rule is simply to divide the logistic regression coefficient by four to derive a probability score. According to Gelman and Hill 2007, 82, the score nicely approximates the impact of the independent variable on the dependent variable, holding potential confounds constant.

69. See Justice Frankfurter's majority opinion in *Baker v. Carr* 1962.

REFERENCES

Anderson, Elijah. 1990. *Streetwise: Race, Class and Change in an Urban Community.* Chicago: University of Chicago Press.

Baker v. Carr, 369 U.S. 186 (1962).

Beckett, Katherine, Kris Nyrop, and Lori Pfingst. 2006. "Race, Drugs, and Policing: Understanding Disparities in Drug Delivery Arrests." *Criminology* 44 (1): 105–37.

Blalock, Hubert M. 1967. *Toward a Theory of Minority Group Relations.* New York: John Wiley.

Blumer, Herbert. 1958. "Race Prejudice as a Sense of Group Position." *Pacific Sociological Review* 1:3–7.

Bobo, Lawrence, and Devon Johnson. 2004. "A Taste for Punishment: Black and White Americans' Views on the Death Penalty and the War on Drugs." *Du Bois Review: Social Science Research on Race* 1:151–80.

Bobo, Lawrence, and James Kluegel. 1997. "Opposition to Race-Targeting: Self-Interest, Stratification Ideology, or Racial Attitudes?" *American Sociological Review* 58: 443–64.

Bobo, Lawrence, James Kluegel, and Ryan Smith. 1996. "Laissez-Faire Racism: The Crystallization of a 'Kindler, Gentler' Anti-Black Ideology." In *Racial Attitudes in the 1990s: Continuity and Change*, edited by Steven A. Tuch and Jack K. Martin, 23–25. Westport, CT: Praeger.

Bonacich, Edna. 1980. "Class Approaches to Race and Ethnicity." *Insurgent Sociologist* 10:9–23.

Borg, Miriam J. 1997. "The Southern Subculture of Punitiveness? Regional Variation in Support for Capital Punishment." *Journal of Research in Crime and Delinquency* 34:25–45.

Buckler, Kevin, Steve Wilson, Deborah Hartley, and Mario Davila. 2011. "Racial and Ethnic Perceptions of Injustice: Does Prior Personal and Vicarious Incarceration Experience Alter the Racial/Ethnic Gap in Perceptions of Injustice?" *Criminal Justice Review* 36:269–90.

Carter, David. 1985. "Hispanic Perceptions of Police Performance: An Empirical Assessment." *Journal of Criminal Justice* 13:487–500.

Chambliss, William, and Robert Seidman. 1971. *Law, Order and Power*. Reading, MA: Addison-Wesley.

Clear, Todd. 2007. *Imprisoning Communities: How Mass Incarceration Makes Disadvantaged Neighborhoods Worse*. New York: Oxford University Press.

Cochran, John, and Mittchell Chamlin. 2006. "The Enduring Racial Divide in Death Penalty Support." *Journal of Criminal Justice* 34:85–99.

Cole, David. 1999. *No Equal Justice: Race and Class in the American Criminal Justice System*. New York: New Press.

Collins, Sharon. 1997. *Black Corporate Executives: The Making and Breaking of a Black Middle Class*. Philadelphia, PA: Temple University Press.

Converse, Philip. 1964. "The Nature of Belief Systems in Mass Publics." *Critical Review: A Journal of Politics and Society* 18:1–74.

Dimock, Michael, and Carroll Dohetry. 2013. "Wider Race Gap in Interest Than for Rodney King, O. J. Simpson: Modest Public Interest in Close of Zimmerman Trial." Washington, DC: Pew Research Center.

Easton, David. 1965. *A Framework for Political Analysis*. Englewood Cliffs, NJ: Prentice Hall.

Eberhardt, Jennifer L., Paul G. Davis, Valerie J. Purdie-Vaughns, and Sheri Lynn Diamond. 2006. "Looking Deathworthy: Perceived Stereotypicality of Black Defendants Predicts Capital Sentencing Outcomes." *Psychological Science* 17:383–86.

Edsall, Thomas B., and Mary D. Edsall. 1990. *Chain Reaction: The Impact of Race, Rights, and Taxes on American Politics*. New York: Norton.

Flanagan, R. J., and M. S. Vaughn. 1996. "Public Opinion about Police Abuse of Force." In *Police Violence: Understanding and Controlling Police Abuse of Force*, edited by W. A. Geller and H. Toch, 113–28. New Haven, CT: Yale University Press.

Gabbidon, Shaun, and Kareem L. Jordan. 2013. "Public Opinion on the Killing of Trayvon Martin: A Test of the Racial Gradient Thesis." *Journal of Crime and Justice* 36:283–98.

Gaertner, Samuel L., and John F. Dovidio. 1986. "The Aversive Form of Racism." In *Prejudice, Discrimination, and Racism,* edited by Samuel L. Gaertner and John F. Dovidio, 61–89. Orlando, FL: Academic Press.

Gelman, Andrew, and Jennifer Hill. 2007. *Data Analysis Using Regression and Multi-level/Hierarchical Models.* New York: Cambridge University Press.

Giles, Michael, and Arthur Evans. 1986. "The Power Approach to Intergroup Hostility." *Journal of Conflict Resolution* 3:469–86.

Goidel, Kirby, Wayne Parent, and Bob Mann. 2011. "Race, Racial Resentment, Attentiveness to the News Media, and Public Opinion toward the Jena Six." *Social Science Quarterly* 92:20–34.

Grasmick, Harold G., John K. Cochran, Robert J. Bursik Jr., and M'Lou Kimpel. 1993. "Religion, Punitive Justice and Support for the Death Penalty." *Justice Quarterly* 32:251–66.

Hagan, John, and Celesta Albonetti. 1982. "Race, Class and the Perceptions of Criminal Injustice in America." *American Journal of Sociology* 88:329–55.

Hagan, John, Carla Shedd, and Monique R. Payne. 2005. "Race, Ethnicity and Youth Perceptions of Criminal Injustice." *American Sociology Review* 70:381–407.

Hansen, Mark. 1992. "Different Jury Different Verdict?" *American Bar Association Journal* 78:54.

Hawkins, Darnell. 1987. "Beyond Anomalies: Rethinking the Conflict Perspective on Race and Criminal Punishment." *Social Forces* 65:719–45.

Henderson Martha, Francis Cullen, Liqun Coa, Sandra L. Browning, and Renee Kopache. 1997. "The Impact of Race on Perception of Criminal Injustice." *Journal of Criminal Injustice* 25:447–62.

Hochschild, Jennifer. 1995. *Facing Up to the American Dream: Race Class and the Soul of the Nation.* Princeton: Princeton University Press.

Jackson, Pamela I., and Leo Carroll. 1981. "Race and the War on Crime: The Sociopolitical Determinants of Municipal Police Expenditures in 90 Non-southern U.S. Cities." *American Sociological Review* 46:290–305.

Jacobs, David, and Jason Carmichael. 2001. "The Politics of Punishment across Time and Space: A Pooled Time-Series Analysis of Imprisonment Rates." *Social Forces* 80:61–89.

Jacobs, David, and Ronald Helms. 1996. "Towards a Political Model of Incarceration." *American Journal of Sociology* 102:323–57.

Kaminski, Robert J., and Eric S. Jefferis. 1998. "The Effects of a Violent Televised Arrest on Public Perceptions of the Police: A Partial Test of Easton's Theoretical Framework." *Policing: An International Journal of Police Strategies and Management.* 21:683–706.

Kent, Stephanie, and Jason Carmichael. 2014. "Racial Residential Segregation and Social Control: A Panel Study of the Variation in Police Strength across U.S. Cities, 1980–2010." *American Journal of Criminal Justice* 39:228–49.

Kent, Stephanie, and David Jacobs. 2005. "Minority Threat and Police Strength from 1980 to 2000: A Fixed-Effects Analysis of Nonlinear and Interactive Effects in Large U.S. Cities." *Criminology* 43:731–60.

Key, V. O. 1949. *Southern Politics in State and Nation*. New York: Knopf.

Kinder, Donald R., and Lynn M. Sanders. 1996. *Divided by Color: Racial Politics and Democratic Ideals*. Chicago: University of Chicago Press.

King, Desmond, and Rogers Smith. 2005. "Racial Orders in American Political Development." *American Political Science Review* 99:75–92.

Lasley, James. 1994. "The Impact of the Rodney King Incident on Citizen Attitudes toward the Police." *Policing and Society: An International Journal* 3:245–55.

Lawrence, Bobo, and James R. Kluegel. 1997. "Status, Ideology and Dimensions of Whites' Racial Beliefs and Attitudes: Progress and Stagnation." In *Racial Attitudes in the 1990s: Continuity and Change*, edited by S. A. Tuch and J. K. Martin, 93–120. Greenwood, CT: Praeger.

Liska, Allen E. 1992. *Social Threat and Social Control*. Albany: State University of New York Press.

Liska, Allen E., Mitchell B. Chamlin, and Mark D. Reed. 1985. "Testing the Economic Production and Conflict Models of Crime Control." *Social Forces* 64:119–38.

Lundman, Richard, and Robert Kaufman. 2006. "Driving While Black: Effects of Race, Ethnicity, and Gender on Citizen Self-Reports of Traffic Stops and Police Actions." *Criminology* 41:195–220.

MacDonald, John, Robert Stokes, Greg Ridgeway, and Jack Riley. 2007. "Race, Neighbourhood Context and Perceptions of Injustice by the Police in Cincinnati." *Urban Studies* 44:2567–85.

Metress, Christopher. 2002. *The Lynching of Emmett Till: A Documentary Narrative*. Charlottesville: University of Virginia Press.

Peffley, Mark, and Jon Hurwitz. 2010. *Justice in America: The Separate Realities of Blacks and Whites*. New York: Cambridge University Press.

Portes, Alejandro, and Ruben Rumbaut. 2001. *Legacies: The Story of the Immigrant Second Generation*. Berkeley: University of California Press.

Radelet, Michael, and Glenn Pierce. 1985. "Race and Prosecutorial Discretion in Homicide Cases." *Law and Society Review* 19:587–622.

Riley, John. 1992. "Race, Defense Lapses Seen as Key to Verdict." *Newsday*, April 30, 4.

Sampson, Robert, and Dawn Bartusch. 1998. "Legal Cynicism and (Subcultural?) Tolerance of Deviance: The Neighborhood Context of Racial Differences." *Law and Society Review* 32:777–804.

Sampson, Robert, and Janet Lauritsen. 1997. "Racial and Ethnic Disparities in Crime and Criminal Justice in the United States." *Ethnicity, Crime, and Immigration* 21:311–74.

Schneider, Anne, and Helen Ingram. 1993. "Social Construction of Target Populations: Implications for Politics and Policy." *American Political Science Review* 87:334–47.

Schuman, Howard, Charlotte Steeh, and Lawrence Bobo. 1985. *Racial Attitudes in America: Trends and Interpretations.* Cambridge, MA: Harvard University Press.

Sigelman, Lee, and Susan Welch. 1991. *Black Americans' Views of Racial Inequality: The Dream Deferred.* New York: Cambridge University Press.

Stewart, Eric A., Eric P. Baumer, Rod K. Brunson, and Ronald L. Simons. 2009. "Neighborhood Racial Context and Perceptions of Police-Based Racial Discrimination among Black Youth." *Criminology* 47:847–87.

Terkildsen, Nayda. 1993. "When White Voters Evaluate Black Candidates: The Processing Implications of Candidate Skin Color, Prejudice, and Self-Monitoring." *American Journal of Political Science* 37:1032–53.

Tonry, Michael. 1999. "Why Are U.S. Incarceration Rates So High?" *Crime & Delinquency* 45:419–37.

Tuch, Steven, and Ronald Weitzer. 1997. "Trends: Racial Differences in Attitudes towards the Police." *Public Opinion Quarterly* 61:642–43.

Turk, Austin. 1969. *Criminality and Legal Order.* Chicago: Rand McNally.

Tyler, Tom. 1988. "What Is Procedural Justice? Criteria Used by Citizens to Assess the Fairness of Legal Procedures." *Law and Society Review* 22:103–35.

———. 1990. *Why People Obey the Law.* New Haven, CT: Yale University Press.

Tyler, Tom, and Jeffrey Fagan. 2008. "Why Do People Cooperate with the Police?" *Ohio State Journal of Criminal Law* 6:231–75.

Unah, Isaac. 2011. "Empirical Analysis of Race and the Process of Capital Punishment in North Carolina." *Michigan State Law Review* 2011:609–58.

Unah, Isaac, and K. Elizabeth Coggins. 2013. "When Governors Speak Up for Justice: Punishment Politics and Mass Incarceration in the United States." *Journal of Political Sciences & Public Affairs* 1:1–12.

Useem, Bert, and Anne Piehl. 2008. *Prison State: The Challenge of Mass Incarceration.* Cambridge: Cambridge University Press.

Warren, Patricia, and Amy Farrell. 2009. "The Environmental Context of Police Profiling." *Annals of the American Academy of Political and Social Sciences* 623:52–63.

Weitzer, Ronald. 2002. "Incidents of Police Misconduct and Public Opinion." *Journal of Criminal Justice* 30:397–408.

Weitzer, Ronald W., and Steven A. Tuch. 1999. "Race, Class and Perceptions Discrimination by the Police." *Crime & Delinquency* 45:494–507.

———. 2002. "Perceptions of Racial Profiling: Race, Class, and Personal Experience." *Criminology* 40:435–56.

———. 2004. "Race and Perceptions of Police Misconduct." *Social Problems* 51:305–25.

———. 2006. *Race and Policing in America: Conflict and Reform.* Cambridge: Cambridge University Press.

Welch, Kelly. 2009. "Parental Status and Punitiveness: Moderating Effects of Gender and Concern about Crime." *Crime & Delinquency* 57 (6): 878–906.

Western, Bruce. 2006. *Punishment and Inequality in America.* New York: Russell Sage Foundation.

Wilson, William J. 1987. *The Truly Disadvantaged: The Inner City, the Underclass, and Public Policy.* Chicago: University of Chicago Press.

Yanich, Danilo. 2004. "Crime Creep: Urban and Suburban Crime on Local TV News." *Journal of Urban Affairs* 26:535–63.

Yates, Jeff, and Richard Fording. 2005. "Politics and State Punitiveness in Black and White." *Journal of Politics* 67:1099–1121.

11

The Zimmerman Verdict

Media, Political Reaction, and Public Response in the Age of Social Networking

CHENELLE A. JONES AND MIA ORTIZ

Recognizing the importance of print and online news sources in the dissemination of information regarding the George Zimmerman verdict, this chapter presents a critical analysis of the impact of such news outlets in the age of social networking. We begin this analysis by discussing the role of print, televised, and online news sources in disseminating information about the verdict. We then examine the role of social media in sharing news and opinions on the verdict. Understanding the role of news 1sources and social media, we then explore their contributions to facilitating collective action. We conclude with a qualitative analysis of the political response to the verdict as well as a discussion on implications for the future.

In this effort, we lay out four questions to guide our analyses:

1. *How was the news of the verdict disseminated via various media outlets?* Online news and social media outlets were quick to broadcast the verdict. We seek to examine differences in the delivery and frequency of how news of the verdict was spread.

2. *How were the responses in the media expressed?* We seek to evaluate the similarities and differences between the responses within the different media outlets. We are also interested in assessing any patterns that exist within those responses.

3. *Did the responses (public, political, etc.) fall along racial and political fault lines?* The death of Trayvon Martin and subsequent criminal justice processing of George Zimmerman have elicited significant debate around the issues of race and racism in America. In

this chapter, we examine whether the reactions to the verdict still reflect a division of race and political affiliation.

4. *Was the use of social media (specifically sites such as Facebook and Twitter) successful in creating and sustaining capacity to launch collective action (e.g., demonstrations and marches) for social and legal change?* Social networking sites are an accessible and efficient form of communication to broadcast information to the public. We aim to evaluate not only how the reactions to the verdict yielded collective action, but also whether such networking sites were helpful in maintaining the public's interest in continuing such action.

In order to explore the aforementioned research questions, we examined 128 newspaper and online news articles written within the first forty-eight hours following the verdict through LexisNexis. We then narrowed our focus and conducted a content analysis on the fifteen largest mainstream online news sources, newspapers, and online news sites for predominate black audiences (see table 11.1). We specifically searched for (1) similarities and differences in how the verdict was reported and (2) themes emerging from responses to the verdict. We found responses to the verdict typically fell into one of the following themes: (1) sympathy, (2) advocacy and demands for justice, (3) what-if scenarios, and (4) rage. Responses adhering to the sympathy theme expressed feelings of pity and sorrow for the Martin's misfortune. Advocacy- and demands-for-justice-themed responses sought change and attempted to galvanize individuals for collective action. Responses that posed what-if scenarios provoked individuals to think how the verdict and responses to it would be different if Martin had not been African American. Responses following the rage theme sought to express anger and dissatisfaction with the verdict.

Print and Online News Reactions to the Verdict

The Zimmerman verdict was announced on the evening of July 13, 2013, and news of the verdict immediately spread through social media and print and online news outlets. Of the 4.9 million tweets posted on Twitter within the first twenty-six hours following the verdict, the Pew Research Center reported a vast majority (39 percent) disseminated news of the verdict without a definitive opinion.[1] Such rapid dissemination demonstrates the effectiveness of social media as a source for breaking news. Print and online news sources were also quick to disseminate news of the verdict.

In addition, polls assessed whether or not the general public agreed with the verdict (see table 11.1). Several polls demonstrated divisions along both racial and political lines.[2] In an NBC/*Wall Street Journal* collaborative poll, 48 percent of respondents said the trial had no effect on their confidence in the criminal justice system, 32 percent of respondents said it decreased their confidence, and 17 percent said it increased their confidence.[3] Among the respondents, 71 percent of African Americans and 48 percent of Democrats stated the trial diminished their confidence in the criminal justice system.[4] In a *Washington Post*/ABC poll, 86 percent of African Americans reported not receiving equal treatment in the criminal justice system.[5] Likewise, in a *Huffington Post* poll, an overwhelming majority (75 percent) of African American respondents indicated they would have found Zimmerman guilty of a crime, whereas only 34 percent of white respondents would have found him guilty.[6] The Pew Research Center assessed reactions to the verdict, and found that 86 percent of African Americans disagreed with it, in comparison to 49 percent of white Americans.[7] A CNN online poll found that 86 percent of African American respondents believed George Zimmerman should have been arrested immediately following the murder of Trayvon Martin.[8] A *USA Today* online poll found that 73 percent of African American respondents believed George Zimmerman would have been arrested immediately if Trayvon Martin had been white, in comparison to only 34 percent of white Americans.[9]

Although racial differences were expressed in opinion polls, many op-ed news articles addressed the racialized context of the verdict and embraced one of the following themes: sympathy, advocacy and demands for justice, what-if scenarios, and rage. Opposite editorial (op-ed) articles encompassing the sympathy theme identified with Trayvon Martin, expressed condolences to the Martin family, and/ or informed parents the situation could have happen to their child. MSNBC's article "I Could've Been Trayvon Martin" addressed the ways pervasive stereotypes influence African Americans and how they interact with other racial groups.[10] HLN's article "Parents: This Is about

Other Trayvon Martins" humanized Trayvon Martin by describing an incident where he saved his father from a grease fire. The article simultaneously attempted to contest the media's attack on his character (an indication of the traditional vilification of African American males in the media) and explain how the verdict had broader implications for the African American community.[11]

Other op-ed articles advocated change, demanded justice, and/or noted disparities within the criminal justice system. NBC News discussed the reactions of various Martin supporters in the article "It's Injustice: Martin Supporters React to Verdict" and indicated that the verdict represented a miscarriage of justice.[12] ABC News examined reactions to the verdict in the op-ed article "Vast Racial Gap on Trayvon Martin Case Marks a Challenging Conversation" and highlighted the existence of different racial perceptions of the criminal justice system.[13] CBS published an op-ed article highlighting racially different perceptions of the verdict and the criminal justice system. The *Huffington Post* published an op-ed article titled "No Justice in Trayvon Martin Killing Case," which addressed disparities in the criminal justice system and noted how privileged individuals often receive preferential treatment.[14] The article also used the verdict as a platform to urge people to advocate change. The *Washington Post* published two op-ed articles, "Young, Black, and Speaking Out after the Trayvon Martin Case"[15] and "Trayvon Martin and the Stolen Youth of Black Children," which decried racial disparities in the criminal justice system.[16]

Some op-ed articles posed what-if questions and challenged their readers to view the situation from a different perspective. CNN's op-ed article "What If Trayvon Martin and George Zimmerman Were White?" challenged readers to question whether or not the Sanford police department would still grant credibility to Zimmerman's version of the events if the offender and victim were both white. It also questioned whether the primarily white, all-female jury would have expressed empathy toward a man who stalked and murdered an unarmed white child.[17] Another op-ed article by CNN, "What about Martin's Right to 'Stand His Ground'?," criticized the media's tabloid-like focus on Trayvon Martin's background. It also questioned the generally accepted framing of the event, which was George Zimmerman acting in self-defense.[18] The author questioned why society placed so much emphasis on George

Zimmerman's fear of Martin and not Martin's fear of Zimmerman. After all, Martin had great reason to fear Zimmerman for both histori- cal reasons and the simple fact that Zimmerman stalked him and failed to identify himself as a neighborhood watchman.[19]

Numerous op-ed articles expressed rage or acknowledged the exis- tence of widespread rage. *USA Today* published two of such articles, "'System Has Failed': Crowds React to Zimmerman Verdict" and "After Zimmerman Verdict, Can Nation Heal Racial Rift?" One article expressed rage over the differential treatment experienced by African Americans in the criminal justice system.[20] The other article exam- ined whether or not the general public can heal from the racial divide witnessed after the verdict.[21] The *New York Times* published an op-ed article titled "The Whole System Failed Trayvon Martin," highlighting structural glitches within the criminal justice system that disadvantage African American males.[22]

In addition to mainstream online new sources, online news sources aimed at predominately African American audiences published op-ed articles promoting the idea that the Zimmerman verdict reflects insti- tutionalized discrimination against African American males. *Grio's* article "Trayvon Martin, Emmett Till and the Shadow of Jim Crow Justice" compared the situation involving Trayvon Martin and George Zimmerman to the situation involving Emmett Till, a teenager who was murdered for allegedly whistling at a white woman.[23] *Grio* identified similarities between Martin and Till because both were brutally mur- dered and their known offenders were acquitted of all charges. Each case demonstrates the devaluation of black life in the criminal justice system. *Root's* article "Trayvon, Race and American Democracy" dis- cussed the need for an open dialogue about race and its impact on American democracy.[24] Last, an article published by *Your Black World*, "The Gift of Trayvon Martin—His Sacrifice Has Awakened a Nation" noted the injustices of the criminal justice system and suggested that the verdict may actually benefit the nation by bringing awareness to institu- tionalized discrimination within the criminal justice system and serve as a means to incite change.[25]

In contrast to the aforementioned op-ed articles, Fox News pub- lished two online articles, "Double Standards and Zimmerman Verdict" and "We Never Should Have Witnessed a Zimmerman Trial," which

TABLE 11.1. Media Headlines Following the Zimmerman Verdict

Source	Poll	Op-ed headline
CNN	Yes	What If Trayvon Martin and George Zimmerman Were White?
		What about Martin's Right to "Stand His Ground"?
Fox News	Yes	Double Standards and Zimmerman Verdict
		We Never Should Have Witnessed a Zimmerman Trial
MSNBC	Yes	I Could Have Been Trayvon Martin
ABC News	Yes	Vast Racial Gap on Trayvon Martin Case Marks a Challenging Conversation
CBS News	Yes	Opinions of Zimmerman Verdict Break along Racial Lines
NBC News	Yes	"It's Injustice": Martin Supporters React to Verdict
HLN	Yes	Parents: "This Is about Other Trayvon Martins"
Huffington Post	Yes	No Justice in Trayvon Martin Killing Case
Wall Street Journal	Yes	The Zimmerman Verdict: New Federal Civil-Rights Charges Would Smack of Double Jeopardy
New York Times	No	The Whole System Failed Trayvon Martin
USA Today	Yes	"System Has Failed": Crowds React to Zimmerman Verdict
		After Zimmerman Verdict, Can Nation Heal Racial Rift?
Washington Post	Yes	Young, Black, and Speaking Out after the Trayvon Martin Case
		Trayvon Martin and the Stolen Youth of Black Children
Grio	No	Trayvon Martin, Emmett Till and the Shadow of Jim Crow Justice
Root	No	Trayvon, Race and American Democracy
Your Black World	No	The Gift of Trayvon Martin—His Sacrifice Has Awakened a Nation

expressed agreement with the verdict. The first article suggested that although the event was tragic, race and tragedy were not on trial and that, based on the evidence presented, the acquittal of Zimmerman was appropriate.[26] The other article questioned whether it was even appropriate to bring charges against Zimmerman since he claimed self-defense.[27]

With the exception of Fox News, op-ed articles following the verdict presented a collective challenge to the notion of equal justice. The themes of sympathy, advocacy and demands for justice, what-if scenarios, and rage all speak to the broader issue of the differential treatment of African Americans within the criminal justice system. Existing research has found differential treatment (i.e., bias and racial profiling), as demonstrated in the case of Trayvon Martin, to contribute to negative perceptions of the criminal justice system.[28] African Americans tend to hold more negative perceptions of the criminal justice system in comparison to other racial groups.[29] Other research has focused on the role of the media in shaping the public's perceptions of the criminal justice system.[30] Tsfati found that consumers who drive the media tend to be attracted to sensationalized stories that elicit emotions.[31] Incidents such as the tragic murders of both Sean Bell and Oscar Grant and video footage capturing the brutal beatings of both Rodney King and Chad Holley are just a few examples of how print and online news stories can elicit emotions and reinforce negative perceptions the criminal justice system. The more recent incident involving Trayvon Martin and George Zimmerman rekindled questions and concerns regarding the equitable treatment of African Americans in the criminal justice system and even prompted a strong political response.

Political Response to the Trayvon Martin Verdict

Media sources not only documented the sentiments of the American populous at large, but also reflected the reactions from members of government. Perhaps, none were as profound (or as historic) as President Obama in his remarks regarding the verdict on July 19, 2013.

Throughout his presidency, President Obama has largely maintained a neutral stance on the issues of race in society. There have been, however, several noted exceptions that have resulted in missteps.[32] In 2009, he held the "beer summit" between Harvard Professor Henry Louis Gates and arresting police officer James Crowley in what could be characterized as a clumsy effort to mediate and quell lingering racial tension. In 2010, the Obama administration was embroiled in controversy as Department of Agriculture director Shirley Sherrod was erroneously forced to resign as a result of an excerpted segment that was posted on a conservative blog that presented Sherrod as being discriminatory against a white farmer. Moreover, there has been growing scrutiny over Obama's reticence in properly addressing the epidemic of gun violence (where African American men are both perpetrator and victim) in his home city of Chicago.[33]

But President Obama's remarks on July 19 were significant in that they marked one of the few occasions when he not only directly discussed the plight of African American men in the United States, but also acknowledged that in a given time and space (prior to his notoriety) he himself may have suffered the same fate as Trayvon Martin. It is further remarkable that no other president has spoken so candidly and personally about a racialized moment in history when he had firsthand understanding of the experience. In many respects, his remarks provide legitimacy to experiences that have historically shaped African American communities for centuries.[34]

Within his speech, Obama shared with the world that the African American community still experiences differential treatment within the criminal justice system. Moreover, he spoke about lived experiences and how the worldview of African Americans continues to be sullied by a painful and bitter American history. In the same vein, President Obama connected the historical role of the past with the societal assumptions that all young black men are dangerous.

In regard to the Zimmerman acquittal, Obama was reticent to discuss or challenge the merits of the outcome; rather he showed reverence to the execution of the legal process: The judge conducted the trial in a professional manner. The prosecution and the defense made their arguments. The juries were properly instructed that in a case such as this reasonable doubt was relevant, and they rendered a verdict. And once the jury has spoken, the decision is final; that's how our system works.[35]

Though he stated that the Department of Justice was reviewing the merits of charging George Zimmerman on the federal level with possible civil rights violations in the death of Trayvon Martin, the president recognized that states, in general, yield the greatest autonomy. Instead President Obama focused his remarks on challenging local communities to work to address the issues of mistrust of law enforcement and others within the justice system and to further challenge the realities of gun violence in our communities.

The reactions to President Obama's remarks were both vast and polarizing largely along political as well as racial lines (although not exclusively) and discussed extensively throughout television and social media. Many of the reactions fell into three distinct camps: those who felt that his remarks were timely, relevant, and appropriately addressed a nation; those who felt that the president's remarks did not go far enough to address the issues of racial injustice and the realities of violent crime; and those who felt that the president should have said nothing as the Zimmerman case was not about race.

Those in consensus with the president's remarks regarding the Zimmerman acquittal felt that this was a watershed moment for this administration, given that the president in the past had been equivocal in his comments regarding race and racial injustices. Supporters such as Reverend Al Sharpton, president of the National Action Network, referred to the president's remarks as a "historic" moment in time as a sitting black president was able to be candid about his thoughts related to race and crime.[36] Former NAACP president Benjamin Jealous referred to the remarks as "a powerful moment."[37] Perhaps the most surprising supporter of the remarks was George Zimmerman's brother, Robert, who stated in an interview that he hoped the president's remarks would serve as a "teachable moment."[38]

In general, critics of the president's comments after the acquittal argued that his comments were divisive and had the potential to fuel civil unrest within the African American community. Conservative commentator Todd Starnes, in a series of Twitter postings, commented that his remarks were "race baiting" in nature, "unprofessional," and an attempt to "tear apart the country."[39] Iowa congressman Steve King charged President Obama with exploiting this matter "as a political issue that should have been handled exclusively with law and order."[40] Other conservative news commentators such as Sean Hannity also weighed in on the president's comments by suggesting that Obama identified with Trayvon Martin because he had indulged in illicit drugs when he was younger.[41]

In addition to the widespread and expected outcry from conservative politicians and cable news hosts, some in the liberal community also voiced dissatisfaction with the tenor of President Obama's remarks on the verdict. Many in this camp not only were underwhelmed by the statements, but also largely felt that the president had mostly ignored the African American community in terms of addressing its most pressing issues: racial injustice and gun violence within the inner city. Two of Obama's most prominent liberal critics, Cornel West and talk show host Tavis Smiley, consistently called on the president to address the social condition of the disenfranchised more aggressively. West was very direct with the president, stating that Obabma was on "limited moral authority" and that he was in essence a "global George Zimmerman," who had done little to employ social justice in matters before and after the death of Trayvon Martin.[42] Similarly, Smiley called the president's comments about the acquittal "as weak as presweetened Kool-Aid."[43] And yet another columnist, Keli Goff of *Root*, said that the president's comments were in fact "offensive," as he failed to declare that race was a central component of Trayvon Martin's death.[44]

Social Media Reaction to the Verdict

For the majority of Americans, political, print, and online news platforms were not readily available for expressing their opinions on the verdict. However, many took to social media (e.g., Twitter) to express their reactions, with 31 percent of tweets opposing the verdict and 7 percent supporting it. Tweets opposing the verdict outnumbered those supporting it four to one. Themes emerging from tweets addressing the verdict mirrored those found in op-ed articles. In addition, many tweets were followed by the hashtags #Justice4Trayvon, #RIPTrayvon, #Hoodies, #IamTrayvon, #JusticeForTrayvonMartin, #MillionHoodies, #StandYourGround, #WeWantJustice, and #Skittles, to name a few.

Similar to op-ed articles, several tweets offered sympathy and prayers. Trayvon Martin's father Tracy Martin tweeted "Even though I am broken hearted my faith is unshattered, I WILL ALWAYS LOVE MY BABY TRAY." His mother Sabrina Fulton tweeted, "Lord during my darkest hour I lean on you. You are all that I have. At the end of the day, GOD is still in control." Russell Simmons, who cofounded Def Jam Records, said, "Prayers for the Martin family. Only God knows what was on Zimmerman mind but the gun laws and stand your ground laws must change." Former U.S. representative Anthony Weiner tweeted, "Keep Trayvon's family in our prayers. Deeply unsatisfying verdict. Trial by jury is our only choice in a democracy." Chairman and CEO of Black Entertainment Television (BET) Debra Lee tweeted, "My heart is broken. Prayers go out to the family of #TrayvonMartin." Some prayers were even followed by the hashtags #PrayersForTrayvon and #PrayersForMartinFamily. Tweets that offered sympathy included those of American filmmaker and actress Lena Dunham, who said, "No. My heart is with Sybrina Fulton, Rachel Jeantel, everyone who loved Trayvon and has been sent the message that his life didn't matter." Actress Sophia Bush tweeted, "The wind is more than knocked out of me. . . . My heart aches for this boy's family. Justice System? I don't think so. #justicefortrayvon." Actress and television cohost Whoopi Goldberg tweeted, "My heart is with Trayvon Martin's family tonight, so my focus on them. No one else really matters."

Other tweets following the verdict called for advocacy and justice. The NAACP started a petition to bring additional charges against George Zimmerman by tweeting, "We can still seek justice for #TrayvonMartin. Sign the #NAACP petition to the Department of Justice." The mayor of New York City Bill DeBlasio tweeted, "Trayvon Martin's death was a terrible tragedy. This decision is a slap in the face to justice. #nojusticefortrayvon." New York City comptroller John C. Liu tweeted, "Our justice system is far from perfect. #Trayvon must not be in vain. May #NoJusticeForTrayvon stir actions toward peace #EndRacialProfiling." Actor Larenz Tate tweeted, "The justice system has FAILED #Trayvon Martin, his parents, his loved ones, and us—the people. #ConfirmationOfaFailedSystem #ZimmermanTrial." Actress Octavia Spencer called for justice by tweeting, "Stop saying the system needs 2 change and JUST CHANGE IT, ppl. YOUR vote matters. Midterm elections! Show up for TrayvonMartin & OscarGrant." Russell Simmons tweeted, "This is not 'only' about race. This is about laws that allow racist acts to go unpunished. We must change laws that promote injustice."

Many tweets expressed outrage. Filmmaker and author Michael Moore tweeted, "Had a gun-toting Trayvon Martin stalked an unarmed George Zimmerman, and then shot him to death . . . DO I EVEN NEED TO COMPLETE THIS SENTENCE?" Journalist and scholar Dr. Marc Lamont Hill expressed his dissatisfaction with the verdict by saying, "Although I predicted and expected this verdict, I find no pleasure in hearing it." Former speaker of the New York City Council Christine Quinn's tweet, "Today's acquittal in the Trayvon Martin case is a shocking insult to his family and everyone seeking justice for Trayvon," suggests people should be offended by the outcome of the trial. NFL players Roddy White and Victor Cruz were more controversial in their expression of outrage by tweeting, "Fucking Zimmerman got away with murder today wow what kind of world do we live in," "All them jurors should go home tonight and kill themselves for letting a grown man get away with killing a kid," and "Thoroughly confused. Zimmerman doesn't last a year before the hood catches up to him."

In addition to the aforementioned themes, several tweets following the verdict expressed relief. George Zimmerman's brother Robert tweeted, "Message from Dad: 'Our whole family is relieved.' Today . . . I'm proud to be an American. God Bless America! Thank you for your prayers!" Kurt Schlicheter tweeted, "Thank God. #Zimmerman free. Now, I think we can all take a moment for the Martin family and keep them in our prayers as well." American conservative and political commentator Ann Coulter simply tweeted "Hallelujah!"

Social media, especially Twitter, proved instrumental for disseminating news of the verdict. Twitter was particularly important for offering a platform for the general public to express their feelings on the verdict. Several tweeters expressed disdain for the verdict and blacked out their profile as a means of showing solidarity and protest for the verdict.[45] Unlike high-profile cases (e.g., the O. J. Simpson trial) that were tried before the development of social media, contemporary high-profile cases have the luxury of social media to galvanize people to show support for victims and protest controversial verdicts. For example, many were open in their support for the Martin family, but George Zimmerman also received a lot of support. His website alone raised nearly eighty thousand dollars for his defense fund.

The Use of Social Media to Galvanize Collective Action

Social media sites such as Twitter and Facebook have been vital tools for communication for nearly two decades, especially with their ability to diffuse information at rapid speed, coupled with their applications on mobile devices through which consumers are constantly alerted to new updates and comments from others. Such sites have been well utilized by an assortment of groups ranging from fringe communities to mainstream organizations.

Scholars who study social movements suggest that collective action is largely attributed to individuals framing their personal experiences to the macro level.[46] In many respects, the Zimmerman acquittal represented the "tipping point" to the conceptualization and framing of past grievances (or injustices) that have affected their communities.[47] In addition, the protests represented an expressive moment of anger over the realization that a young African American man's life is still devalued despite the best efforts of the civil rights movement of the twentieth century. The "I am Trayvon" identity, which has been a hashtag on Twitter and Facebook and to which President Obama alluded in his July 2013 remarks, emerged as an opportunity to put a face to a group experience and garner support for collective action.

Through the use of Twitter, Facebook, and organizations such as the Trayvon Martin Organizing Committee, information about the rallies was spread virally to the masses. The protests had three important goals: (1) to challenge the legitimacy of the verdict, (2) to repeal Stand Your Ground laws, and (3) to encourage the Department of Justice to charge Zimmerman with civil rights violations in the wrongful death of Martin.

Protests following the Zimmerman verdict occurred in many forms. Some blacked out their social media profile pictures, others started petitions to bring federal charges against George Zimmerman, youth organizations such as the Dream Defenders launched sit-ins in Florida's capitol, and advocacy groups such as the National Action Network (NAN) launched a series of rallies. Although most protests could be described as collective action because they sought to raise awareness and effectively change Stand Your Ground laws and the ways in which African Americans are treated within the administration of justice, many took the form of normative action as demonstrated by the NAN rallies and the change.org petition calling for the federal prosecution of George Zimmerman.

Marches and Rallies

In addition to its utility in fostering public discourse in response to the Zimmerman acquittal in the virtual realm, social media have been critical to the organizing of street rallies, marches, and other physical methods of protests throughout the country. The use of social media (specifically Facebook, Twitter, as well as the blogosphere) has been integral to the immediate diffusion of emotional expression and information postverdict. In real time, these platforms allowed the world to connect with one another in this shared experience through the "creating, tagging, and sharing content . . . which may facilitate becoming more informed, engaged citizens."[48]

Al Sharpton was the principal architect of a hundred-city rally on Saturday, July 20. Individuals met at the federal courts to demand the federal government charge George Zimmerman with civil rights violations in the death of Martin. Sharpton along with Martin's mother, Sabrina Fulton, and celebrities Jay Z and Beyoncé, rallied with thousands in front of NYPD's One Police Plaza in protesting the verdict. In Miami, Martin's father, Tracy Martin, was the keynote speaker at the steps of the federal courthouse.

Throughout the country, the emergence of collective action was vast and immediate. New Yorkers marched into Times Square in response to the verdict. In Los Angeles, a major interstate was occupied by protestors for nearly an hour.[49] In New York's Time Square and Union Square people rallied against injustices.[50] In Atlanta nearly eight hundred motorcyclists rallied to protest injustices.[51] At a Chicago rally Auricka Gordon Taylor drew the connection between the deaths of her cousin Emmett Till and Trayvon Martin: " 'We've gone from approved killings in Mississippi in 1955 to approved killings in Florida in 2013,' said Taylor. '[Till's] murder illuminated what was being done to blacks in 1955. Now with Trayvon Martin, it's also another illumination. It's demonstrating to our young people that your rights are being stripped away. It's open season on black children.' "[52] The most violent of demonstrations occurred in downtown Oakland as protestors threw bottles at police, attacked news reporters and drivers, broke windows, and committed other acts of vandalism, flag burning, and obstruction of traffic.[53] For Oakland, this set of demonstrations compounded an already volatile situation given the city's history of police misconduct and high homicide rates among African American men. In South Central Los Angeles, thirteen people were arrested due to unlawful assembly. However, given the extensive reach of the protests across the country, most cities experienced calm protests with relatively few arrests.

The role of social media in the organization and facilitation of demonstrations following the verdict signified a new era in collective action and represented a shift in protests as compared to demonstrations of the past, namely during the civil rights era. Although social media played a significant role in galvanizing people to protest, it proved ineffective in sustaining the movement. Little change has resulted from the rallies and protests immediately following the verdict. Federal charges were not brought against George Zimmerman, and the controversial Stand Your Ground laws in Florida remain in place. In fact, the Florida House of Representatives recently passed the Threatened Use of Force bill (CS/HB89), which expands Stand Your Ground provisions. Although birthed from the case involving Marissa Alexander, who received nearly twenty years in prison after firing warning shots, the proposed legislation expands the circumstances under which an individual can brandish a gun and/or fire a warning shot to protect himself or herself from danger.

The protests and demonstrations following the verdict in the Zimmerman trial did not produce the legislative and legal changes that followed other social movements (e.g., the Civil Rights Act of 1964). The inability of contemporary protests to facilitate change following the verdict can be attributed to several factors including lack of a strategic plan, strong opposition, economic limitations, and lack of commitment from the general population. Whereas during the civil rights movement protests were strategically organized, economically supported, and sustained by the commitment of several individuals, protests following the Zimmerman verdict missed several of these elements and as such were unsuccessful in facilitating substantive change.

Despite the protests' failure to produce substantial changes across the country, there remains significant promise in the use of social media and its ability to bring communities together in times of struggle. Beyond their ability to galvanize, websites such as Facebook and Twitter create the opportunity for people to express their rage, disappointment, and uncertainty regarding societal developments in anonyomous and quasi-anonymous ways. What is achieved here is the opportunity for catharsis: to be able to express emotions without resorting to violence and destruction. Moreover, these sites, at the very least, provide the opportunity for communities to connect and to be informed of future activities.

Conclusion

In this chapter, we discussed the role the media have played after the verdict in the George Zimmerman murder trial. In revisiting the guiding questions that were stated earlier in this chapter, we found that the reactions to the verdict were widely disseminated across print, online, and social media outlets. Reactions to the verdict were polarized between emotions of anger and relief but were also sharply divided by race: whites generally favored the verdict, blacks found it to be an injustice and violation of Martin's civil rights. Moreover and unsurprisingly, political reactions (i.e., conservative and liberal) to the outcome of this trial were also sharply divided.

Furthermore, the extensive influence of social media websites following the verdict cannot be underestimated. This chapter discussed social media's tremendous power as not only a source of breaking news and information, but also a cathartic way to express a wide range of emotions in the virtual world. Social media allowed the average and the infamous to lay claim to an identity of a slain youth though the adoption of the hashtag #IamTrayvon. The power of social media in spurring communities to come together in solidarity following the verdict, as demonstrated through hoodie photos, blacked-out profiles, and rallies, is profound. While the collective behaviors of protest and marching did not lead to legislative changes to Stand your Ground, social media sites should not be undervalued in creating a safe online space for everyone to express rage and other emotions without consequences. Perhaps it is through such sites that more strategic conversations regarding social change may continue and ultimately lead to effective social change.

NOTES

1. Pew Research Center 2013a.
2. Conner 2013.
3. Ibid.
4. Ibid.
5. Cohen and Bals 2013.
6. Swanson 2013.
7. Pew Research Center 2013b.

8. CNN Political Unit 2013.

9. Alcindor 2013.

10. Nicholas 2013.

11. Loiaconi 2013.

12. NBC News 2013.

13. Langer 2013.

14. Strickland 2013.

15. Brown 2013.

16. Capehart 2013.

17. Vivian 2013.

18. Francis 2013.

19. Ibid.

20. Neale 2013.

21. Alcindor 2013.

22. Blow 2013.

23. Kelley 2013.

24. Joseph 2013.

25. Watkins 2013.

26. Thomas 2013.

27. Lott 2013.

28. Cochran and Warren 2012; Rocque 2011; Sherman 2010; Weitzer and Tuch 2004.

29. Rocque 2011; Weitzer and Tuch 2004.

30. Mason 2007; Tsoudis 2000.

31. Tsfati 2003.

32. Tumulty 2010.

33. Jeffries 2013.

34. Obama 2013.

35. Ibid.

36. Edwards 2013.

37. Jealous 2013.

38. Knickerbocker 2013.

39. Ibid.

40. Fox News 2013.

41. Knickerbocker 2013.

42. Goodman 2013.

43. Eldridge 2013.

44. Goff 2013.

45. Clayton 2013.

46. Benford and David 2000.

47. Ibid.

48. Gleason 2013.

49. Luscombe and Siddique 2013.
50. Robinson 2013.
51. *Atlanta-Journal Constitution* 2013.
52. Knowles 2013.
53. Schwartz 2013; Alston, Quintana, and Klapper 2013.

REFERENCES

Alcindor, Y. 2013. "Poll Shows Racial Divide on Views of Trayvon Martin Case." *USA Today.* http://usatoday30.usatoday.com/news/nation/story/2012-04-05/trayvon -martin-poll/54047512/1.

Alcindor, Y., and L. Copeland. 2013. "After Zimmerman Verdict, Can Nation Heal Racial Rift?" *USA Today.* http://www.usatoday.com/story/news/nation/2013/07/14/ nation-moves-forward-after-zimmerman-trial/2516189/.

Alston, J., Sergio Quintana, and Kira Klapper. 2013. "Oakland Rally for Trayvon Martin Turns Violent." KGO-TV, July 14. http://abclocal.go.com/kgo/story?id=9172087. Accessed February 19, 2013.

Associated Press. 2013. "Jurors Find George Zimmerman Not Guilty of 2nd-Degree Murder; Judge Releases Zimmerman." Fox News. http://www.foxnews.com/ us/2013/07/13/jurors-find-george-zimmerman-not-guilty-2nd-degree-murder -judge-releases/.

Atlanta-Journal Constitution. 2013. "Protesters Rev Motorcycles for Trayvon Martin." http://www.myajc.com/photo/news/protesters-rev-motorcycles-trayvon-martin/ pwfHD/. Accessed February 19, 2014.

Barlow, M. H. 1998. "Race and the Problem of Crime in Time and Newsweek Cover Stories, 1946 to 1995." *Social Justice* 25 (2): 149–83.

Benford, R. D., and A. S. David. 2000. "Framing Processes and Social Movements: An Overview and Assessment." *Annual Review of Sociology* 26:611–39.

Blow, C. 2013. "The Whole System Failed Trayvon Martin." *New York Times.* http:// www.nytimes.com/2013/07/16/opinion/the-whole-system-failed.html?_r=0.

Botelho, G., and H. Yan. 2013. "George Zimmerman Found Not Guilty of Murder in Trayvon Martin's Death." CNN. http://www.cnn.com/2013/07/13/justice/ zimmerman-trial/.

Brown, D. 2013. "Young, Black, and Unsettled after the Trayvon Martin Case." *Washington Post.* http://www.washingtonpost.com/local/young-black-and-unsettled-after -the-trayvon-martin-case/2013/09/07/b7f9cdd6-0434-11e3-a07f-49ddc7417125_ story.html.

Callanan, V. J. 2012. "The Effects of Crime-Related Media on Public Perception and Fear of Crime: Examining Race/Ethnic Differences." *Sociological Perspectives* 55 (1): 93–115.

Capehart, J. 2013. "Trayvon Martin and the Stolen Youth of Black Children." *Washington Post.* http://www.washingtonpost.com/blogs/post-partisan/wp/2013/07/15/ trayvon-martin-and-the-stolen-youth-of-black-children/.

Clayton, T. 2013. "Social Media 'Blacks Out' for Trayvon." *Root.* http://www.theroot. com/blogs/the_grapevine/2013/07/blackout_for_trayvon_social_media_supports_ trayvon_martins_family.html.

CNN Political Unit. 2013. "CNN Poll: Majority Call for Arrest in Trayvon Martin Shooting." *CNN.* http://www.cnn.com/2012/03/26/justice/florida-teen-shooting -poll/.

Cochran, J. C., and P. Y. Warren. 2012. "Racial, Ethnic, and Gender Differences in Perceptions of Police: The Salience of Officer Race Within the Context of Racial Profiling." *Journal of Contemporary Criminal Justice* 28 (2): 206–27.

Cohen, J., and D. Bals. 2013. "Zimmerman Verdict Poll: Stark Reaction by Race." *Washington Post.* http://www.washingtonpost.com/politics/race-shapes-zimmerman -verdict-reaction/2013/07/22/3569662c-f2fc-11e2-8505-bf6f231e77b4_story.html.

Coltrane, S., and M. Messino. 2000. "The Perpetuation of Subtle Prejudice: Race and Gender Imagery in 1990s Television Advertising." *Sex Roles* 42 (5/6): 363–89.

Conner, T. 2013. "America's Race Relations Take Hit after Zimmerman Verdict, NBC News/WSJ Poll Finds." *NBC.* http://www.nbcnews.com/politics/first-read/ americas-race-relations-take-hit-after-zimmerman-verdict-nbc-news-v19644475.

Davis, J., and O. Gandy. 1999. "Racial Identity and Media Orientation: Exploring the Nature of Constraint." *Journal of Black Studies* 29 (3): 367–97.

Desmond-Harris, J. 2013. "Zimmerman Walks: Black Life Not Valued." *Root.* http:// www.theroot.com/articles/culture/2013/07/zimmerman_verdict_reactions_black_ life_not_valued.html.

Edwards, B. 2013. "Al Sharpton: Historic Statement." Politico.com. http://www.politico .com/story/2013/07/al-sharpton-historic-statement-obama-trayvon-martin-94492 .html.

Eldridge, D. 2013. "Tavis Smiley: Obama's Race Speech 'Weak as Kool-Aid.' " *Washington Times,* July 21. http://www.washingtontimes.com/news/2013/jul/21/tavis-smiley -obamas-race-speech-weak-kool-aid/.

Entman, R. 1990. "Modern Racism and the Images of Blacks in Local Television." *Critical Studies in Mass Communication* 7:332–45.

Eschholz, S. 2002. "Racial Composition of Television Offenders and Viewers' Fear of Crime." *Critical Criminology* 11:41–60.

Essence.com. 2013. "Celebrity Reactions to Trayvon Martin Tragedy." July. http:// photos.essence.com/galleries/celebrity-reactions-trayvon-martin-tragedy/.

Fox, R., R. Van Sickel, and T. Steiger. 2007. *Tabloid Justice: Criminal Justice in an Age of Media Frenzy.* Boulder, CO: Lynne Reiner.

Fox News. 2013. "Transcript of Rep. Steve King." July 18. http://www.foxnews.com/ on-air/hannity/2013/07/19/reps-king-rush-debate-zimmerman-verdict.

Francis, M. 2013. "What about Martin's Right to 'Stand His Ground'?" *CNN.* http:// www.cnn.com/2013/07/11/opinion/francis-zimmerman-trial/.

Gilens, M. 1996. "Race Coding and White Opposition to Welfare." *American Political Science Review* 90:593–604.

Gleason, B. 2013. "Occupy Wall Street: Exploring Informal Learning about a Social

Movement on Twitter." *American Behavioral Scientist* 57 (7): 966–82. http://go
.galegroup.com.libserv-prd.bridgew.edu/ps/i.do?id=GALE%7CA343977588andv=2
.1andu=mlin_s_bridcollandit=randp=AONEandsw=wandasid=75ba6b68e386e
93015ad96786bd030ec.

Goff, K. 2013. "Obama Fails Black American and Trayvon." *Root*, July 14. http://www
.theroot.com/blogs/blogging_the_beltway/2013/07/obama_fails_black_america_
and_trayvon.html.

Goodman, Amy. 2013. "Transcript of Democracy Now. Cornel West: Response to Trayvon Martin Case Belies Failure to Challenge 'New Jim Crow.'" July 23. http://www
.popularresistance.org/cornel-west-responds-to-barak-obama-on-trayvon-martin/.

Hawkins, D. F. 1983. "Black and White Homicide Differentials: Alternatives to an Inad-
equate Theory." *Criminal Justice and Behavior* 10:407–40.

HLN. 2013. "Zimmerman Found Not Guilty: Do You Agree?" HLN. http://www.hlntv
.com/poll/2013/07/12/do-you-agree-verdict.

Jeffries, M. P. 2013. "Obama's Chicago Speech Can't Address Gun Violence Unless It
Takes on Race." *Atlantic*. http://www.theatlantic.com/politics/archive/2013/02/
obamas-chicago-speech-cant-address-gun-violence-unless-it-takes-on-race/
273200/.

Johnson, G. B. 1941. "The Negro and Crime." *American Annals of the American Academy of Political and Social Science* 217:93–104.

Jones, Eunique Gibson. 2013. "I am Trayvon Martin Campaign." http://rollingout
.com/photos/i-am-trayvon-martin-photo-campaign-by-eunique-gibson-jones/
attachment/i-am-trayvon-martin-photo-campaign-11/.

Joseph, P. 2013. "Trayvon, Race and American Democracy." *Root*. http://www.theroot
.com/articles/culture/2013/07/trayvon_martin_race_and_american_democracy
.html.

Kelley, B. 2013. "Trayvon Martin, Emmett Till and the Shadow of Jim Crow Justice."
Grio. http://thegrio.com/2013/07/17/trayvon-martrin-emmett-till-and-the-shadow
-of-jim-crow-justice/.

Knickerbocker, B. 2013. "Political World Reacts to Obama's 'Trayvon' Moment." *Christian Science Monitor*, July 20.

Knowles, F. 2013. "Sunday Rally, March in Chicago to Protest Acquittal in Trayvon
Martin Case." *Chicago Sun-Times*. http://www.suntimes.com/news/metro/21322301
-418/sunday-rally-march-in-chicago-to-protest-acquittal-in-trayvon-martin-case
.html. Accessed February 19, 2014.

Kovaleski, S. 2012. "Trayvon Martin Case Shadowed by Series of Police Missteps." *New
York Times*. http://www.nytimes.com/2012/05/17/us/trayvon-martin-case-shadowed
-by-police-missteps.html?pagewanted=alland_r=0.

Langer, G. 2013. "Vast Racial Gap on Trayvon Martin Case Marks a Challenging Conversation." ABC. http://abcnews.go.com/blogs/politics/2013/07/vast-racial-gap-on
-trayvon-martin-case-marks-a-challenging-conversation/.

Loiaconi, S. 2013. "Parents: This Is about Other Trayvon Martins." HLN. http://www
.hlntv.com/article/2013/07/19/nancy-grace-trayvon-martin-parents-interview.

Lott, J. 2013. "We Never Should Have Witnessed a Zimmerman Trial." Fox News. http://www.foxnews.com/opinion/2013/07/14/never-should-have-witnessed-zimmerman-trial/.

Luscombe, R., and H. Siddique. 2013. "George Zimmerman Acquittal Leads to Protests across US Cites." *Guardian*, July 15. http://www.theguardian.com/world/2013/jul/15/trayvon-martin-protests-streets-acquittal. Accessed February 19, 2014.

Mason, P. 2007. "Misinformation, Myth and Distortion." *Journalism Studies* 8:481–96.

May, C. 2013. "NAACP on Obama's Trayvon Martin Remarks: 'This Is a Powerful Moment.'" *Daily Caller*, July 19. http://dailycaller.com/2013/07/19/naacp-plans-to-use-presidents-comments-to-fight-stand-your-ground-laws/.

Mendelberg, T. 1997. "Executing Hortons: Racial Crime in the 1988 Presidential Campaign." *Public Opinion Quarterly* 61:134–57.

Metress, C. 2003. "'No Justice, No Peace': The Figure of Emmett Till in African American Literature." *MELUS* 28 (1): 87. http://go.galegroup.com.libserv-prd.bridgew.edu/ps/i.do?id=GALE%7CA103996927andv=2.1andu=mlin_s_bridcollandit=randp=AONEandsw=wandasid=8702aeb70b1dfc0dae3f0b7f840fe350.

NBC News. 2013. "It's Injustice: Martin Supporters React to Verdict." NBC. http://www.nbcnews.com/news/us-news/its-injustice-martin-supporters-react-verdict-v19460930.

Neale, R. 2013. "'System Has Failed': Crowds React to Zimmerman Verdict." *USA Today*. http://www.usatoday.com/story/news/nation/2013/07/13/zimmerman-jury-deliberations-draw-crowds/2514307/.

Nicholas, V. 2013. "I Could've Been Trayvon Martin." MSNBC. http://www.msnbc.com/msnbc/i-could-have-been-trayvon-martin.

Obama, B. 2013. "Remarks by the President on Trayvon Martin." July 19. http://www.whitehouse.gov/the-press-office/2013/07/19/remarks-president-trayvon-martin.

Oliver, M. B. 1994. "Portrayals of Crime, Race, and Aggression in 'Reality-Based' Police Shows: A Content Analysis." *Journal of Broadcasting and Electronic Media* 38:179–92.

Omansky, K. 2013. "I Am Not Trayvon Martin and You Aren't Either." *Policymic*, July 17. http://www.policymic.com/articles/55191/i-am-not-trayvon-martin-and-you-aren-t-either. Accessed February 19, 2014.

Pew Research Center. 2013a. "Straight News Accounts, Anger Dominates Twitter Response." Washington, DC: Pew Research Center.

———. 2013b. "Whites Say Too Much Focus on Race, Blacks Disagree: Big Racial Divide over Zimmerman Verdict." http://www.people-press.org/2013/07/22/big-racial-divide-over-zimmerman-verdict/.

Robinson, K. 2013. "Trayvon Martin Protests Sweep Times Square, and Spread across the Nation." July 14. http://www.policymic.com/articles/54535/trayvon-martin-protests-sweep-times-square-and-spread-across-the-nation.

Rocque, M. 2011. "Racial Disparities in the Criminal Justice System and Perceptions of Legitimacy: A Theoretical Linkage." *Race and Justice* 1 (3): 292–315.

Sakuma, A. 2013. "George Zimmerman Found Not Guilty in Death of Trayvon Martin."

MSNBC. http://www.msnbc.com/msnbc/george-zimmerman-found-not-guilty -death.

Schwartz, C. 2013. "Oakland's Trayvon Martin Protests Underscore City's History of Racially Charged Violence." *Huffington Post*, July 15. http://www.huffingtonpost .com/2013/07/14/oakland-trayvon-martin_n_3595505.html. Accessed February 19, 2014.

Seay, B. 2013. "I Am Not Trayvon Martin." *Huffington Post*, July 16. http://www .huffingtonpost.com/bob-seay/i-am-not-trayvon-martin_b_3603241.html. Accessed February 19, 2014.

Sherman, L. 2010. "Defiance, Compliance and Consilience: A General Theory of Criminology." In *The Sage Handbook of Criminological Theory*, edited by E. McLaughlin and T. Newburn, 360–91. Thousand Oaks, CA: Sage.

Singerman, D. 2013. "Youth, Gender, and Dignity in the Egyptian Uprising." *JMEWS: Journal of Middle East Women's Studies* 9 (3): 1. http://go.galegroup.com/ps/i.do?id= GALE%7CA344154964andv=2.1andu=mlin_s_bridcollandit=randp=AONEandsw= wandasid=a7fdfb5439817e2a7fd3b91fod6d9976.

Sniderman, P., T. Piazza, P. Tetlock, and A. Kendrick. 1991. "The New Racism." *American Journal of Political Science* 35 (2): 423–47.

Strickland, J. 2013. "No Justice in Trayvon Martin Killing Case." *Huffington Post*. http:// www.huffingtonpost.com/joy-strickland/no-justice-in-trayvon-mar_b_3596623 .html.

Swanson, E. 2013. "George Zimmerman Poll Finds Divide over Not Guilty Verdict." *Huffington Post*. http://www.huffingtonpost.com/2013/07/17/george-zimmerman -poll_n_3612308.html.

Thomas, C. 2013. "Double Standards and Zimmerman Verdict." *Fox News*. http://www .foxnews.com/opinion/2013/07/16/double-standards-and-zimmerman-verdict/.

Thorson, K., K. Driscoll, B. Ekdale, S. Edgerly, L. Thompson, A. Schrock, and C. Wells. 2013. "YouTube, Twitter and the Occupy Movement." *Information, Communication and Society* 16 (3): 421–51.

Tsfati, Y. 2003. "Do People Watch What They Do Not Trust?" *Communication Research* 30:504.

Tsoudis, O. 2000. "Does Majoring in Criminal Justice Affect Perceptions of Criminal Justice?" *Journal of Criminal Justice Education* 11:225–36.

Tumulty, K. 2010. "A Place for Race on Obama's Agenda." *Washington Post*. http://www .washingtonpost.com/wp-dyn/content/article/2010/07/22/AR2010072201691.html.

Van Stekelenburg, J., and B. Klandermans. 2010. "The Social Psychology of Protests." *Sociopedia*. http://www.surrey.ac.uk/politics/research/researchareasofstaff/ isppsummeracademy/instructors/Social%20Psychology%20of%20Protest,%20Van %20Stekelenburg%20%26%20Klandermans.pdf.

Vivian, A. 2013. "What If Trayvon Martin and George Zimmerman Were White?" CNN. http://www.cnn.com/2013/07/25/opinion/vivian-zimmerman-verdict/.

Watkins, B. 2013. "The Gift of Trayvon Martin—His Sacrifice Has Awakened a Nation."

Your Black World. http://www.yourblackworld.net/2013/07/black-news/dr-boyce
-the-gift-of-trayvon-martin-his-sacrifice-has-awakened-a-nation/.

Weitzer, R., and S. Tuch. 2004. "Race and Perceptions of Police Misconduct." *Social Problems* 51:305–25.

Wright, S. C., D. M. Taylor, and F. M. Moghaddam. 1990. "The Relationship of Perceptions and Emotions to Behavior in the Face of Collective Inequality." *Social Justice Research* 4 (3): 229–50.

12

Read between the Lines

What Determines Media Coverage of Youth Homicide?

HEATHER M. WASHINGTON AND VALERIE WRIGHT

On February 26, 2012, Trayvon Martin, a seventeen-year-old unarmed teen in Sanford, Florida, was fatally shot by a twenty-eight-year-old neighborhood watchman, George Zimmerman. The shooting was initially catapulted into the media spotlight on March 7, 2012, and national coverage followed after Martin's father held a press conference on March 8, blaming Zimmerman for his son's death and criticizing the Sanford Police Department for not arresting him. The media continued to cover Martin's killing for the duration of Zimmerman's trial, and several factors contributed to the media's interest in the fatal altercation: the fact that the shooting occurred in a gated community, the age and racial/ethnic dissimilarity of Martin and his killer, questions about Martin and Zimmerman's demeanor on the evening of the incident, the mystery surrounding the incident with regard to what occurred, Zimmerman's behavior before he assumed the neighborhood watchman position, and Zimmerman's claims of self-defense that raised questions about whether Martin was to blame for his own demise. In many respects, both Martin's death and the media coverage thereof are not representative of youth homicides in general. However, the incident raises questions regarding how "typical" youth homicides are covered in the media, and whether the amount and the content of coverage are similar across all youth homicide victims, especially with regard to victims' race and gender.

Such inquiries are important given that the media play a significant role in shaping the public's awareness and imagination about crime. This is achieved via the way in which the media portray criminal events, crime victims, and criminal offenders, and the frequency with which criminal events are reported. Historically, violent crimes, especially homicides, receive the most media coverage, constituting more than 40 percent of all crime stories in some media outlets.[1] This is true although homicides occur much less frequently than other crimes in the United States.[2]

The available research suggests that media coverage is not consistent across all homicide events and victims. Some homicides are not covered by media outlets, and those that do receive media attention vary with regard to the amount of coverage they receive.[3] It is well documented that extralegal factors related to homicide victims dictate the extent to which homicides receive media coverage and, more importantly, how facts are presented and contextualized in the media. In fact, victims' race is one of the most robust predictors of media coverage, with white victims overwhelmingly receiving more media coverage than African American and Hispanic victims.[4] Much of the selectivity mirrors the social structure of society and is representative of the inequitable patterns related to race and gender stratifications that are commonplace in American society. When blacks, especially black males, are in the media, their stories are more likely to include a script that portrays them as violent perpetrators,[5] and as more menacing than whites.[6] Such typifications by media outlets provide a prototype that can confirm existing stereotypes in the minds of the public by providing stories that feel familiar and predictable to their audiences.[7]

Victims' gender also influences media attention, with females more likely to receive media coverage than their male counterparts.[8] Cases involving young victims and elderly victims also garner a considerable amount of attention relative to those involving middle-aged adults.[9] As such, when looking at youthful homicide cases in the media, existing theories assert that there is no expectation to observe variation by race and gender because youth, as a population, are generally considered worthy and blameless victims.

Overall, the available perspectives view inconsistencies in media coverage across homicides as a function of media outlets' assessment of the newsworthiness of each case. Other scholars note the importance of being a "worthy victim" as a predictor of coverage, in addition to victims' race and gender. Victims who are deemed blameless are more likely to receive coverage and garner feelings of compassion from the community relative to those victims who are viewed as having contributed to their own death.[10] Typically, when victims are at fault for any of the circumstances surrounding their death, they are more likely to be discredited and have some blame attributed to them. Thus, more often than not, media resources are allocated to cover the stories of victims who are perceived as vulnerable, blameless, and thus undeserving of their fate.[11] However, some scholars rule out these perspectives in favor of instrumental explanations such as the amount of space that is available to cover the event, the extent to which known facts about the case are available, and other events that are occurring simultaneously that might overshadow the importance of a particular case such as a national or local catastrophe.[12] To these scholars, media selection bias is simply a function of practicality rather than the result of subjective decisions that place importance on one case over another.

The current study uses data from homicide reports from two police departments matched with articles from one newspaper. We use these data to (1) explore whether blameworthiness, race, and gender contribute to divergent coverage among youthful homicide victims in the media and (2) investigate how the number of newspaper articles as well as the content of the articles (i.e., how the story is presented to the audience) might differ at the intersection of victims' race and gender. In doing so, we extend existing research by using data from Seminole County, Florida, which includes the city of Sanford, which has not been the focus of prior work but has received media attention because of the Trayvon Martin killing. In addition, we contribute to current scholarship by focusing only on youthful homicide victims and by exploring variation in the amount and content of the media's reporting of youth homicides.[13]

Background

Crime, the Media, and Public Perception

Most individuals will not become victims of crime, and few individuals experience homicides involving those who are close to them. It is for these reasons that most individuals must rely on secondhand information to shape their knowledge about crime, crime victims, and the criminal justice system's response to crime.[14] As such, media construction of homicides and homicide victims plays a significant role in shaping public awareness and beliefs about criminal events and those involved in them.[15]

A large and growing body of literature documents disparities in media reporting of homicides. The media's interest in particular homicide events, to the neglect of others, could adversely affect the public's perceptions and fear of crime. If, for example, the media focus on homicide cases that involve white, female, blameless victims, such a portrayal of homicide might lead to an increase in fear among white women, even though most homicide victims are African American males. Conversely, if black male homicide victims are portrayed as violent offenders killed by individuals who are merely "standing their ground," such propaganda could contribute to biases in the minds of members of the general public and potential jurors alike.

Disparate coverage of homicide cases in the media can also contribute to stereotypes concerning victims' and offenders' demographic characteristics. If white women are predominately portrayed as victims of crime, these individuals become the standard for achieving "ideal" victim status. Such a depiction might limit public sympathy for black and male victims. Moreover, frequent coverage of cases involving white victims, to the neglect of black victims, might also convey to the public that some lives are worth more than others.

Determinants of Newsworthiness among Homicide Cases

Newsworthiness, as a concept, is difficult to define in part because of its subjectivity. As Meyers notes,[16] "there are no hard-and-fast rules about what constitutes the news, and reporters and editors themselves are often vague about how they separate what to cover from what to ignore within the vast pool of occurrences that could, potentially, be news." For this reason, scholars have attempted to capture newsworthiness in a variety of ways including the actual selection of certain cases over others,[17] and the relative frequency of reporting on specific events.[18]

Most scholars generally agree that newsworthiness is best understood by looking at the choices made with regard to what cases receive coverage.[19] Basically, cases that are covered in the media are newsworthy; if they were not newsworthy, they would have probably been ignored by the media. There are gradations of newsworthiness within this framework, however. Some homicides receive only one news article. Others are selected for follow-up coverage. Still others receive frequent and repeated front-page coverage.[20]

Pertinent to this study, the available literature points to blameworthiness as one factor that helps to explain such variation.[21] One way to assess blameworthiness is by considering whether victims constitute "ideal victims,"[22] who are seen as completely undeserving of, and thus not to blame for, their own criminal victimization.[23] Such victims typically include individuals who are white, young, and/or elderly, have high socioeconomic status, and those who are murdered by a stranger.[24] These victims tend to generate collective mourning from their communities and across the nation and may even generate social and/or political change (e.g., Megan's Law, AMBER Alerts).[25] On the other end of the continuum are victims who are black, male, drug-addicted, or homeless or who have otherwise been marginalized and are thus unable to achieve "ideal" victim status. As such, these victims are less likely to garner public sympathy, social change, and even media coverage.[26]

In addition to victims' blameworthiness, race and gender contribute to their location on the victim hierarchy and thus the amount and type of coverage they receive. Victims who are racial/ethnic minorities are typically denied ideal victim status, which relegates them to the bottom of the hierarchy. As such, media coverage of homicides involving black victims is relatively scant when compared to that of their white counterparts.[27] Recent research suggests that relative to their actual rates of victimization, African Americans are underrepresented and whites are overrepresented as crime victims in media outlets.[28] And not only are blacks and Hispanics less likely to receive media coverage in general, but when media attention is given, blacks are four times more likely than whites to be portrayed as suspects rather than victims of crime.[29]

Overall, the available research shows white victims are more likely than minority victims to receive extensive coverage,[30] to have articles about their victimization appear on the front page of the newspaper,[31] and to have longer articles.[32] It is important to note, however, that some research finds no differences in media coverage among whites and blacks, but this is the exception, not the rule.[33] Schildkraut and Donely's work focused on homicides in Baltimore, Maryland, a city that is majority African American, has a relatively high homicide rate, and has a significant portion of homicide victims who are black.[34] It is possible that these facts tainted the results of their study since there is research to suggest that in areas where homicides are more prevalent and homicide victims are predominately African American, journalists may consider homicides ordinary and thus not newsworthy.[35]

With regard to victims' sex, female status trumps male status on the victim hierarchy. As such, homicides involving female victims are more likely to be reported than those involving male victims.[36] The intersection of gender and race is important to consider, however, since not all female homicide victims receive the same amount of coverage. For example, recent studies find that among female victims, white victims receive more coverage than their black counterparts.[37]

The Current Study

Several limitations of prior work impede our understanding of how and why some news stories are highly covered while others receive no coverage. First, little research focuses exclusively on homicides involving young individuals. This is a significant limitation in that persons under twenty-five are significantly more likely to fall victim to homicide than are their older counterparts, who have been the focus of much research on the determinants of the media's coverage of homicides.[38] As such, exploring variation in media reporting of youth homicides is a needed and pertinent area of research.

In addition, few studies systematically examine the validity of the aforementioned perspectives jointly.[39] That is to say, studies tend to focus exclusively on finding support for one perspective over the other, with little or no interest in showing the extent to which multiple perspectives might play a role. For example, studies typically focus on the impact of race or gender on media coverage, but fail to examine the impact of other factors that have been shown to be predictors of coverage such as victim blameworthiness.[40]

Prior work is also limited in that the window of study is often short. Most studies examining media reporting have an analysis period that is shorter than one year. So it is possible that extant research findings are the result of variations in the number of actual homicide incidents and the reporting of such events in a given year. Studying a longer period of time diminishes the likelihood that the results are biased by such irregularities. This study focuses on homicides over a decade, which allows us to avoid some of the issues plaguing scholarship using a shorter time frame.

The current study has three goals. First, we seek to identify legal (i.e., blameworthiness) and nonlegal (i.e., victims' race and gender) determinants of media coverage of youth homicides in Sanford, Florida. Second, we explore whether there are differences in media coverage by and at the intersection of victims' race and gender. Our research differs from previous work that would hypothesize little variability in coverage of homicides involving youthful victims. Instead of seeing youth homicide victims as a homogenous group, we expect variation in the amount and type of media coverage documenting homicides involving youthful victims. Specifically, cases involving white female victims should receive the most coverage compared to those that include victims who are black and/or male. We also predict that cases in which victims are deemed blameless will receive more coverage than cases in which the victims are implicated either wholly or partially in their own death.

Data and Method

Data

This study utilizes police report data from forty closed homicide cases from 2000 through 2012 handled by the Seminole County, Florida, Sheriff's Office as well as the Sanford, Florida, Police Department. The police reports include both the offender's and the victim's name, age, and race as well as information about the weapon used, manner of death, whether there was a known suspect, whether or not the case had been cleared by an arrest, and other pertinent information related to the offense.

The newspaper articles are from the *Orlando Sentinel*, which covers Seminole County, Florida, where the Trayvon Martin homicide occurred. We explored the possibility of using other newspapers that receive readership in Seminole County, but chose to rely solely on the *Orlando Sentinel* for two reasons. First, it is the primary newspaper of

Orlando, covering Lake, Orange, Osceola, and Seminole Counties. Second, smaller, local newspapers covering the area, such as the *Sanford Herald,* only cover cases that occur in their specific locale. Including these newspapers would bias the results because cases that occurred outside of the city limits would not receive coverage.[41] For these reasons, we rely on one newspaper covering a large area rather than several smaller newspapers covering less geographical space.

The *Orlando Sentinel* has an average weekday paper circulation of 161,837 as well as a Sunday circulation of 270,040. In addition to its paper circulation, it is accessed daily by 419,400 people online and receives 23.6 million page views monthly. In Seminole County alone, 210,000, or 63 percent of adults, read the newspaper in print or online over the course of a week.[42]

Seminole County is located between Orange County to the south and Volusia County to the north and covers over three hundred square miles. It is part of the Greater Orlando metropolitan area. According to the latest census (2012), Seminole County is home to 430,838 residents, who compose roughly 2 percent of the entire population in Florida. With regard to race, Seminole County is mostly white (65.52 percent), 11.8 percent African American, and 18.2 percent Hispanic.[43] The county's median household income is $58,577, and nearly 11 percent of the population lives in poverty.[44] The city of Sanford, which occupies 22.96 square miles, is the county seat of Seminole County and a port city in central Florida. The U.S. Census Bureau reported that the city had a population of 54,651, with whites composing 45 percent, followed by African Americans (30.5 percent) and Hispanics (20.2 percent). The median household income in Sanford is $43,514, considerably lower than the median income for the whole county. Furthermore, compared to Seminole County as a whole, almost twice as many Sanford residents live in poverty (20.1 percent).

Analytic Strategy

The homicide data are matched with online news stories about homicides reported in the *Orlando Sentinel.*[45] Forty homicides involving youthful victims are available in the police report data. The victims range in age from zero to twenty-five years. Victims' names were used

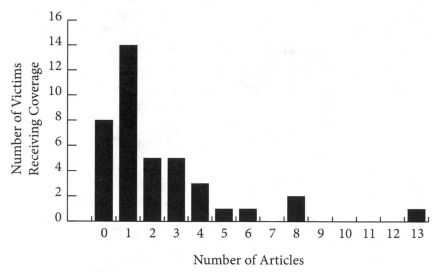

Figure 12.1. Distribution of the newspaper articles ($N = 91$) across the homicide victims ($N = 40$).

as the search criteria to identify articles. Only articles that included the victim's name and that made mention of the victim's homicide were retained. Figure 12.1 presents the distribution of the number of articles across victims. As shown in the figure, among the forty victims, eight did not have any articles written about their homicide, and thus these eight victims are not included in the analysis. The remaining thirty-two victims received between one and thirteen articles covering their death. The focus of our study is the ninety-one articles that covered the thirty-two victims.

We conducted content analysis on the newspaper articles, coding them for indications of blame attributed to the victim, offender, and both parties. Reliability of the coding was checked by comparing the authors' codes for each article. In rare cases of disagreement, we discussed why one code was or was not chosen, thus the codes we report are the result of the consensus reached. Data were gathered on blameworthiness as well as the number of articles. Within these categories, whenever possible, we conducted means tests to examine whether significant differences exist between racial and gender groups with regard to the information coded from the newspaper. Thus, the results presented speak to the broader themes identified and variation in the media's reporting on those themes by victim's race and gender.[46]

Newspaper and Homicide Report Coding

The newspaper content and homicide reports were coded as follows.[47] *Blameworthiness* is a measure of who was deemed responsible for the homicide in each article without any consideration of the victim's characterization. This was coded as being attributed solely to the offender, solely to the victim, or jointly to both the victim and the offender. The *number of articles* that included the victim's name was recorded, and this ranged from eight victims having zero articles to one victim having thirteen articles written about their homicide.

Information on victim's age, race, and gender was coded using police reports. *Age* is the victim's age in years. We included postadolescent victims because this age group is more likely than their middle-age and older adult counterparts to be victims of crime. Victim's *race* was coded solely using information from the homicide reports, which categorized victims as white, black, or unknown.[48] *Gender* captures whether the victim was male or female.

Results

Sample Characteristics

Table 12.1 provides an overview of our unit of analysis, media stories about youthful homicides in the *Orlando Sentinel* ($N = 91$ articles), in addition to the characteristics of the homicide victims themselves ($N = 40$). As shown in the table, over half (56.04 percent) covered white victims and the majority of articles (80.22 percent) covered male victims. Most (56.04 percent) articles suggest that the offender is solely to blame for the victim's death, although in over a quarter of the articles (27.47 percent) both the victim and the perpetrator are deemed blameworthy. Slightly fewer than 10 percent of articles indicate that the victim was solely responsible for his or her own death, and in six articles (6.60 percent) neither the victim nor the offender is implicated.

TABLE 12.1. Descriptive Statistics for Newspaper Articles and Homicide Victims

	Newspaper articles		Homicide victims	
	n/Mean (*SD*)	%	*n*/Mean (*SD*)	%
Race				
White	51	56.04	17	42.50
Black	34	37.36	18	45.00
Unknown	6	6.60	5	12.50
Total	91	100.00	40	100.00
Gender				
Male	73	80.22	33	82.50
Female	18	19.78	7	17.50
Total	91	100.00	40	100.00
Age	17.63 (6.51)		16.80 (7.45)	
Blame				
Offender only	51	56.04	17	42.50
Shared	25	27.47	6	15.00
Victim only	9	9.89	5	12.50
Not specified	6	6.60	4	10.00
No coverage	—		8	20.00
Total	91	100.00	40	100.00
Number of articles	—		2.28 (2.67)	
Avg. number of words	397.34 (240.89)[a]		352.23 (196.04)[b]	

[a] This statistic pertains only to the 32 victims who received at least one article covering their homicide.
[b] This number represents the average number of words in the articles per victim.

Results from the Content Analysis

COVERAGE BY RACE AND GENDER

Newspaper coverage varied across victim race and at the intersection of race and gender. In terms of race, a disproportionate number of articles covered homicides involving white victims compared to black victims. Figure 12.2 illustrates the distribution of articles by victim race and shows that while articles covering white victims ranged from one to thirteen, the range for blacks is only one to six. Despite the fact

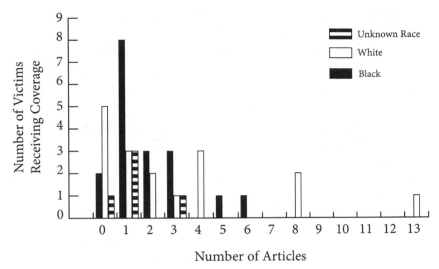

Figure 12.2. Distribution of articles by victims' race.

TABLE 12.2. Descriptive Statistics by Race (UA = Articles)

	Articles on white victims (n = 51)		Articles on black victims (n = 34)	
	n/Mean (SD)	%	n/Mean (SD)	%
Gender (p < .001)				
Male	37	72.55	34	100.00
Female	14	27.45	0	0.00
Total	51	100.00	34	100.00
Age (p < .001)	16.76 (5.83)		21.32 (2.83)	
Blame (ns)				
Offender only	28	54.90	17	50.00
Shared	15	29.41	10	29.41
Victim only	4	7.84	5	14.71
Not specified	4	7.84	2	5.88
Total	51	100.00	34	100.00
Number of articles (p < .001)	7.15 (4.12)		3.17 (1.83)	
Avg. number of words in article (ns)	433.76 (224.83)		368.68 (267.75)	

Note: There were six articles about victims (two males and four females) in which we did not have information about their race in the police reports.

that blacks composed 45 percent of homicide victims, they were represented in only 37.36 percent of the articles. Conversely, whites were 42.50 percent of homicide victims but were represented in 56.04 percent of the articles. On average 7.15 articles were devoted to white victims, while only 3.17 articles covered blacks, a difference that is significant at $p < .001$.

With regard to gender, there are no significant differences in terms of the number of articles covering male and female victims. However, we looked at the interaction of race and gender and found that there are significant racial differences in the amount of newspaper coverage devoted to male victims. On average 7.65 articles covered the homicides of white males, over double those covering black male victims (3.18). An analysis of racial differences in homicide stories covering female victims is not possible given that black females are not represented in our sample of newspaper articles stories.

TABLE 12.3. Descriptive Statistics by Gender (UA = Articles)

	Articles on male victims ($n = 73$)		Articles on female victims ($n = 18$)	
	n/Mean (SD)	%	n/Mean (SD)	%
Race ($p < .001$)				
White	37	50.68	14	77.78
Black	34	46.58	0	0.00
Unknown	2	2.74	4	22.22
Total	73	100.00	18	100.00
Age (ns)	17.96 (6.36)		16.28 (7.14)	
Blame ($p < .001$)				
Offender only	35	47.95	16	88.89
Shared	24	32.88	1	5.56
Victim only	8	10.96	1	5.56
Not specified	6	8.21	0	0.00
Total	73	100.00	18	100.00
Number of articles (ns)	5.38 (4.12)		5.11 (2.83)	
Avg. number of words in article (ns)	392.73 (249.61)		416.06 (206.99)	

TABLE 12.4. Descriptive Statistics by Male Gender and Race (UA = Articles)

	Articles on white male victims $(n = 37)^a$		Articles on black male victims $(n = 34)$	
	n/Mean (SD)	%	n/Mean (SD)	%
Victim age (p < .001)	15.76 (6.54)		21.32 (2.83)	
Blame (ns)				
Offender only	16	43.24	17	50.00
Shared	14	37.84	10	29.41
Victim only	3	8.11	5	14.71
Not specified	4	10.81	2	5.88
Total	37	100.00	34	100.00
Number of articles (p < .001)	7.65 (4.46)		3.18 (1.83)	
Avg. number of words in article (ns)	427.30 (232.71)		368.68 (267.75)	

^{a} There were two articles about male victims in which race was not specified in the police reports.

RACE, MALES, AND BLAMEWORTHINESS

Nearly half (47.95 percent) of the articles covering males placed the blame solely on the offender, and one-third (32.88 percent) of the stories placed blame on both the offender and the victim (see table 12.3). Blame does not determine amount of media coverage per se; however, our content analysis reveals differences in how blame was contextualized by victims' race. In all instances where blame was shared, both the offender and the victim were engaging in a felonious offense and the victims willingly placed themselves in a dangerous situation. Interestingly, black male victims who were partially responsible for their own demise were portrayed as thugs, while white males who shared blame were portrayed as youth who made a poor decision.

Among the ten articles on black male victims that portrayed the victims as having shared blame for their own killing, the language used in the article made it glaringly apparent that the victim contributed to their own death: "robbers," "suspects," "gunman," "bad guys," "attackers," "intruder," and "criminal." For example, one article covering the shooting death of a black male, titled "Victim Turns Gun on Attackers, Kills Teen Firing Semiautomatic Pistol," implicates the young man who was killed in the exchange.[49] The article goes on to state that "a 19-year-old man is dead after he fired a semiautomatic pistol at a boxed-in motorist who then shot him back."[50]

Another article covering the homicide of a different black male is titled "Homeowner Kills Would-Be Intruder in Seminole County."[51] In covering the incident, the article states, "While his wife, Pamela, dialed 911, Carlton Montford opened the door and came face-to-face with a masked man, dressed all in black. And when that man came at Montford, he fired, hitting him in the chest—a wound that proved fatal."[52] The opening lines of a newspaper story covering yet another black male state, "An attempted armed robbery of an Internet café in Seminole County early Tuesday left one of the suspected robbers dead and deputies combing Pine Hills for his accomplices. Gary Bryant, 21, was one of two men who walked into the Allied Veterans Internet Café at 3030 East Semoran Boulevard about 1 a.m. and later ended up dead after a shoot-out with a security guard."[53]

Some white victims shared blame with their accomplices, however they were not depicted as thugs in the newspaper stories. In fact, even when an article made it clear that a white male youth was killed during the commission of a felony, he was portrayed as someone who merely had a lapse in judgment, rather than as a criminal. Fourteen articles covered white male victims who shared blame with their perpetrator. The narratives suggested that they were naïve and deemphasized their role while heightening the role of the people who were arrested for the shooting. As such, the stories referred to the killing as an incident involving "buddies" who had a "plot to kill" or were engaged in "a robbery that turned deadly." For instance, considerable newspaper coverage was given to a seventeen-year-old white male who was killed "as he rode in the back seat of a car traveling down Interstate 4 during a drug deal that turned into a robbery."[54] Another article suggested the victim was merely there to purchase drugs and died scared at the hands of a robber, even after he cooperated by handing over his cash. The article quoted the suspect: " 'He was afraid to die. He took off his shoes, pulled out the money and handed it over,' Johnson said."[55] The majority of articles covering the homicide portrayed the white teen victim (who was purchasing drugs) as a scared boy who was intimidated by his black associates, and who made a mistake that cost him his life.

Another article portrayed a white male victim as slain by a friend who was visiting him from Seattle. According to the newspaper article, "The Sheriff's Office said the shooting was the result of a dispute between the men."[56] Despite the implication that the victim's death was the result of a mutual dispute prior to the shooting, most of the articles covering the homicide minimized the victim's contribution to the dispute and the events that led to his death.

GENDER AND BLAMEWORTHINESS

The content analysis revealed differences in the way in which females compared to males were portrayed in the media with regard to victim blameworthiness. In fact, 88.89 percent of articles covering female homicide victims placed the blame solely on the offender; only 47.95 percent of the articles covering male victims completely excluded the victims from blame. This difference between males and females with regard to blameworthiness was statistically significant at $p < .05$.

Eighteen articles covered the homicides of six female victims. Unlike the males described above who were more likely to be partially or wholly responsible for their own death, female victims were rarely implicated. For instance, the murder of a teenage girl who was kidnapped at knifepoint garnered a considerable amount of coverage. One article written shortly after her murder reads, "At some point, authorities think Davis abducted Malave from the dealership at knifepoint, took her to his Pine Hills home and killed her."[57] A subsequent article closer to the defendant's trial also pointed to the perpetrator's blame: "There is no question that Davis committed the crime. He gave a confession on the day of her death, Oct. 29, 2009. And his defense attorneys have conceded that he committed the crimes."[58] Other articles covering this homicide reiterated Davis's blameworthiness by holding him legally and solely accountable for Malave's murder. "A judge on Monday gave the death penalty to William Davis III."[59]

It should be noted that there are two homicides in which female victims were held wholly or partially to blame for the events that led to their demise. In such cases these victims received minimal coverage, with only one article devoted to each of their stories. In one instance, the victim was shot after asking to participate in a game of Russian roulette. According to the arrest affidavit, "One witness told police Oglesby asked Alvarez to play Russian roulette and told him 'she didn't care if she died.'"[60]

In another case, the victim was portrayed as a troubled young woman with a checkered past who came to her former boyfriend's house with bad intentions. "Some neighbors interviewed Sunday said Oglesby was there to rob Priest; others say she was looking for a fight." The article goes on to state, "Her reputation as a troublemaker lingered. . . . It was a messed-up situation, but she put herself there. . . . Oglesby has a criminal record in the county that includes battery charges in two separate incidents and a DUI."[61] The excerpts from the article clearly suggest that the victim initiated the violent altercation that led to her demise. On the whole, among the female victims, those who were blameless were newsworthy and those who were implicated in their own death were less worthy of media attention.

Discussion

Trayvon Martin's murder garnered much media attention both locally and nationally. This study explored the determinants of media coverage of homicides involving more "typical" teen victims—those whose homicides were not catapulted into the national spotlight but who did receive media coverage in their own locales. Data from police records in Seminole County and Sanford, matched with online newspaper stories from the *Orlando Sentinel*, were used to explore whether victims' race and gender, both independently and jointly, explain divergent media coverage of youthful homicides. Because victim blameworthiness is an important contributor to media coverage, we coded the newspapers for indications of blame (i.e., offender only, victim only, and shared blame) and explored race and gender differences in media coverage within this categorical theme.

Our findings underscore the importance of victims' race and gender as determinants of media coverage. With regard to race, we find significant differences in the amount of media coverage that youthful homicides receive, with white youth receiving a disproportionate amount of coverage. Gender differences in media coverage were not statistically significant, however we find more nuanced patterns when we explore media coverage at the intersection of race and gender. More specifically, our results reveal differences in the content of the newspaper articles documenting homicides involving black and white male youth who share blame with their perpetrators. Black male youth were criminalized and portrayed as thugs, whereas white male youth managed to retain their "ideal victim" status despite being killed while they were engaging in a felonious offense. On the whole, female victims who were not responsible for their deaths in any way received the most media coverage. The media, on the other hand, seemed to punish females who were wholly or partially to blame for their own deaths, with these victims receiving only one newspaper article and no follow-up coverage.

Although we did not systematically examine newspaper articles about Trayvon Martin's murder, the findings presented here regarding blame, race, and gender might help us understand the media's fascination with Martin's case. We speculate that blame played a significant role in determining media coverage of Martin's murder, especially early on in the case. In fact, from the beginning, disputes regarding who was to blame for Martin's death became the catalyst for the case itself and the media coverage that followed. The early coverage of the case featured Martin's parents as well as others who blamed Zimmerman and called for him to be held accountable. As media coverage of the case intensified, more stories regarding blame began to emerge, with some even suggesting that Martin was wholly or partially responsible for his own demise.

In the same way that the black males in our sample who shared blame with their perpetrators were portrayed, later stories about Martin's killing began to characterize Martin as the aggressor in the altercation, an illegal drug user, and a trouble youth who engaged in several infractions while at school. Indeed, for a time the stories about Martin's case became almost as much about Martin's character (i.e., whether he was a troubled youth who was to blame for his own death) as about Zimmerman's role in the events that led him to kill Martin. The disagreement about blame and the light that was cast on Martin's character might have contributed to increased media coverage.

On the whole, our analysis adds to the larger body of work documenting divergent patterns of coverage by victims' race and gender. Our focus on youthful homicide victims and the way in which race and gender interact to produce patterns of media coverage, in particular, is an important addition to extant scholarship. Nevertheless, there are limitations to the current study that provide avenues for future research.

First, future research should replicate our study, and others focusing on homicides more generally, in other areas of the country. This will provide a more complete picture of the determinants of media coverage among youthful homicides, and allow us to better compare whether the same factors are at play across locales. Second, this study leaves questions unanswered about media reporting of homicides among a large proportion of Seminole County and Sanford residents: Hispanics. This is true despite the fact that Hispanics constitute a large percentage of the population in these areas (i.e., 18.2 percent and 20.2 percent in Seminole County and Sanford, respectively). We did not intentionally exclude Hispanic victims from our study; in fact, several victims' surnames suggested Hispanic heritage. However, Hispanic ethnicity could not be confirmed since the homicide reports coded victims' race as white, black, or unknown. Victims having Hispanic surnames were reported as white in the homicide reports. One of the ways in which future research could extend this study is by exploring whether the patterns found in this study apply to Hispanic victims and those of other races.

Third, our study has limited representation of female homicide victims. It is not surprising that male victims made up the largest proportion of our sample given general patterns of homicide with regard to gender. However, having few female victims in our sample hindered our ability to thoroughly examine gender differences in media reporting of juvenile homicides. An important goal of future work should be to explore differences in media reporting by gender and at the intersections of race and gender. We are aware of only one recent study that has explored the latter issue.[62] Exploring this issue is important given that race trumps other statuses (i.e., gender and class) in the United States.

Fourth, there are a few interesting but supplemental findings that should be investigated more thoroughly in future research. For instance, contrary to arguments offered in studies examining the hierarchy of victimization, our findings suggest that younger victims actually receive less coverage than their older counterparts. Interesting, too, is the fact that the majority of the younger victims were white and blameless. The limited number of cases involving these young juveniles did not allow us to fully investigate media coverage among them. However, if these patterns of coverage are true, such findings refute what is predicted by victim hierarchy assertions in that the victims were young, white, and blameless. Future work should explore variation by victim's age in the media's reporting of juvenile homicides.

Finally, future research should explore the determinants of media inattention. Eight of the cases included in the homicide data received no media coverage, and the only clear pattern that emerged with regard to why these cases were excluded from the media spotlight was that the facts of the case were sparse. For example, a suspect was not identified in a few of the cases that failed to receive coverage. This suggests that when a case has a great deal of ambiguity, it is unlikely to be covered because the who, what, why, when, and where questions cannot be fully answered, and most newspapers strive to include this basic information.[63]

Appendix

Examples of Article Titles Characterizing the Homicide Events When Victims Shared Blame with Their Perpetrator(s)

Whites	Blacks
3rd Man Held in Slaying	Video Released from Fatal Shootout at Internet Café
Friend May Face Life if He Knew about '06 Plot to Rob Lake Brantley Teen	Casselberry Man Charged with Murder in Internet Café Shootout
Informants Testifies in Murder Trial of High School Buddy	Seminole Jury Convicts Man in Internet Café Killing
Drug Dealer Convicted in Lake Brantley Student's Killing	Trial Starts in 2007 Drive-by Shooting
2 Sentenced to Life in Prison in Sanford Teen Slaying	Witness: Dealers Began Shooting
Man Critical after Shooting Inside Condo	For Seminole Killer, Life in Prison
Key Witness in Lake Brantley High Murder Is Missing	Homeowner Kills Would-Be Intruder in Seminole County

NOTES

1. Humphries 1981; Paulsen 2003; Pollak and Kubrin 2007.
2. Gruenewald, Pizarro, and Chermak 2009; Paulsen 2003; Pritchard 1985.

3. Gruenewald, Pizarro, and Chermak 2009; Meyers 1997; Weiss and Chermak 1998.

4. Pritchard and Hughes 1997; Weiss and Chermak 1998.

5. Chiricos and Eschholz 2002; Gilliam and Iyengar 2000.

6. Chiricos and Eschholz 2002.

7. Lundman 2003.

8. Buckler and Travis 2005; Lundman 2003; Paulsen 2003.

9. Carrabine et al. 2004.

10. Christie 1986.

11. Greer 2004.

12. Chermak 1995.

13. We would like to thank Frankie Bailey, James Chriss, Jody Miller, Ruth Peterson, and the editors of this volume for their helpful comments on previous versions of this book chapter. We also thank the Criminal Justice Research Center at Ohio State University and the Racial Democracy, Crime and Justice Network for their support.

14. Surette 1992; Pollak and Kubrin 2007.

15. Chermak 1994; Maguire, Sandage, and Weatherby 1999; Surette 1992.

16. Meyers 1997, 18.

17. Weiss and Chermak 1998.

18. Chermak 1995.

19. Clayman and Reisner 1998.

20. Entman and Rojecki 2000; Meyers 1997.

21. Christie 1986; Sorenson, Manz, and Berk 1998.

22. Christie 1986; Greer 2004; Valier 2004.

23. Christie 1986.

24. Sorenson, Manz, and Berk 1998.

25. Greer 2004.

26. Greer 2004; Valier 2004.

27. Pritchard and Hughes 1997; Weiss and Chermak 1998.

28. Dixon, Azocar, and Casas 2003.

29. Chiricos and Eschholz 2002; Poindexter, Smith, and Heider 2003.

30. Paulsen 2003; Weiss and Chermak 1998.

31. Lundman 2003.

32. Buckler and Travis 2005; Gruenewald, Pizarro, and Chermak 2009; Lundman 2003; Paulsen 2003; Weiss and Chermak 1998.

33. Schildkraut and Donley 2012.

34. Ibid.

35. Blau 1991; Pritchard 1985; Simon 1991.

36. Buckler and Travis 2005; Lundman 2003; Paulsen 2003.

37. Lundman 2003; Paulsen 2003; Peelo et al. 2004.

38. Cooper and Smith 2011.

39. See Schildkraut and Donley 2012 for an exception.

40. E.g., Buckler and Travis 2005; Paulsen 2003; Sorenson, Manz, and Berk 1998. See Schildkraut and Donley 2012 for an exception.

41. We explored the possibility of using articles from the *Sanford Herald*. Personal correspondence with a representative from the newspaper informed us that homicides that occur outside the city boundaries would not be covered. Several homicide cases occurred outside of the city of Sanford.

42. Information about the *Orlando Sentinel* comes from their advertising and subscription website. The web address is http://www.orlandosentinelmediagroup.com/AF/ReaderDemo.aspx.

43. Although Seminole County and the city of Sanford, Florida, have a sizable proportion of Hispanic residents, police reports coded the race of the victims only as white, black, or unknown.

44. The Census Bureau calculates poverty in both Seminole County and Sanford from 2008 to 2012.

45. We analyzed only the text of the articles; we excluded obituaries and photos.

46. It is important to note that the results of this study center on the number of homicide stories covering youth homicides ($N = 91$) rather than the number of youth homicide victims ($N = 40$). As such, the stories presented in the 91 articles are grouped by the categories that emerged from the content analysis and not by homicide victims. We only use victims' information to group the articles by victims' race and gender.

47. In instances where the homicide reports and newspapers were inconsistent, we relied on the information from the newspaper articles.

48. Despite some of the victims having Hispanic surnames (e.g., Gonzales), they were coded as white by the police in the homicide reports. Although there were indications in the articles that suggested the race/ethnicity of the victim, assuming a race or ethnicity that was in direct conflict with the information recorded in the official police documents may have biased our results. For example, a victim could have been adopted by or married someone with a Hispanic surname.

49. *Orlando Sentinel*, December 18, 2010.

50. *Orlando Sentinel*, December 18, 2010.

51. *Orlando Sentinel*, June 20, 2009.

52. *Orlando Sentinel*, June 20, 2009.

53. *Orlando Sentinel*, June 20, 2009.

54. *Orlando Sentinel*, August 27, 2010.

55. *Orlando Sentinel*, May 8, 2008.

56. *Orlando Sentinel*, November 18, 2007.

57. *Orlando Sentinel*, November 1, 2009.

58. *Orlando Sentinel*, May 3, 2012.

59. *Orlando Sentinel*, December 17, 2012.

60. *Orlando Sentinel*, September 21, 2004.

61. *Orlando Sentinel*, March 15, 2011.

62. I.e., Lundman 2003.

63. Ricketson 2004.

REFERENCES

Blau, R. 1991. *The Cop Shop: True Crime on the Streets of Chicago*. Reading, MA: Addison-Wesley.

Buckler, K., and L. Travis. 2005. "Assessing the News Worthiness of Homicide Events: An Analysis of Overage in the *Houston Chronicle*." *Journal of Criminal Justice and Popular Culture* 12:1–25.

Carrabine, E., P. Iganski, M. Lee, K. Plummer, and N. South. 2004. *Criminology: A Sociological Introduction*. London: Routledge.

Chermak, S. M. 1994. "Body Count News: How Crime Is Presented in the News Media." *Justice Quarterly* 11 (4): 561–82.

———. 1995. *Victims in the News: Crime and the American News Media*. Boulder, CO: Westview.

Chiricos, T., and S. Eschholz. 2002. "The Racial and Ethnic Typification of Crime and the Criminal Typification of Race and Ethnicity in Local Television News." *Journal of Research in Crime and Delinquency* 39:400–420.

Christie, N. 1986. "The Ideal Victim." In *From Crime Policy to Victim Policy*, edited by E. Fattah, 17–30. Basingstoke: Macmillan.

Clayman, S. E., and A. Reisner. 1998. "Gatekeeping in Action: Editorial Conferences and Assessments of Newsworthiness." *American Sociological Review* 63:178–99.

Cooper, A., and E. L. Smith. 2011. "Homicide Trends in the United States, 1980–2008." Washington, DC: Bureau of Justice Statistics.

Dixon, T. L., C. L. Azocar, and M. Casas. 2003. "The Portrayal of Race and Crime on Television Network News." *Journal of Broadcasting & Electronic Media* 47:498–523.

Dorfman, L., and V. Schiraldi. 2001. "Off Balance: Youth, Race, and Crime in the News." Washington, DC: Youth Law Center.

Entman, R., and A. Rojecki. 2000. *The Black Image in the White Mind: Race and Media in America*. Chicago: University of Chicago Press.

Ericson, R. V., P. M. Baranek, and J.B.L. Chan. 1991. *Representing Order: Crime, Law, and Justice in the News Media*. Toronto: University of Toronto Press.

Ferrell, J. 2005. "Crime and Culture." In *Criminology*, edited by C. Hale, K. Hayward, A. Wahidin, and E. Wincup, 157–75. Oxford: Oxford University Press.

Fishman, M. 1980. *Manufacturing the News*. Austin: University of Texas Press.

Gans, H. 1979. *Deciding What's News: A Study CBS Evening News, Newsweek and Time*. New York: Pantheon Books.

Gilliam, F. D., and S. Iyengar. 2000. "Prime Suspects: The Influence of Local Television News on the Viewing Public." *American Journal of Political Science* 44:560–73.

Gilliam, F. D., Jr., S. Iyengar, A. Simon, and O. Wright. 1996. "Crime in Black and White: The Violent Scary World of Local News." *Harvard International Journal of Press/Politics* 1:6–23.

Graber, D. 1980. *Crime News and the Public*. Chicago: University of Chicago Press.

Greer, C. 2004. "Crime, Media and Community: Grief and Virtual Engagement in Late Modernity." In *Cultural Criminology Unleashed*, edited by J. Ferrell, K. Hayward, W. Morrison, and M. Presdee, 109–18. London: Cavendish.

Gruenewald, J., J. Pizarro, and S. M. Chermak. 2009. "Race, Gender and Newsworthiness of Homicide Incidents." *Journal of Criminal Justice* 37 (1): 262–72.

Humphries, D. 1981. "Serious Crime, News Coverage and Ideology: A Content Analysis of Crime Coverage in a Metropolitan Paper." *Crime & Delinquency* 27:191–205.

Jewkes, Y. 2004. *Media and Crime*. London: Sage.

Johnstone, W. C., D. F. Hawkins, and A. Michener. 1994. "Homicide Reporting in Chicago Dailies." *Journalism Quarterly* 71:860–72.

Lundman, R. J. 2003. "The Newsworthiness and Selection Bias in News about Murder: Comparative and Relative Effects of Novelty and Race and Gender Typifications on Newspaper Coverage of Homicide." *Sociological Forum* 18:357–86.

Maguire, B., D. Sandage, and G. A. Weatherby. 1999. "Crime Stories as Television News: A Content Analysis of National, Big City and Small Town Newscasts." *Journal of Criminal Justice and Popular Culture* 7:1–14.

Marsh, H. L. 1991. "A Comparative Analysis of Crime Coverage in Newspapers in the United States and Other Countries from 1960–1989: A Review of the Literature." *Journal of Criminal Justice* 19:67–79.

Meyers, M. 1997. *News Coverage of Violence Against Women: Engendering Blame*. Thousand Oaks, CA: Sage.

Paulsen, D. J. 2003. "Murder in Black and White." *Homicide Studies* 7:289–317.

Peelo, M., B. Francis, K. Soothill, J. Pearson, and E. Ackerly. 2004. "Newspaper Reporting and the Public Construction of Homicide." *British Journal of Sociology* 33:256–75.

Poindexter, P. M., L. Smith, and D. Heider. 2003. "Race and Ethnicity in Local Television News: Framing, Story Assignments, and Source Selections." *Journal of Broadcasting and Electronic Media* 47:524–36.

Pollak, J. M., and C. E. Kubrin. 2007. "Crime in the News: How Crimes, Offenders and Victims Are Portrayed in the Media." *Journal of Criminal Justice and Popular Culture* 14 (1): 1–25.

Pritchard, D. 1985. "Race, Homicide, and Newspapers." *Journalism Quarterly* 62: 500–507.

Pritchard, D., and K. D. Hughes. 1997. "Patterns of Deviance in Crime News." *Journal of Communication* 47:49–67.

Reiner, R., S. Livingstone, and J. Allen. 2000. "No More Happy Endings? The Media and Popular Concern about Crime since the Second World War." In *Crime, Risk and Insecurity*, edited by T. Hope and R. Sparks, 107–24. London: Routledge.

Ricketson, Matthew. 2004. *Writing Feature Stories: How to Research and Write Newspaper and Magazine Articles*. London: Allen and Unwin.

Schildkraut, J., and A. Donley. 2012. "Murder in Black: A Media Distortion Analysis of 2010 Homicides in Baltimore." *Homicide Studies* 16 (2): 175–96.

Simon, D. 1991. *Homicide: A Year on the Killing Streets*. Boston: Houghton Mifflin.

Sorenson, S. B., G. P. Manz, and R. A. Berk. 1998. "News Media Coverage and the Epidemiology of Homicide." *American Journal of Public Health* 88:1510–14.

Surette, R. 1992. *Media, Crime, and Criminal Justice: Images and Realities*. Pacific Grove, CA: Brooks/Cole.

Valier, C. 2004. *Crime and Punishment in Contemporary Culture*. London: Routledge.

Weiss, A., and S. M. Chermak. 1998. "The News Value of African-American Victim: An Examination of the Media's Presentation of Homicide." *Journal of Crime and Justice* 21:71–88.

Afterword

Reducing Racialized Violence and Deracializing Justice

DORIS MARIE PROVINE AND RUTH D. PETERSON

Trayvon Martin's violent death at the hands of George Zimmerman and the legal process and publicity that ensued provide an opportunity to consider how race matters in the United States. The contributors to this volume consider the role that race and racism likely played in every aspect of the case, from Zimmerman's pursuit of young Martin to the jury's verdict at the end of the criminal trial. The media and public reaction to the case were also inflected with racialized assumptions and stereotypes, and so they are, quite appropriately, part of the scholarly analysis undertaken here.

The violent encounter between Zimmerman and Martin and the legal system's response to it involved more than a clash between two men of different racial backgrounds. The majority-white neighborhood in which the confrontation took place, the age and gender of these two men, the time of day, and other factors were also part of the violent scenario that ensued. Most important, perhaps, is the fact that our racially stratified society views young black and Latino men as probably poor, potentially violent, and likely to be disaffected with mainstream values. As Gau and Jordan point out, the failure of society's primary institutions—its schools, job markets, and commitment to personal security—foster an oppositional culture among many disadvantaged youth, which in turn fosters fear in the mass public and hypersurveillance by police. Confrontations between individuals who have learned to distrust each other can, and do, sometimes lead to violence (e.g., see Like, Sexton, and Porter in this volume).

This volume arose out of the conviction of editor Devon Johnson and her co-editors, Patricia Y. Warren and Amy Farrell, that a thorough understanding of this case could begin to fill a significant gap in contemporary scholarship on the racial dynamics that characterize violent encounters between individuals of different racial and ethnic backgrounds. They issued a call for papers that would shed light on the dynamics and contexts that give rise to such events, the implications for criminal justice processing, and the perceptions and reactions of the media and the public. The result is *Deadly Injustice: Trayvon Martin, Race, and the Criminal Justice System*. Individually and collectively, the chapters here offer insights into the role of race in incidents like the confrontation between Martin and Zimmerman, how criminal justice agencies react, how the mass media cover the story, and the ways that different publics perceive, interpret, and react to such events.

Lethal encounters that cross the social, economic, and racial boundaries that separate segments of American society are not rare. For example, the media have recently drawn attention to a series of incidents between white police officers and African American men, often youth from disadvantaged neighborhoods.[1] The number of lethal incidents between representatives of law enforcement and minority men has led to a social movement, Black Lives Matter, and to some soul searching in political and law enforcement circles about how to prevent lethal encounters. Zimmerman was not a member of any law enforcement service, but news reports made it clear that he saw himself, and was perceived by some, as a representative and enforcer of law and order.

It is not only the lethal encounters themselves but also the response of the legal system that draws attention to how race matters in American society. The systems in place for examining these confrontations do not inspire trust in every community. Blacks and whites differ significantly in their views about the tendency of police to use excessive force on minority citizens and the devotion of law enforcement to good relations with all segments of society. The same is true for opinions about the fairness of the criminal justice system as a whole. Several chapters (see, e.g., Sykes et al., Rios, Unah and Wright) in this volume speak to this issue of trust in law enforcement.[2]

In addition to its substantive insights, this volume sets the stage for future work on situations where racial and ethnic differences are believed to play a role. Recognizing the importance of race and ethnicity in shaping understanding is, we believe, a key to lessening the frequency of lethal incidents involving people of different racial and ethnic groups. However, arriving at such an understanding is difficult in a society divided along racial lines by economic status, education, and opportunity. This very real challenge has not tempered the determination of the authors of these chapters to bring about a more accurate understanding of how race affects crime, criminal justice, and public perceptions of the system's capacity for justice. The remainder of this essay therefore identifies and comments on some of the central lessons of the volume, and offers additional directions that we believe researchers should consider in light of the findings presented here.

Evolving Patterns of Racial Bias

The case that inspired this volume involved the killing of an African American youth by an individual whom the U.S. Census Bureau would classify as white, of Latino origin. The site was a predominantly, but not exclusively, white community. Was racism implicated in this killing and the response by criminal justice authorities (the police, the jury, etc.)? And if so, how? To begin to answer this fundamental question, it is essential to situate racism in its contemporary context. That is the primary goal of the chapters in the first section of this volume. The authors all argue, in various ways, that the racial dynamics that manifest themselves in violent encounters today are unlike those that prevailed in an earlier era of white on black killings.

Consider, for example, the 1955 death of Emmett Till, a fourteen-year-old African American youth murdered by Roy Bryant and his half brother.[3] They had been disturbed by Till's reported flirtation with Bryant's wife. The case aroused national attention in part because Till's mother opted for an open casket at his Chicago funeral, putting the grisly circumstances of her son's killing on full display. The Mississippi trial resulted in the acquittal of both killers, though, protected by double jeopardy, they later admitted their guilt. That killing and like events of that era reflected a racism that was inscribed in law, justified in public policy, and enforced through violence that was condoned and tolerated by white society. During this period, the manifestation of racial animus throughout much of the United States was constant, unrelenting antagonism based on skin color and racial heritage.

The chapters in this volume indicate that this constellation of oppressions no longer prevails. Racism works in more insidious ways and without open tolerance for its practice. The authors describe the core of contemporary racism in terms of racial aversion and latent bias, which often operates at an unconscious level (see Drakulich and Siller; Gau and Jordan; Like, Sexton, and Porter; Russell-Brown; Sykes et al.). Contemporary racism, in other words, is more about the reactive side of individual minds than conscious racial animus. An underlying theme is that the "new racism" is manifest in *fear* of those who are constructed as racially or ethnically different, especially young males from racial Other groups who are perceived as criminally dangerous. Russell-Brown evokes the image of the *criminalblackman* to describe this fear-based image.[4] Contemporary racism therefore, is context-specific, arising when the elements of a situation provoke fear. As Like, Sexton, and Porter show in their chapter, while such situation-based fears are most often associated with perceived racial Others, fear-escalated violence can also occur in nonracial situations where perceived difference signals dangerousness.

The concept of implicit bias suggests a racial dynamic that plays out at an individual level, in the minds, generally, of whites faced with ambiguous situations in which conflict and perhaps violence are possible. The chapters in this volume, however, go further to identify structural and institutional arrangements that are part of violent cross-racial encounters. Particularly important in shaping fears associated with implicit bias is the neighborhood or other immediate environment in which the encounter occurs. Both Drakulich and Siller, and Sykes et al. view neighborhood context (i.e., racial composition, and safe versus unsafe areas) as a prime for dangerousness. The immediate environment, in other words, becomes the filter through which the actions and intentions of black and/or Hispanic males are interpreted. Their findings comport with Elijah Anderson's thinking regarding what he terms the "Iconic Ghetto."[5] Anderson proposes that disadvantaged urban areas become iconic, symbolizing the impoverished, crime-prone, drug-infested, violent area of the inner city where, in the minds of many Americans, "the Black people live." The media and mass culture help to hype this fear-inducing image, which then serves as a powerful source of stereotypes, prejudice, and discrimination that burdens black Americans. The fear-inducing Iconic Ghetto also leads to violent encounters and lethal outcomes like the death of Trayvon Martin.[6]

Other works in this volume, though sometimes less explicit about the particular structural and institutional characteristics in situational violence, view these incidents and their aftermaths as occurring within a racialized social fabric. This suggested link among neighborhoods and other structural arrangements, fear of the racial Other, and lethal violence deserves more investigation. It is important to locate the structures and circumstances that maintain racial residential and social separation, and thereby permit iconic images to go unchallenged. The key to reducing violent cross-racial incidents and the social divisions they tend to perpetuate lies in looking more closely at the structures that maintain our current racial organization.

Reactions of Criminal Justice Institutions to the "New Racism"

One of the lessons of this volume is that implicit bias and neighborhood and legal context reinforce one another. These aspects of lethal encounters between whites and racial Others are easy to miss or deny. Despite decades of social psychological research suggesting the significance of implicit bias against racial Others, many whites deny its existence.[7] Context can play a paradoxical role, allowing legal authorities, juries, and some segments of the public to justify a violent reaction to perceived danger, which itself has a racial component (see, e.g., Gau and Jordan). Acting on one's racially inflected fears may be interpreted as a "commonsense" approach to protect one's personal safety. At the institutional level, the intertwining of racial bias and context-specific fears helps to justify initiatives like New York City's "stop and frisk" policy.[8] The dangers associated with certain neighborhoods make it easy to deny that race is involved in the deployment of law enforcement personnel, even when racial targeting is part of the formula for maintaining community safety. In this situation it is easy to downgrade the culpability of those who harm (or kill) racial Others.

The chapters in this volume suggest some of the ways that criminal justice institutions/processes (legislative processes, policing, the courts, and the penal system) may be implicated in racial bias, and how "commonsense" solutions become mechanisms that leave room for biases that favor whites at the expense of Others (particularly blacks and Latinos). These "commonsense" solutions become taken-for-granted institutional norms. Stand Your Ground laws like the one in Florida that factored into the Zimmerman trial are a good example. Russell-Brown and Jones-Brown and Fradella show that these laws, which are common throughout the United States, open the door to racial bias. Russell-Brown demonstrates that they abandon the traditional reasonable man standard, which attempts to set an objective test of liability for harm, in favor of a personal fear standard. Because fear of crime in the United States is closely associated with fear of racial minorities, Stand Your Ground laws offer protection to whites whose violence harms blacks, Hispanics, and other racial minorities. This "commonsense" policy, however, works in only one direction (Jones-Brown and Fradella). Harris makes a similar point in arguing that Stand Your Ground laws make it easier for police and citizens to act on implicit bias because of the perceived association of race with crime. The solution, he suggests, is training that makes law enforcement officers and citizens aware of implicit bias. This awareness can lessen the potential for lethal violence in situations like the confrontation between George Zimmerman and Trayvon Martin.

These and related findings from the volume suggest that criminologists should give more attention to the question of whether legal institutions and the processes they control are sensitive to the role of implicit racial bias. This kind of analysis can pose many obstacles, as Farrell et al. point out in their chapter on race in the context of acquittals. Often the information available to researchers is limited, with important elements of decision making remaining, in effect, a black box that cannot effectively be scrutinized with the tools and information available.

The role of the unconscious in producing harm is acknowledged to some extent in civil cases claiming negligence, and even in some kinds of discrimination suits where statutes provide that disproportionate outcomes can be an indication of racial or other bias. The standards that prevail in criminal justice, however, are heavily weighted toward conscious intent. The Supreme Court's own jurisprudence is part of the problem. Proving racial bias in sentencing, for example, requires a showing of a malicious intent to discriminate. This is true even when the Court accepts as valid the statistics underlying a showing of racial disparity in sentencing. The majority opinion in *McCleskey v. Kemp*, a 1987 death penalty case, suggests that the Court fears a "slippery slope" in which various kinds of bias might also be shown to affect sentences.[9] The failure of the Supreme Court to acknowledge the role of fear-based, less conscious, context-specific racial bias means that evidence of racial disproportion, even severe racial imbalance, is not actionable without evidence of conscious racial motivation.[10] So from the Court's current perspective, the significant racial disproportion associated with the war on drugs is, legally speaking, a nonissue.[11]

We hope that future scholars will take up the challenge that the authors of this volume pose to critically investigate the full complexity of criminal justice processes as they operate in an era of subtle, even unconscious, racial bias. Part of this complexity involves the intersections between forms or systems of oppression, domination, or discrimination. Kimberle Crenshaw deployed the term "intersectionality" in a seminal 1989 article that illustrated the difficulties courts were having addressing discrimination against women of color—they were attempting to choose between sex discrimination and race discrimination.[12] We must, she argued, stop conceptualizing discrimination along single-axis frameworks and accept that discrimination occurs in the intersectionalities of identity. The lesson here is that research on encounters with police, courts, and corrections must take account of the ways that race intersects with various other identities, including gender, class, age, education, disability, and other categories of disadvantage. This work must begin with an appreciation that certain individuals and groups, at certain times and in certain places, are more vulnerable than others to encounters with violent outcomes, and that they are also likely to suffer differential processing within justice organizations.

The analyses herein offer another caution to researchers investigating the legal system's response to violent incidents. Because they are implicit and often unrecognized, contemporary forms of racism may operate in a cascading fashion, linking the loosely coupled stages of the criminal justice system in ways that can create harm to disadvantaged groups and individuals. Police, prosecutors, judges, and probation officers can be assumed to be equally susceptible to racialized fears, which means that their individual decisions can cascade into hard-to-penetrate racial disadvantage.

Finally, the Trayvon Martin case is a reminder that legal doctrines and policies can also play a role in producing racially biased outcomes. The problems of subjective criteria for excusing harmful behavior (see Russell-Brown) and single-axis analytical frames have already been noted. The good news is that laws and policies can also be crafted to avoid racial and other forms of bias. An example is the decision of some cities and police departments to resist the federal government's urging that local law enforcement become a "force multiplier" in the federal effort to increase immigration enforcement. Asking police officers to assist in detecting immigrants with perilous or nonexistent legal status risks local commitments to community policing, which is based on trusting relationships with police, and can encourage some officers to engage in pretextual stops to query immigration status. Scholarship attentive to the complexity of race and justice, as evidenced by the work in this volume, has the potential to help policy makers avoid or lessen the prevalence of implicit racial bias.

Perceptions of Injustice

Trayvon Martin's death and the trial of George Zimmerman for killing him drew a lot of attention from the media and public. Several chapters analyze media representations of the case and how different audiences responded (see Jones and Ortiz on the trial, Washington and Wright on youthful homicides in the area, and Rios, Sykes et al., and Unah and Wright on racial patterns in, perceptions of, and reactions to crime and the treatment of authorities). Collectively the articles yield a number of interesting points. The mass media, as Jones and Ortiz demonstrate, can and sometimes do publicize a range of voices in covering an event like this. However, Washington and Wright show that homicides of white and female youth garner more media coverage because members of these groups are presumed to be less responsible for their own deaths than black and male youth. Once again, fear of Russell-Brown's *criminalblackman* influences the framing of events, in this case the perception of victims of violence. Prevailing racial attitudes make it difficult to envision black male youth, especially disadvantaged youth, as wholly innocent victims; indeed, they are likely to be characterized as thugs and criminals. There is a parallel difficulty for female victims of rape and sexual violence—under some circumstances, for example, acquaintance rape, the victim tends to be presumed to be at fault for her own victimization.

The studies in this group also reveal deep divisions across race lines in perceptions of discrimination in the criminal justice system and neighborhood policing. Not surprisingly, these broader perceptions tend to be associated with racial and ethnic differences in reactions to the Martin-Zimmerman incident and the court's handling of the case. For example, Unah and Wright find a racial gradient in perceptions regarding the Martin-Zimmerman case, whereby blacks more than Hispanics, and Hispanics more than whites, are likely to believe that (1) Zimmerman would have been arrested earlier had he killed a white person, (2) the justice system is biased against blacks, and (3) the Zimmerman verdict is unjust.

Concluding Thoughts

This book makes a valuable contribution to the literature on racialized violence, often committed in the name of reestablishing order and maintaining public safety. Zimmerman justified his actions in these terms. In this sense, the killing of Trayvon Martin is connected to a recent series of deaths of unarmed black men by police officers committed to maintaining safety on American streets.[13] The circumstances of these killings are ambiguous enough to occasion sharp disagreement over what actually happened and how legal officials and the legal system as a whole should have responded.

While the sharp racial divisions in American society over cases like this are distressing, public attention and debate about race, violence, and justice are important. The public's attention to and disagreement over the circumstances of these incidents encourage, and sometimes force, discussions about how to do better. As Rios shows, harsh encounters with police and other authorities can provoke critical reflection and positive action, and that is occurring with increasing frequency as a critical mass of young black and Latino men have been killed by police and vigilantes. The coalitions that have formed in Ferguson, Missouri, to discuss local court practices, police training, diversity within law enforcement, and related matters are a healthy and welcome development. They suggest that racial justice, along with racism, is in a constant state of evolution.

The contributors to this volume emphasize the personal growth that must occur if this society is to overcome contemporary racism, with its subtle, deniable consequences for disadvantaged groups and individuals. In the spirit of promoting positive change, they make a variety of suggestions, including training of the public and criminal justice officials to recognize the role of implicit bias so that they can take corrective steps in their policies and practices. Law and legal doctrine can also be rethought to make the law less vulnerable to discrimination. These are important and basic moves in the pursuit of justice for all Americans.

The structural and institutional elements of law and our systems of justice also need critical attention. Structures that foster or tolerate discrimination are still in place because they reflect "commonsense" understandings of racial, economic, gender, and ethnic differences. The power of institutions to perpetuate stereotypes cannot be underestimated. The fact that so many violent racial encounters have occurred recently, in Detroit, Ferguson, New York, Dayton, Cleveland, and elsewhere, should remind us of the urgency of this issue. We believe that scholars like the broad array of contributors to this volume have an important part to play in sensitizing policy makers and the public to what needs to be done and what a wholehearted commitment to racial justice can achieve.

NOTES

1. The fatal shooting of Michael Brown by officer Darren Wilson in Ferguson, Missouri, may have garnered the most coverage, but other such deaths include the following killings: Rumain Brismon by a Phoenix Police Department officer; John Crawford by Beaver Creek, Ohio, Police Department officers; Jonathan Ferrell by Charlotte Police Department officers; Ezell Ford by a Los Angeles Police Department officer; Eric Garner by Officer Daniel Pantaleo (New York Police Department—NYPD); Akai Gurley by officer Peter Laing (NYPD); Darrien Hunt by Utah officers; Tamir Rice by officer Timothy Loehman (Cleveland Police Department). Information on "victims" and officers is from http://www.huffingtonpost.com/2014/12/15/police-killing-black -men_n_6277020.html and http://www.motherjones.com/politics/2014/08/3-unarmed -black-african-american-men-killed-police.

2. See also Blow 2015.

3. Crowe 2003; Wright and Boyd 2011.

4. Russell-Brown 1998, 2008.

5. Anderson 2012.

6. Ibid.

7. E.g., Wise 2008.

8. In the 1990s, police officials in New York City changed their traditional "stop and question" policy in favor of a policy that allowed officers to stop, question, *and then frisk* a pedestrian for weapons and other contraband. The majority of those stopped were black or Latino men, with the vast majority of those found to have done nothing wrong. This stop and frisk policy has now been ruled by a federal judge to constitute indirect racial profiling and thereby to be unconstitutional.

9. McCleskey, an African American male, was convicted of armed robbery and murder; his victim was a white police officer. The Court said that the "racially disproportionate impact" of the Georgia death penalty law was not enough to overturn the verdict without a showing of "a racially discriminatory purpose." *McCleskey v. Kemp* 1987.

10. This is in contrast to the standard in other areas of law, such as employment discrimination. In these cases, racially (or gender- or other status-based) disproportionate outcomes are deemed to indicate discriminatory treatment.

11. For a fuller treatment of this issue, see Provine 2007.

12. Crenshaw 1989.

13. See note 1 of this essay for examples.

REFERENCES

Anderson, Elijah. 2012. "The Iconic Ghetto." *Annals of the American Academy of Political and Social Science* 642:8–24.

Blow, Charles M. 2015. "Beyond 'Black Lives Matter.'" *New York Times*, February 9, A17.

Crenshaw, Kimberle. 1989. "Demarginalizing the Intersection between Race and Sex: A Black Feminist Critique of Antidiscrimination Doctrine, Feminist Theory and Antiracist Politics." *University of Chicago Legal Forum* 1989:139–67.

Crowe, Chris. 2003. *Getting Away with Murder: The True Story of the Emmett Till Case.* New York: Dial Books.

McCleskey v. Kemp, 481 U.S. 279 (1987).

Provine, Doris Marie. 2007. *Unequal Under Law: Race and the War on Drugs.* Chicago: University of Chicago Press.

Russell-Brown, Katheryn. 1998. *The Color of Crime: Racial Hoaxes, White Fear, Black Protectionism, Police Harassment, and Other Macroaggressions.* New York: New York University Press.

———. 2008. *The Color of Crime: Racial Hoaxes, White Fear, Black Protectionism, Police Harassment, and Other Macroaggressions.* 2nd ed. New York: New York University Press.

Wise, Tim. 2008. *Speaking Treason Fluently: Anti-racist Reflections from an Angry White Male*. Berkeley, CA: Soft Skull Press.

Wright, Simeon, and Herb Boyd. 2011. *Simeon's Story: An Eyewitness Account of the Kidnapping of Emmett Till*. Chicago: Chicago Review Press.

ABOUT THE CONTRIBUTORS

LAWRENCE D. BOBO is W.E.B. Du Bois Professor of the Social Sciences at Harvard University. He holds appointments in the Department of Sociology and the Department of African and African American Studies. His research focuses on the intersection of social inequality, politics, and race and has appeared in the *American Sociological Review*, the *American Journal of Sociology*, *Social Forces*, the *American Political Science Review*, the *Journal of Personality and Social Psychology*, *Social Psychology Quarterly*, and *Public Opinion Quarterly*. He is an elected member of the National Academy of Science as well as a Fellow of the American Academy of Arts and Sciences and the American Association for the Advancement of Science.

KEVIN M. DRAKULICH is Associate Professor in the School of Criminology and Criminal Justice at Northeastern University. His research focuses on questions related to race, inequality, and crime, including the social processes related to crime and its consequences across communities; perceptions of crime, disorder, and social control within communities; and perceptions of race, crime, control, and related policies more broadly. He is a 2014 recipient of the National Institute of Justice's W.E.B. Du Bois Fellowship as well as the 2014 New Scholar Award from the American Society of Criminology's Division on People of Color and Crime. His recent work has appeared in *Social Problems*, *Social Science Research*, *Journal of Interpersonal Violence*, *Punishment & Society*, and *Race and Justice*.

AMY FARRELL is Associate Professor in the School of Criminology and Criminal Justice at Northeastern University. Her scholarship seeks to understand arrest, adjudication, and criminal case disposition practices. In addition, her research examines jury outcomes, particularly the factors that predict and explain acquittals. She also studies police legitimacy and law enforcement responses to new crimes, such as hate crime and human trafficking. She was a co-recipient of the National Institute of Justice's W.E.B. Du Bois Fellowship on crime, justice, and culture in 2006.

HENRY F. FRADELLA is Professor and Associate Director of the School of Criminology and Criminal Justice at Arizona State University. He specializes in the social scientific study of courts and law. His research and teaching focus on the historical development of substantive, procedural, and evidentiary criminal law, including courtroom acceptability of forensic and social scientific evidence, especially forensic psychological/psychiatric testimony. His work also includes the evaluation of law's effects on human behavior; the dynamics of legal decision making; and the nature, sources, and consequences of variations and changes in legal institutions or processes.

JACINTA M. GAU is Associate Professor in the Department of Criminal Justice at the University of Central Florida. Her research focuses on policing, with an emphasis on police-community relations, procedural justice and police legitimacy, and race issues. In addition, she studies racial discrepancies in jury composition. Her work has appeared in numerous academic journals, and she is the co-author of *Key Ideas in Criminology and Criminal Justice* as well as author of *Statistics for Criminology and Criminal Justice* (second edition).

JASON GIOVIANO is a graduate student completing his master's degree in sociology at DePaul University. He received his undergraduate degree in sociology from Northern Illinois University, and is currently employed in the nonprofit sector as the Research Manager for a Chicago-based operations management organization. His research interests include neighborhood effects and mass incarceration.

DANIEL GIVELBER is Professor of Law Emeritus at the Northeastern University School of Law, where he also served as Dean from 1984 to 1993. He is the co-author (with Amy Farrell) of *Not Guilty: Are the Acquitted Innocent?* He has written and litigated extensively in the area of capital punishment.

DAVID A. HARRIS is Distinguished Faculty Scholar and Professor of Law at the University of Pittsburgh School of Law. His scholarly interests include police behavior and regulation, law enforcement, and national security issues and the law. He is the leading national authority on racial profiling. His 2002 book, *Profiles in Injustice: Why Racial Profiling Cannot Work*, and his scholarly articles in the field of traffic stops of minority motorists and stops and frisks have influenced the national debate on profiling and related topics.

DEVON JOHNSON is Associate Professor in the Department of Criminology, Law, and Society at George Mason University. Her current research focuses on punishment preferences and perceptions of police legitimacy in the United States and the Caribbean, with an emphasis on understanding racial and ethnic differences in public opinion. She also studies public views about counterterrorism strategies and airport security. She has received awards for her research from the American Association for Public Opinion Research and the Law and Society Division of the Society for the Study of Social Problems.

CHENELLE A. JONES is Assistant Professor of Criminology and Criminal Justice at Ohio Dominican University in Columbus. She received her Ph.D. from Texas Southern University in Administration of Justice. Her research interests include race and crime, policing, juvenile delinquency, and the administration of justice. Her most recent work has appeared in the *Journal of Juvenile Justice*, and she is the co-editor of *A Critical Analysis of Race and the Administration of Justice*.

DELORES JONES-BROWN is Professor in the Department of Law, Police Science and Criminal Justice Administration at John Jay College, City University of New York. She is the founding Director of the college's Center on Race, Crime and Justice. Her scholarly interests center around issues related to race, crime, and the application of law, with a special emphasis on policing, police-community relations, and youth. She is the author or co-editor of four books: *Race, Crime and Punishment, The System in Black and White: Exploring Connections between Race, Crime and Justice, Policing and Minority Communities: Bridging the Gap*, and *African Americans and Criminal Justice: An Encyclopedia*, released in July 2014. She is a former prosecutor, and her recent work focuses on the implications of stop and frisk policing in New York City.

KAREEM L. JORDAN is Associate Professor in the School of Criminology and Justice Studies at the University of Massachusetts Lowell. His research interests include juvenile justice and race/ethnicity and crime. His most recent publications have appeared in the *Journal of Juvenile Justice, Journal of Crime and Justice*, and *Youth Violence & Juvenile Justice.*

TOYA LIKE is Associate Professor of Criminal Justice and Criminology at the University of Missouri, Kansas City. Her research focuses on racial and ethnic variations in violent victimization and the intersections of race, ethnicity, gender, and class in crime and victimization. Her work has appeared in journals such as *Crime & Delinquency, Race and Justice*, and *Deviant Behavior* as well as in edited books including *The Many Colors of Crime: Inequalities of Race, Ethnicity and Crime in America* and *The Oxford Handbook on Ethnicity, Crime and Immigration.*

MIA ORTIZ is Assistant Professor in the Criminal Justice Department at Bridgewater State University. She received her Ph.D. from the Graduate Center of the City University of New York. Her research interests include quality-of-life offending, pretrial release, specialized courts, and juvenile delinquency. Her most recent work has appeared in the *Journal of Experimental Criminology* and the *Journal of Drug Issues.*

RUTH D. PETERSON is Emerita Professor of Sociology and former Director of the Criminal Justice Research Center at the Ohio State University. Her research focuses on community conditions and crime, racial and ethnic inequality in patterns of crime, and the consequences of criminal justice policies for racially and ethnically distinct communities. She is co-author of *Divergent Social Worlds: Neighborhood Crime and the Racial-Spatial Divide* and co-editor of *The Many Colors of Crime.* She is also the co-organizer of the Racial Democracy, Crime, and Justice Network and its Crime and Justice Summer Research Institute: Broadening Perspectives and Participation.

ALEX R. PIQUERO is Ashbel Smith Professor of Criminology at the University of Texas at Dallas. He has published over three hundred peer-reviewed articles in the areas of criminal careers, criminological theory, and quantitative research methods. In addition, he has collaborated on several books. He has received numerous awards including the American Society of Criminology's Young Scholar Award, and has been named a Fellow of both the American Society of Criminology and the Academy of Criminal Justice Sciences. He has also received several other research, service, and teaching awards including the University of Texas System Regents' Outstanding Teaching Award in 2014.

NICOLAS PITTMAN has a master's in sociology from DePaul University. He received his undergraduate degree in sociology from the University of Illinois at Urbana-Champaign. His research explores the intersection of deviance, education, race and ethnicity, and social policy. He has participated in academic conferences focusing on education policy, race, and deviance, and is planning on pursuing a Ph.D. in the future.

SAVANNAH PORTER received her bachelor's degree in criminal justice and criminology with a minor in Spanish from the University of Missouri–Kansas City. She is former Vice President of the National Criminal Justice Honor Society, Alpha Phi Sigma. Her research interests include issues around civil rights and social action. She has participated in training from the Kansas Division of the International Association for Identification.

DORIS MARIE PROVINE is Professor Emerita of Justice and Social Inquiry in the School of Social Transformation at Arizona State University. Her areas of interest reflect her background in law and political science. Much of her research focuses on courts and policies related to them. Most recently she has examined policies concerning unauthorized immigration and the interaction of local police and federal officials in the enforcement of federal immigration law. She is the principal author of *Policing Immigrants* (in press) and sole author of "The Morality of Law: The Case Against Deportation of Settled Immigrants," and other work on unauthorized immigration. She is also author of *Unequal Under Law: Race and the War on Drugs.*

VICTOR M. RIOS is Associate Professor in the Department of Sociology at the University of California, Santa Barbara. His research focuses on juvenile justice, social control, masculinity, and race and crime. He is author of the award-winning book *Punished: Policing the Lives of Black and Latino Boys*, and the forthcoming *Missing Fire: Gangs Across Institutional Settings.*

JORDYN L. ROSARIO is a Ph.D. student in the College of Criminology and Criminal Justice at Florida State University in Tallahassee. She received her B.A. in sociology and criminal justice in 2009 from the University of Georgia and her M.S. in criminology in 2012 from Florida State University. Her research interests include victimization, stratification, and the intersection of gender, race/ethnicity, and social class.

KATHERYN RUSSELL-BROWN is Chesterfield Smith Professor of Law and Director of the Center for the Study of Race and Race Relations at the University of Florida, Levin College of Law. She teaches, researches, and writes on issues of race and crime and the sociology of law. Her article, "The Constitutionality of Jury Override in Alabama Death Penalty Cases," was cited by the U.S. Supreme Court in *Harris v. Alabama* (1995). Her books include *Criminal Law* (2015), *The Color of Crime*, second edition (2009), *Protecting Our Own: Race, Crime and African Americans* (2006), and *Underground Codes: Race, Crime, and Related Fires* (2004).

LORI SEXTON is Assistant Professor of Criminal Justice and Criminology at the University of Missouri, Kansas City. Her research interests lie at the intersection of criminology and sociolegal studies, with a specific focus on prisons, punishment, and the lived experience of penal sanctions among transgender prisoners. Her work has been funded by the National Science Foundation, the National Institute of Justice, and the Fletcher Jones Foundation, and has been published in *Punishment & Society*, *Critical Criminology*, *Justice Quarterly*, and *Criminology & Public Policy.*

LAURA SILLER is a doctoral student in criminology at Northeastern University. She received a master's in Criminal Justice from Northeastern University. She has worked as a Research Assistant at Northeastern's Institute on Race and Justice. Her research centers on the relationship between race, ethnicity, and violent crime. Her current work involves the intersection of community structural imbalance and domestic violence.

BRYAN L. SYKES is Assistant Professor of Criminology, Law and Society (and by courtesy, Sociology and Public Health) at the University of California, Irvine, and a Research Affiliate in the Center for Demography and Ecology at the University of Wisconsin–Madison and the Center for Evidence-Based Corrections at UC Irvine. His research focuses on the intersection of demography, health, social inequality, and mass incarceration. His work has appeared in several issues of the *Lancet* and the *Annals of the American Academy of Political and Social Science.*

ISAAC UNAH is Associate Professor of Political Science at the University of North Carolina at Chapel Hill. His research and teaching interests focus on judicial institutions and their influence on public policy and bureaucratic behavior. His research has been published in leading political science, law, and interdisciplinary social science journals. His book, *The Courts of International Trade: Judicial Specialization, Expertise, and Bureaucratic Policymaking* (1998), examines the role of specialized courts in U.S. trade policy implementation. From 2005 to 2007 he served as Program Director for the Law and Social Sciences Program at the National Science Foundation.

PATRICIA Y. WARREN is Associate Professor in the College of Criminology and Criminal Justice at Florida State University. Her research explores the varied ways in which race, ethnicity, and social class influence sentencing and policing outcomes. Her recent work has appeared in *Criminology, Journal of Research in Crime and Delinquency,* and *Criminology and Public Policy.*

HEATHER M. WASHINGTON is Assistant Professor in the School of Criminal Justice at the University at Albany, SUNY. Her current research focuses on the consequences of incarceration for individuals and their families with an emphasis on the impact of parental incarceration on multiple indicators of youths' well-being. She also studies how residential neighborhood environments influence residents' involvement in crime, delinquency, and other problem behaviors.

VALERIE WRIGHT is Assistant Professor in the Department of Sociology and Criminology at Cleveland State University. She has a diverse background in research, policy evaluation, advocacy, and teaching. Her research broadly focuses on racial disparities in the criminal justice system and includes studies on the media's portrayals of crime, prosecutorial handling of backlogged rape kits, and perceptions of injustice. Her book, *Could Quicker Executions Deter Homicides?*, examines whether long waits on death row have implications for the deterrent value of capital punishment.

INDEX

ABC, 277

ABC News, 89

Acquittal, 166–180, 328; role of race, 169–179

Adjudicatory asymmetry, 166

Adolescents, 185, 192–201; perceptions of discrimination, 192–201

Affect Misattribution Procedure (AMP), 39

Alexander, Marissa, 127, 289

Allport, Gordon, 33, 45

AMBER Alert, 302

The American Jury, 168

American Legislative Exchange Council, 128

American National Election Studies, 37

Anderson, Elijah, 24, 31, 65, 326

Araujo, Edward, 97

Araujo, Edward, Jr. *See* Araujo, Gwen

Araujo, Gwen, 3, 81, 88–90, 97–105

Atlanta, Georgia, 288

Austin, Mark D., 188

Baba, Yoko, 188

Bailey, F. Lee, 235n44

Baker, Houston, 64

Baker v. Carr, 267

Baldus study, 126–127

Baltimore, Maryland, 4, 189, 302–303

Barker, Justin, 255

Bartusch, Dawn, 251

Baxley, Dennis, 120

Beard v. United States, 117

Beaver Creek Police Department, 332n1

Becker, Howard, 60, 68

Beer summit, 281

Bell, Derrick, 215

Bell, Sean, 281

Bertalan, Olivia, 94

Bias crimes. *See* Hate crimes

Biology, 82–83, 86; of race, 84–85; of sex, 83, 97–100, 102

Black codes, 130–131

Black criminality, xi, xiii, 2, 32, 59, 132–134, 137, 155, 160, 217–218, 231; assumption of, 78, 137, 146–147, 155, 179, 217–218, 224, 231, 234n18; benefit to whites, 218, 248; "criminalblackman," 132, 326, 330; fears of; 3, 14, 130, 134, 156, 179, 188, 216, 227, 279, 326–327, 329–330; internalization of, 60, 68; role of official statistics, 9, 134, 217; stereotype of, xiii, 2, 9, 25, 85, 88, 130, 132–134, 155, 157, 160, 162n40, 190–191, 216–217, 219–220, 226–227, 234n26, 235n34

Black Entertainment Television, 284

Black Lives Matter, 224

Blackstone, William, 168

Blalock, Hubert, 186

Blogs, 89, 287

Bloom, Lisa, 94

Blumer, Herbert, 32, 186

Brady Campaign, 121

Brewer, Lawrence Russell, 233n4, 234n24

Brismon, Rumain, 332n1

Broken windows theory, 26, 48n13

Bronx County Supreme Court, 172–173

Brown, Michael, xi-xii, 47n1, 59, 78, 105, 180, 234n7, 332n1

Brown, Nichole, 98

Brown v. United States, 117

Bryant, Gary, 312

Bryant, Roy, 325

Bobo, Lawrence, 33, 248

Botelho, Greg, 94, 96

Buckler, Kevin, 252

Bumpurs, Eleanor, xi

Burden of proof, 166

Bureau of Justice Statistics, 167

Burglary, 87, 94, 186–187

Bush, Jeb, 119, 121

Bush, Sophia, 285

Byrd, James, 229, 233, 233n4, 234n24

California, 223, 229

Cardozo, Benjamin, 118

Caulfield, Phillip, 96

Cazares, Jason, 97

Centers for Disease Control and Prevention, 192

Change.org, 287

Charlotte Police Department, 332n1

Cheng, Cheng, 129, 150–151

Chicago, Illinois, 189, 250, 281, 288

Chicago Tribune, 89

Cincinnati, Ohio, 254

Civil Rights Act of 1964, 230 289

Clark, Marcia, 224

Class, xi, 3, 26, 28, 31, 33–34, 62, 64, 67, 69, 76–77, 81–82, 86–88, 91, 93, 97, 103, 220, 222, 226, 228–229, 233, 316, 329; inequality, 86, 195, 226

Cleveland, Ohio, 105, 332

Cleveland Police Department, 78

CNN, 89, 277–278

Cobinna, Jennifer E., 84

Cochran, Johnnie, 223–224, 228, 235n44

Cognitive processes, 27–30, 42–43, 154–156, 187; affect, 29, 33, 45; availability, 27; priming effect, 28, 39, 43, 45, 188,

202; representativeness, 28; stereotyping, 28–30; substitution, 28–29, 42

Collective action, 275, 286–290

Collective efficacy, 188

Collective racialization, 75

"Commonsense" reactions, 327–328, 332

Community-based theories, 190

Comparative relativism, 251

Confederate flag, 18

Confederate States of America, 231

Conflict theory, 247–248

Convict-lease system, 201

Correll, Joshua, 157–159

Cosby, Bill, 43

Coulter, Ann, 286

Cox, Rodney, 120

Crawford, John, 332n1

Crenshaw, Kimberle, 329

Criminal justice system: bias in, xiii-xiv, 4, 46, 85, 179–181, 216–217, 256–258, 260–263, 267, 281, 327–332; disparate treatment of people of color xiv, 4, 65, 134–135, 160, 179–181, 186–187, 201–203, 216, 247–248, 250–252, 277–282, 288, 333n8; legitimacy of, 2–4, 171, 246, 253, 267, 277; perceptions of, xii, 3–4, 246–253, 260, 263, 266–267, 277–278, 281, 324–325, 331; racialization of, 2, 8

Critical race theory, 115

Crowley, James, 281

Crump, Benjamin, 93

Cruz, Victor, 285–286

Culture of suspicion, 8

Danger/dangerousness: assumption of, 3, 78, 102–103, 282; evaluating, 23–25, 27, 29–30, 34, 42–43, 103–104; perception based on appearance, 8–10, 96, 103; role of race, 23–25, 32–33, 42, 85, 158, 326

Danger/dangerousness of Black males, 8, 85, 88; perceptions of 2, 24, 27, 33–34, 36, 44–46, 81–83, 85–87, 91, 96–97,

99–102, 105, 155–156, 158–159, 179, 202, 282, 326–327; potential, 10–11; social construction of, 91

Darden, Christopher, 224

Davis, Angela, 73

Davis, Jordan, 47n1

David, William, III, 313

Dayton, Ohio, 332

Dean, Shellie, 92

Death penalty, 127, 186, 222, 333n9

DeBlasio, Bill, 285

Debrabander, Firmin, 96

Def Jam Records, 284

Defendants, 165–166, 168–180, 216, 218–219, 222, 224; race of, 165, 169–180, 222, 234n18

Department of Justice, 1, 282, 285, 287

Dershowitz, Alan, 235n44

Detroit, Michigan, 332

Deviant politics, 73

Diallo, Amadou, xi

Discrimination, xi, 3, 9, 32, 46–47, 179, 185–186, 191–204, 249–250, 326–328, 332, 333n10; conscious intent, 328–329; employment, 9, 18, 31, 63, 65, 86, 186, 202, 249, 333n10; in education, 9, 63, 65, 86, 186, 202, 249

Donley, Amy M., 302–303

Dr. Michael M. Krop High School, 91

Drakulich, Kevin M., 2, 326

Dream Defenders, 287

Dred Scott v. Sandford, 236n63

Drugs, 34–38, 75, 104, 229, 248, 283, 312, 315

Du Bois, W.E.B., 46, 201–202

Duncan, Birt, 155

Dunham, Lena, 285

Easton, David 246, 254

Eberhardt, Jennifer, 221

Ecological contamination, 190–191

Ecological fallacy, 10

El Dorado County, California, 98

Erwin v. State, 117

Evidence, 168, 172–174, 224, 226; of racial bias 223–224, 228–229, 328–329; strength of, 173

Explicit racial bias, xiv, 9, 12–13, 24–27, 29–30, 32, 34–47, 51n70, 152–153, 157, 160, 185, 223, 227, 325

Facebook, 276, 286–287, 289

Factual innocence, 166

Fallacy of objectivity, 216

Farrell, Amy, xii, 3, 170, 253, 323, 328

Fear of crime, 25, 87–89, 136, 150, 186, 188–189, 301; perception of, 89, 301; role of race, 14, 130, 134, 150, 156, 188; social construction of, 89

Federal Bureau of Investigation, 1, 43, 64

Femininity, 83–84, 99

Feminist scholarship, 83

Fenstermaker, Sarah, 86

Ferguson, Missouri, xii, 4, 78, 105, 180, 234n7, 331–332, 332n1

Ferrell, Jonathan, 332n1

Flash mobs, 64–65

Florida, xii, 3, 115, 118–124, 127–128, 132, 135–137, 146–147, 149–150, 229–231, 237n87, 238n92, 328; legislature, 119–121, 127

Florida Carry, 127

Florida Coalition to Stop Gun Violence, 121

Florida Prosecuting Attorneys Association, 121

Florida Republican Party, 119–121

Florida State's Attorney Office, 236n60

Fradella, Henry F., 3, 328

Frankfurter, Felix, 297

Forbes, 89

Ford, Ezell, 332n1

Fox News, 89, 279–280

Fulton, Sybrina, 91, 284–285, 288

Fuhrman, Mark, 223, 228

Gallup News Service, 256–257

Gallup poll, 245, 256–260

Gangs, 34–38, 64, 69, 75

Garner, Eric, xi–xii, 59, 78, 105, 180, 233n7, 234n25, 332n1

Gated community, 94, 101, 134, 146, 298

Gates, Henry Louis, 281

Gau, Jacinta M., 2, 323, 326–327

Gay panic defense, 100

General Social Survey, 12

Gender, 2–4, 81–88, 91, 97–103, 105, 199–200, 203, 227, 229, 233, 237n71, 263, 265, 298–304, 306–316, 323, 329; discrimination, 203, 329; hierarchy, 84, 99; inequality, 83–84; roles and norms, 83–84; social construction of, 83, 93; violence, 84

Gideon v. Wainwright, 238n92

Gioviano, Jason, 3

Giroux, Henry, 62, 67

Givelber, Daniel, 3, 170

Goetz, Bernhard, 134

Goff, Keli, 284

Goff, Phillip, 133–134, 155–157

Goffman, Erving, 31–32

Goidel, Kirby, 255

Goldberg, Whoopi, 285

Goldman, Ronald, 167, 221–223

Google, 89–90

Google News, 89–90

Grant, Oscar, 47n1, 59, 73–74, 281, 285

Greene, Dionte, 105

Grio, 279

Group conflict, 32–33, 44–45, 266

Group position, 32–33, 44–46, 249–250, 266

Group trait theory, 186

Guardian, 105

Guerrero, Sylvia, 97

Gun control, 119, 121, 132

Gun ownership, 96; rights of gun owners 119–120, 130–132; role of race, 130–132

Gurley, Akai, 332n1

Hagan, John, 247, 250

Hagedorn, John, 67

Hammer, Marion, 119–121, 128

Hannity, Sean, 283

Harris, David A., 3, 218

Hate crimes, 85, 103–105, 229

Hayhoe, Arthur, 121

Heteronormativity, 84, 98–99, 101

Heuristic devices, 9–10, 154–156

High-profile cases. *See* Salient crime events

Hill, Marc Lamont, 285

Historical inequalities, xi–xii, 31–33, 44–47, 63, 216–217, 248, 266, 279, 282

HLN, 277–278

Hoekstra, Mark, 129, 150–151

Holder, Eric, xiv

Hollander, Jocelyn A., 84, 87

Holley, Chad, 281

Homicide, 117, 120, 124, 128–129, 148–149, 151–152, 161n10, 298–317, 319n41, 319n46, 330; double homicide, xii–xiv; media coverage, 298–317, 330; youth homicide, 4, 298–299, 303–305, 307, 314–316, 319n46, 330

Homosexuality, 84, 98–100, 103

Hooded sweatshirt, 1, 7, 92–93, 96, 103, 165, 224, 290

Huffington Post, 89, 277–278

Hunt, Darrien, 332n1

Hurricane Ivan, 120

Hurricane Katrina, 128

Hypercriminalization, 60, 63, 77

"I am Trayvon Martin," 1, 287

Iconic ghetto, 31, 326–327

Identity, 82–83, 86–87, 97, 104, 247, 329; class, 86; deviant, 82–83, 85; gender, 105, 221; racial, 84–85, 221–222, 256; sexual, 84, 98, 105

Ideomotor effects, 157–158

Illinois v. Wardlow, 217

Implicit association test, 153–154, 162n30

Implicit bias, 2, 9, 12–13, 18–20, 23–25, 27–30, 32, 37–47, 51n68, 116, 133–134, 137, 147, 153–160, 190, 221, 227, 235n27, 326–330, 332; blindness to race, 18–19, 32, 147, 160, 249; in the criminal justice system, 29, 147, 156–160, 248, 328–329; prevalence of, 12, 154; rationalization for, 13; role of media, 9; role of politicians, 9; solutions to, 19–20, 44, 332

Incarceration, 62, 64, 71, 73, 75–76, 97, 135, 195, 248–249, 252

Indianapolis, Indiana, 191

Ingram, Helen, 248

Injustice, 47, 78, 167, 180–181, 219, 234n7, 245–258, 266–267, 278–279, 283, 285, 287–288, 290; perceptions of, 245–258, 266–267; role of race, 245–256, 266–267

Innocence Project, 235n36

Institutional discrimination, 279, 325–327, 332

Inter-group conflict. *See* Group conflict

Interracial crime 15–16, 74, 92, 95, 125–129, 133, 135–136, 142n48, 151–156, 159–160, 175–180, 218–224, 230, 233, 256–258, 260, 263, 265–266, 298

Intersectionality 2–3, 81–83, 87–89, 91, 99, 101–105, 303–304, 308–310, 315–316, 329

Ito, Lance 224

Jackman, Mary R., 32, 44

Jackson, Jesse, 246, 267n4

Jackson, Jimmie Lee, xi

Jackson, Michael, 216

Jay Z, 288

Jealous, Benjamin, 283

Jeantel, Rachel, 104, 226, 228, 237n68, 285

Jefferis, Eric S., 254

Jena, Louisiana, 255

Jena Six, 255

Jim Crow, 45, 47, 93, 279

Johnson, Devon, xii–xiv, 3, 248, 323

Jones, Chenelle A., 3, 330

Jones-Brown, Delores, 3, 328

Jordan, Kareem L., 2, 323, 326–327

Judge satisfaction 3, 168, 170–174, 177–180

Judges, 15, 124, 128, 149, 166–180, 182n29; decision-making, 3, 15–16, 149, 165–181, 329; impact of race 15–18, 165, 170–181

Juries, xi, xiii–xiv, 165–180, 181n4, 181n16, 182n25–26, 182n28–29, 218–227, 229–233; group similarity, 18; hung juries, 182n28, 232; liberation hypothesis, 17, 168–170; racial composition of, 170–172, 182n26, 220–221, 225–228, 278; relating to defendants, 17–18, 156, 170–171, 220–221; role of race in decision-making, 15–16, 19, 165, 170–180, 181n4, 182n25, 228, 301, 329; severe treatment of people of color, 8; small juries 229–233, 238n90, 238n95

Jus, 135

Kahneman, Daniel, 30, 154

Kalvens, Harry, 168–170

Kaminski, Stephanie, 254

Kansas City, Missouri, 105

Kardashian, Robert, 236n44

Keene, David, 130

Kelley, Robin, xii, 64

Kerner Commission. *See* National Advisory Commission on Civil Disorders

King, Martin Luther, Jr., 131–132, 267n4

King, Rodney, xi, 134, 215, 219–221, 224–225, 228, 253–254, 269n56, 281

King, Steve, 283

Knowles, Beyonce, 288

Ku Klux Klan, 131

Kuhn, Ashley, 150

Labeling process, 60, 68, 77

Laing, Peter, 332n1

Lake Mary, Florida, 92

Lane, Jodi, 150

Lasley, James, 254

Latino Paradox, 197

Lawson, Tamara, 149
Lee, Cynthia, 147
Lee, Debra, 284
Leidman, Frank, 228
Lex, 135
LexisNexis, 89–90, 276
Like, Toya Z., 3, 84, 323, 326
Link, Bruce G., 33
Lipsitz, George, 62
Liu, John C., 285
Loehman, Timothy, 332n1
Lopez, Andy, 59, 65
Los Angeles, California, 288
Los Angeles Police Department, 134, 219–220, 254, 332n1
Los Angeles Superior Court, 171–173
Los Angeles Times, 89
Louisiana, 231
Lynching, 63–64, 186, 201–202, 216–217

MacDonald, John, 251
Macroaggression, 136
Magidson, Michael, 97–98
Malcolm X, 62
Manassas, Virginia, 91
Mandatory-minimum sentences, 135
Mann, Bob, 255
Maricopa County Superior Court, 172–173
Marschall, Mellisa J., 190
Martin, Tracy, 91, 96, 284, 288, 298
Martin, Trayvon, xi–xiv, 1–4, 7–8, 15–18, 20, 23–24, 27, 30–31, 41, 43, 46–47, 59, 61, 78, 81, 88–97, 101–105, 115, 130, 134, 136, 146, 156, 161n4, 165, 185–191, 199, 202, 216–218, 224–229, 235n34, 236n63, 245–246, 253, 255–256, 260, 262–264, 266, 275–288, 290–291, 298, 300, 304, 315, 323–324, 327–328, 330–331; culpability of, 92–93, 95–96, 105, 226–228, 298, 315
Marxism, 247
Masculinity, 83–84, 99–102, 224–226, 236n64; hypermasculinity, 226

McDonald's, 98
McClellan, Chandler, 129, 151
McCleskey v. Kemp, 126–127, 329, 333n9
McVeigh, Timothy, 233n4
Media, 1, 3, 23, 41, 59, 81, 85, 88–95, 97, 100–101, 103–105, 168–169, 181n16, 217, 222, 225–226, 245, 252–257, 263, 275–290, 298–317, 323–324, 326, 330
Media response, 4, 275–286, 290; news polls, 277; newsworthiness, 301–303, 314; online news, 275–277, 279, 281, 305, 314; op-ed news articles, 277–280, 284; political response, 3, 281–284, 290; representations of people of color, 29, 85, 226, 278, 301–302, 311–313, 315; selection bias, 300; social media, 1, 4, 59, 228, 275–277, 282, 284–287, 289–290
Megan's Law, 302
Men of color: criminalization of, 62–68, 72–78, 93, 104, 226, 278, 315, 326, 330; dangerousness, 3, 8, 85–86, 88, 93–94, 146, 234n26, 235n34, 282; discrimination against, 199–200, 202, 279; mistrust of the system, 65, 324; police treatment of, 2–3, 11, 13–14, 61, 63, 70–71, 85, 104, 199, 203, 226; profiling of, 93; racialization of, 69; sentencing disparities, 16, 329; violence against, 59, 93, 104, 323, 331; violent stereotype, xiii, 9, 11, 13, 84–86, 88, 162n40, 179, 226–227, 234n26, 235n34, 299, 311–312, 315, 323, 326, 330
Mendelberg, Tali, 189
Merel, Jose, 97–98
Meritocracy, 18, 86
Meyers, Marian, 301
Miami, Florida, 91, 96, 121, 288
Miami-Dade County Public Schools, 91
Microaggression, 136
Miller, Jody, 84
Miller, Tyisha, xi
Miscegenation, 230
Misogyny, 73, 99, 101

Mob violence, 9
Mohammed, Selina A., 187
Moore, Michael, 285
Montford, Carlton, 312
Moral panic, 23
Mormon Church, 231
MSNBC, 89, 277
Muha, Michael J., 32, 44
Muhammad, Khalil Gibran, 217–218
Mullins, Dexter, 93

NAACP, 94, 283, 285
Nabors, Jaron, 97–98
National Action Network, 283, 287
National Advisory Commission on Civil
    Disorders, 230
National Center for State Courts, 165, 171–
    172, 174, 178, 180
National Opinion Research Center, 12, 192
National Rifle Association, 119–120, 127–
    128, 130–132; influence of race, 130–132
National Survey of Children's Health, 192–
    195, 197–198
NBC, 277
Neighborhood watch, 7, 27, 92, 94, 96,
    128, 142n55, 146, 165, 186, 191, 202, 226,
    279, 298
Neighborhoods, 23–26, 28–47, 185–204,
    248, 251, 323, 326; disadvantage, 26, 31,
    194–196, 198, 202, 251, 323, 326; disor-
    der, 24–26, 37, 42–43, 45–46, 48n13,
    188–190, 196, 199; perceptions of
    crime, 2, 23–26, 29–30, 32–47, 48n13,
    50n61, 51n68, 51n70, 103, 188–192,
    202, 327; racial composition of, 23–26,
    32, 36–37, 42, 50n63, 189–191; racial
    stereotypes of, 25, 189; safety, 3, 186,
    192–193, 195–201; trust in neighbors,
    190, 194
Nelson, Debra, 141n3
New York, New York, xii, 105, 288, 327,
    332, 333n8
New York Daily News, 96

New York Police Department, 78, 288,
    332n1
New York Times, 89
Newark, California, 3, 97
Nine-millimeter handgun, 93–94
NPR, 89

Oakland, California, 73, 288
Oakland Police Department, 59, 68
Oakland Tribune, 89
Obama, Barack, xiv, 1, 46, 78, 245–246,
    281–284, 287
O'Hara, Mark, 95, 116
Ohio Supreme Court, 117
Oliver, Eric J., 189
Oliver, Pamela, 75
Oppositional culture, 9–10, 323
O'Reilly, Bill, 96
Orlando, Florida, 304–305
Orlando Sentinel, 89, 304–305, 307, 314,
    319n42
Ortiz, Mia, 3, 330

Padilla, Felix, 67
Pager, Devah, 189
Pantaleo, Daniel, 332n1
Parent, Wayne, 255
Payne, Monique R., 247, 250
Payne, Yasser, 66
Peaden, Durrell, 120–121
Pensacola, Florida, 120
People v. Tomlins, 118
Perceptions of crime, 2, 23–27, 31–34, 37–
    47, 89, 188, 202, 253
Perceptual shorthand, 8–10; role of stereo-
    types, 16; in sentencing decisions, 16
Pew Research Center, 255, 276–277
Phelan, Jo C., 33
Philadelphia, Pennsylvania, 64–65
Phoenix Police Department, 332n1
Piliavin, Irving, 190
Piquero, Alex, 3
Pittman, Nicolas, 3

Play, 64–65; criminalization of, 65

Plea bargaining, 167–168

Police: accountability, 77, 253; attitudes towards, xi, 3–4, 11–15, 248, 250–251, 253–254, 266, 282, 324; brutality, 60–61, 63, 67, 73–75, 248, 253–254; community policing, 330; conflict with people of color, xii-xiii, 2–3, 9, 13–15, 59, 323; decision-making, 8–9, 123, 128, 136, 157–159, 329; enhanced scrutiny of people of color, 8, 14, 251–252; force multiplier, 330; hostility towards, 14, 73; immigration enforcement, 330; mistreatment of people of color, xi-xiv, 14, 47, 61, 63, 65, 77, 85, 104, 191, 199, 202, 217, 233n7, 248–253, 267, 288, 323, 333n8; perceptions of neighborhoods, 190–191, 331; rationalization of actions, 11, 13–14, 19, 60, 162n53, 234n25, 327; role in self-defense, 123, 128, 139–140; school-based, 77; surveillance by, 13–15, 71, 186, 199, 226, 248, 251, 323; symbolic importance of, 14; training, 127–128, 156–159, 331–332; violence committed by, xii–xiii, 59–61, 63, 65, 74, 77, 104, 191, 217, 220–221, 234n7, 250, 253, 323, 331

Political correctness, 18

Porter, Savannah, 3, 323, 326

Portes, Alejandro, 249

Poverty, 9, 13, 60, 69, 86, 188–189, 195, 251, 305, 319n44, 326

Prejudice, 11–13, 17, 19–20, 24–25, 31–33, 44–45, 47, 94, 96, 150, 152–153, 186–187, 192, 195–201, 217, 228–229, 249

Prison industrial complex, 73

Privilege, 32, 84–86, 278

Procedural justice, 253

ProPublica, xiii

Protection of Persons/Use of Force bill. See Stand Your Ground

Protests, 1, 4, 287–290

Public opinion, 3, 246, 253, 255–257; racial bias, 8, 19, 255

Punishment, 63–66, 72, 76, 170, 186–187, 248

Punitive social control, 59–66, 69, 73, 76–78

Quillian, Lincoln, 189

Quinn, Christine, 285

Quinney, Richard, 67

Quinnipiac University, 132

Race, xi-xiv, 1–4, 7–8, 15–19, 23–27, 30–31, 33–34, 37, 40–47, 62, 78, 81–82, 85–88, 91, 97, 103, 115–116, 122, 125–128, 131–135, 137, 146–147, 150–157, 159–160, 165, 169–180, 189–191, 196–203, 215–223, 226–229, 233, 245–258, 260–267, 275–287, 298–316, 323–332; inequality, 96, 196, 218, 226, 230; social construction of, 85, 93

Race baiting, 283

Racial gradient thesis, 246–247, 249, 252, 255–256, 260, 262–266, 331; position of Hispanics, 249, 260, 262, 265–267, 331

Racial profiling, 10, 13, 19–20, 61, 92–93, 135, 146, 161n4, 190, 216–218, 248, 250, 253, 281, 333n8

Racial segregation, xiv, 9, 18, 31, 188, 202, 230, 248, 250–251; consequences of, 188

Racial solidarity, 74–75

Racial taboos, 223

Racialized policing, xiv, 3, 11–14, 19, 147, 152–153, 156–160, 191, 267

Racism, xi, xiii, 30–31, 62, 85, 153, 224, 231, 245, 285, 323, 325–326, 329, 332; color-blind, 32, 160; contemporary, 326, 329, 332; cultural, xi, xiii; laissez-faire, 32–33; overcoming, 332; postracial era, 18; symbolic, 32

Ragsdale, Brian, 187

Rape, 87, 330–331

Raudenbush, Stephen W., 189

Reasonable suspicion, 217
Reisif, Michael D., 191
Resistance, 60, 66–76; authority views of, 68–69; as deviance, 66, 69, 72; crimes of, 67, 69–72, 76; rationalization of, 71–72, 76; resilience skills, 66
Resistance identities, 67, 75; subculture of, 76
Reuters, 94
Rice, Tamir, xi, 65, 78, 105, 332n1
Richardson, L. Song, 133–134, 155–157
Rios, Victor M., 2, 324, 330–331
Rioting, 219, 225, 229, 254, 269n56, 288
Rivera, Geraldo, 96
Robbery, 87
Rodriguez, Dylan, 62
Roman, John, 128–129, 151–152, 160
Root, 279, 284
Rorschach test, 39
Rosario, Jordyn, 3
Routine activities perspective, 185
Rumbaut, Ruben, 249
Russell-Brown, Katheryn, 3, 215, 222, 224, 326, 328, 330
Russian roulette, 313–314

Sagar, H. Andrew, 155
Saks, Michael J., 232
Salient crime events, 47n1, 59, 88–90, 97, 103–104, 134, 167, 171, 180, 219–220, 246, 252–256, 266, 281, 286
Sampson, Robert, 31–32, 189, 251
San Francisco Chronicle, 89
San Francisco Examiner, 228
San Jose Mercury News, 89
Sanford, Florida, 1, 7, 91–92, 96, 116, 147, 159, 186, 189, 202, 236n60, 245, 256, 260, 263, 278, 298, 300, 305, 314, 316, 319n41, 319n43, 319n44
Sanford Herald, 89, 305, 319n41
Schildkraut, Jaclyn, 302–303
Schilt, Kristen, 84, 99
Schlicheter, Kurt, 286

Schneider, Anne, 248
Schofield, Janet Ward, 155
Scott, Rick, 127
Seattle, Washington, 189
Seattle Neighborhoods and Crime Survey, 34–38
Seattle Police Department, 34
Seattle Times, 89
Self-control, 187–188, 194, 196, 199
Self-defense, 1, 7, 15, 47n1, 92–93, 95, 97, 115–130, 132–140, 148–150, 161n12, 225, 227–229, 278, 280, 298, 328; Castle Doctrine, 117–120, 122, 148, 150, 161n13; deadly force, 116–123, 126, 133, 135, 137–140, 146, 148–149, 156, 160, 161n12; English common-law, 116–118, 124; imminent threat, 15, 123, 138, 140, 148; justifiable force, 122–124, 126–128, 132–133, 136, 142n48, 152; presumption of fear, 122, 132, 137–139, 328; presumption of reasonableness, 122, 137, 328; reasonable fear; 116, 118–119, 134, 149; rule of retreat, 116–119, 122, 148–149, 161n12, 161n13
Sellin, Thorsten, 217–218, 234n13
Seminole County, Florida, 189, 300, 304–305, 312, 314, 316, 319n43, 319n44
Sentencing, 16, 64, 127, 134–135, 166–167, 328–329
September 11, 2001, 128
Seven-Eleven, 92
Sexism, 99
Sexton, Lori, 3, 323, 326
Sexual assault, 87, 234n18, 330–331
Sexual orientation, 81, 84–88, 91, 98–102
Sharpton, Al, 283, 288
Shedd, Carla, 247, 250
Shepard, Matthew, 103–104
Sherrod, Shirley, 281
Shooter bias, 157
Sierra Nevada, 98
Siller, Laura, 2, 326

Simi Valley, California, 215, 221–222, 225–226

Simmons, Russell, 284–285

Simpson, Nicole Brown, 167, 221–223, 227, 237n71

Simpson, O. J., 166–167, 169, 181n8, 215–216, 220–224, 227–229, 233, 235n44, 236n46, 236n55, 237n71, 286

Skittles, 92–93

Skogan, Wesley, 150, 188

Slavery, xiv, 46–47, 93, 130–131, 137, 250

Slave codes, 130–131, 137

Slave patrols, 131, 142n55

Smiley, Tavis, 283–284

Smith, Douglas A., 191

Social consciousness, 66, 73

Social death, 60, 62–63, 77

Social distance, 2, 219–220, 224, 226–228, 230, 234n21, 249

Social incapacitation, 60, 62–63

Social institutions, 193, 195–196, 199

Social mobility, 63

Social movement, 60, 67, 75–76, 104, 286, 290

South Carolina, 231

Spencer, Octavia 285

St. Petersburg, Florida ,191

Stand Your Ground, xii, 3, 47n1, 96, 115–116, 118–130, 132–140, 141n4, 146–152, 156, 159–160, 225, 230–231, 237n84, 278, 287, 289–290, 301, 328; creation of, 119–12; deterrent effect; 124, 149–151; expungement, 127; immunity, 116, 120, 123–124, 140, 149–150, 160; opposition to 121, 124, 150–151; racial impact of, 124–129, 134, 136–137, 146–147, 150–152, 159–160; role of police, 123, 128, 139–140, 149

Standard of proof. See Burden of proof

Starnes, Todd, 283

State v. Zimmerman, 226

Staten Island, New York, 4, 180

Statistical discrimination, 9, 29, 32–33, 44–45, 134

Status, 82–85, 88, 97, 99, 101, 103, 105

Stefani, Gwen, 97

Steffensmeier, Darrell, 179

Stereotype threat, 185–188, 192, 202–203; consequences of 186–187

Stewart, Eric A., 191

Stop and frisk, 11, 327, 333n8

Stigma, 10, 31–33, 44–45, 99, 188, 203; of places, 31; tribal, 31

Stolle, Dietlind, 190

Superior Court of the District of Columbia, 172–173

Supplementary Homicide Report, 128

Surveillance, 2, 13–15, 71, 186–188, 192, 199, 202

Suspicion heuristic, 133–134, 155–156, 221, 224, 227, 231, 234n26, 235n34

Swidler, Anne, 69

Sykes, Brian L., 3, 324, 326, 330

Symbolic assailant, 8–10

Symbolic interactionism, 82, 87–88, 91, 99, 104

Tampa Bay Times, 124

Task Force on Citizen Safety and Protection, 127–128

Task Force on 21st Century Policing, 78

Tate, Larenz, 285

Taylor, Auricka Gordon, 288

Tennessee v. Garner, 123

Tekin, Erdal, 129, 151

Terrill, William, 191

Terrorism, 128

Texas, 231

Threat, 7–8, 24–25, 27, 63–64, 86, 89, 92, 94, 96, 100, 102; assessment of, 88, 97, 102–104; perceptions of, 3, 81, 83, 87–88, 91, 96–97, 99, 100–101, 105, 122, 132–134, 137, 155–156, 249

Threatened Use of Force bill, 289

Thug imagery, 224–225, 228, 236n52, 311–312, 315, 330
Till, Emmett, 24, 46, 48n6, 279, 288, 325
Timoney, John, 121
Tobar, Hector, 94
Trans panic defense, 100–101
Transgender, 81, 97, 99, 102
Trayvon Martin Organizing Committee, 287
Tversky, Amos, 154
Twin Lakes, Florida, 91–92
Twitter, 276, 283–287, 289; hashtags, 284–285, 287, 290

Unah, Isaac, 3, 324, 330–331
Unified Sportsmen of Florida, 119
Uniform Firearms Act, 131
University of Chicago, 192
Urban Institute, 128, 152
U.S. Census Bureau, 34, 305, 319n44, 325
U.S. Constitution, 160, 231
U.S. Supreme Court, 61, 117–118, 123, 126–127, 217, 231–232, 236n63, 238n92, 267, 328–329
USA Today, 89, 256, 277
Utah, 231, 332n1

Ventura County, California, 220
Verdicts, 17, 165–173, 177–178, 180, 229, 231, 233; accuracy of, 3, 170–173, 177–178, 180; nonunanimous, 229, 231, 233, 238n90
Victimization, 35–36, 81, 87, 94, 185, 298–303, 330–331; blameworthiness, 299–300, 302–304, 306–307, 311–317, 327, 330; by police, 14; ideal victim, 301–302, 330; perceptions of, 91–92, 94–95, 189–190, 330; risk of, 25, 87, 185; worthy victim, 299
Vigilantism, 59–61, 63–64, 77, 93–94, 116, 121, 124, 130–131, 201–202
Von Bulow, Claus, 215

Vulnerability, 96–97, 100, 102; assessment of, 81, 83, 87, 91, 103–104; perceptions of, 82–83, 87, 89, 91, 99, 101, 105

Wall Street Journal, 89, 277
Walnut Park, 69
Walker, Tricia Elam, 93
War on Drugs, 135, 329
Warning shots, 127, 289
Warren, Patricia, xii, 3, 253, 323
Washington, Heather M., 3, 330
Washington Post, 89, 277–278
Weiner, Anthony, 284
Werthman, Carl, 190
West, Candace, 83, 86
West, Cornel, 283–284
West, Don, 95
Westbrook, Laurel, 84, 99
White, Roddy, 285–286
White, Terry, 221
Wildemuth, Barbara M., 91
Williams, David R., 187
Williams, Patricia, 135
Williams v. Florida, 231–232
Wilson, Darren, 180, 332n1
Workman, James, 120
Wright, Valerie, 3–4, 324, 330–331
Wyoming, 103

Yan, Holly, 94
Yanich, Danilo, 252
Your Black World, 279
Youth control complex, 60, 63, 66, 72

Zeisel, Hans, 168–170
Zero-tolerance policies, 64, 77
Zhang, Yan, 91
Zimmerman, Don H., 83
Zimmerman, George, xi-xii, 1–4, 7–8, 15–18, 20, 23, 27, 30–31, 43, 47, 81, 88, 90–97, 101–104, 115–116, 129, 133–134, 136, 141n3, 141n4, 146–147, 159–160, 165,

Zimmerman, George (*cont.*)
171, 179–180, 185–187, 190–191, 199,
202, 215–218, 220, 225–229, 231–233,
235n34, 235n43, 236n60, 236n63,
236n64, 245–246, 255–258, 260–
267, 275–290, 298, 315, 323–324, 328,
330–331; arrest of, xii, 1–2, 47, 95, 116,
136, 147, 236n60, 245–246, 255–258,
260, 263, 331; charges against, 15, 136;
desire to be a police officer, 96, 146;
ethnicity of, 1, 15, 48n2, 91, 95, 101;
injuries of, 92, 96; stalking by, 94;
victimization of, 94–95
Zimmerman, Robert, 283, 286

Zimmerman-Martin trial, 2–3, 23, 93, 104,
116, 146, 179, 225–229, 232–233, 245, 261,
282, 298, 232, 328, 330; acquittal of Zimmerman, xi-xii, 2–3, 95, 104, 147, 165, 171,
215, 229, 232, 245–246, 255–256, 260, 280,
282–287; attacks on Martin's character,
15, 17, 96, 226–228, 315; evidence, 116,
161n4, 226, 280; jury, xii, 2, 7, 15–18, 116,
141n3, 141n4, 156, 165, 225–228, 236n64,
256, 278, 282, 286, 323; media coverage, 23; role of race, 16–18, 30, 165, 179;
special prosecutor, 1, 136, 147; verdict,
xii, 3, 17–18, 93–94, 156, 165, 225, 255–258,
260–261, 263–266, 275–288, 290, 323